LAW, RIGHTS AND DISCOURSE

A philosophical system is not what one would expect to find in the work of a contemporary legal thinker. Robert Alexy's work counts as a striking exception. Over the past 29 years Alexy has been developing, with remarkable clarity and consistency, a systematic philosophy covering most of the key areas of legal philosophy. Kantian in its inspiration, his work admirably combines the rigour of analytical philosophy with a repertoire of humanitarian ideals reflecting the tradition of the Geisteswissenschaften, rendering it one of the most far-reaching and influential legal philosophies in our time. This volume has been designed with two foci in mind: the first is to reflect the breadth of Alexy's philosophical system, as well as the varieties of jurisprudential and philosophical scholarship in the last three decades on which his work has had an impact. The second objective is to provide for a critical exchange between Alexy and a number of specialists in the field, with an eye to identifying new areas of inquiry and offering a new impetus to the discourse theory of law. To that extent, it was thought that a critical exchange such as the one undertaken here would most appropriately reflect the discursive and critical character of Robert Alexy's work. The volume is divided into four parts, each dealing with a key area of Alexy's contribution. A final section brings together concise answers by Robert Alexy. In composing these, Alexy has tried to focus on points and criticisms that address new aspects of discourse theory or otherwise point the way to future developments and applications. With its range of topics of coverage, the number of specialists it engages and the originality of the answers it provides, this collection will become a standard work of reference for anyone working in legal theory in general and the discourse theory of law in particular.

Law, Rights and Discourse

The Legal Philosophy of Robert Alexy

Edited by

George Pavlakos

•HART•
PUBLISHING

OXFORD AND PORTLAND, OREGON
2007

Published in North America (US and Canada) by
Hart Publishing
c/o International Specialized Book Services
920 NE 58th Avenue, Suite 300
Portland, OR 97213-3786
USA
Tel: +1 503 287 3093 or toll-free: (1) 800 944 6190
Fax: +1 503 280 8832
E-mail: orders@isbs.com
Web Site: www.isbs.com

Hart Publishing, 16c Worcester Place, Oxford, OX1 2JW
Telephone: +44 (0)1865 517530 Fax: +44 (0)1865 510710
E-mail: mail@hartpub.co.uk
Website: http://www.hartpub.co.uk

British Library Cataloguing in Publication Data

Data Available

ISBN-13: 978-1-84113-676-9 (hardback)

Typeset by Columns Design Ltd, Reading
Printed and bound in Great Britain by
TJ International Ltd, Padstow, Cornwall

Alexander Peczenik (1937-2005)

Preface

This volume springs from a workshop on the discourse theory of law which was held on 11 and 12 June 2004 at Queen's University, Belfast under the auspices of the Forum for Law and Philosophy. The event constituted the second in a series of Workshops in Analytical Jurisprudence that regularly invite state of the art papers to address key issues in legal philosophy. The choice of the topic of the second volume was dictated by the intent to highlight the close links between schools of analytical jurisprudence beyond territorial or any other barriers formally conceived. In that respect, Robert Alexy's work is, perhaps, the best proof for the absence of such barriers, thereby demonstrating the potential for a fertile dialogue between English-speaking and 'continental' or 'other' schools of analytical legal theory that has yet to be explored in its full potential.

The essays which comprise the volume are original contributions that were either presented at the workshop or specially commissioned for the collection. Both the workshop and, subsequently, the book would not have been possible if it were not for the generous financial support of the British Academy, Social and Legal Studies, the Queen's Law School, the Manchester Law School and the Publications Fund of the Faculty of Social Sciences at Queen's. Most of the editing of the book and the writing up of my portions were completed in 2005 when I was an Alexander von Humboldt Research Fellow at the University of Kiel. To these organisations I owe my profound thanks.

Both the workshop and the subsequent composition of this book have been intellectually most stimulating and rewarding. All of the workshop participants have contributed to the editing and shaping of this volume, and all came up with insightful comments and suggestions which proved invaluable for improving the final result. However, a number of people deserve special mention, for without them the book would have never found its way to the publisher: Emmanuel Melissaris was a splendid co-organiser of the Belfast workshop and a most incisive advisor in the later stage of the preparation of the collection. Bonnie Litschewski Paulson and Stanley L Paulson, in their characteristic intellectual manner, have provided tremendous help with the editing of the volume as well as numerous suggestions to individual authors and myself without which the end product would have been much poorer; Gerard Conway offered valuable editorial help concerning some of the chapters written by non English-speaking scholars; Richard Hart, as ever, provided his unhampered support and expert advice throughout the preparation of the book; my wife, Estelle, has been a constant source of energy and inspiration during the entire project. It is, however, Robert Alexy who has instilled life into this collection, by investing enormous amounts of energy to synthesise the various contributions in his replies. His dedication to the entire undertaking and attention to detail during the various stages of the preparation of the book has not only made a huge difference to the final result, but has also been a most rewarding intellectual experience for me personally.

Sadly, despite his lively engagement with the conference in Belfast, Aleksander Peczenik did not live to complete his contribution. His sudden death was a shock to all of us, friends, colleagues and former students. The gap he left behind will be difficult to fill both in personal and academic terms, given his pioneering work in legal argumentation and his deep knowledge of discourse theory. This book is dedicated to him.

Contents

List of Contributors

Robert Alexy is Professor for Public Law and Legal Philosophy at the Christian Albrechts University of Kiel.

Stefano Bertea is a Lecturer in Legal Theory at the University of Leicester.

Giorgio Bongiovanni is Professor of Jurisprudence at the University of Bologna.

Bartosz Brożek is a Lecturer in Jurisprudence at the University of Krakow.

Maeve Cooke is Professor of Philosophy at University College Dublin.

Jonathan Gorman is Professor of Moral Philosophy at Queen's University Belfast.

Carsten Heidemann holds a PhD in legal philosophy from the University of Kiel and practises as a barrister in Kiel.

Mattias Kumm is Professor of Law at New York University.

Sir Neil MacCormick is the Leverhulme Personal Research Professor and Regius Professor of Public Law and the Law of Nature and Nations at the University of Edinburgh.

George Pavlakos is Research Professor in Globalisation and Legal Theory at the Faculty of Law, University of Antwerp.

Joseph Raz is Professor at Columbia University and Research Professor at Oxford University.

Julian Rivers is Senior Lecturer in Law at the University of Bristol.

Antonino Rotolo is a Reader in Jurisprudence at the University of Bologna.

Corrado Roversi is a Lecturer in Jurisprudence at the University of Bologna.

Giovanni Sartor is the Marie-Curie Professor of Legal Informatics and Legal Theory at EUI in Florence and Professor of Legal Informatics at the University of Bologna.

Jan Sieckmann is Professor of Public Law at the University of Bamberg.

Philippos Vassiloyannis is a Lecturer in the Philosophy of Law at the University of Athens.

Introduction

GEORGE PAVLAKOS*

A PHILOSOPHICAL SYSTEM is not what one would expect to find in the work of a contemporary legal thinker. Robert Alexy's work counts as a striking exception. Over the past 29 years Alexy has been developing, with remarkable clarity and consistency, a systematic philosophy covering most of the key areas of legal philosophy.[1] Kantian in its inspiration, his work admirably combines the rigour of analytical philosophy with a repertoire of humanitarian ideals reflecting the tradition of the *Geisteswissenschaften*, rendering it one of the most far-reaching and influential legal philosophies of our time.

It would hardly be an exaggeration to say that the publication, in 1978, of *A Theory of Legal Argumentation*, Alexy's first book, marked a decisive turn in contemporary jurisprudential discussion. Parting company with debates conducted as head-on confrontations between positivists and non-positivists, Alexy argues that law's nature is best understood in the light of a theory of legal argumentation (or discourse). Here, the concept of rational argumentation functions as an overarching concept, inviting a dialogue between analytical positivism and the variants of natural law theory. For Alexy, as for analytical positivism, law is predominantly a social practice, albeit one that has the structure of rational argumentation. In developing the latter, Alexy argues that law is essentially related to the other forms of practical reasoning (morality and ethics) in virtue of sharing a common discursive structure with them.

This insight of an underlying rational structure pertaining to the different types of practical discourse does not count as the rejection of the

* I am indebted to Stanley L Paulson for valuable suggestions on both content and style.

[1] The core of his work consists of three monographs: R Alexy, *Theorie der juristischen Argumentation. Die Theorie des rationalen Diskurses als Theorie der juristischen Begründung* (Frankfurt am Main, Suhrkamp, 1978) and in English translation by N MacCormick and R Adler, *A Theory of Legal Argumentation* (Oxford, Clarendon Press, 1985); R Alexy, *Theorie der Grundrechte* (Frankfurt am Main, Suhrkamp, 1985) and in English translation by J Rivers, *A Theory of Constitutional Rights* (Oxford, Oxford University Press, 2000); finally, R Alexy, *Begriff und Geltung des Rechts* (Freiburg etc, Alber, 1992); and in English translation by B Litschewski Paulson and S L Paulson, *The Argument from Injustice: A Reply to Legal Positivism* (Oxford, Clarendon Press, 2002).

institutional character of law, for legal argumentation remains tied to the institutional arrangements of particular legal systems. Thus the outcomes of legal argumentation are correct relative to a particular institutional framework, a condition suggesting that law be understood as a *special case* of a general practical discourse that comprises moral and ethical discourse (Alexy's so-called 'special case thesis').

At the same time, the common discursive structure of law and morality allows for a communication of standards between the two domains, a thesis that is most commonly found amongst natural lawyers. In contrast to natural law theory, however, the focus in Alexy's work marks a decisive shift: instead of conceiving of law and morality as self-contained domains that may interact on occasion, the idea of an underlying rational structure makes possible a dynamic understanding of the boundaries between law and morality. What belongs to the legal domain and what to the moral domain cannot be settled by mere reference to institutional facts but has to be established within a rational discourse. To that extent, legality emerges as a concept in need of justification, one that stems only in part from the institutional facts of a legal system, requiring an appeal to substantive arguments that are moral in character.

AIMS AND STRUCTURE OF THE VOLUME

The volume has been designed with two foci in mind: the first is to reflect the breadth of Alexy's philosophical system, as well as the varieties of jurisprudential and philosophical scholarship in the last three decades on which his work has had an impact. The second objective is to provide for a critical exchange between Alexy and a number of specialists in the field, with an eye to identifying new areas of inquiry and offering a new impetus to the discourse theory of law. To that extent, it was thought that a critical exchange such as the one undertaken here would most appropriately reflect the discursive and critical character of Robert Alexy's work.

The volume has been divided in four parts, each dealing with a key area of Alexy's contribution. A final section brings together concise answers by Robert Alexy. In composing these, Alexy has tried to focus on points and criticisms that address new aspects of discourse theory or otherwise point the way to future developments and applications.

A Debate on Legal Positivism

This first part of the volume was not originally to be. An initial reading of Joseph Raz's chapter, 'The Argument from Justice, or How not to Reply to

Legal Positivism',[2] suggested that it seemed to fall neatly into what is now the second part of the volume, where the chapter would have taken its place, alongside the other essays addressing issues of law and morality. When, however, Robert Alexy began preparing his reply, it became clear that Raz's chapter was far too comprehensive to be dealt with in the space of a short reply. Here was a clear case for a daring editorial intervention! After considering the matter for a while, and in the light of some valuable advice from Stanley L Paulson and Bonnie Litschewski Paulson, I decided it would be appropriate to ask Robert Alexy to compose an extensive reply, which would then be included alongside Joseph Raz's chapter in a separate section. The two essays, taken together, address a number of key issues with respect to the nature and the state of contemporary legal philosophy and they offer answers that are bound to influence the way we think about these issues. The result is that the exchange has something of the character of a landmark philosophical debate, which would have been lost had Alexy confined himself to a brief reply. In addition, the exchange reconstructs, in retrospect, the debate between Raz and Alexy that had been scheduled for the 2005 IVR World Congress in Granada but that had to be cancelled owing to Joseph Raz's illness at the time.

Although the two chapters take up concrete points from Alexy's *The Argument from Injustice*, the scope of the exchange extends far beyond that book, addressing a number of key issues in contemporary jurisprudential debates. Here are the main highlights of the exchange.

The importance of definitions and, more generally, of conceptual analysis in legal philosophy is put to the test in the example of the definition of the positivist concept of law. Joseph Raz[3] declares his general suspicion vis-à-vis such definitions, for they fail, in his view, to capture the subtlety of positivist thinking. Most notably, he argues that the content of the separation thesis, which is put forward by Alexy as representing the main feature of positivism, cannot be adequately captured in terms of a conceptually necessary link between law and morality, or its denial, for there are a number of different types of conceptual connection between law and morality to which positivists might well subscribe. Contrariwise, Alexy[4] argues for the meaningfulness of definitions along the lines of Kant's recommendation that a definition produce a system within which the various essential properties of the *definiendum* fit together. Moreover, Alexy argues that conceptual connections between law and morality comprise a comprehensive aspect that cannot leave positivism untouched. Despite the complexity of the exchange, the reader is provided with a

[2] J Raz, 'The Argument from Justice, or How Not to Reply to Legal Positivism' (this volume).
[3] Raz, above n 2.
[4] R Alexy, 'An Answer to Joseph Raz' (this volume).

wealth of stimulating argument on the question of the significance of conceptual analysis in legal theory generally and with respect to the separation thesis in particular.

What role, if any, does the distinction between observer and participant play vis-à-vis the concept of law? The two authors go some way toward arguing that the distinction could only then be of importance for the explication of law's nature if it were possible to show that the distinction served to demarcate different concepts of law. For in that case, the concept of law corresponding to the participant's viewpoint would include elements (presumably moral) not found in the concept corresponding to the observer's viewpoint. What is disputed by the two authors is whether observer and participant may indeed share different concepts and what the content of such different concepts would come to.

Are legal utterances connected with a claim to correctness? Raz[5] thinks that this is nearly as trivial as to say that every intentional action claims its own meaningfulness. Yet he remarks that correctness conceived of in this manner may well remain relative to an agent's subjective purposes and evaluations, so that even a group of bandits might well be raising the claim by issuing a command. Conversely, Alexy[6] submits that there is an objective dimension linked to the claim, one requiring reference to intersubjective criteria of correctness. Assuming that this is true, might it be a way to illustrate Hart's distinction between law and orders backed by threats? More generally, might it be possible to extend this conclusion beyond law, into other domains of intentional action?

Next, there is the issue of extreme injustice: when does a legal precept cease to be law? In adopting the so-called 'Radbruch Formula', Alexy argued in his *Begriff und Geltung des Rechts*[7] that extremely unjust law is deprived of its legal character for reasons that are internal to the legal system. From this, he went on to conclude that the concept of law incorporates moral elements. Raz argues that the fact that judges often set aside grossly unjust precepts on legal grounds scarcely counts as proof that the concept of law contains moral elements, for it is possible to take account of these grounds in ways that are altogether compatible with positivism.[8] In order that the claim entails the moral implications that Alexy reads into it, Raz continues, one would have to argue that for all legal systems, the law necessarily gives judges legal power to set aside immoral laws. This, in turn, would require a still further argument to the effect that law necessarily raises a claim to moral correctness. As Raz remarks, however, the most one can claim of law is that it raises a claim to

[5] Raz, above n 2.
[6] Alexy, above n 4.
[7] Alexy, *The Argument from Injustice*, above n 1.
[8] Raz, above n 2.

legitimate authority. While the latter is a moral claim, it is far from being a claim to moral correctness. Moreover, legal officials may well be aware both that the rules they apply are morally wrong and that these rules are morally binding on them and their subjects.[9] In view of the above, for an official to set aside a legal precept on grounds of moral wrongness (even to an extreme degree) is not enough. The official would have to know that that precept had ceased to claim legal authority. And given that the claim to legitimate authority, at least on Raz's view, is a necessary property of legality, this seems to be impossible. Judges' own attitudes attest to this: even when they think that a precept is grossly unjust, they rarely think that the law authorises them to set it aside.

Alexy objects that the claim to correctness, which is necessarily raised by law, points to the dual character of law: law is at the same time authoritative and ideal. To each of the two dimensions there corresponds a distinct value: certainty in the case of authoritativeness, justice in the case of the ideal dimension. Now, Alexy maintains, if certainty happens to prevail most of the time, this is for reasons moral in nature (given that certainty is itself a value). Thus it ought to follow that whenever reasons obtain that outweigh those underpinning certainty, then one should recognise justice as taking priority over certainty. Thus the matter of whether certainty or justice takes priority is one that can be resolved only by reference to moral reasons. And this is enough to show that the claim raised by law is a claim to moral correctness.

Finally the debate touches upon the idea of incorporation of non-legal standards by the law: at what point does the incorporation of moral standards into a legal system take place? Does it take place, so to speak, too late, namely after the legal system has already been constituted as a positive normative order, with its own legal rules specifying the conditions of incorporation (Raz)? Or does the incorporation come, so to speak, too early, namely before and for the purpose of the constitution of the legal system, with the effect that morality is already incorporated in a constituted positive legal order (Alexy)?

Law and Morality

The essays of the second part focus on more particular aspects of the concept of law and the relation between law and morality; Alexy addressed both topics extensively in his monograph *The Argument from Injustice*.[10] The chapters in this section attempt to answer such questions as: whether

[9] *Ibid.*
[10] Alexy, above n 1.

law is a special case of morality, whether law necessarily raises a claim to moral correctness; and whether there are objective answers possible in law.

Neil MacCormick[11] unravels the hidden implications behind the talk of law's raising a claim to correctness with a view to defending an original interpretation of the relation between law and justice or morality, one that draws on his recent book *Institutions of Law*.[12] The gist of his argument is that the connection between law and claims to justice can be made out in its strongest if we stop confusing law's real or institutional aspect with its ideal aspect, one that ought to be attributed to the practice of those individual and collective agents who 'use' the law. The argument unfolds as follows: first he argues that law as such is incapable of raising any claim whatever, for institutional normative orders are states of affairs, incapable of making any kind of claim. Then he moves on to contend that it is only legislators, adjudicators and legal persons who can raise claims within an institutional legal order. The author employs the speech act theory of Austin and Searle to show that the meaningfulness of legal utterances cannot be secured unless reference is made to standards that care for the happy employment of legal speech acts. Reference to such standards brings out the ideal dimension of law, namely its necessary affinity with ideas of the common good, justice and morality. Thus, it is by creating, applying and interpreting the law that we come to realise its commitments to ideals of justice and morality. Contrariwise, any talk of law's raising a claim to moral correctness is a damaging metaphor that is bound to lead to a confusion that disarms law from its critical dimension: in claiming that law raises claims we come to confuse law's real and ideal aspects, thereby thinking that law aspires to replace or substitute morality. Far from being true, this claim must be driven out of legal theory for the danger of distorting the fact that moral or practical disagreement is pervasive in legal practices. In concluding, MacCormick finds himself in more agreement with Alexy's understanding of the proposition that law makes claims to correctness than that of Raz.[13]

Stefano Bertea[14] puts forward a non-positivist account of legal certainty in his chapter, a concept that more than any other is assumed by positivists to undermine non-positivist explications of law. The chapter begins with an appraisal of the importance of certainty and its potential conflict with the value of justice, the other fundamental value enshrined in legal systems. This aspect of the law—certainty and justice, both of them fundamental

[11] N MacCormick, 'Why Law Makes No Claims?' (this volume).

[12] N MacCormick, *Institutions of Law* (Oxford, Oxford University Press, 2007).

[13] MacCormick explicitly formulates his thesis in order to include Raz's view that law raises a necessary claim to legitimate authority, which MacCormick treats as being in the neighbourhood of Robert Alexy's claim to correctness.

[14] S Bertea, 'How Non-Positivism Can Accommodate Legal Certainty?' (this volume).

values in law, and yet each of them colliding with the other—has been a source of serious theoretical problems, for reasons that are not far to seek. Both certainty and justice enjoy a fundamental status. Thus, any comprehensive theory of law needs to make sense of both, even if their relationship is one of conflict. Next, Bertea considers whether non-positivism can suitably accommodate certainty and hence be a genuinely general theory of law. Here he examines the specific version of non-positivism advanced by Robert Alexy with an eye to determining whether it can explain law's claim to certainty. The argument proceeds by introducing Alexy's theses on the nature of law and on legal certainty. The reconstruction is aimed at explaining the strategy Alexy adopts on the relationship between law and certainty, and at showing how the need to account for certainty contributes importantly to shaping his non-positivism. This Bertea follows up with a generalisation of the argument, going beyond Alexy and showing how non-positivism may well explain legal certainty. This, in turn, shows inter alia that non-positivism can legitimately aspire to be a comprehensive theory of law.

George Pavlakos' chapter[15] juxtaposes two of the most influential contemporary cognitivist theories in legal philosophy: Ronald Dworkin's interpretivism and Robert Alexy's discourse theory of law. Despite the fact that both thinkers address the possibility of right answers in law, their respective accounts begin from premises that are, prima facie, hard to reconcile. It may appear that the idea of a right answer might well be an illusion, for objective answers cannot be reached by endorsing conflicting ideas of objectivity. In the first part of the chapter, Pavlakos considers the conditions of objectivity in Dworkin's theory and identifies a series of difficulties that give rise to an insurmountable dilemma. The dilemma arises from alternative readings of 'interpretive theory', both of which are rejected after due consideration: either the content of interpretive theory is determined by the practice of the legal community or by some special substance that is intrinsic to legal phenomena. The former reading seems to be incompatible with Dworkin's criticisms of Hartian positivism; conversely, for the latter to work, one would have to assume that legal concepts are rigid designators that depict certain (mysterious) legal essences. This, then, is the dilemma that the two interpretations give rise to: either objectivity evaporates (communal practice), or it emerges in such strong form that it proves to be unattainable (legal essentialism). In the second part of the chapter Alexy's account of objectivity is taken up with an eye to addressing the dilemma. The discourse theory of law is reconstructed with a view to illustrating the deep structure of legal argumentation ('discursive grammar'). Discursive grammar is, then, shown

[15] G Pavlakos, 'Two Concepts of Objectivity' (this volume).

to underpin legal practice and to specify criteria for determining the validity of normative propositions—but without succumbing to the dilemma. The chapter concludes that the ostensible incompatibility between interpretivism's account of objectivity and that offered by the discourse theory of law can be bridged by substituting Alexy's philosophically more elaborate idea of a discursive grammar for Dworkin's less illuminating idea of a substantive theory.

Philippos Vassiloyannis[16] aims in his chapter to assess Alexy's thesis that legal discourse is a special case of moral discourse. He argues that the transition from moral to legal discourse is not only possible but, indeed, necessary for reasons moral in nature. The author claims that by subscribing to a procedural version of discourse ethics, akin to that of Jürgen Habermas, Alexy opens up his theory to the charge of reproducing the positivist distinction between law and morality or, in any case, to the charge that law has its own internal morality, one that is incompatible with any other normative sub-system. In conclusion, the author warns that a procedural discourse ethics, aside from failing to be Kantian in the desired way, runs the risk of being Kantian in a number of undesired ways: first, with respect to Kant's rejection—rather Hobbesian in spirit—of the right to civil disobedience; and, secondly, with respect to Kant's claim that it is conceptually impossible for the sovereign to commit an injustice.

Constitutional Rights

The second part of the volume is devoted to Alexy's arguments in *A Theory of Constitutional Rights*.[17] Amongst the questions addressed by the authors are: whether the idea of rights as optimisation requirements can capture the moral claims usually expressed in the language of classical liberal theory; what the advantages are of a structural account of political morality for adjudication; whether the theory of legal discourse can guarantee an impartial justification of rights, and, finally, whether an absolute justification of rights is compatible with a procedural theory of justification.

Mattias Kumm[18] poses the question in his chapter of whether it is plausible to claim that liberal political morality exhibits an optimisation structure of the sort suggested by the linkage between principles and proportionality analysis, as defended by Alexy in his *A Theory of Constitutional Rights*.[19] To address the question, the author examines three

[16] P Vassiloyannis, 'Discourse-Ethics, Legal Positivism and the Law' (this volume).
[17] Alexy, above n 1.
[18] M Kumm, 'Political Liberalism and the Structure of Rights' (this volume).
[19] Alexy, above n 1.

distinct ideas associated with the priority of rights within the liberal political tradition and assesses their implications for the structure of rights. The first concerns the priority of rights over the general good or general interest (the 'anticollectivist' dimension of political liberalism). This idea is easily expressed within the structure of rights as optimisation requirements, whereas competing structural accounts are less successful. The second concerns the priority of rights over the impositions of perfectionist ideals, religious or secular (the 'antiperfectionist' dimension of political liberalism). This idea, too, can be given expression within the optimisation structure suggested by Alexy, but the structure needs to be complemented by the idea of excluded reasons. To the extent that perfectionist concerns are deemed off limits for the purposes of establishing political justice, perfectionist arguments are categorically excluded as reasons that justify infringements on liberty—they are not balanced against them. With that qualification, however, the structure remains intact. The third idea concerns the strong restrictions placed on the use of a person as a means to bring about some otherwise desirable end without that person's consent (the 'anticonsequentialist' or deontological dimension of political liberalism). The chapter concludes that there is *no single moral structure* that adequately expresses the structure underlying the range of individual moral claims that are conventionally expressed using the language of rights. Instead, it is possible to discern *three distinct structures*. Nonetheless, Alexy's conception of rights as optimisation requirements is a useful model of the moral structure exhibited by the vast majority of constitutional rights cases in liberal democracies.

In the Postscript to the *Theory of Constitutional Rights* and in subsequent articles, Alexy demonstrates that the doctrine of proportionality is compatible with two categories of discretion, structural and epistemic. In responding to this view, Julian Rivers sets himself a twofold purpose in his chapter.[20] First, he seeks to establish the existence of four basic types of discretion implicit in the doctrine of proportionality. These are termed policy-choice discretion, which is a structural discretion based on the interrelationship of the tests of necessity and balancing; cultural discretion, which is a structural discretion based on disagreements about relative abstract values of constitutional 'goods'; scalar discretion, which is a mixed structural-epistemic discretion based on the relative crudeness or refinement of value-classifications; and expertise discretion, which is an epistemic discretion related to the processes by which empirical data are established and the degree of certainty with which associated beliefs may be held. Although suggesting certain modifications in Alexy's theory, Rivers' account remains fairly close to the original. The author's second

[20] J Rivers, 'Proportionality, Discretion and the Second Law of Balancing' (this volume).

purpose is to demonstrate that, while the existence of discretion is a possible part of the doctrine of proportionality, its scope is determined by the competence of different political institutions. The theory as such is open to a variety of possible scopes of discretion. In the light of both typical features of legal arrangements for the protection of fundamental rights, as well as judicial discussions of discretion and variable standards of review in international, European and domestic law, the theory seeks to identify the main factors affecting the scope of discretion permitted to legislatures and executive bodies vis-à-vis proportionality under a regime of judicial review. Thus, Rivers seeks both to apply Alexy's theory to problems of judicial reasoning and clarify a significant area of confusion in contemporary jurisprudence.

Jan-Reinard Sieckmann takes up the argument of the claim to correctness in Alexy's theory along with its use within the discursive justification of human rights.[21] The analysis points to two basic problems; first, the inadequacy for a discursive theory of justification of a semantics that is restricted to assertions and propositions, and, secondly, the necessity of distinguishing between rational justification based on the long-term self interest of individuals, and the moral justification of human rights. Conversely, it is argued that a more adequate account of a necessary claim to correctness is possible within a model of principles, which conceives of them as normative arguments whose conclusions have the status of normative claims that are to be weighed and balanced against each other. This model provides a foundation for the justification of norms and, in particular, of human rights.

Inconsistency among legal principles may exist prior to their application in particular cases and may continue to exist thereafter. Inconsistencies are removed for particular decisions. The situation is the same for rights—both human rights, and rights granted under constitutions. Alexy reasons that we need to specify pragmatic rules of rational discussion which govern the procedure of justification, but even these do not determine a single outcome.[22] Jonathan Gorman[23] shows this in his chapter by analysing in detail the contrast between interpersonal moral disagreement and intrapersonal moral puzzlement, showing that their structures are not analogous. Interpersonal disagreement raises the moral problem of toleration, but puzzlement does not. The essence of disagreement lies in the mere contingency that another person disagrees. Toleration qua concept has a three-person justification situation built into it, and an accurate specification of the applicability of the concept minimally requires three separate

[21] J-R Sieckmann, 'Human Rights and the Claim to Correctness in the Theory of Robert Alexy' (this volume).

[22] See in general Alexy, *A Theory of Legal Argumentation*, above n 1.

[23] J Gorman, 'Three-Person Justification' (this volume).

codes: the code of one party, the conflicting code of the other, and the necessarily distinct code of the judge. Judicial decisions are a special case of three-person justificatory discourse. This discourse requires a range of concepts such as toleration, which are appropriate to such discourse. By contrast, the codes of competing parties cannot properly use such concepts. In view of the above, Gorman concludes that Alexy's conditions for discourse in general, which are typically two-person conditions, are not sufficient for our understanding here.

Discourse and Argumentation

The third part of the book addresses the issue of rationality in legal discourses with an eye to Alexy's first book, *A Theory of Legal Argumentation*.[24] The topics discussed in this part concern the nature and limits of legal rationality; the epistemic conditions for legal knowledge; the nature of discursive correctness as a regulative ideal; the differences between a teleological and a deontological conception of legal reasoning; the relation between unjust and self-contradictory normative sentences; the compatibility of a discourse theory as a theory of validity of normative propositions with its role as a sociological theory of practices of communication; and, finally, the problems in a theory of legal argumentation that are linked to the formalisation of weighing principles.

In her contribution, Maeve Cooke[25] takes stock of the philosophical background of discourse theory with an eye to arguing that neither Habermas' nor Alexy's conceptions of legal validity live up to the requirements of discourse theory. The thesis that the law is open to criticism, not just from the outside but from within the system of law itself, is central to the discourse theories of law proposed by Alexy and Habermas. In this way they distance themselves from legal positivism. Alexy and Habermas disagree, however, as to how the context-transcending component of law's claim to correctness should be understood. Alexy assimilates legal correctness (in the context-transcending sense) to the correctness of moral norms. Habermas rejects this as a 'moralisation' of legal validity; instead, he ties legal correctness to the substantial unity of practical reason in the democratic decision-making process. Cooke argues that the result is a contextualist interpretation of law's claim to correctness that is at odds with the antipositivist orientation of Habermas' legal theory. Conversely, she calls for an approach that neither assimilates legal to moral validity (Alexy) nor curtails the context-transcending force of legal validity claims (Habermas). For this purpose, she proposes a model of practical reasoning

[24] See Alexy, above n 1.
[25] M Cooke, 'Law's Claim to Correctness' (this volume).

in which legal decisions claim neither moral validity nor general acceptability in a given democratic order, but rather *practical rationality*: correctness in a context-transcending sense that represents a complex interplay of moral, ethical and pragmatic elements.

In his contribution,[26] Giovanni Sartor considers two ideas that play a fundamental role in the thought of Robert Alexy: the idea of dialogue and the idea of teleological reasoning, with an eye to posing a philosophical conflict and to providing a pragmatic reconciliation between them. It is first argued that dialogues (and, in particular, ideal dialogues) cannot provide a foundation for practical reasoning, for we must choose whether to engage in dialogue and how to structure our dialogues according to practical reasoning, and, in particular, according to teleological reasoning. However, important teleological considerations underlie the practice of dialectical procedures, and, in particular, the kinds of procedure that have been presented and defended by Alexy in his theory of legal reasoning.

Giorgio Bongiovanni, Antonino Rotolo and Corrado Roversi[27] attempt to clarify the conditions of the claim to correctness by making explicit the interaction between the semantic and pragmatic dimensions of norms. In Alexy's theory of practical discourse, the claim to correctness is necessarily raised by all normative speech acts in so far as they ought to be open to justification. If agent x gives expression to a norm N, x must be ready to justify N in the context of a practical discourse. Rejecting this thesis entails rejecting the very possibility of argumentation and so, of meaningfully giving expression to N. In performing this task the authors develop an inferential semantics by using the framework developed by Robert Brandom in *Making It Explicit*. In this context, it is shown that the semantic content of practical assertions depends on the role they play as premises or conclusions in argumentation, and it is shaped with respect to their inferential correctness. Hence, giving expression to a norm N means committing oneself with respect to N's discursive conditions of appropriateness. Thus, the claim to correctness means, inter alia, a claim to propositional content. What is more, the notion of normative self-contradictoriness—itself of key importance for the justification of the claim to correctness—may be explained in terms of different degrees of semantic meaninglessness.

In his chapter,[28] Carsten Heidemann brings out a potential contradiction lurking in the discourse theories of Habermas and Alexy. On the one hand, discourse theory is, according to Habermas, the legitimate successor of *prima philosophia* and, as such, a theory of objective validity in a strong

[26] G Sartor, 'Varieties of Dialogues and their Teleological Justification' (this volume).

[27] See G Bongiovanni *et al*, 'The Claim to Correctness and Inferentialism: Alexy's Theory of Practical Reason Reconsidered' (this volume).

[28] C Heidemann, 'The Concept of Validity in a Theory of Social Action' (this volume).

sense. On the other hand, it is first and foremost a sociological theory of communication practices, with the aim of reconstructing the internal perspective of those who participate in those practices. These aspects are hard to reconcile with one another. As a theory of objective validity, discourse theory cannot make plausible why it is that the validity of (normative) sentences ought to depend on the performance of a discourse. As a theory of social interaction, it cannot—conversely—make plausible why the results of felicitous de facto social interaction ought to be regarded as objectively valid. What is missing in discourse theory is a convincing justification for the equation of 'a normative sentence which is agreed upon under certain conditions' with 'an objectively valid normative sentence'. This shortcoming leads to a number of collateral problems, regarding, in particular, the nature of the 'input' into the normative discourse.

Bartosz Brożek pursues in his chapter[29] two ends: first, to determine precisely the role of the 'weight formula' and the 'subsumption scheme' within the framework of Robert Alexy's theory of legal argumentation; and, secondly, to analyse the logical mechanisms of both modes of reasoning. Contrary to Alexy's explicit claims, Brożek argues that the weight formula and the subsumption scheme do not count as two distinct forms of legal argumentation. In order to substantiate this thesis, he distinguishes between two levels or layers of legal discourse: the level of constructing arguments and the level of comparing them. He claims that the subsumption scheme is at work at the former level, the weight formula at the latter. Moreover, he argues that there is no balancing—and hence no application of the weight formula—without recourse to the subsumption scheme. All of this leads to serious logical puzzles, for it turns out that classical logic—favoured by Alexy—is incapable of handling the relationship between the weight formula and the subsumption scheme. It is a central claim of the chapter that legal discourse ought to be modelled on the use of a defeasible logic. It is here that one has the resources needed to account for the two-level idea of argumentation.

[29] B Brożek, 'The Weight Formula and Argumentation' (this volume).

Part I

A Debate on Legal Positivism

1

The Argument from Justice, or How Not to Reply to Legal Positivism

JOSEPH RAZ

PROFESSOR ROBERT ALEXY wrote a book whose avowed purpose is to refute the basic tenets of a type of legal theory which 'has long since been obsolete in legal science and practice'. The quotation is from the German Federal Constitutional Court in 1968.[1] The fact that Prof Alexy himself mentions no writings in the legal positivist tradition [in English] later than Hart's *The Concept of Law* (1961) may suggest that he shares the court's view.[2] The book itself may be evidence to the contrary. After all why flog a dead horse? Why write a book to refute a totally discredited theory? Perhaps Alexy was simply unlucky. The burst of reflective, suggestive and interesting writings in the legal positivist tradition reached serious dimensions only in the years after the original publication of his book, when Waldron, Marmor, Gardner, Leiter, Shapiro, Murphy, Himma, Kramer, Endicott, Lamont, Dickson, Bix and others joined those who had made important contributions to legal theory in the positivistic tradition in the years preceding the original publication of Alexy's book: Lyons, Coleman, Campbell, Harris, Green, Waluchow and others, who are still among the main contributors to legal theory in the positivist tradition. It is a great shame that nothing in these writings influenced the arguments of the book.

[1] Cited by R Alexy in *The Argument from Injustice: A Reply to Legal Positivism* (Oxford, Clarendon Press, 2002) original German publication as *Begriff und Geltung des Rechts* (Freiburg and Munich, Alber, 1992).

[2] The Federal Constitutional Court's reference is narrower than I made it appear. It refers to 'statutory positivism'. Since the case, and the passages from which the citation is extracted, are used by Alexy to show how the dispute between legal positivists and their opponents bears on legal practice, I thought it fair to assume that he took the court's statement to imply something like the following: a legal positivist theory of law requires 'statutory positivism'. Since 'statutory positivism' is false it follows that so is any theory in the legal positivist tradition.

Perhaps this regret is misplaced. After all 'positivism' in legal theory means, and always did mean, different things to different people. What Radbruch, one of Alexy's heroes, meant when he first saw himself as a legal positivist and then recanted was not the same as what 'legal positivism' means in Britain (and nowadays in the United States as well) among those who engage in philosophical reflection about the nature of law. Perhaps Alexy is simply addressing himself to a German audience, and refuting, or attempting to refute, legal theories of a kind identified in Germany as 'legal positivism'. Perhaps, though his references to Hart show that he does not intend it that way.

My aims in this chapter are, however, reasonably clear. My main purpose is to explore whether any of Alexy's arguments challenge any of the views which I have advocated. Subsidiary aims are, first, to clarify why what Alexy says is legal positivism is not what is understood as such in the English speaking world, so that some of Alexy's sound points find no target; secondly, to try and clarify some of his arguments which I found, at least initially, rather obscure. Given the prominence of Alexy's book I will refer only to it, and will not consider his other publications.

IDENTIFYING LEGAL POSITIVISM

According to Alexy the common feature of all legal positivist theories is 'the separation thesis which says that the concept of law is to be defined such that [*sic*] no moral elements are included. The separation thesis presupposes that there is no conceptually necessary connection between law and morality ... The great legal positivist Hans Kelsen captured this in the statement, "thus the content of the law can be anything whatsoever"'.[3]

It is a pity that the only support for this claim is a statement of Kelsen's which is manifestly false according to Kelsen's own theory. Since Kelsen regards the law as consisting of norms directing courts to apply sanctions for breach of duties,[4] it follows (a) that the law can consist only of norms, (b) that it must address courts, (c) that it must stipulate for the application of sanctions, and (d) that their application must be conditional on certain conduct taking place. All these are, according to Kelsen's theory, necessary restrictions on the content of the law. Perhaps they do not violate the separation thesis as Alexy understands it, but they certainly do not support it, and, as I said, they show Kelsen's statement cited by Alexy to be false by Kelsen's own lights.

[3] Alexy, above n 1 at 3.

[4] See H Kelsen, *Pure Theory of Law*, 2nd edn (M Knight (trans), Berkeley and Los Angeles, University of California Press, 1967) para 28(a) (pp 114–17).

I should explain why Kelsen's statement cited by Alexy does not, even if true, support the separation thesis. But first we need to ponder what that thesis is. In the course of clarifying the thesis the irrelevance to it of Kelsen's claim will become clear. It says, according to Alexy, that 'the concept of law is to be defined such that no moral elements are included'—presumably in the definition. And as the definition is a proposition, the elements referred to must be concepts. So the thesis is that no moral concepts feature in the definition of law.

Given that it is highly debatable what are moral concepts, this is an unpromising way of identifying legal positivism. Many normative and evaluative concepts are common to moral and non-moral discourse. There are moral and non-moral reasons, duties, rights, virtues, offences, rules, laws, and so on. There are difficulties in demarcating the realm of morality, and distinguishing between it and the non-moral domain,[5] which is but one reason why I see little to be gained in trying to identify which concepts are moral concepts. My own writings on the law may highlight another problem with this way of understanding the separation thesis. I maintain that necessarily the law claims to have legitimate authority, and that that claim is a moral claim.[6] It is a moral claim because of its content: it is a claim which includes the assertion of a right to grant rights and impose duties in matters affecting basic aspects of people's life and their interactions with one another. Does it follow that I believe in a definition of law which includes moral concepts? Not necessarily. So far as I remember I did not advance a definition of law. I was merely arguing about some of its necessary features.

It was Hart who convinced many legal theorists that the concentration on defining law in some earlier writings about the nature of law is unproductive. He wrote about this in his inaugural lecture in 1953, and again in *The Concept of Law* in 1961.[7] Without going into detail, definitions normally aim to demarcate the boundaries of what is defined, to identify a set of features possession of which is necessary and sufficient for the defined concept to apply to their possessor. Three relevant conclusions follow: first, that concepts may admit of more than one definition (in other words, there can be more than one set of necessary and sufficient

[5] I argued that the task is without theoretical significance in *Engaging Reason* (Oxford, Oxford University Press, 1999), chs 11 & 12. T M Scanlon's *What We Owe to Each Other* (Cambridge Mass, Belknap Press, 1998) is an interesting case. His theory proposes an account of an important moral domain: wronging others. But it acknowledges that morality is much wider, and makes no attempt to identify its boundaries. Domains such as supererogation, virtue, duties which are not owed to other people are left untouched.

[6] My first publication including these points is *Practical Reason and Norms*, 1st edn (Oxford, Oxford University Press, 1975) and 2nd edn (1999) ch 5.

[7] The explanation I give below is close to the reasons why *The Concept of Law* avoids definitions, but not to Hart's earlier argument.

conditions for the application of the concept). Secondly, arguably some concepts do not have definitions, or at least no known definitions of this kind, at all, since there are no known or knowable and informative features which constitute necessary and sufficient conditions for their application. Finally, there is no theoretical justification to focus on the definition of the concepts rather than on their necessary features, some of which may not figure in any sensible definition of them. At any rate, the question arises: what is special about the features which figure in a definition? Why should they be at the core of the separation thesis, whereas other necessary features of the concepts are not?[8]

So let us try to reformulate the separation thesis to meet these points. Possibly it would then be the proposition that a theory belongs to the legal positivist tradition if and only if it maintains that the necessary features of the law can be stated without the use of any moral concepts. By this thesis my writings on the nature of law do not belong to the legal positivist tradition, since they ascribe to the law as an essential feature that it claims legitimate authority, and the concept of legitimate authority is a moral one.

I do not care whether my views are classified with legal positivism, as they commonly are, or not. I believe that the classification of legal theories as legal positivist or non-legal positivist, which underpins the structure of Alexy's book, is unhelpful and liable to mislead. And in a way my remarks here are meant to illustrate this point. But I know of no one who thinks that the fact that a theory of the nature of law makes claims which can only be made with the use of moral concepts shows that it does not belong to the legal positivist tradition.

Arguably, Alexy himself does not understand the separation thesis to mean what it means given his statement of its content. As we saw he believes that 'the separation thesis presupposes that there is no conceptually necessary connection between law and morality'. But the proposition that the definition of law does not contain moral elements, ie can be articulated without the use of moral concepts, does not presuppose that there is no conceptually necessary connection between law and morality.

I will again use my own work to illustrate the point. In *Practical Reason and Norms*[9] I argued (reformulating the point in a way I now find clearer and more accurate) that even if all the law's essential features can be stated without the use of moral concepts it may be the case that that it has those features entails that it has some moral merit. At different times when repeating this point I instanced Lon Fuller's and John Finnis' theories, not ones ever considered to belong to the legal positivist tradition, as possible

[8] There is the additional question: should we focus on the necessary features of the law or of the concept of law? But I will not stop to consider it here.

[9] See above n 6.

examples, though whether they are depends on certain interpretive questions regarding their claims. These theories, among the central examples of natural law theories in recent times, at the very least show the possibility of both meeting Alexy's test for being legal positivist theories, and being at the centre of the natural law tradition. We should conclude either that legal positivists can be natural lawyers, and vice versa, that is that the classification of theories into legal positivist and others is misleading and unhelpful, or that Alexy's separation thesis is not the test for being a legal positivist. I am inclined to accept both conclusions.

I do not wish to ignore the fact that something in the general neighbourhood of Alexy's separation thesis is sometimes put forward as a defining mark of legal positivism. It is commonly understood to state that whether or not the law of any country taken in general, or each one of its legal rules taken singly, has any moral merit is a contingent matter. I will call this the 'contingency thesis'. It should not be confused with what Alexy mentions as the presupposition of the separation thesis, namely the absence of a conceptually necessary connection between law and morality. For example, it is a conceptual point about the law that it can be morally evaluated as good or bad, and as just or unjust, just as it is a conceptual fact about black holes that propositions like 'this black hole is morally better or more just than that' make no sense. So there are conceptually necessary connections between law and morality which no legal positivist has any reason to deny.

What, then, are we to say of the contingency thesis? It is false, and Alexy of course agrees with its rejection. But the interesting point is that it is false for reasons which have no relevance to the main theses of theories of law in the positivist tradition. It cannot therefore be taken as a defining feature of this tradition. John Gardner dubbed the association of legal positivism with this thesis as one of the myths about positivism.[10] It is easy to see why. It is a necessary fact, for example, that rape cannot be committed by the law.[11] There are naturally an indefinite number of necessary moral properties that the law of any country must have if it has this one, or others similar to it. Such truth as there is in Fuller's claims that some of the formal, in themselves non-moral, necessary features of the law, such as its reliance on general standards, restrict its ability to be arbitrary, shows those features to be among those which establish a necessary connection between law, specified without reference to morality, and morality.

It would be evident to all that the fact that the law necessarily has moral properties of the kind illustrated (and there are other more interesting

[10] See J Gardner, 'Legal Positivism: 5 /12 Myth' (2001) 46 *American Journal of Jurisprudence* 199 at 222.

[11] See this example and more generally on the issue J Raz, 'About Morality and the Nature of Law' (2003) 48 *American Journal of Jurisprudence* 1.

examples) does not invalidate anything which I or any theorist within the legal positivist tradition ever held dear. You can now see why Kelsen's assertion that the law can have any content whatsoever, even if true, lends no support to Alexy's separation thesis, or to any of its reformulations and modifications that we examined. It is even consistent with the rejection of the contingency thesis.

These reflections may help explain why I am referring not to 'legal positivism', but to 'theories in the positivist tradition'. Theories belong to a tradition by their frame of reference, sense of what is problematic and what is not, and by similar historical features which do not presuppose that they all share a central credo. But possibly there is a fairly important thesis which is common to all the theories within the tradition of legal positivism. If so, then it is likely to be 'that determining what the law is does not necessarily, or conceptually, depend on moral or other evaluative considerations about what the law ought to be in the relevant circumstances'.[12] Andrei Marmor, whose formulation this is, calls it 'the separation thesis', and as it is much more successful in getting at the common core of the positivist tradition, when referring to the separation thesis without qualification it is this thesis I will have in mind. I believe it to be correct. Indeed I have endorsed, under the name of the 'sources thesis' in *The Authority of Law*,[13] a stricter thesis, namely that the identification of law never requires the use of moral arguments or judgements about its merit; although the sources thesis was not endorsed by Hart, and is not endorsed by many writers within the positivist tradition, those who are now variously known as inclusive positivists, or soft positivists.

OBSERVERS AND PARTICIPANTS

What has all this to do with Alexy's refutation of legal positivism? Alexy's failure to define legal positivism in a way which would apply to many of the theories of law commonly known as positivist does not entail that he failed to refute theories belonging to that tradition. It only means that some of his arguments, aimed as they are at refuting his separation thesis, are not relevant to that task. Even when successful they do not refute legal positivism in the sense in which the term is used in the English-language tradition of legal thought, especially in its contemporary meaning. Nevertheless, some of Alexy's arguments, if sound, would undermine the success of theories in that tradition, which, as I indicated, is best identified by Marmor's separation thesis. Ignoring the rest, I will try to examine those arguments. What are they?

[12] A Marmor, *Positive Law and Objective Values* (Oxford, Clarendon Press, 2001) 71.
[13] J Raz, *The Authority of Law* (Oxford, Clarendon Press, 1979).

They are preceded by a long series of distinctions not all of which I understand. One distinction which is put to instant use by Alexy has to be confronted. It is the distinction between the participant's and the observer's perspective. The participant's perspective is that 'adopted by one who, within the legal system, participates in disputation about what is commanded, forbidden, and permitted in the legal system, and to what end this legal system confers power'.[14] It is contrasted with 'the observer perspective', namely that 'adopted by one who asks . . . how decisions are actually made in a certain legal system'.[15] This characterisation is multiply puzzling. What for example is it to participate in a disputation about the law 'within the legal system'? What is it to participate in such a disputation without or outside the legal system? If I[16] write an article about the German law regarding the rights of asylum seekers in Germany for a British magazine am I within the legal system or outside it? Would my article, if presented to a German court as part of an interpretative argument about German law, turn into one written from within, whereas until then it was one written from outside? I suspect that the phrase 'within a legal system' is better omitted. It adds nothing but confusion to the characterisation of the distinction.

Similarly, I suspect that 'participates in disputation' is not intended to mean what it means. If I publish an article expressing a view about what German law is on certain matters (eg that there is, or there is not local income tax in Germany), or if I explain German law to my students I do not participate in any disputation. But a lawyer could make the very same points, express the very same propositions when arguing before a court, and what determine the truth of his assertion are the same factors which determine the truth of my assertion. I can see no way of distinguishing the disputant's perspective from mine, and as Alexy does not explain what the difference may be I will assume that there is none, and that the participant's perspective has nothing to do with participation in disputations.

The way Alexy uses the distinction[17] makes clear that his typical participant is not so much someone participating in a disputation as a judge, or court, deciding a case. But again, leaving aside the fact that a court's decision is binding on the litigants, and as such has the effect of law-making between them, and focusing exclusively on the reasons the court gives in support of its decision, we cannot see here any evidence of a special perspective. Normally we expect a court to be as faithful to the truth about the law as we do a litigating lawyer, an academic scholar or a

[14] Alexy, above n 1 at 25.

[15] *Ibid.*

[16] To remove doubt let me admit that I am not German, never lived in Germany and have no academic qualifications in German law.

[17] eg Alexy, above n 1 at 42.

foreign commentator. Whatever their other aims, when stating what German law is they all normally[18] have the same aim: to state truly how German law is.

The next puzzle is this: is the 'observer's perspective' one which those inquiring 'how decisions are actually made' should adopt if they are to succeed in finding the answer to their question? Or does it consist simply in inquiring how decisions are actually made, so that adopting it is no more than asking that question? A parallel question arises regarding the participant's perspective. To make vivid the difference think of a methodological claim in anthropology: some anthropologists claim that to understand a culture one must adopt the point of view of its participants; that the explanation of a culture misses its target if it does not explain the meanings rituals had for the people who engaged in them. Here we have a clear separation between (a) the subject of inquiry (the rituals of a particular population) and (b) the method of inquiry (explaining the meaning the rituals have for the members of that population). Providing statistics about the impact of the ritual on economic productivity may be interesting, but will not—according to this claim—constitute an explanation of the ritual.

At no point does Alexy say anything which can be taken as assigning any content to the two perspectives. He does not specify different methodologies as being employed by their practitioners. We are thus forced to the supposition that having these perspectives is simply seeking or endorsing propositions or views about what the law is ('participant's perspective') or about how courts actually decide cases ('observer's perspective'). I will assume that to be his view, odd though it is to say that a class of truths identified by their subject matter constitutes a perspective. It would be odd, eg, to think that those interested in physics and those interested in the pay and status of physicists adopt, just by the fact that they have different subjects, two different perspectives. And Alexy gives us no more reason for assuming that his 'participant and observer perspectives' are perspectives.[19]

Given that we are given no choice but to assume that the difference between the observer's and the participant's perspective is the subject matter of their inquiry there is no reason to expect them not to be able to share the same concepts. One or the other of them may find that some concepts crop up more often in his inquiries, but there is no principled

[18] The qualification allows for cases in which they aim to deceive, or just do not care about the truth of their utterances. Such cases exist but are necessarily parasitical on the normal case.

[19] Unless his reference to the alleged similarity of his distinction to Hart's between the internal and external point of view is taken to be one. But that would be a mistake. The two distinctions bear no similarity to each other. Hart's internal point of view marks the position of a person who endorses a set of norms or reasons. There is nothing of that in Alexy's 'participant's perspective'.

reason why they should diverge in any way in their concepts. It is therefore surprising to find Alexy claiming that the statement:

> *A* has not been deprived of citizenship according to German law, although all German courts and officials treat *A* as denaturalized . . .[20] as a statement of an observer contains a contradiction.[21]

Given that being contradictory is a property of statements or of propositions and not of the relations between them and those who make or express them, it is odd that the statement is contradictory 'as a statement of an observer'. If Alexy means that the same statement can be made either from a 'participant's' or from 'an observer's perspective' then, given that it is the same statement, if it contains a contradiction if made from one point of view it does so if made from any point of view.

Moreover, given the way the observer's perspective was defined it is odd to regard this as an observer's statement. Surely, it consists of two component statements; the first, being about what the law is, is—by Alexy's definition—a participant's statement, while the second is an observer's statement, since it is about what legal institutions actually do. Taken together they imply that the officials are flouting the law by the way they treat A. This is, we assume, unfortunate, but it is hardly a contradiction. If I am right so far then Alexy's conclusion that the observer has a special concept of law and that his statement avoids contradiction because of that cannot be sustained. There may well be more than one concept of law in current use, but no reason is given here, nor anywhere else in the book, for thinking that 'participants' and 'observers' are committed by their role to use different concepts. That is, the study of what the law is, and the study of how judges deal with cases, can use the same concepts. Indeed they had better use the same concepts (though they may use more than one) since the second (the study of how judges actually deal with cases) is meant to tell us, among other things, what happens to the law (the very same law we study when we are 'participants') in the hands of the courts. All this has the unfortunate consequence that Alexy's statement that 'the separation thesis is essentially correct from the observer's perspective'[22] is not supported by his own analysis. I will return to Alexy's use of the distinction between the two perspectives below.

[20] Alexy, above n 1 at 29–30.
[21] *Ibid* at 30.
[22] *Ibid* at 35.

THE CORRECTNESS THESIS

Alexy states that while his argument is one from injustice its foundations are in the more basic thesis, the thesis of correctness, which says—and this is all we are ever explicitly told about it—that the law as a whole, and each of its norms and decisions, claim to be correct.[23] I assume that the thesis is not explained because Alexy thinks that it is too obvious to require explanation. Let me explain my difficulties.

You may say that the claim made by the law is that it is correct as law, that it is what the law should be. The claim made by any legal decision is that it is correct qua legal decision. I am, it claims, what I should be. The decision claims: I am the decision that I should be. This sounds plausible, but how is it to be understood, and how does Alexy establish this conclusion? A natural reading is to take it to be a special case of a more general thesis: every speech act presents itself as doing something: stating how things are, raising a question, expressing goodwill, making a promise, giving advice. In presenting itself as such an action it claims to be, in the circumstances of the case, correct as an action of that kind.

This thesis can be explained as an instance of a still more general thesis applying to all intentional actions, which explains reference to 'the claim made by a speech act' by reference to a commitment of the speaker, or, more generally, the agent: the agent commits himself to the action's being correct, or appropriate. That means that if an agent acts intentionally and is proven to have acted inappropriately or unwisely, or in some other way to have acted as he should not have, he must, once convinced of his mistake, believe that he should not have acted as he did, on pain of irrationality. In this sense every intentional action 'claims', that is commits its agent to, its own correctness. As is evident the thesis merely means that (a) actions of different kinds are subject to evaluation as actions of those kinds (though perhaps also to other evaluations as well), and (b) it is part of the concept of intentional action that one who performs an intentional action knows that his action is subject to assessment by the standard applying to actions of that kind (the kind under which it is intentional).

The law is not an action, but it is the product of intentional actions, and it is common to attribute to the product of an action some of the properties of the action. For example, if the agent states that things are thus and so, then he commits himself to the statements not only that it was right to state that they are thus and so, but also that they are thus and so, namely that the proposition expressing his statement is true. Thus the law-maker commits himself that the act of making this law was appropriate, and this can be taken as a commitment that the law thus made is as it should be.

[23] *Ibid* at 35–6.

There are two difficulties in understanding Alexy's correctness thesis in this way. First, my interpretation of the correctness thesis renders it, I think, true, but at the cost of taking it to be a general thesis about intentional actions and their products, thus denying that it says anything special about the law. Alexy, by way of contrast, rather than taking the thesis to be an instance of a wider one, regards it as perhaps special to the law. At any rate he denies that it applies to the actions of 'a bandit system'.[24] But surely if the bandits act intentionally as bandits their actions manifest the thesis: bandits are committed to the claim that what they do is appropriate (being self-enriching, looking after their own children, wreaking revenge, or whatever are the considerations which explicitly or implicitly they take to establish the appropriateness of their actions). Perhaps some bandits are guilt-ridden, believing themselves to be always in the wrong. Perhaps some bandits are motivated by self-hate, and a desire for self-debasement which leads them subconsciously to want to do the wrong thing. One doubts that such motivations are more prevalent among bandits than among the judges of the High Court, but it does not matter. People who are so motivated manifest as clearly as others that they share the commitment that their actions be correct. For only through the violation of this commitment can they realise their self-debasing desires. More interesting is the possibility that the bandits do not think of their actions in the way Alexy describes them. They may think of them as Christian actions, they may act intending to act in a Christian way (perhaps that is how Robin Hood and his band intended their actions). In that case they are claiming correctness by that standard, ie by the standard of Christianity. Their actions may not be intentional under the description 'bandit actions', and they may not be claiming correctness by those standards, if there are such.

The second difficulty in understanding Alexy's correctness thesis along the lines I suggested is that he thinks (or implies) that the correctness thesis involves, though it is not exhausted by, a claim that the law is morally correct.

These difficulties notwithstanding, I think that my interpretation is the right interpretation of what is true in the correctness thesis, for there is something true in it, and that Alexy is at least half aware of it. For no sooner has he invoked as an example of the correctness claimed by the law a claim to justice,[25] than he concedes[26] that 'a positivist can endorse the argument from correctness and nevertheless insist on the separation thesis' (this is, of course, Alexy's separation thesis). Alexy explains that, among

[24] *Ibid* at 34.
[25] *Ibid* at 36–7.
[26] *Ibid* at 39.

other reasons, the legal positivist can 'maintain that the claim to correctness, having trivial content lacking moral implications, cannot lead to a conceptual connection between law and morality'. Taken literally, as I think it should be, these points allow that if there is an argument against positivism, the correctness thesis does not contribute to it (for 'a positivist can endorse' it, etc).

I think that Alexy is right on this point. The inability of the correctness thesis to yield substantive results is worth understanding properly: the correctness thesis, as I explained and generalised it, is not empty, but it is formal. It is also a conceptual truth. It marks the nature of purposive activity (and its products). Having a purpose involves subjecting oneself to some standards of correctness, standards establishing that the purpose is worth adopting and pursuing, etc. It is a conceptual thesis not specifically about the law (though it applies to the law) but about the nature of purposes, intentional actions and their products, ie that in being endorsed by their agents, who could in principle reject them, they commit their agents to standards of appropriateness.

The thesis is formal in that it does not determine what standards apply. Obviously, since it is so general, applying to all purposeful conduct, it cannot do that. Different standards apply to different activities and pursuits. It is the nature of various activities, and of the circumstances in which they are undertaken, which determines which standards apply to them. If the law is committed to standards of justice this follows from the nature of law, not from the nature of purposeful activity. It follows that nothing can be learnt from the correctness thesis about the nature of law. Rather, once we have established, in light of other arguments, what is the nature of law, and only then, will we be able to conclude which commitments the law makes, or what claims it makes. The correctness thesis, being a formal thesis, while true, affords no specific help in elucidating the nature of law. I will return to Alexy's use of the thesis below.

THE ARGUMENT FROM INJUSTICE

Alexy aims to vindicate Radbruch's formula, namely:

> The conflict between justice and legal certainty may well be resolved in this way: The positive law, secured by legislation and power, takes precedence even when its content is unjust and inexpedient, unless the conflict between statute and justice reaches such an intolerable degree that the statute, as a 'lawless law' must yield to justice.[27]

[27] See G Radbruch, *Rechtsphilosophie III. Vol 3 of the Gustav Radbruch Gesamtausgabe* (A Kaufmann (ed), Heidelberg, CF Mueller, 1990) 89.

On its face this passage is ambiguous between two positions: it could mean, consistently with legal positivism, that it is the duty of the court to refuse to apply a statutory provision which is grossly unjust.[28] Alternatively, it can mean that the law necessarily (for I assume that Radbruch was not writing merely about German or any other specific legal system), contains a legal norm instructing the courts to refuse to apply laws which perpetrate gross injustices (either because every legal system contains a rule dictating that grossly unjust law is not law, or because every legal system contains a legal rule, which overrides all others, which directs judges to disregard unjust rules even if they are law).[29] I am no Radbruch scholar, but I assume that Alexy is right in ascribing to Radbruch the second view. In any case this is the view which Alexy defends.

Surprisingly, his defence, elaborate and often subtle, takes the form of disputing, often successfully, a large number of unsuccessful arguments against the Radbruch formula. To find in the book any argument for the thesis is hard. But that is what I would try to do.

Alexy argues thus:

> Take the substantive thesis that there are good legal reasons for the judge not to apply Ordinance 11 . . . Given this presupposition it would be unsatisfactory for the judge to say that Ordinance 11 is law. He must characterise his decision as 'law' since he is deciding on the basis of legal reasons. Since his decision contradicts Ordinance 11, then if he were also to classify Ordinance 11 as 'law', he would be characterizing contradictory norms as 'law'. . . . This contradiction can be resolved without difficulty if the judge says that Ordinance 11 is indeed prima-facie law but in the end not law at all. What is expressed thereby is that, in the course of the norm-applying procedure, Ordinance 11 is denied legal character. If there are good legal reasons for not applying Ordinance 11 then not only is it possible for the judge to say that the Ordinance is in the end not law, it is necessary that he do so in order to avoid a contradiction.[30]

Given that there can be legal reasons for the judge to invalidate Ordinance 11—their existence is a contingent matter—the concept of law may include moral elements.[31]

There is, however, nothing in the argument, assuming *arguendo* that it is sound when understood as Alexy intends it, to show that the concept of law includes moral elements. It only shows that the law includes such elements, ie that the law can include a norm that grossly unjust laws are

[28] Legal positivists are more likely than natural lawyers or other non-legal positivists to affirm that sometimes courts have (moral) duties to disobey unjust laws.

[29] One may regret that Radbruch did not consider some related issues. For example, what if refusing to apply the unjust law would itself yield grossly unjust results, as can be the case; or, what if the law is not grossly unjust, but its application to a particular case is? To simplify matters, I will myself ignore all such relevant but complicating factors.

[30] Alexy, above n 1 at 42.

[31] Alexy, above n 1 at 42.

invalid, if, for example, the legislature passes a statute to that effect. On that assumption, consistent with everything in the argument, the concept of law need include nothing but that the law is whatever the legislature legislates. When the legislature instructs a court to use its power to set aside grossly unjust laws the court should use its judgement on moral matters to decide which laws to set aside.

This seems consistent with Alexy's observation that one can describe what happened in the case as 'derogating judge-made law'.[32] Is there anything in the quotation to explain why that is not the correct description of the situation? Alexy says that the judge 'must characterise his decision as "law" since he is deciding on the basis of legal reasons'. How are we to understand this? Perhaps Alexy means that the judge must hold his decision to be legally binding. That is so, however, not because he is deciding on the basis of legal reasons, but because he has the legal power to determine the matter litigated before him. That makes his decision binding in law, and it is so binding even if it is mistaken in law, that is, even if it is not correctly based on legal reasons. Perhaps Alexy means not merely that the court's decision is binding, but that it is in fact also a correct application of legal reasons (ie the assumed legal rule empowering the court to set aside a grossly unjust law).

This too is consistent with the hypothetical situation as well as with legal positivism. By assumption there are two conflicting rules involved here: Ordinance 11 and the rule which directs the courts to set aside any rule which is grossly unjust. Lots of issues remain unspecified. We know that the second rule, by its nature and content, overrides the first. So the correct decision according to the law is for the court not to follow Ordinance 11. The important point is that whatever the content of the legislated rule against unjust rules, the example poses no difficulty for my explanation of the nature of law, nor for any other which allows, indeed insists, that courts have the power, sometimes in virtue of legal rules, sometimes independently of them, to change law, for example on the ground that it is grossly unjust.[33]

The example imagines one such situation. The second law, instructing courts to disregard grossly unfair laws, directs the court to set aside Ordinance 11. When doing so the court both makes law, and (by that very act) it also follows law. There is nothing here which cannot be described by either observer or participant. There are, of course, other cases as well.

[32] See Alexy, above n 1 at 41.

[33] For a more recent and more nuanced explanation of this power see my 'Incorporation by Law' (2004) 10 *Legal Theory* 1. In dealing with this and similar situations, Alexy applies his distinction between the participant's and the observer's perspectives. My observations here illustrate why it is not needed, by showing how such situations can be described without reference to it.

There are cases in which the law denies the courts law-making powers on certain matters, and they, defying the law, nevertheless assume such power, perhaps for good moral reasons. In such cases they may not be free to acknowledge that they change the law. They may well be advised to disguise the true nature of their action, and pretend that the law has always been as they now say it was. This is not the situation Alexy invites us to examine. But let it be observed that while such situations are real enough they hardly justify postulating a special perspective. Lying or pretending that things are other than one knows them to be is not to be confused with the existence of any perspective.

Is there anything in the example which is inconsistent with legal positivism? I see nothing of this kind. If we assume that the rule giving the courts power to set aside grossly unjust laws can exist in some legal systems and not exist in others then its existence can only be a matter of social fact, for by assumption there is no moral difference between these systems which would justify its existence in one, but not in the other. To argue against legal positivism Alexy needs to show not only that the courts of any and all legal systems should set aside unjust laws, but that necessarily the law gives them this power as a legal power, so that its exercise can never be a violation of the law.

It is not clear what reasons Alexy has for that claim. Andrei Marmor has suggested to me that implied in the book is something like the following argument:

(1) The law essentially makes a claim to its moral correctness.
(2) From the participant's point of view, this claim to moral correctness forms part of the reasons to follow the law, and in the case of judges, to apply it.
(4) Since a grossly unjust law cannot be morally correct (ex hypothesis), judges ought to interpret the law so that grossly unjust law is rendered invalid.
(5) Therefore, from the internal point of view, from the point of view of judges, unjust law is not law.[34]

Neither Marmor nor I are sure that this is a correct presentation of Alexy's underlying thought. But something like it may be the best argument to be culled from the book. How good is it?

Something like the first thesis is true. I remarked earlier that while it is true that the law, like all intentional actions and their products, can be said to make a claim to correctness, whether the claim is to moral correctness depends on an argument, not provided by Alexy, about the nature of the

[34] Private communication (from notes prepared by him for a debate with Alexy at IVR World Congress, Granada, Spain, 27 May 2005). I have left out the third step in his argument.

institution. I have argued[35] that the law claims to have legitimate authority, in the sense that legal institutions both act as if they have such authority, and articulate the view that they have it. This is, of course, a moral claim but it is not a claim to moral correctness. It is in the very nature of authoritative rules that they are binding even if not correct. So authorities (police, courts, administrative agencies) can be aware both that the rules they apply are morally wrong, and that they are morally binding on them and on their subjects. Of course, if they have power (whether legally sanctioned power or not) to change them or to refrain from applying them they may have to do so.[36] But that is not always the case, and when it is such actions are not always authorised by law, hence it is not true that the law makes a claim to moral correctness.

A more serious mistake creeps into the second proposition. It is generally true that participants, if this means officials such as judges, administrators, police and the like, generally follow the law not because it *claims* to be morally legitimate, but because they think that *it is* morally legitimate. The claim by itself is neither here nor there. To examine the rest of the argument we need to assume that while unjust laws may be morally binding, grossly unjust laws cannot be, that is we need to assume that grossly unjust laws are not only morally deficient, they also exceed any legitimate (ie morally binding) authority which anyone may have. Will that assumption vindicate the conclusion that officials (ie Alexy's participants) are always morally justified in refusing to apply such laws? Not necessarily, for as was observed above, the evil flowing from not applying them may sometimes be worse than the evil of applying them. Suppose that we succeed in identifying a class of cases such that relative to any given authority they (a) lie beyond the legitimate power of that authority, and (b) it would be right not to follow them. The possible existence of such a class of cases is not surprising, at least not to anyone who believes that legitimate political and legal authority is always limited. The question is whether this can lead to the conclusion that no grossly unjust law is law, or that courts have inherent legal power to set such laws aside? Clearly the assumptions do not in themselves entail such a conclusion. Such an inference requires the additional premise that law can never be unjust in these ways. But after all, the whole argument is about the truth of that premise. Does looking at matters as they appear to the officials change matters? No, for officials just like other people may, and should, believe that some laws should be set aside, but it does not follow that they think

[35] The reader will be glad that I will not repeat the arguments here yet again. They have been adumbrated in *Practical Reasons and Norms*, above n 6, *The Authority of Law*, above n 13, *Ethics in the Public Domain* (Oxford, Clarendon Press, 1985).

[36] But not always, as the evil caused by changing a bad law may be greater than that of allowing it to stand and applying it.

that they are authorised by law to set them aside. If it would turn out that officials, qua officials, must believe that about the law, we may have the beginning of an argument towards Radbruch's formula. But Alexy does not provide any reason to think that they must think that. Clearly not all judges do think that, as the statements of various judges that they are morally bound to obey the law come what may show. Legal positivists claim that they should not think that, for to do so would be to confuse their moral duty to set aside such laws with their legal duty. Alexy does not agree, but I fail to find the argument.

Alexy has much more to say. Many of his arguments have to do with claims that the world would be morally better if the concept of law had this feature or that (eg positivistic versus non-positivistic features). I cannot see how any such arguments can help establish what features the concept of law does have. Much of what Alexy says in these contexts involves both conceptual confusions and highly speculative empirical assumptions. Let me give but one example. Alexy maintains that 'if there are notions of justice which are rationally justifiable, then one who rationally justifies his view that an action is unjust can be said to know this. Now the following principle applies: the more extreme the injustice the more certain the knowledge of it'.[37] First a conceptual point: one can argue rationally to a mistaken conclusion, that is, having reached a false belief (which one arrived at by reasoning) and having irrationally accepted a belief are not necessarily co-extensive notions. Can knowledge (as distinct from belief) be more or less certain, that is admit of degrees (this too is a conceptual point)? Is it true that the greater the injustice the less likely we are to make mistakes about it being an injustice? There is some empirical evidence to doubt the last claim. Many will admit that slavery as practised by Muslims and Christians in the sixteenth and seventeenth centuries was among the greatest injustices of those times, yet it was not among the most obvious injustices to the people who engaged in it. The repression of women or of gays in many cultures provides similar examples. I think we are lucky that such arguments do not bear on the question of the nature of law.

I do not find any arguments put forward by Alexy which can refute Marmor's separation thesis. I suspect that Alexy feels that his question is the right one to ask for he is aware of only one other, namely, the clarification of linguistic usage, which he claims correctly cannot settle the issue. He seems unaware of a theoretical task of explaining the nature of a social institution we have, which is neither a question of linguistic usage, nor the question of which linguistic usage would be, if it prevails, morally better.

[37] See Alexy, above n 1 at 52.

THE ARGUMENT FROM PRINCIPLE

Alexy finds another argument, completely independent of the argument from injustice, for a necessary connection between law and morality. As pointed out, my own view, and the separation thesis, are consistent with the existence of such necessary connections. They may, however, be inconsistent with the kind of connection Alexy aims to establish, and it may, therefore, be of interest to find out whether he succeeds, and if so what kind of connection he establishes.

As a first step in a complex argument he claims that all developed legal systems include principles, which he understands, following Dworkin, to be standards which can be realised to varying degrees.[38] Naturally, so can rules. The idea is, however, that sometimes realising a principle to less than the highest degree is not a violation of that principle, whereas failing to conform completely to a rule is a breach of that rule. Perhaps we can identify principles with prima facie reasons, whereas rules are conclusive reasons. Alexy discusses here only principles whose function or role is to instruct courts how to decide cases to which conflicting reasons apply.

It is not implausible to expect that all developed legal systems include principles. Alexy's argument to that effect does not, however, secure that conclusion. It is roughly that because of the thesis of correctness, 'in all legal systems in which there are doubtful cases that give rise to the question of striking a balance, it is legally required to strike a balance and thereby to take principles into account. Thus, in all legal systems of this kind, principles are, for legal reasons, necessary elements of the legal system'.[39] This argument can be generalised to establish that every legal system contains various kinds of laws: in all legal systems in which deciding a case requires enforcing a duty there are duty-imposing rules, in all legal systems in which deciding a case requires protecting a right there are right-protecting rules, etc. All such arguments have a core of good, if unexciting, sense. In all these cases it is plausible to suppose that legal systems include legal standards of varying kinds, which are needed for the resolution of practical disputes. Since such practical disputes involve conflicts of rights, duties, etc, it is plausible to expect the law to have rules on these matters.

This observation is not, however, an argument for the inevitable presence of such rules in all legal systems. Does not Alexy provide such an argument? His argument, unfortunately, is not valid, for it concludes that the law of a country includes principles from the sole premise that the courts are required, by law, to apply principles. That is a non-sequitur. The courts of Britain are required by law to apply standards of foreign law, and many others which are not parts of the law of the land in Britain. Alexy's

[38] See Alexy, above n 1 at 70.
[39] *Ibid* at 74.

argument here confirms the suspicion mentioned above that he fails to conceive of the possibility that standards which courts are required by law to apply may nonetheless not be part of the legal system which requires their application.

The rest of the argument does not add much. Alexy relies on his correctness thesis to claim that laws, eg principles, which are morally wrong, or incorrect, should be changed. For reasons explained earlier the correctness thesis does not establish that conclusion. To establish it one has to establish that the law should be morally correct. That is not an empty, trivial conclusion. But it can be established, and indeed, I know no one who disputes it. It is a blemish in the law that it is morally defective, unjust, etc. If this establishes anything regarding the credentials of legal positivism it establishes that Alexy's separation thesis, which he so laboriously undermined by his argument to this conclusion, has nothing to do with legal positivism. After all it was Bentham, the founder of legal positivism in Britain, who did more than anyone to argue that the law should be moral, and expose the moral deficiencies of the law of his day.

Paradoxically, the generally critical tone of this chapter is more a result of agreement than of disagreement. To be sure I find some of the book's central contentions unsupported by its arguments, and some of them are, I think, wrong. But to a considerable degree the critical tone of this chapter is due to the large measure of agreement with Alexy. On many matters he is wrong not in the views he takes, but in thinking that he is contradicting legal positivists in taking them. It would, however, be a bad mistake to think that my aim was to defend legal positivism. I see Alexy's book as a missed opportunity, the opportunity to go beyond the dispute about legal positivism. The very fact that so many issues, including several that Alexy takes up, which are or were thought to characterise the divide between legal positivist and other accounts of the nature of law, serve no such purpose shows that legal theorists both on the legal positivist and the opposing side have advanced the discussion about the nature of law beyond the point where legal positivism is an illuminating category in such discussions. Perhaps it is time not to refute legal positivism, but to forget the label and consider the views of various writers within that tradition on their own terms.

2

An Answer to Joseph Raz

ROBERT ALEXY*

THE RECENT DEBATE in the English-speaking world on the concept and nature of law has produced a wealth of theories showing that law is a far more complex matter than many had believed earlier. To acknowledge the degree of sophistication achieved in our day is not, however, to accept Joseph Raz's thesis:

> that legal theorists both on the legal positivist and the opposing side have advanced the discussion about the nature of law beyond the point where legal positivism is an illuminating category in such discussions.[1]

Precisely the opposite, I believe, is true. The divide between legal positivist and non-positivist theories of the nature of law will be an illuminating category for as long as law exists. The reason for this lies in the dual nature of law, which stems from the fact that law is, on the one hand, factual in nature and, on the other, ideal. The relation between law as fact and law as an ideal is the most important issue in explaining its nature. Non-positivists claim that the factual dimension is internally connected with the ideal dimension; positivists—in any case today, and in considerable numbers—do not grow tired of stressing the important relations between the real and the ideal, but they insist that the ideal remains essentially external to what the law is. In order to answer the question of what the essence of law is, the positivist refers only to facts, while the non-positivist, in contrast, refers to both facts and ideals. I think that this difference is significant enough to warrant the labels 'positivism' and 'non-positivism', rather than 'forget[ting]' them, as Joseph Raz recommends.[2] This is the background against which I would have my rejoinder to Raz's reply to my critique of legal positivism in *The Argument from Injustice* seen.

* I should like to thank Stanley L. Paulson for suggestions and advice on matters of English style.

1 J Raz, 'The Argument from Justice, or How Not to Reply to Legal Positivism' (this volume) 17 at 35.

2 *Ibid.*

SEPARATION THESIS

According to Raz's first objection, the arguments put forward in *The Argument from Injustice* do not address legal positivism, for, Raz contends, I am attacking a thesis that is not common to the legal positivists. I have called this thesis the 'separation thesis'. At the end of his discussion of my attempt to identify positivism by means of this thesis, Raz presents a 'separation thesis' formulated by Andrei Marmor. Raz believes Marmor's formulation, first, 'to be correct', and, secondly, to be 'possibly ... a fairly important thesis which is common to all the theories within the tradition of legal positivism'.[3] Perhaps it will help in making clear what is at issue if I begin with Marmor's formulation of the separation thesis. It runs as follows:

> This thesis basically maintains that determining what the law is does not necessarily, or conceptually, depend on moral or other evaluative considerations about what the law ought to be in the relevant circumstances.[4]

The separation thesis is expressed in *The Argument from Injustice* as follows:

> All positivistic theories defend the *separation thesis,* which says that the concept of law is to be defined such that no moral elements are included. The separation thesis presupposes that there is no conceptually necessary connection between law and morality, between what the law commands and what justice requires, or between the law as it is and the law as it ought to be. The great legal positivist Hans Kelsen captured this in the statement, 'Thus, the content of the law can be anything whatsoever.'[5]

The second sentence of this quotation from *The Argument from Injustice* is quite close to Marmor's formulation. There might be differences where Marmor's distinction between 'determining what the law is' and 'considerations about what the law ought to be' and my distinction between 'the law as it is and the law as it ought to be' are concerned, but these differences, if they exist at all, seem to be of minor importance. If, however, Marmor's formulation is, as Raz says, successful in getting at the 'common core of the positivist tradition',[6] and if no relevant differences exist

[3] *Ibid* at 22.

[4] A Marmor, *Positive Law and Objective Values* (Oxford, Clarendon Press, 2001) 71. Raz adds to this that his 'sources thesis', as presented in *The Authority of Law* (Oxford, Clarendon Press, 1979) 47, is 'a stricter thesis', for it not only says that the law does not necessarily depend on moral arguments, but, what is far more, that such a dependence necessarily does not exist. Marmor's formulation is the contradictory of the connection thesis, which says that what the law is necessarily depends on moral arguments. The separation thesis, as the contradictory of the connection thesis, is indeed the common core of exclusive and inclusive positivism. It is implied by exclusive as well as by inclusive positivism.

[5] R Alexy, *The Argument from Injustice: A Reply to Legal Positivism* (B Litschewski Paulson and SL Paulson (trans), Oxford, Clarendon Press, 2002) 3.

[6] Raz, above n 1 at 22.

between Marmor's formulation and mine, as quoted above, then the reply to positivism in *The Argument from Injustice* hits its target. It does, at any rate, in so far as the concern is with the common core of the positivist tradition as depicted by Marmor's formulation—that is, the separation of the law as it is from the law as it ought to be. Exactly this is, indeed, the main target of my reply. The Radbruch formula is the most striking example. It says that extreme injustice is not law. Thus, the law in the way it actually stems from its social sources, that is, the 'law as it is', is connected with the 'law as it ought to be'. The former notion then depends on the latter notion.

To be sure, Raz, in objecting that the separation thesis as presented in *The Argument from Injustice* does not correctly identify legal positivism, is not concentrating on the distinction between the 'law as it is' and the 'law as it ought to be'. Rather, the main tenets of Raz's objection are three points connected with this distinction in the paragraph at page 3 of *The Argument from Injustice*, quoted above. These three points concern (1) Kelsen's content-thesis, (2) the idea of a definition of law, and (3) the concept of a necessary connection between law and morality.

Kelsen's Statement

Hans Kelsen's famous statement, 'Thus, the content of the law can be anything whatsoever',[7] is adduced as a paradigmatic formulation of the separation thesis as understood in *The Argument from Injustice*. Raz maintains, first, that this statement of Kelsen's is 'manifestly false according to Kelsen's own theory'[8] and, secondly, that, 'even if true, [it] lends no support to Alexy's separation thesis'.[9] Only the first of these two arguments will be considered here. The second argument will be taken up in the context of Raz's general thesis about necessary connections between law and morality.

Kelsen's statement that the content of the law can be anything whatsoever is, Raz claims, false according to Kelsen's own theory, for there 'are, according to Kelsen's theory, necessary restrictions on the content of the law'.[10] These necessary restrictions on the content of law are said to follow from Kelsen's concept of law, which implies:

[7] H Kelsen, *Pure Theory of Law* (*Reine Rechtslehre* (1960)), 2nd edn (M Knight (trans), Berkeley and Los Angeles, University of California Press, 1967) para 34(c) (at 198) (trans altered); see also H Kelsen, *Introduction to the Problems of Legal Theory* (*Reine Rechtslehre* (1934)), 1st edn (B Litschewski Paulson and SL Paulson (trans), Oxford, Clarendon Press, 1992) para 28 (at 56).

[8] Raz, above n 1 at 18.

[9] *Ibid* at 22.

[10] *Ibid* at 18.

> (a) that the law can consist only of norms, (b) that it must address courts, (c) that it must stipulate for the application of sanctions, and (d) that their application must be conditional on certain conduct taking place.[11]

Are these four conditions really restrictions of the *content* of the law?

The concept of content, like the concept of form, is notoriously vague. Perhaps even more important, the two concepts are in constant danger of being confused with other concepts. Thus, the distinction between form and content is often conflated with that between abstract and concrete. Kelsen's thesis that law consists of norms is, for instance, more abstract than the thesis that law consists of general norms, for Kelsen's thesis refers to general as well as to individual norms. If, however, one of these theses is formal, both are. Something similar applies in the case of the thesis that law consists of norms that are authoritatively issued, that is, that are issued by some authority or other. This thesis is more abstract than the thesis that the authority must be democratically legitimised in order to be able to issue law.

John Gardner has pointed out that the distinction between form and content is often conflated with a third distinction, namely, that between source-based criteria of legal validity and merit-based criteria.[12] Source-based criteria of legal validity are criteria of a '*merit*-independent type'.[13] This makes it possible to cast Gardner's distinction in slightly more abstract terms by giving it the form, so to speak, of the difference between merit-based and merit-independent criteria of legal validity. The decisive point is that merit-based criteria can be applied not only to the content of law but also to its form. Examples of formal merits are generality and enactment as the result of a democratic procedure.

If in the light of these three distinctions we consider the four features of the law that Raz ascribes to Kelsen, the first conclusion is that all of them are formal. The concept of content in Kelsen's famous statement is used as a concept that is contrasted with the concept of form. This becomes quite clear if one reads the sentence following the statement of Kelsen's quoted above:

> There is no human behaviour that would be excluded simply by virtue of its substance from being the content of a legal norm.[14]

This suffices to show that it is not true that Kelsen's statement is false by Kelsen's own lights. Kelsen is referring not to formal features of law as set out by Raz but to its substance.

[11] *Ibid.*
[12] J Gardner, 'Legal Positivism: 5 ½ Myths' (2001) 46 *American Journal of Jurisprudence* 199 at 208.
[13] *Ibid* at 209.
[14] Kelsen, *Pure Theory of Law*, above n 7 at para 34(c) (at 198) (trans altered).

Even if one were to interpret 'content' in Kelsen's statement as 'merits', not a great deal would change. As already noted, there exist formal merits. But the four restrictions introduced by Raz are so abstract that they hover far above the field where merits and demerits come into play. There seems to be a rule that says: the more abstract the formal properties of law, the less significant their moral relevance. Where the cases of consisting of norms and of being addressed to courts are concerned, this seems to be quite clear. Less clear, but clear enough, is the matter in the case of law's being conditioned on certain conduct. Doubts might arise in the case of sanctions. One can consider the fact that law is connected with sanctions as either a merit or a demerit. This ambivalence, however, shows that the concept of a sanction does not suffice, by itself, to establish a restriction on merits. Therefore, even if for 'content' one were to substitute 'merits', Kelsen's statement would not be rendered false according to his own theory. At most, there would be some doubts respecting sanctions.

The Idea of a Definition of Law

Raz's second objection to the separation thesis as per my ascription of it to legal positivism concerns the idea of a definition of law. I do indeed use the concept of a definition in order to explain the separation thesis. Repeating it here:

> All positivistic theories defend the *separation thesis*, which says that the concept of law is to be defined such that no moral elements are included.[15]

Raz's critique begins with the remark that it 'was Hart who convinced many legal theorists that the concentration on defining law … is unproductive'.[16] He himself 'did not advance a definition of law'.[17] His main reason for this is that:

[15] Alexy, above n 5 at 3.

[16] Raz, above n 1 at 19. Stanley L Paulson has drawn my attention to the fact that Hart does offer something like a definition of the existence of a legal system—and this in the terms of classical analysis, that is, by means of conditions necessary and jointly sufficient: 'There are therefore two minimum conditions necessary and sufficient for the existence of a legal system. On the one hand, those rules of behaviour which are valid according to the system's ultimate criteria of validity must be generally obeyed, and, on the other hand, its rules of recognition specifying the criteria of legal validity and its rules of change and adjudication must be effectively accepted as common public standards of official behaviour by its officials.' See HLA Hart, *The Concept of Law,* 2nd edn (Oxford, Clarendon Press, 1994) 116. To be sure, the question of whether Hart intended to give a definition in the paragraph quoted as well as the question of how closely Hart's characterisation of the existence of a legal system approximates his characterisation of law as such remain open. Nonetheless, one can say that Hart's own work raises doubts about the claim that he really considers definitions related to the concept of law in all respects as 'unproductive'.

[17] Raz, above n 1 at 19.

> there is no theoretical justification to focus on the definition of the concepts rather than on their necessary features, some of which may not figure in any sensible definition of them.[18]

The reply to this depends on how one determines the relation between definition, concept, and the nature of things. It is impossible to go into detail here. A handful of remarks must suffice.

Definitions can be introduced for a variety of purposes. A rather unpretentious one is the demarcation of what is defined. An example is the definition of human being as (naturally) a featherless biped. Definitions of this kind can easily be distinguished from definitions that claim to grasp the essence of what is defined. The definition of human being qua rational animal is an example. Definitions of this kind represent a rather pretentious enterprise. For, even if they correctly express our actual common understanding of the concept, they are always in danger of failing. The reason for this is that concepts relate not only to socially established rules of meaning, but also to the nature of things. The nature of law consists of its necessary properties. Every definition of the concept of law is in danger of failing to grasp these properties adequately. For this reason, one can never be certain about whether a definition is correct or not, even if it captures perfectly our use of language. This might suggest that one ought to refrain from defining the concept of law at all, and ought to concentrate, instead, on certain essential or necessary features of the law or on a list of such features. But in doing so, a decisive element of our understanding of the nature of law would remain beyond reach. For an explanation of the nature of law, it is not enough that some of its necessary properties, or a list of them, be presented. These properties must be fitted together in a system. A definition of law that seeks to grasp the nature of law must represent the attempt to set out the core of such a system. Naturally, this cannot take place at the beginning of an analysis of the nature of law, but perhaps it can take place at the end.[19]

Necessary Connections

The remarks about definition, concept, and nature concern method and, to a certain degree, style. Raz's substantial point is that the separation thesis qua thesis that the concept of law has to be defined such that no moral elements are included is not a true description of the positivist tradition, for, he is arguing, legal positivism is compatible with the existence of necessary connections between law and morality. According to Raz, the

[18] *Ibid* at 20.

[19] See I Kant, *Critique of Pure Reason* (W S Pluhar (trans), Indianapolis and Cambridge, Hackett, 1996) B 759.

number of necessary connections between law and morality is 'indefinite'.[20] Now it is not possible to work through an indefinite number of things. I will therefore confine myself to four examples presented by Raz.

Raz's first example consists of normative and evaluative concepts that 'are common to moral and non-moral discourse'.[21] It is doubtless true that normative concepts that are common to moral and legal discourse do exist. There are, for instance, moral as well as legal obligations. But the point to be made here is similar to that which has been made with respect to Kelsen's formal properties of law. The mere fact that there exist legal as well as moral obligations says nothing about any moral content that law must necessarily have or not have in order to be valid or invalid. To put it another way, it in no way renders legal validity or legal correctness dependent on any moral merits or demerits.

The last point can be generalised. The separation thesis as ascribed to legal positivism in *The Argument from Injustice* concerns the separation of both legal validity and legal correctness from any moral merits or demerits. Exactly this is what is meant by the separation of the 'law as it is' from the 'law as it ought to be'.[22]

In light of this background, it is not difficult to show that a further example of Raz's fails, again, to distinguish the separation thesis as a thesis about the relation between legal validity or legal correctness on the one hand, and moral merits and demerits or moral correctness and incorrectness on the other. This second example concerns a conceptually necessary relation that law has to morality which black holes do not have:

> it is a conceptual point about the law that it can be morally evaluated as good or bad, and as just and unjust, just as it is a conceptual fact about black holes that propositions like 'this black hole is morally better or more just than that' make no sense.[23]

It is, indeed, a conceptual point about the law that it can be morally evaluated, whereas this is not possible in the case of black holes. To this extent, then, there exists a conceptually necessary relation between law and morality that does not exist between morality and physical objects. But does this relation really count as a connection? It is, in any case, not a connection that makes legal validity or legal correctness dependent on moral merits. The relation between law and the possibility of its moral evaluation is simply a condition of the possibility of such a dependence, a possibility that as such entails nothing whatever about any necessary dependence of legal validity or legal correctness on moral merits. Still, I

20 Raz, above n 1 at 21.
21 *Ibid* at 19.
22 Alexy, above n 5 at 3.
23 Raz, above n 1 at 21.

must concede that it is possible to understand the expression 'conceptually necessary connection between law and morality' in such a way that it is not restricted to any dependence on moral merits and demerits but refers also to the possibility of being assessed according to moral criteria. Perhaps I should have been more explicit, namely, in noting that I did not intend to include the latter instead of assuming that this would become clear from the rest of the sentence.

Raz's third example is far more interesting. It directly concerns law's moral merits. Raz's argument runs as follows:

> even if all the law's essential features can be stated without the use of moral concepts it may be the case that that it has those features entails that it has some moral merit.[24]

An example of this—here Raz refers to Fuller—is law's 'reliance on general standards'.[25] Now, law's reliance on general standards does, indeed, restrict one's 'ability to act arbitrarily',[26] and avoiding arbitrariness is a moral merit, but is it also true that generality is a necessary or essential feature of law from the point of view of positivism? According to Gardner, it is a 'half-myth' that positivity as such has any moral merits and a myth that legal positivism is necessarily associated with criteria stemming from the rule of law, such as generality.[27] On this point Gardner is right: he is, at any rate, if it is true that according to legal positivism 'whether a given norm is legally valid ... depends on its sources, not its merits'.[28] Law's generality—like the other requirements of Fullers 'inner morality of law'[29]—is a 'formal moral criteri[on]'.[30] Failure to meet this criterion does not deprive norms of their legal validity if legal validity is understood exclusively as source-based. Being source-based does not imply being general. Generality, therefore, is a contingent property of positive law. It is, as a formal merit, demanded by morality, but it is not implied by positivity. For this reason it does not provide an example of a connection between law and morality that every legal positivist must accept qua legal positivist as a necessary connection.

The fourth example is the most interesting one. It concerns law's claim to legitimate authority. It is one of Raz's main theses about the nature of law 'that necessarily the law claims to have legitimate authority, and that

[24] *Ibid* at 20.
[25] *Ibid* at 21.
[26] *Ibid*.
[27] Gardner, above n 12 at 204–8.
[28] *Ibid* at 201.
[29] LL Fuller, *The Morality of Law*, rev edn (New Haven, Yale University Press, 1969) at 42 and 46–91.
[30] Alexy, above n 5 at 31.

that claim is a moral claim'.[31] Here a necessary connection between law and morality, a connection concerning the merits of law, is indeed at stake. Raz believes that it is possible, on the one hand, to assume that the law is necessarily or essentially connected with a moral claim and, on the other, to defend legal positivism.[32] I think that it is not possible to do both. This issue goes, however, far beyond the question of whether positivism can be identified by means of the separation thesis. It is one of the questions determining which is right, positivism or non-positivism. Raz considers this issue in the third part of his chapter, where he discusses the correctness thesis. I return to the issue in the third section of the present chapter, where I address the correctness thesis.[33]

PARTICIPANTS AND OBSERVERS

Raz's second objection concerns the distinction between the observer's perspective and the participant's perspective. This distinction plays a central role in my reply to positivism. I do not claim that the separation thesis is wrong from both perspectives. It is wrong only from the perspective of the participant. By contrast, from the observer's perspective it is correct.

It is understood that the participant is found within a certain legal system; the observer, for his part, is referring to that legal system. The difference between their perspectives is that the participant asks and adduces arguments on behalf of what he deems to be the correct answer to a legal question in the legal system in which he is found, whereas the observer asks and adduces arguments on behalf of a position that reflects how legal questions are actually decided in that legal system. Raz objects that there is not really a difference here. One may take a court:

> a litigating lawyer, an academic scholar, or a foreign commentator. Whatever their other aims, when stating what German law is they all normally have the same aim: to state truly how German law is.[34]

There are, indeed, cases in which the observer and the participant can use the same proposition, for instance, the sentence 'In Germany, every person can raise a constitutional complaint on the ground that his constitutional

31 Raz, above n 1 at 19.

32 *Ibid* at 20.

33 On three further examples, see J Raz, 'About Morality and the Nature of Law' (2003) 48 *American Journal of Jurisprudence* 1 at 3. One of them is law's inability to commit rape, which is also mentioned in our text. I do not discuss it here, for I already have considered it together with the two other examples elsewhere. See R Alexy, 'Agreements and Disagreements: Some Introductory Remarks' in M Escamilla and M Saavedra (eds), *Law and Justice in a Global Society* (Granada, University of Granada, 2005) 739–40.

34 Raz, above n 1 at 23–4.

rights have been infringed by public authority'. But as soon as this sentence poses a question of interpretation, the difference between the two perspectives comes to the fore. For example, under what conditions can an omission on the part of the legislator be classified as an infringement of a constitutional right by a public authority against which a constitutional complaint may be raised? This question is highly contested. The participant will give one answer; it claims to be legally correct and is supported by arguments. The answer may well be in opposition to the established practice of the Constitutional Court. The observer, qua observer, can only describe the practice of the Constitutional Court and the debate in which the Court is engaged. He cannot engage in argument on the question of which answer is legally correct. As soon as he does that, he ceases to be an observer and becomes a participant. Raz is right in pointing out that a participant not only 'participates in disputation'.[35] As the proposition about constitutional complaints in Germany shows, there are, indeed, sentences that can be used both by observers and participants. But they are embedded in different contexts. The participant's context is defined by the question 'What is the correct legal answer?', the observer's by the question 'How are legal decisions actually made?'.

Can one describe perspectives in this way by means of questions? According to Raz a question, or a subject matter identified by it, does not suffice to constitute a perspective. For a perspective Raz seems to be demanding 'different methodologies'.[36] Now it is true that I have not specified different 'method[s] of inquiry'[37] in my explanation of the two perspectives. I think, however, that they are obvious. In the case of the participant, the methods are the rich means of legal argumentation. In the case of the observer, they comprise all the methods of empirical description, namely, for describing the law qua social practice. This suggests that Raz's comparison of the distinction between participants and observers with that between 'those interested in physics and those interested in the pay and status of physicists'[38] falls short of the mark. If one wishes to make a comparison in the field of physics, one ought to distinguish those who are asking for the truth of physical theories and those, for example, historians of physics, who are asking for the genesis, the dissemination, and the decline of physical theories without showing any real interest in their truth. It is, I think, not odd to speak in this case about two perspectives.

[35] *Ibid* at 23.
[36] *Ibid* at 24.
[37] *Ibid.*
[38] *Ibid.*

In my explanation of the participant's perspective I say that the disputation of participants takes place 'within a legal system'.[39] Raz maintains that this phrase 'adds nothing but confusion to the characterisation of the distinction'.[40] Perhaps I ought to have gone into greater detail. Legal systems are not only systems of norms but also systems of procedures.[41] The procedures may or may not be institutionalised. The most general non-institutionalised legal procedure is discourse about what the law of the land says. Whoever adduces an argument on this question takes part in this discourse and is, in this sense, 'within a legal system'.

Raz maintains not only that there is not really any difference between observer and participant but also that even if there were a difference between them, there would be 'no reason to expect them not to be able to share the same concepts'.[42] For this reason he finds my claim, namely, that the following sentence, 'as the statement of an observer, contains a contradiction',[43] surprising:

> *A* has not been deprived of citizenship according to German law, although all German courts and officials treat *A* as denaturalized and support their action by appeal to the literal reading of a norm authoritatively issued in accordance with the criteria for validity that are part of the legal system efficacious in Germany.[44]

Raz contends that contradictoriness is a property of propositions, not of the relations between them and those who make them. He therefore considers it odd that being contradictory might depend on whether the proposition is made by an observer or a participant. One would have to agree with Raz on the point about oddity if the statement made by an observer and by a participant did, indeed, express the same proposition. But—the rub—precisely this is not the case. When uttered by an observer our sentence expresses a different proposition than the same sentence as uttered by a participant. The reason underlying this difference is that the expression 'law' in the first part of the quoted sentence represents one concept when used by the observer and another when used by the participant. When used by the observer it expresses a positivistic concept of law that refers exclusively to social sources or, in other words, to authoritative issuance and social efficacy. When used by a participant it expresses a non-positivistic concept that comprises not only social sources but also moral correctness.

The second part of the quoted sentence refers to a chain of legal sources: (1) a practice of courts and officials, (2) a norm authoritatively issued and

39 Alexy, above n 5 at 25.
40 Raz, above n 1 at 23.
41 See Alexy, above n 5 at 24–5.
42 Raz, above n 1 at 24.
43 Alexy, above n 5 at 30.
44 *Ibid* 29–30.

(3) criteria for validity, that is, criteria that are recognised as such in a socially efficacious legal system. If an exercise of state power is grounded in this way on legal sources it is, according to an exclusively source-based concept of law, part of the law of the land. To say, at the same time, that it is, according to that concept, not part of the law of the land involves a contradiction. Things are completely different where the expression 'law' expresses a non-positivistic concept of law that includes morality: in our example, the Radbruch formula. If the exercise of state power, which is the object of the statement, is extremely unjust, the participant can say that it is not a part of the law of the land, in spite of the fact that it would be deemed to be so if a positivistic concept of law were applied. If the observer and the participant use different concepts of law, then there is not even a hint of oddity in the claim that the sentence is contradictory when uttered by an observer, and not contradictory when uttered by a participant.

To be sure, one could pose the question of why the observer and the participant use different concepts of law in the first place. Raz comes quite close to posing this question when he maintains that 'no reason is given here, nor anywhere else in the book, for thinking that "participants" and "observers" are committed by their role to use different concepts'.[45] The reply to this is as follows: if the answer of a participant to the question of what the law is—at least in cases that cannot be solved by simple subsumption—involves considerations about what the law ought to be, then he has to presuppose a concept of law that includes not only a factual but also an ideal dimension. In contrast to this, the observer's answer to the question of what the law is does not in any case involve considerations about what the law ought to be.[46] If it did, the party would not remain an observer. Therefore, he must be presupposing a concept of law that refers only to the factual dimension of law and excludes the ideal dimension. This is a positivistic concept of law.

It is very easy to recognise that the correctness of this reply depends on the question of whether the participant (at least in the class of cases that cannot be solved simply by subsumption) really has to refer to considerations about what the law ought to be in order to be able to say what the law is. This question is the *leitmotif* that connects the three arguments from correctness, from injustice and from principles.

[45] Raz, above n 1 at 25.

[46] This is not to say, however, that the observer's considerations cannot include considerations about what the participants he observes think the law ought to be. One might call such considerations 'indirect' or 'third person' considerations about what the law ought to be by contrast to the direct and first person consideration of the participants.

THE ARGUMENT FROM CORRECTNESS

The argument from correctness is the basis of my reply to positivism. As a reply, the argument would be considerably weakened if it had to be granted that it did not contribute anything to the elucidation of the nature of law. Exactly this is stated by Raz: 'nothing can be learnt from the correctness thesis about the nature of law'.[47] For the argument from correctness (or, as Raz calls it, the correctness thesis):

> is a conceptual thesis not specifically about the law (though it applies to the law) but about the nature of purposes, intentional actions and their products.[48]

Every intentional action commits its agent to 'standards of appropriateness',[49] and on this point one can agree with Raz. What is more, it is true that if the argument from correctness said no more than this, it would indeed afford 'no specific help in elucidating the nature of law'.[50] But it does say more.

This becomes quite clear as soon as one considers Raz's assessment of what is described in *The Argument from Injustice* as a 'bandit system'.[51] Bandits, if they act intentionally, are indeed committed to the claim that what they do is appropriate. But the general claim to appropriateness that is reflected in all intentional actions is different from the claim to correctness. Raz mentions 'being self-enriching' as a possible standard of the appropriateness of the bandit's action.[52] This is a standard that does not claim to be accepted by all who are affected by the bandits' activities—not, for instance, by their victims—but only by the bandits themselves. The matter is completely different in the case of the claim to correctness. The claim to correctness is a claim that is addressed to all. It is similar to the claim to truth in so far as both are claims to objectivity. As a claim to objectivity in law it does not claim, as universalistic morality does, to be acceptable to all without any further qualification. It claims to be acceptable to all who take the point of view of the legal system in question. This means that law is an enterprise that is intrinsically connected with the idea of objectivity. Objectivity is an essential feature of law, a feature that is not shared by purposeful activity as such, for purposeful activity as such is compatible with the complete subjectivity of the purposes at issue, exactly as the bandit example illustrates.

Raising a claim to correctness qua objectivity does not, as such, imply raising a claim to moral correctness. If, however, one adds certain premises

47 Raz, above n 1 at 28.
48 *Ibid.*
49 *Ibid.*
50 *Ibid.*
51 Alexy, above n 5 at 33–4.
52 Raz, above n 1 at 27.

that are not easily contested, the claim to moral correctness is indeed implied. This is quite clear in cases in which the authoritative material allows for more than one decision. The decision to be made in such an 'open' sphere is the decision of a normative matter that cannot be based on standards of positive law, for if it could be based on such standards, it would not be a decision in an 'open' sphere. If it is to be based on any standard at all, that is, if it is not to be an arbitrary decision, it must be based on other normative standards. Legal decisions often concern questions of distribution and balance. Questions of correct distribution and balance are questions of justice, for justice is nothing other than correctness in distribution and balance. Questions of justice, however, are moral questions. Raz raises the question of how one is to understand the doctrine that the claim to correctness involves the claim that the law is morally correct.[53] Perhaps the preceding remarks suggest the lines along which this might be understood.

Once an argument is adduced, one can always try to construct a counter-argument. In the case of the argument from correctness, several possibilities are open to the positivist. Two strategies are of special interest. Both begin with the endorsement of the argument of correctness and continue by contesting the claim that it has any power to undermine positivism. I attempt to counter the first strategy by means of the argument from injustice, the second by means of the argument from principles. Raz contends, however, that my saying in *The Argument from Injustice* that a 'positivist can endorse the argument from correctness and nevertheless insist on the separation thesis'[54] amounts to my conceding that the correctness thesis does not contribute to an argument against positivism.[55] I concede, however, no such thing. Perhaps I should have made the point more clearly, namely, by saying that a 'positivist could endorse' the correctness thesis rather than saying a 'positivist can endorse' it.[56]

THE ARGUMENT FROM INJUSTICE

The argument from injustice, in its shortest form, says that extreme injustice is not law. The best-known variant of the extreme injustice thesis is Radbruch's formula. The Radbruch formula is a kind of litmus test on

[53] *Ibid.*
[54] Alexy, above n 5 at 39.
[55] Raz, above n 1 at 27–8.
[56] This applies to the English as well as to the German version.

the question of whether a theory of law is positivistic or non-positivistic. One who accepts the thesis that extreme injustice is not law has bid farewell to positivism.[57]

Raz's critique of the extreme injustice thesis begins with an analysis of an example that I have used in vindicating the extreme injustice thesis. The example concerns a case in which, on the one hand, Ordinance 11 applies, but, on the other, 'good legal reasons'[58] say that this ordinance ought not to be applied. A judge who grounds his decision on these good legal reasons cannot say that both Ordinance 11 and his decision are, at one and the same time, law. In order to avoid contradiction, he has to say that Ordinance 11 is not law.

Raz argues that this hypothetical situation only shows 'that the law can include a norm that grossly unjust laws are invalid'.[59] This inclusion is said to be a 'matter of social fact'.[60] Therefore, there is nothing 'in the example which is inconsistent with legal positivism'.[61]

The reply misses the point of the example. The point of the example is that the clause 'good legal reasons' refers to authoritative as well as to non-authoritative reasons. The extreme injustice thesis refers to the second class of reasons. The example shows that if there are reasons of the second kind, that is, non-authoritative legal reasons, they affect the concept of law essentially. This appears to be an analytical truth.

Of course, the hypothesis that there are such legal reasons does not count as proof of their existence. Raz, therefore, is right to maintain that in order to argue against legal positivism, it is not enough to show that it would be *morally* right not to follow grossly or extremely unjust law or that it lies beyond the legitimate power—that is, the *morally* legitimate power—of any given authority to issue extremely unjust laws.[62] These two

[57] That adherence to the extreme injustice thesis entails the rejection of positivism does not mean that the rejection of this thesis entails adherence to positivism. By virtue of the argument from correctness it is possible to reject the extreme injustice thesis and to remain a non-positivist.

[58] Alexy, above n 5 at 42.

[59] Raz, above n 1 at 29–30.

[60] *Ibid* at 31.

[61] *Ibid*. Raz refers not only to a power of the court transferred by 'legal rules', but also to a power 'sometimes independently of them, to change law, for example on the ground that it is grossly unjust' (Raz, above n 1 at 30). If this independence of legal rules counts as an independence from social facts, then Raz has, with this, crossed the border into non-positivism, even if the court's power to set aside extremely or grossly unjust laws independently of legal rules only 'sometimes' exists.

[62] Raz makes the additional point that the evil flowing from not applying extremely unjust law may sometimes be worse than the evil of applying them (Raz, above n 1 at 32). It is not clear what kinds of cases he has in mind here. I should like simply to remark that there are cases in which, on the one hand, what Raz says about the extent of evil is true, but, on the other, that the extreme injustice thesis, if it applies at all, applies here. Consider a statute requiring that one be sentenced to death on ethnic grounds, and compare a situation in which sentencing one person to death can save a hundred others from being treated in the same way.

assumptions about moral rightness or legitimacy do not, as such, entail the conclusion that no extremely or grossly unjust law is law, that is, they do not entail the extreme injustice thesis. According to Raz, '[s]uch an inference requires the additional premise that law can never be unjust in these ways'.[63] It does not matter whether this requirement is, indeed, an additional premise that connects the two assumptions with the extreme injustice thesis as conclusion, or whether it is simply another way of expressing the conclusion. The decisive point is that 'the whole argument is about the truth of that premise'.[64]

Raz argues that I provide no reason for thinking that the extreme injustice thesis is true or for the claim that owing to the extreme injustice thesis officials, qua officials, must believe that they are 'authorised by law' to set aside extremely unjust laws.[65] Perhaps I have still not made my argument clear enough. It can be divided into two parts: a theoretical part and a normative part.

The theoretical part concerns the nature of law. The claim to correctness, which is necessarily raised by law, comprises an institutional or authoritative dimension as well as an ideal or critical one. This implies that it belongs to the nature of law that it have a double character. Law, at the same time, is essentially authoritative and essentially ideal. It is, of course, possible to provide a description of the law of a land that pays heed solely to its institutional or authoritative dimension, and this is precisely what our observer does. But—and this is the telling point—such a description is restricted to a single necessary aspect of law. In restricting oneself to just one of the necessary aspects of a thing, one cannot grasp its nature.

That the claim to correctness, which is necessarily connected with the law, has two dimensions implies that law is necessarily connected with two kinds of values or principles, those of the authoritative dimension of law and those of its ideal dimension. The most abstract value or principle of the authoritative dimension is legal certainty, the most abstract value or principle attached to the ideal dimension is justice. Law would not be law if it did not comprise these principles, which, as principles or values, say what law ought to be. This implies that it is impossible to say what the law is without saying what it ought to be. Indeed, it is true that law is a social

It shall be assumed that the evil of not applying the statute with respect to one person is, in this constellation, worse than the evil of applying it. But this does not imply that the statute must be considered for that reason alone as valid law, whereas it would not be legally valid for reasons of extreme injustice if sentencing the one saved no one. This shows that the question of the legal validity of a statute has to be separated from considerations concerning the balance of evil in a concrete case.

[63] Raz, above n 1 at 32.

[64] *Ibid*.

[65] *Ibid* at 33.

institution. Its being a social institution does not, however, preclude its being a moral entity. Law is a part of reality that refers necessarily to the ideal.

If this is a correct explanation of the nature of law, the theoretical task of explaining the nature of law necessarily includes a normative task. If justice as well as legal certainty is a part of the nature of law, a participant in the legal system, when confronted with extremely unjust law, say Ordinance 11, must ask himself whether justice as a necessary element of law prevents him from applying it, or whether legal certainty prevents him from following the lines of substantial correctness. The answer to this question requires that one strike a balance between these two principles. The result of this balancing or weighing is that the principle of legal certainty precedes justice even if the law is unjust, save for one sort of case: that in which the threshold of extreme injustice is crossed. The reason for the general priority of legal certainty over justice is the moral value and legitimacy of authoritativeness.[66] But if moral reasons are relevant as reasons for abiding by the law, then moral reasons must also be relevant as reasons against abiding by the law; and if reasons of the same kind stand on both sides of a problem, then it is always possible that sometimes those on the one side will prevail, and sometimes those on the other. Thus, the possibility cannot be excluded that the moral reasons on the side of legal certainty will be outweighed by moral reasons on the side of justice. Precisely this is the case when the threshold of extreme injustice is crossed. That happens when human rights are grossly violated.[67] In this way, the Radbruch formula is vindicated by normative arguments that are embedded in theoretical arguments.

The reproach that I have not offered any argument in favour of the thesis that extreme injustice can never be law is Raz's main point with respect to the extreme injustice thesis. Raz adds to it further objections that are directed against arguments I have put forward in the discussion of this thesis. They address deep philosophical questions, and it goes without saying that I can only offer some brief comments here.

The extreme injustice thesis presupposes that it is possible to know whether a law is, or is not, extremely unjust. In order to show that this is possible, I have connected the concept of rational justification with that of knowledge: 'If there are notions of justice that are rationally justifiable, then one who rationally justifies his view that an action is unjust can be said to know this.'[68] Raz objects that 'one can argue rationally to a mistaken conclusion'.[69] In theoretical discourse this is an obvious truth,

66 See on this J Raz, 'Incorporation by Law' (2004) 10 *Legal Theory* 1 at 8–10.
67 See Alexy, above n 5 at 58.
68 *Ibid* at 52.
69 Raz, above n 1 at 33.

but in practical discourse, too, Raz's thesis is correct: it is, at any rate, correct if one understands 'argue rationally' as referring to the degree of rationality that one can actually achieve in real discourses. There will always be the possibility of error. If, however, one reads 'argue rationally' as, in Raz's words, giving 'adequate or completely vindicatory support by reason',[70] then a rather close relation between rational argument and knowledge emerges. This is not the place to discuss how close this relation is, and it is not the place to consider the connection between real and ideal discourses either. I want simply to remark that the concepts of rational argument and knowledge are intrinsically intertwined just as the other concepts found in the objectivity family—truth, correctness, intersubjectivity, reality, and the like—are.

THE ARGUMENT FROM PRINCIPLES

The argument from injustice focuses on an exceptional situation, that of a statute that is unjust in the extreme. My reply to positivism adds to this a further argument that concerns the everyday life of law. Specifically, it is an argument that addresses the question of legal argumentation in the open area of the positive law. Due to the complexity of legal argumentation, this argument can be presented in different ways. Perhaps its most interesting version is the argument from principles.

The argument from principles holds, first, that all legal systems, beginning at a minimal level of development, necessarily comprise principles; secondly, that the necessary presence of principles in the legal system leads to a necessary connection between law and some morality or another, and, thirdly, that this, together with the claim to correctness, leads to a necessary connection between law and moral correctness.[71]

Raz's critique of the argument from principles is confined to two points. The first concerns the first step of the argument, that is, the thesis:

> that in all legal systems in which there are doubtful cases that give rise to the question of striking a balance, it is legally required to strike a balance and thereby to take principles into account. Thus, in all legal systems of this kind, principles are, for legal reasons, necessary elements of the legal system.[72]

According to Raz, this is merely a special case of a general form of argument establishing 'that every legal system contains various kinds of laws'.[73] The first step of the argument from principles is said to have the same structure as the argument: 'in all legal systems in which deciding a

[70] J Raz, *Engaging Reason* (Oxford, Oxford University Press, 1999) 159.
[71] Alexy, above n 5 at 74–81.
[72] *Ibid* at 74.
[73] Raz, above n 1 at 34.

case requires enforcing a duty there are duty-imposing rules'.[74] There is, however, an important difference. The step from the enforcement of a duty to a duty-imposing rule does not involve any interesting shift from one concept to another. There is such a shift, however, in the case of the argument from principles. The argument begins with the possibility of striking a balance, proceeds from this to its necessity, and arrives, finally, at the concept of a principle. It is difficult to say whether this is as 'unexciting'[75] as the step from a duty to a duty-imposing rule. Here it suffices to say that the two arguments have quite different structures, a point that emerges clearly from the fact that the step from the concept of balancing to the concept of a principle is sound only if some fundamental theses of the theory of balancing are true.

Raz's second point, however, has to be taken far more seriously. It concerns the concept of incorporation. The fact that the courts of a country are required, by law, to apply principles, no more incorporates these principles into the law of that country than does the requirement that the courts of a country are to apply, as a matter of law, standards drawn from foreign law.[76] Thus, Raz is arguing, conflict-of-law doctrines show that the law can require the application of certain standards without thereby turning these standards into the law of the land.[77] This applies not only to foreign law but also to moral principles.

The validity of this argument depends essentially on what is meant by saying that the courts are required 'by law' to apply principles. In case of foreign law, 'by law' means 'by positive law'. The same is, in principle, true with respect to inclusive positivism, for the inclusion must be a matter of positive law if inclusive positivism is to remain a species of positivism.[78] Things look completely different, however, from the standpoint of non-positivism. The clause 'by law' acquires the meaning of the clause 'by the nature of law'. The overarching concept of law, that comprises the authoritative dimension of law as well as the ideal, necessarily and essentially includes moral principles. With respect to the function of 'so-called incorporating laws', Raz has remarked: 'Given that morality applies anyway, their function cannot be to incorporate it'.[79] To this it can be added that morality, by virtue of the nature of law, is already incorporated.

[74] *Ibid.*
[75] *Ibid.*
[76] *Ibid.*
[77] Raz, above n 66 at 10.
[78] See J Coleman, 'Authority and Reason' in RP George (ed), *The Autonomy of Law* (Oxford, Clarendon Press, 1996) 316.
[79] Raz, above n 66 at 17.

Part II

Law and Morality

3

Why Law Makes No Claims

NEIL MACCORMICK

THERE HAS ARISEN a famous dispute concerning what law claims. One view says that it claims correctness, hence cannot but have a minimum moral content. The other view says it claims legitimate authority, since it provides a source of reasons enabling people to solve co-ordination and other problems they couldn't solve by trying to act on the non-legal reasons that are relevant to the problems. But this entails no conceptually required minimum moral content for law. The former view is that of Robert Alexy,[1] the latter, that of Joseph Raz.[2] Each view phrased as I have phrased it is, however, based on a mistake. For law claims nothing. To say law claims anything, meaning this literally, is a category mistake. There is no entity 'law' which is capable of performing speech acts of this sort.[3] Alexy and Raz both acknowledge this point, if somewhat grudgingly, but continue to use what must then be a metaphor of law's 'claiming' correctness or respectively authority. With great respect to two friends, thinkers from whose work I have learned enormously, I shall argue that saying this kind of thing metaphorically is unhelpful. There are hidden implications about he character of law that lurk in the metaphor.

[1] R Alexy, *Begriff und Geltung des Rechts* (Freiburg and Munich, Alber, 1994) conveniently restated in English in 'My Philosophy of Law' in L Wintgens (ed), *The Law in Philosophical Perspectives* (Dordrecht, Kluwer, 1999) 23–45 at 24.

[2] See J Raz, *The Authority of Law* (Oxford, Clarendon Press, 1979) 28–33, esp at 30; *Ethics in the Public Domain* (Oxford, Clarendon Press, 1994) 194–221, chapter entitled 'Authority, Law, and Morality'.

[3] Alexy expressly concedes this point (above n 1 at 24). 'In a strict sense, claims can only be raised by subjects having the capacity to speak and to act. The fact that the law raises a claim to correctness can therefore only mean that it is raised by those who work in and for the law, creating, interpreting, applying, and enforcing it.' Raz, in *Ethics in the Public Domain* (above n 2) moves yet closer to expressly personifying law as an active agency, at 199: 'The claims the law makes for itself are evident from the language it adopts and from the opinions expressed by its spokesmen, i.e., by the institutions of the law.' In his recent *Justice in Robes* (Cambridge Mass, Belknap Press, 2006), Dworkin takes on the personification involved in Raz's idea that law raises a claim to legitimate authority (at 199–200).

Law considered generically is a kind of normative order; specifically, it is institutional normative order.[4] Among the elements to be found in institutional normative orders are normative sentences issued by various authoritative institutions enacting certain rules into law, and these rules are sometimes known as 'laws'. Jurists of various kinds (judges, professors, scholars and the like) state propositions of law, and these propositions may be said, controversially or not, to be evidentiary or constitutive of what the law is in a particular jurisdiction. When a normative order exists somewhere, and a fortiori an institutional normative order, a certain state of affairs obtains among a certain group or society of people associated with a certain territory (state law), or a certain religion (canon law, Shari'a, the Talmud etc), or a certain organised sport (golf, football, cricket, etc). The state of affairs comprises human acts and interactions distributed through space and time which can be envisaged as orderly on the ground that most acts and interactions are carried out or deemed to be carried out with a certain orientation to laws and the law, whichever species or instance of law one has in mind. Not merely are they so oriented, they are by and large in conformity with what is prescribed in relevant norms.

The existence of a normative order is thus a state of affairs, like peace, or the aftermath of a hurricane or Tsunami, or a functioning market economy. States of affairs do not have intentions, do not make claims, and are incapable of performing speech acts. They should be distinguished from entities that can have intentions, can make claims, can perform speech acts. This should be insisted on, even though such entities can do such things only in the context of certain kinds of state of affairs (existence of a language community at least, and possible existence of a state with a working legal order, or a seriously observed religion, or a community of golfers or cricketers or footballers, football fans, commentators and the like).

In a state which has (and indeed is partly constituted by) a territorially effective legal order,[5] this entails the existence of various agencies defined and established through complex sets of norms-in-force. These must include at least: courts, legislative organs and executive government with subordinate administrative agencies. Moreover, as a scheme of imputation of rights, duties, powers and other legally determined relations and relational properties, the law must also contain provisions as to what entities are capable of being the subject of such imputation. Human beings,

[4] For a fuller account of this thesis, see N MacCormick, *Institutions of Law* (Oxford, Oxford University Press, 2007). Compare N MacCormick, *Questioning Sovereignty* (Oxford, Clarendon Press, 1999) ch 1 and *Rhetoric and the Rule of Law* (Oxford, Oxford University Press, 2005) ch 1.

[5] Compare MacCormick, *Questioning Sovereignty*, above n 4 at chs 2 and 3, *Institutions of Law*, above n 4 at ch 5.

at least upwards of a certain minimum level of maturity, are naturally among the law's 'persons', being indeed classed in many schemata as 'natural persons'. Other group and corporate entities of various kinds may also count as persons, that is, as points of imputation of acts and resultant rights, duties and powers. Persons in private law and public agencies of various kinds in public law are the beings recognised as having the capacity to act in the law.[6]

State law is highly institutionalised and to some degree effectively coercive. This gives it a special place among instances of institutional normative order. It creates the conditions in which relative civil peace is possible, if not always satisfactorily secure and widespread. This is important, since only with a reasonable degree of civil peace can there flourish other forms of institutional and non-institutional normative order, including supra- or trans-state orders such as confederations (eg, the European Union) or international sporting associations (eg, FIFA), and the supreme instance of non-institutional normative order, autonomous morality.

In turn, the law-making, law-applying and governmentally acting institutions or agencies of the state have a particularly salient role. Legislatures make laws. Everywhere, this is a fairly long drawn-out process involving preliminary inquiries and consultations followed by several stages of formal legislative debate with opportunities for amendments to be made to the originally proposed text before the final vote on the basis of which the text is finally enacted. Usually, there are further procedural steps required before a legislative act comes into force as a binding law. Nearly all such legislative procedures take place in public at nearly all their stages. Absence of publicity in legislative proceedings is a matter for adverse comment and calls for special justification, such as some public emergency. The law-making of the Council of Ministers of the European Union is suspect on this account, though some defend it on the ground of the international (or intergovernmental) and partly diplomatic character of the process. The still unadopted draft Constitution of the European Union lays down a principle of publicity of all law-making acts in the Union that would have, and might yet, set these concerns to rest.

Enacted laws have to be applied by courts in the context of properly laid criminal charges or properly formulated and lodged civil claims. The process of law application, at least in contested cases, frequently involves issues of interpretation of legal texts, and the judiciary must resolve these, normally giving in public the reasons for the interpretation they adopt and apply in deciding individual cases. Such judicial decisions always have some influence or authority as precedents, and in some legal systems

[6] See MacCormick, *Institutions of Law*, above n 4 at ch 5.

judicial precedents are formally acknowledged as sources of binding legal rules in certain conditions. Ministers of the central government and subordinate executive officials, as well as relatively independent law-enforcement agencies (police forces, customs authorities and the like) see to the implementation of the laws. In doing so, they exercise discretionary powers conferred on them by the constitution or other laws, being answerable before the legislature for the wise exercise of discretion and being controllable by the judiciary as far as concerns the legality of their acts. The legality of governmental action, including due attention to any requirements in the constitution or in ordinary law concerning respect for fundamental human rights, is a condition for the existence of a 'law-state' or *Rechtsstaat.*

To a very large extent, the acts of higher agencies of government—in legislature, executive and judiciary—are confined to those that fall within the category of 'speech acts'.[7] What they do, they do by issuing formal linguistic utterances. The physical implementation of the law's requirements occurs much further down the chain of public responsibility, or indeed occurs simply through citizen compliance with enacted laws. Any claims to correctness or authority associated with law will thus be found in the context of these speech acts.

Both Alexy and Raz, in fact, impute to a personified 'law' the acts of those engaged in legislating, judging and ministerially executing laws and legal powers. These, they contend, constitute a coherent set of activities only to the extent that all the human actors actually orient their acts toward a single constitutional framework in a certain largely shared understanding of that framework. The overall coherence and co-ordination of many and disparate human acts makes it reasonable, even necessary, to impute them to some single common point of reference, and thus to 'the law'. Hence any claims or conditions that attach to the relevant human speech acts can also be imputed to the law itself.

Indeed, there is a vital point in this contention. To be sure, the possibility of the coherence and co-ordination of many diverse acts cannot be taken for granted. Some single point of imputation may indeed be sought. A more obvious contender for such a single point of imputation would, however, surely be 'the state' rather than the law itself, at any rate in the case of state-law. The state is commonly personified as an acting subject, and the actions that are imputed to it are all legally oriented human acts of a governmental kind. Only, however, if one accepts the rather contentious

[7] JL Austin 'Performative Utterances' in JL Austin, *Philosophical Papers* (JO Urmson and GJ Warnock (eds), Oxford, Clarendon Press, 1961) 220–9. Compare Austin, *How to Do Things with Words* (Oxford, Clarendon Press, 1962); see also J Searle, *Speech Acts* (Cambridge, Cambridge University Press, 1969).

proposition of Hans Kelsen that the law and the state are identical,[8] the same object viewed in different ways, does the transition over from imputing many acts to a single state also justify imputing them to a personified law. Quite apart from any other possible reservations that might be expressed towards this Kelsenian thesis, in the particular present context of a collection of essays about Robert Alexy's work it is relevant to observe that the identity of law and state entails that every state is a law-state or *Rechtsstaat*.

Contrariwise, it seems important to acknowledge that states as political entities can either be or fail to be law-states. The governance of states, through the conduct of those who exercise effective power within them, may be governance with full and fair respect for constitution and sub-constitutional law, or it may to a lesser or greater extent fail to respect constitutionality and legality. Law, in this light, sets a potential, and often an actual, constraint on official action. It is not simply the state by another name, but a possible framework that constrains and channels state action, that is, the acts of persons holding superior governmental positions within the state, whether legislative, executive or judicial. What matters is the character of the constraints that an aspiration to legality would put upon their acts and ways of acting . We can then ask what if any implications flow from the fact that persons exercising authority in the state do, or purport to, act under law and with a view to lawfully making new laws or to implementing and giving effect to laws, whether newly made or already existing laws. A law-state is a political achievement, not a tautology.

Thus it remains, in my respectful submission, misleading to impute speech acts to 'the law' itself.[9] But it is illuminating to consider what are the presuppositions and implications involved in the performance of acts-in-law by those who carry on the highest business of government in a law-state. In common with any form of speech act, there are presuppositions, or preparatory conditions, that have to be in place before such acts can be genuinely performed at all. The blowing of a whistle can signify a referee's decision only if we presuppose an ongoing game of football (or other like game), conducted under established rules of football, and only if we suppose the whistle-blower to have been appropriately empowered to act as referee. So too in the case of state action, there are necessary presuppositions of anything counting as an act of legislation, or an act of

[8] See Hans Kelsen, *The Pure Theory of Law* (Berkeley, Cal, University of California Press, 1967) 279–319, discussed in MacCormick, *Questioning Sovereignty*, above n 4 at 21–2.

[9] I share this view with Carsten Heidemann, 'Law's Claim to Correctness' in S Coyle and G Pavlakos (eds), *Jurisprudence or Legal Science?* (Oxford and Portland, Hart Publishing, 2005) 127–46. Heidemann is yet less persuaded than I about the degree to which a legislator's claim to being legally correct necessarily evinces some aspiration to justice, at least a purported aspiration to justice

participating in a legislative proceeding. It is presupposed that the legislature functions within some kind of state or state-like organisation. For this activity to be meaningful presupposes the existence of a constitution that defines the composition and functions of the legislature, and regulates, or provides for the regulation of, elections to membership of the legislature.

In general: all purported acts of legislation involve an implicit claim (or sometimes indeed an express one) on the part of all those participating that each is constitutionally empowered to play the relevant role in the legislature. And only if the claim is in fact a justified one in the prevailing conditions are the conditions for 'felicity' in a law-making utterance satisfied. Purporting to legislate involves the claim; successfully doing it presupposes that the claim is sound or justified. Much the same goes for purported acts of adjudication or of executive decision-making. The authority to do such things must be found in or derived from the constitution. Acts that purport to be adjudicative or executive involve an implied claim to have been constitutionally placed in office and relevantly empowered. The only valid acts are those in relation to which the conditions are actually satisfied.

In all these respects, the proposition that governmental acts-in-law presuppose the authority of the actor, and thus involve an implicit claim by the actor to have appropriate authority, is obviously true. It is also important notwithstanding its obviousness. Does it also follow, as Raz claims, that the claim to be authoritative involves a claim to be establishing morally sound reasons for citizens' actions such as to pre-empt the citizen's own recourse to moral reasons? Is it the case that legislation supplants moral reasoning by citizens to the extent that it is valid? This is highly implausible. Certainly, in future legal disputes on this subject matter, legal decision-makers will have to have regard to the enacted law rather than (though not necessarily to the total exclusion of) considerations of the moral or other policy grounds which motivated the majority in the legislature to enact it. Certainly, one point of legislation in subject matters which are under dispute among the citizens of a state, is that for practical purposes in relation to the governance of the state, legislation closes the argument for the time being. Smoking in public may be harmful and unpleasant, or it may be the exercise of an elementary liberty. But once the issue becomes contested whether or not to ban the smoking of tobacco in 'enclosed public spaces', the legislature has to reach some decision, and that settles the matter as a question of law. The morality or otherwise both of the activity, smoking, and of the legislative decision, to ban or not, remains, however, as much an open question as ever it was before. In this sense, though some moral authority may attach to the activity of law-making, and to its output, laws, it is in no sense pre-emptive or exclusionary moral authority. If the state in question has a fair and democratic constitution, this fairness and democratic character should be taken seriously even by those who disagree with the particular decision. Exceptional cases excepted, those who support democratic institutions and take their part in them as voters always have strong, though not always overriding, moral reasons to respect even those legislative decisions with which they disagree. They have reason to go along with them, if only under protest and while seeking to organise a new majority to bring about repeal or amendment, or while articulating some new constitutional interpretation that would permit a challenge to the validity of the legislation under the constitution.

This does not seem to confirm or support Raz's broader claims about law's claim to authority, based on what he calls the 'service conception of authority'.[10] At least some legislators may be presumed to adhere to some more or less Kantian version of the autonomy of moral agents as foundational to moral reasoning and judgement.[11] If they do, they will themselves firmly reject any suggestion that they are in the business of settling moral issues for their fellow-citizens. It will be sufficient for them to claim that they do have the authority conferred on them by the constitution, that they are exercising it within the constitutional limits that apply, and that they in good faith believe the legislation to be necessary for promoting some aspect of the common good consistently with a proper regard for justice.

The latter considerations move us closer to endorsing something like the Alexian 'claim to correctness', while not buying into Raz's version of a 'claim to authority'. Again, it is to be insisted that the claim is that of the law-maker, not that of the law itself. Nevertheless, the law-maker's claim is one that depends on a certain understanding of the character of that which the law-maker purports to make, namely, a law.

In other places, I have pointed out that many British statutes bear names that are variations on 'Administration of Justice Act', dealing in various ways with the organisation of the system of courts and the regulation of practice in them. Many pieces of legislation have in their time roused great protest concerning the injustice of the provisions contained in them. For example, legislation promoted by the Thatcher administration in the United Kingdom in the 1980s introduced a new and hotly contested form of local taxation known as the 'community charge', but universally pilloried by its opponents as the 'poll tax'. Should the legislation not then have had the title 'Unjust Poll-Tax Act 1987' or something of the kind? Would that not have made more intelligible its speedy repeal by the successor Conservative administration of John Major? Why are there not 'Administration of Injustice Acts', if sometimes law is indeed unjust?

[10] See Raz, *Ethics in the Public Domain*, above n 2 at 198–9.
[11] Compare MacCormick, *Institutions of Law*, above n 4 at ch 14.

A part of the answer to these rhetorical questions is simply to draw attention to the constraints of political rhetoric. It would be politically self-defeating to introduce legislation whose title apparently acknowledges the correctness of the critique mounted by the government's opponents. The government that proposes legislation to the Parliament in any state does so by way of implementing a policy programme that its supporters commend as serving justice and the common good. It would be politically absurd to deny that aim in the very words of one's legislation.

Yet the point goes beyond mere political rhetoric, and comes to rest on the considerations that dictate the canons of political rhetoric. Why ought politicians in legislatures to be claiming that they serve justice and the common good? One answer might be that no one would vote for them if they did not, except possibly in a context of sharply divisive class politics where it might be sufficient to assert that one is pursuing class interests. Surely, however, in that case it would be necessary at least implicitly to be arguing that the class interest ought to be favoured in order to overcome some established injustice. In legislative politics, there is always some underlying claim about just demands and the demands of justice.

That this is so indicates that law is unthinkable without some ascription of value-laden functions to it. Law is for the securing of civil peace so far as possible; civility requires a common sense of justice, for there is no peace where there is injustice. Certainly, what justice requires may be and often is deeply controversial, dividing people sharply into opposing political camps. Nevertheless, to openly proclaim the maintaining or the maximising of injustice as the point of law is to maintain what is not seriously sustainable. Even in all the contests of political debate, whoever puts forward a legislative programme purports to be laying out a reasonable and reflectively justifiable conception of justice and the common good for the community to which the (draft) legislation is addressed. So those who purport to legislate do not merely evince a presupposition that the conditions for their exercising constitutional authority exist. They also evince a supposition that what they do will in some way enhance the common good of the community, either in a way that squares with or indeed in a way that actively procures some needed element of justice in the community. An openly avowed belief that one's actions would violate basic and minimal requirements of justice would be inconsistent with the sincerity conditions[12] implicit in performing the legislative role.

All this depends on some unstated premises and arguments, but these can be stated and justified, as I have attempted to do elsewhere.[13] The upshot is that I come to conclusions far from incompatible with those of

[12] Compare Searle, above n 7.

[13] This chapter expresses in compressed form arguments that I have attempted to develop in full in *Institutions of Law*, above n 4, particularly in Part IV of that book.

Robert Alexy, but by a somewhat different route. In particular, I agree that a well-founded conception of law, such as I claim to have achieved in my version of the institutional theory of law, has to include a version of the Radbruch formula. Whatever violates basic requirements of justice according to any reasonably assertable conception of justice ought not to be recognised as law. In itself, this is vague and highly contestable. But in the contemporary world there are established human rights instruments, notably in Europe the European Human Rights Convention. These provide a positivised means of establishing in an interpersonal and interstatal context an identifiable limit beyond which legislators and governments cannot go, and which all judges ought to respect by virtue of their office as such, albeit taking account of their own constitutional position and tradition.

This partly lies behind, and partly receives support from, reflection on the felicity conditions and sincerity conditions that apply to speech acts that are acts-in-law by way of legislating, adjudicating and deciding in an executive capacity. Is this because law itself expresses a claim to correctness? This seems to me an unhelpfully metaphorical way of expressing what can be stated more clearly. It is, of course, true that any speech act implicitly carries with it a claim to its correctness. In the case of legislative speech acts this ostensibly trivial point acquires seriousness from the point at which one asks what it is to act correctly in the capacity of a legislator. The answer offered here is that this requires an at least implicit and more often an explicit orientation to a sincerely held conception of justice and the common good.

To this extent and in this sense, we can accept that the claim or pretension to correctness implicit in acts of law-making entails reference to justice, that is, to some reasonable conception of justice. Law-makers who act cynically from other concealed motives or brutally for other expressed motives may be able to operate in a system which can successfully coerce a population into a large degree of observance of the laws they purport to make. But what they make, under whatever name they make it, need not and should not be acknowledged as other than gravely defective law, if law at all, by analysts or observers not in thrall to their enforcement apparatus. This 'claim to correctness', if such it be, is that of the law-maker, not that of the 'law'.

4

How Non-Positivism Can Accommodate Legal Certainty

STEFANO BERTEA*

INTRODUCTION

LEGAL CERTAINTY OCCUPIES a central place in law's domain. The very act of setting up a legal order reflects, among other things, a demand for certainty: by subjecting conduct to the governance of rules, the law limits the range of permissible behaviour and legitimises certain expectations, thus reducing contingency and complexity and superimposing an order on human interactions that would otherwise have in them a wide potential for unpredictability and chaos.[1] So legal certainty—the law's ability to make behaviour more predictable and expectations more reliable—is not just one among several ideals by which legal practices can be assessed: it is a fundamental and necessary value of law. This seems to support the view that the principle of certainty forms an indispensable legal pair with the claim to justice: certainty and justice form a couplet that no well-developed system of laws can ignore, since we cannot have a working legal order unless its rules (or a core set of them) are certain and its norms, procedures, and outcomes (or the bulk of them) are correct.[2] But certainty and justice stand more often than not in a conflictive relationship: achieving a greater degree of certainty within a legal system can easily

* Funding for this research has been provided by the Alexander von Humboldt Foundation. I wish to express my indebtedness to Robert Alexy, Francesco Belvisi and George Pavlakos for their helpful remarks on previous drafts of this chapter. Needless to say, responsibility for the views expressed herein, as well as for any errors of form or content, rests solely with me.

[1] These aspects are explored in Z Bańkowski, *Living Lawfully: Love in Law and Law in Love* (Dordrecht, Kluwer, 2001) 39–42.

[2] For a similar view see J Habermas, *Between Facts and Norms* (Cambridge, Polity, 1996 (orig edn 1992) 194–7, though he is not a lone voice in this.

cause us to give up some of its correctness. In sum, at the core of law lies an essential dichotomy between the principle of legal certainty and the claim to justice.

This feature of certainty and justice—both of them being fundamental values in law, and yet each colliding with the other—has been a source of serious theoretical problems. And the reason is not far to seek: because both bear a fundamental status, any comprehensive theory of law needs to make sense of both, no matter if the relationship they stand in is conflictive or otherwise. Different general approaches to law have dealt with the essential dichotomy, but by and large they have been skewed toward either certainty or justice, giving only a partial account of the other. The attitude toward the essential dichotomy can be generalised: granted, we are taking out the broad brush on a large and distinguished body of literature here, but legal positivism can generally be said to more easily accommodate the certainty of law and non-positivism its claim to justice.

Legal positivism understands the law as chiefly a body of entrenched general standards that can be imposed on specific cases without recourse to deliberative reasoning, the regulative ideal being to secure for the law the highest degree of predetermination and certainty there is to be had. But this approach ultimately fails to take seriously the claim to justice associated with law, thus allowing a radical divergence between law and justice. So, unsurprisingly, even extremely unjust norms can be qualified as legal on a positivist view, so long as they have been properly enacted and are socially efficacious. This amounts to making justice an altogether extra-legal standard and denying it as an element constitutive of law. In a positivist framework, then, the essential dichotomy is made into a less problematic (and theoretically less interesting) contrast between a legal value and an extra-legal one. This solution comes at the cost of oversimplifying the legal domain, however, as it can be appreciated in the standard positivist claim that legal theorists should not really concern themselves with matters of justice (these falling beyond their scope and competence), a claim that drastically narrows down the ambit of legal theory and causes it to bear little relevance on the public discussion about issues of practical import.

Non-positivism, in contrast, makes central the thesis that 'law consists of more than the pure facticity of power, orders backed by threats, habit, or organized coercion. Its nature comprises not only a factual or real side, but also a critical or ideal dimension.'[3] Non-positivism can thus acknowledge the existence as well as the legal significance of the essential dichotomy, but—as critics allege—only in a distorted, and hence inadequate, way. The claim that implicit at any level in legal practice is a demand for justice

[3] R Alexy, 'On the Thesis of a Necessary Connection between Law and Morality: Bulygin's Critique' (2000) 13 *Ratio Juris* 138.

suggests an attitude whereby certainty is subordinated to justice and made worthy of protection only derivatively, that is, only insofar as certainty proves compatible with justice and functional to it. There is hardly a case that could be made for non-positivism if it did actually stage such a subordination: no theory can be truly comprehensive if it fails to account for *all* of the fundamental features of law, and since non-positivism aspires precisely to such comprehensiveness, it must explain the ideal side of law (and the connected claim to justice) without thereby forsaking its *factual* side (and the connected claim to certainty).

Here, I will assess whether non-positivism can suitably accommodate certainty and hence be a genuinely general theory of law. I will do this by looking at a specific version of non-positivism—Robert Alexy's—and seeing whether it can explain law's claim to certainty. This argument will proceed by selectively introducing Alexy's theses on the nature of law and on legal certainty,[4] in a reconstruction aimed at explaining the strategy by which Alexy works out the relationship between law and certainty, and at showing how the need to account for certainty contributes importantly to shaping his non-positivism. I will follow this up by generalising the argument beyond Alexy and showing how non-positivism can well explain legal certainty in an analytic and sophisticated way; which in turn shows, among other things, that non-positivism can legitimately aspire to be a comprehensive theory of law.

ALEXY'S NON-POSITIVIST THEORY OF LAW

Alexy articulates a rationalist conception of law based on discourse theory. On this conception, not only is the existence of law rationally required, but its structure and substance are deeply conditioned by practical reason, too. The existence of law is rationally required insofar as we need to have a system of laws in place to make up for the shortcomings of practical reason. For, not all controversies on normative issues for which a rational solution is required can be worked out by practical reason alone; some issues remain unresolved, and the only way we can overcome this practical indeterminateness—and solve specific disputes—is if we can rely on general norms created through a set of pre-established rule-governed procedures.[5] Alexy, then, presents the law as an institutionalisation of practical reason, that is, as a formal instantiation, specification and supplementation of

[4] For a more exhaustive introduction to Alexy's conception of law, see S Bertea, *Certezza del diritto e argomentazione giuridica* (Soveria Mannelli, Rubbettino, 2002) 189–255.

[5] The practical indeterminateness of practical reason, connected with the whole problem of knowledge, is considered by Alexy to be one of the main reasons for setting up a system of law. On this question, as well as on the other problems for which law is offered as a remedy, see R Alexy, 'My Philosophy of Law: The Institutionalisation of Reason' in LJ Wintgens (ed),

practical reason. However, on this view reason does not completely retreat when its service is done in creating a legal system, but rather simply it acknowledges its need to be complemented. Thus, although there are disparate contents that the law can take as an institution shaped and constitutively constrained by reason, it cannot take just any content. Contrary to the key positivist thesis that 'any content whatever can be law',[6] this means that law's autonomy from reason is only partial; which lends from the outset a non-positivist flavour to Alexy's theoretical enterprise.

There is a typical structure that legal systems will present when understood as institutionalisations of practical reason, a structure consisting of different levels. At a high and abstract level stands the constitution: not a constitution positivistically conceived (ie a supreme norm enacted by the highest power) but rather a constitution designed to integrate and contextualise the main rules and principles of rational discourse. This implies that constitutions have a minimal necessary content: they must incorporate the basic human rights (a substantial requirement) and the form of democracy (a procedural requirement).[7] Still, a constitution cannot alone ensure determinateness in the practical sphere, and so a further normative level is needed: the level of legislation. Legislation is an authoritative statement enacted by a competent institution: it accords with the constitutional provisions directly and with the directives of practical reason indirectly. Thus, the legislator's freedom of choice, though it does not vanish altogether, receives from the outset a double delimitation.[8] But even here, constitutional and legislative norms combined do not suffice to implement practical reason and make it conclusive. Practical determinateness can be achieved only at a further normative level: that of legal discourse within the framework set up by constitutional and legislative provisions. Legal discourse—a practice aimed at assessing and comparing alternative solutions to the controversies arising in a system of law—is a special case of practical reasoning: at the same time as it uses reason to address normative issues (this makes it a standard case of rational discourse), it proceeds under a set of more demanding and limiting constraints and conditions (and it is these conditions that make legal discourse a special case of

The Law in Philosophical Perspective (Dordrecht, Kluwer, 1999) 23–45 at 32--3. In this regard Alexy follows I Kant, *The Metaphysics of Morals* (Cambridge, Cambridge University Press, 1996) 124.

[6] H Kelsen, *Pure Theory of Law* (Berkeley and Los Angeles, University of California Press, 1967 (orig edn 1960)) 198.

[7] Alexy, above n 5, esp at 35–8.

[8] On the rational necessity of legislation see A Aarnio, R Alexy and A Peczenik, 'The Foundation of Legal Reasoning' (1981) 12 *Rechtstheorie* at 273–4.

rational discourse).[9] So the structures and forms of legal reasoning differ from those of rational reasoning on practically relevant subjects, but without coming into contrast with them.[10] The forms of legal reasoning may be more or less institutionalised: in legal-theoretical and dogmatic discussions among academics, the practice of legal reasoning is open-ended; but when taken into the hands of decision-making institutions called on to settle controversies by authority, it takes on formal constraints—controversies could not find any final conclusion unless further constraints are placed on the rational discourse by which they are worked out. These constraints do not all have a rational foundation, to be sure, but their use in the law 'does not entail a farewell to reason, though',[11] for even here, where legal reasoning is institutionalised, its forms comport with the basic criteria of rational discourse on practical matters.

From these remarks emerges a concept of law based on the connection thesis, which stipulates a conceptually necessary connection between law and rational morality. The two main arguments on which Alexy grounds the connection thesis are the argument from correctness and that from extreme injustice.[12] The argument from correctness derives the conceptually necessary connection between law and rational morality from the fact that legal systems necessarily raise a claim to correctness. The argument from extreme injustice is basically a sophisticated restatement of the 'Radbruch formula', whereby an extremely unjust provision is not only morally defective but also legally invalid: authoritative directives cease to exist as law when they overpass the point of extreme injustice. On this view, then, the law cannot be made totally independent of critical morality, since there are different sorts of standards that laws must meet before they can qualify as valid: not only systemic, procedural and social standards, but also moral ones. These arguments go into a conception of law that combines three basic elements: what has been issued (authoritative issuance), what is efficacious (social efficacy), and what is morally right (moral correctness). And this in turn yields a definition of law as a:

[9] See Aarnio, Alexy and Peczenik, above n 8 at 274–8. Alexy's theory of legal reasoning takes up the forms of justification typically used in law and proceeds from the 'special case thesis', on which see R Alexy, *A Theory of Legal Argumentation* (Oxford, Clarendon Press, 1989) 14–20; and R Alexy, 'The Special Case Thesis' (1999) 12 *Ratio Juris* 374.

[10] These structures and forms are analysed in detail in Alexy, *A Theory of Legal Argumentation*, above n 9. For a summary statement, see in particular *ibid* at 297–302.

[11] Aarnio, Alexy and Peczenik, above n 8 at 278.

[12] For a synthetic exposition, see R Alexy, 'Law and Correctness' (1998) 51 *Current Legal Problems* 205–21; R Alexy, 'A Defence of Radbruch Formula' in D Dyzenhaus (ed), *Recrafting the Rule of Law: The Limits of Legal Order* (Oxford and Portland, Oregon, Hart Publishing, 1999) 15–39; and R Alexy, 'The Nature of Arguments about the Nature of Law' in LH Meyer, SL Paulson and TW Pogge (eds), *Rights, Culture, and the Law* (Oxford, Oxford University Press, 2003) 3 at 9–16.

> system of norms that (1) lays claim to correctness, (2) consists of the totality of norms that belong to a constitution by and large socially efficacious and that are not themselves unjust in the extreme, as well as the totality of norms that are issued in accordance with this constitution, norms that manifest a minimum social efficacy or prospect of social efficacy and that are not themselves unjust in the extreme, and, finally, (3) comprises the principles and other normative arguments on which the process or procedure of law application is and/or must be based in order to satisfy the claim to correctness.[13]

This non-positivist definition of law maintains that the legal system consists of norms (in the form of either rules or principles), but that it also embodies the rational procedures necessary to understand, compare, apply and justify such norms.[14] This is to argue that duly enacted and socially efficacious directives do not make up the whole of the legal domain: the law consists of much more than the structured set of its constituent norms; it consists, too, in a level of reasoning and procedures by which these norms get their structure. This level amounts to a rational component of law that must be taken into account and, ultimately, incorporated in any comprehensive conception of law. Therefore, in essence, Alexy's view brings reason to bear as a component of the legal domain in so loosening the link between law and authoritative issuance.

ALEXY'S POSITION ON LEGAL CERTAINTY

In the last section I clarified that in Alexy's conception, law is an instantiation of practical reason. In like manner, Alexy looks at legal certainty (*Rechtssicherheit*): the certainty the law seeks to secure is a specification and implementation of rational certainty (*Gewißheit*), ie it is designed to complement and remedy the limited certainty provided by rational discourse. So we have to look at Alexy's conception of *rational* certainty before we can move on and understand what he means by *legal* certainty. Rational certainty (ie the certainty that rational discourse will provide) can be equated with rational determinacy, meaning the ability of a procedure to lead to stringent conclusions and hence make possible a rational agreement on practical issues. In discourse theory, a conclusion is stringent when it is either 'discursively necessary' or 'discursively impossible', that is, when the criteria of rational discourse require a given

[13] Alexy, *The Argument from Injustice* (Oxford, Clarendon Press, 2002) 127.

[14] On this point see R Alexy, 'Idée et structure d'un systéme du droit rationnel' (1988) *Archives du philosophie du droit* 23 at 36–8; and R Alexy, 'Sistema juridico, pricipios juridicos y razon practica' (1988) 5 *Doxa* 139 at 148–9. On the distinction between rules and principles, and on the rational procedure by which to handle norms (the procedure of balancing), see R Alexy, *A Theory of Constitutional Rights* (Oxford, Oxford University Press, 2002) 44–110; R Alexy, 'The Nature of Arguments about the Nature of Law', above n 12 at 3–16; and R Alexy, 'Balancing, Constitutional Review, and Representation' 3 I-CON 572-81.

conclusion, or when they rule it out unequivocally. In either case, practical reasoning helps us to arrive at univocal, and hence certain, answers to practical dilemmas. In fact, 'several judgements of value and of obligation as well as several rules are stringently required and flatly excluded by the rules of discourse'.[15] This is the reason why we can use the rules and forms of rational discourse to settle normative controversies: because they increase 'the probability of reaching agreement on practical issues'.[16] Even so, there will be practical matters that the structures and procedures of rational discourse cannot settle conclusively, failing to produce any permanent agreement. For, it may well be that 'two incompatible normative statements or rules can be justified without violating any of the rules of discourse'.[17] There is only so much certainty that rational discourse can secure: between the discursively necessary and the discursively impossible lies the discursively possible, the realm inhabited by anything that can be justified without acting inconsistently with the standards of rational discourse. And since at least a few of these normative standards are mutually incompatible, rational reasoning lets in a margin of indeterminacy, failing to yield any certain solution as to what course of action ought to be taken. It is here that we must turn to other forms of guidance. But we can do so on the condition that we do not thereby come into contrast with the standards of practical rationality. Legal systems are paradigmatic instantiations of such complementary institutions providing us with guidance in the practical sphere; which by analogy makes legal certainty the necessary complement of rational certainty.

We can see, then, that the question of legal certainty occupies a central position in Alexy's thought. In the end, it is a demand for certainty that justifies the transition from purely rational to legal discourse: a legal order is required because it can contribute to reducing the uncertainty surrounding matters of practical relevance. Legal certainty is thus made to bear a close connection with the law, but even more importantly, it does so as a value, an end worthy of pursuit. Conceiving of certainty as a value, as opposed to a fact, of law allows Alexy to avoid hypostatising the connection between law and certainty as well as the importance of certainty itself. Thus, in showing how legal systems can become more determinate by expanding the realm of certainty—the discursively necessary and the discursively impossible—he points out that no such system can ensure a conclusive answer to every possible controversy where a practical matter is at issue.[18] The law can reduce, but not eliminate, the

[15] Alexy, *A Theory of Legal Argumentation*, above n 9 at 207.

[16] *Ibid* at 206.

[17] *Ibid* at 207.

[18] See, in this regard, Alexy, 'Sistema juridico, pricipios juridicos y razon practica', above n 14 at 150–1.

number of unanswerable practical questions. This makes legal certainty a regulative idea: all legal systems present some degree of uncertainty, and they must strive to replace as much of it as possible with determinacy. However, although Alexy does not hypostatise legal certainty, he does assign to it a value that cannot be compromised. For Alexy legal certainty is a 'material legal universal', meaning that it is one of law's 'necessary properties', one of the *universalia juris*, ie the elements that law needs to have if it is to be conceived as an institutionalisation of practical reason.[19] In fact, if we accept that the law arises out of a demand for certainty, then at least part of law's justification will have to lie in its ability to remedy the unavoidable uncertainty of practical rationality. Yet even here, important as certainty may be in its being a necessary property of law, it does not figure as the *only* value of law—it must therefore be weighed against other values that may come into conflict with it.[20]

With these preliminary philosophical considerations in place, we can move on to Alexy's treatment of the more specific and technical aspects of the certainty that can be secured by having a system of law in place. As a special case of rational certainty, legal certainty is likewise concerned with determinateness: legal directives are determinate when their addressees can come to know exactly what they are and what they prescribe and entail. This kind of knowledge is both general and particular. We have certainty when we know the abstract norms making up a given legal order, but we also need to know how these norms can be applied to specific contexts yielding concrete decisions that are rationally determinate. There are various mechanisms that legal systems offer in this effort to achieve a satisfactory degree of general and specific certainty. Alexy lays stress on three of them: internal justification, dogmatic reasoning and precedent. By internal justification is meant the component of legal justification that is 'concerned with the question of whether an opinion follows logically from the premises adduced as justifying it'.[21] In support of the legal syllogism (and answering the scepticism it tends to draw forth) Alexy strenuously defends the view that legal justification may on certain occasions require showing that a conclusion, say, a statement with which a dispute is settled, follows logically from a set of valid legal premises.[22] The use of deductive

[19] R Alexy, 'Law, Discourse and Time' Beiheft 64 *Archiv fur Rechts- und Sozialphilosophie* (1995) 101 at 102. These necessary properties of law that 'exist in all legal systems and all law must possess independently of time and space in order to be a legal system or law' (*ibid* at 101) include formal as well as substantive elements. Among the formal elements are the concepts of obligation, prohibition and permission; among the substantive ones is that of certainty. Accordingly, Alexy calls legal certainty 'a universal value' (*ibid* at 108).

[20] On this aspect see Alexy, above n 13 at 52.

[21] Alexy, *A Theory of Legal Argumentation*, above n 9 at 221.

[22] The legal syllogism is criticised in the seminal works of T Viehweg, *Topik und Jurisprudenz* (München, Beck, 1954); C Perelman and L Olbrechts-Tyteca, *The New Rhetoric: A Treatise on Argumentation* (Notre Dame, Notre Dame University Press, 1969

reasoning in legal justification is not only possible but also valuable, as it contributes to increasing the overall certainty of law: 'articulating universal rules facilitates consistency in decision-making and thereby contributes towards justice and legal certainty'.[23] Thus, Alexy's insistence on the importance of deductive reasoning in law ultimately reflects a demand for certainty. Dogmatic reasoning and the doctrine of precedent, too, come in the service of legal certainty: they do so by providing stability. Dogmatic reasoning enables this function by serving the 'principle of universalisability', regarded not only as 'an elementary aspect of the principle of justice' but also as the root of legal certainty;[24] the practice of following precedent, for its part, in addition to serving stability, directly provides 'legal certainty and the protection of confidence in judicial decision-making'.[25] These remarks show that Alexy understands the certainty of law to depend heavily on the rationality of the argumentation used in running the legal system. The rationality of legal reasoning strengthens legal certainty and undermines it if endangered: others things being equal, the closer legal reasoning comes to the ideal of rational discourse, the more certain will be the legal system in which such reasoning is regularly carried out. There can be no certainty without rationality.[26]

The preceding remarks put us in the best position to appreciate that not only is Alexy quite aware of the pride of place certainty enjoys in the legal domain but also that he assigns to legal certainty an equally prominent role in his own theory—a non-positivist theory of law, mind you. This fact shows that there is nothing in Alexy's theory to prevent it from giving a sophisticated and detailed account of legal certainty. A closer look at Alexy's non-positivism will enable us to see how it does this. Under the

(Orig ed 1958)); and C Perelman, *Logique juridique. Nouvelle rhetorique* (Paris, Dalloz, 1976) as well as in the more recent contributions of JM Makau, 'The Supreme Court and Reasonableness' (1984) 70 *Quarterly Journal of Speech* 379; RD Rieke, 'The Judicial Dialogue' (1991) 5 *Argumentation* 39; M Maneli, *Perelman's New Rhetoric as Philosophy and Methodology for the Next Century* (Dordrecht, Kluwer, 1993); and DA Herbeck, 'Critical Legal Studies and Argumentation Theory' (1995) 9 *Argumentation* 719.

[23] Alexy, *A Theory of Legal Argumentation*, above n 9 at 230. See also R Alexy, 'Legal Expert Systems and Legal Theory' in H Fiedler *et al* (eds), *Expert Systems in Law* (Tübingen, Tübingen University Press, 1988) 69–74 at 69.

[24] Alexy, *A Theory of Legal Argumentation*, above n 9 at 266.

[25] *Ibid* at 277. Cf Alexy, above n 19 at 109.

[26] It is important to note that on Alexy's view the link between certainty and rationality is complex and non-linear. In other words, rationality cannot without distortion be equated with absolute certainty: 'it is not the generation of certainty which constitutes the rational character of jurisprudence but rather its conformity to a number of conditions, criteria, or rules' (Alexy, above n 9 at 293). Couple this with Alexy's statement that compliance with rules which instantiate the demands of practical reason 'does certainly not guarantee the conclusive certainty of all results' (*ibid* at 179), and you get the conclusion that a procedure can be rational and still fail to achieve a satisfactory level of certainty.

single label *non-positivism* comes a wide variety of theories of law,[27] all of them joined by a fundamental tenet which is the connection thesis, the proposition that in the definition of law moral elements must be included. What marks these theories apart is their construction of the connection thesis, and this is the ground on which can be tested their ability to provide an account of legal certainty, and so a comprehensive explanation of law. This is admittedly rather blunt, but Alexy's non-positivism can be distinguished from other versions by two features. The first of these, the 'source-family thesis', says that the law is source-based, meaning that the law is a social institution whose existence and content depend, among other things, on authoritative enactment.[28] This means that the law carries within it the conditions of its own institutionality and efficacy, and hence that moral correctness—though a necessary condition for a standard to qualify as law—is not sufficient to this end.[29] The second distinctive feature of Alexy's non-positivism consists in the kind of connection it establishes between law and morality, distinguishing a classifying connection from a qualifying one. In both cases the connection is conceptually necessary. But in a classifying connection, a norm or system of norms that should fail given criteria of rational morality could not be classified as a legal norm or system. In a qualifying connection, such a failure would instead be less consequential, bringing a legal defect but not invalidating the norm or system of norms.[30] And this is Alexy's position: a norm can be valid even if it breaches critical morality. The exception comes only in the event of a serious breach: the only way a socially efficacious norm duly enacted by a competent authority can be made legally invalid on moral grounds is if this norm is unjust in the extreme.[31]

These two distinctive features of Alexy's non-positivism can both ultimately be explained as attempts to accommodate the demands of certainty associated with the existence of law. Let us consider first Alexy's distinction between a classifying and a qualifying connection of law and morality. Any version of non-positivism based on an unqualified connection thesis

[27] Among the different types of non-positivism, we have various versions of natural law theory as well as of interpretivism.

[28] On the source-family thesis see R Alexy, 'Effects of Defects: Action or Argument? Thoughts about Deryck Beyleveld's and Roger Brownsword's *Law as a Moral Judgement*' (2006) 19 *Ratio Juris*, 169-179; and R Alexy, 'The Separation between Law and Morality: A Debate between Robert Alexy and Andrei Marmor', unpublished paper prepared for IVR World Congress, Granada, Spain, 27 May 2005.

[29] The main contemporary versions of natural law theory disagree with this thesis. See D Beyleveld and R Brownsword, *Law as a Moral Judgement* (London, Sweet and Maxwell, 1986) 159–64.

[30] Not all versions of non-positivism draw the distinction between a classifying and a qualifying connection. For a sophisticated version of non-positivism that does not rely on this distinction, see Beyleveld and Brownsword, above n 29.

[31] See Alexy, above 13 at 40–62.

will be vulnerable to the criticism that it cannot adequately account for legal certainty. For, an opponent of non-positivism might argue, moral standards cannot unqualifiedly be incorporated into the law without thereby jeopardising the law's ability to guarantee a satisfactory degree of certainty. Especially in a pluralist society, where deep controversy is always surrounding moral standards and making it difficult to validate them, the opponent would continue, the incorporation of morality into the law has the effect of making the law subjective and arbitrary, thus reducing the overall degree of certainty that a legal system can warrant. This argument is sensible enough, but it only applies to an unqualified connection thesis: it cannot be brought against a version of non-positivism based on the distinction between a qualifying and a classifying connection of law and morality. Alexy makes this point by observing that 'the more extreme the injustice, the more certain the knowledge of it'.[32] So, since on Alexy's version of the connection thesis, a norm gets invalidated only when extremely unjust, and since there is usually little doubt as to when injustice is extreme, no radical uncertainty is likely to get passed onto the law. Alexy does acknowledge that 'there may well be cases . . . in which one cannot say with complete certainty whether or not the extreme injustice is at hand', but he also adds that this can scarcely be considered an argument against his moderate non-positivism, because it is only on rare occasions that we cannot tell whether we are looking at a case of extreme injustice.[33] Alexy's qualified incorporation of morality into law, then, does not involve sacrificing certainty beyond what is reasonable. His distinction between a qualifying and a classifying connection of law and morality can therefore be interpreted as designed to retain the connection thesis without thereby having to let go of legal certainty.

We can further appreciate the role of certainty as a defining feature of Alexy's non-positivism if we consider Alexy's discussion of the criteria for the validity not only of single norms, but also of the legal system as a whole. In his treatment, Alexy takes up specifically the question whether the failure of fundamental norms to fulfil the requirements of morality can carry consequences extending to the system as a whole. Contrary to Martin Kriele's 'extension thesis',[34] Alexy argues that a legal system will still be legal even if its fundamental substantive norms lose that status in consequence of infringing standards of justice. The reason why Alexy rejects the extension thesis is that to do otherwise would amount to forsaking legal certainty. The extension thesis implies that a mildly unjust norm (one that does not carry out any extreme injustice) will become

[32] *Ibid* at 52.

[33] *Ibid* at 52.

[34] See M Kriele, *Recht und praktische Vernunft* (Göttingen, Vandenhoeck & Ruprecht, 1979) 125–6.

invalid simply by virtue of belonging to a system whose fundamental norms do effect an extreme injustice. But this is tantamount to destroying the certainty of law.[35] The legal system as a whole cannot ensure any reasonable degree of certainty if it suffers the general consequences deriving from any moral defectiveness of its constituent norms. Thus, even if it is a fundamental norm that carries out the injustice, the system should still not suffer in consequence. In conclusion, if we cannot extend to the legal system as a whole the consequences of applying to individual norms the argument from injustice, the reason has to do with the importance that Alexy accords to certainty in law.

This central role assigned to certainty is also the reason behind the other distinctive feature of Alexy's non-positivism, namely, the source-family thesis. This thesis is best viewed in relation to Alexy's theory of validity. Alexy distinguishes three basic concepts of validity—sociological, ethical and juridical validity—which connect with three defining elements of law—social efficacy, correctness of content and authoritative issuance. Of these three elements, it is only correctness of content, and hence ethical validity, that a non-positive account needs in any strict sense in order to be coherent. Still, Alexy chooses to embrace a more wide-ranging definition of legal validity which takes all three elements combined: if a normative system is to be legally valid, it must be the product of an authority (juridical validity), it must be socially efficacious (sociological validity), and it cannot be unjust in the extreme (ethical validity). Now, this wide definition of legal validity—as dependent on institutional and sociological elements in addition to ethical ones—can be understood as driven by a concern to secure legal certainty. In fact, other things being equal, a system of norms based on institutional, social and moral requirements will yield greater legal certainty than a system whose validity depends on moral standards alone. In the case that the validity of legal systems would hold independently of institutional and social considerations, nothing prevents legal systems from giving place to absolute uncertainty, and we would therefore end up having a valid but uncertain system. Correspondingly, certainty would be irrelevant to the justification of a legal system. This is not acceptable to Alexy. In his framework, the law's connection with certainty can be loosened, but not eliminated altogether. It is in order to secure certainty, then, that Alexy brings institutional and social elements into his definition of legal validity.

That this is so can further be appreciated by looking at the way Alexy describes the relationship obtaining among the three basic components of

[35] In the words of R Alexy in *The Argument from Injustice*, above n 13 at 65, 'legal certainty would be too severely compromised if a norm below the threshold of extreme injustice were to forfeit its legal character because it somehow shares in the injustice of the whole system and is therefore typical of it'.

legal validity. He describes this relationship as asymmetric, in that the two non-institutional components do not carry equal weight at system level. A set of authoritative norms that by and large is socially efficacious and not morally defective will be legally valid. So we have a positive criterion of legal validity and a negative one. The positive criterion—social efficacy—is satisfied if the legal system exerts its dominance and can prevail on other coercive systems of norms should an open conflict with them break out in society.[36] The negative criterion—the system should not present any extensive moral defect— is a straightforward instantiation of the connection thesis. But the point is that, of these two criteria, only the positive one is strictly a requirement of legal validity: no normative system would be valid that should largely fail to exert social efficacy, but a system might still be valid if it were to present a wide moral defect. So, at systemlevel, 'there is an asymmetry between the relation of legal and social validity and the relation of legal and moral validity in that the legal validity of a legal system as a whole depends more on social validity than on moral validity'.[37] Again, in Alexy's conceptual framework a feature of the legal domain (the asymmetry between social efficacy and moral correctness) is dictated by a concern for certainty: certainty requires not only three components of legal validity, but also a ranking among these components—'authoritative issuance must be joined by social efficacy and correctness of content not in a general, equally weighed, relation'.[38]

CONCLUSION

We have seen in this chapter how the main features of Alexy's account of the law connect with the notion of certainty despite the non-positivist matrix of this account: not only does this notion contribute significantly to shape the peculiar traits of Alexy's non-positivist theory of law, but it also helps give Alexy's theory the distinctive traits that mark it off from other non-positivist theories. The moderate non-positivism put forward by Alexy can acknowledge the importance of legal certainty, and give it priority over other fundamental legal values in a number of circumstances, without thereby making law the mere product of authority in the positivist fashion. And it can even be argued, more boldly, that this need to bring out the central role of certainty in law is actually the whole point of Alexy's theory, the reason why it steers a middle course that stands clear of both legal positivism and the most radical forms of non-positivism.

36 This is the 'dominance criterion', introduced by N Hoerster, 'Die rechtsphilosophische Lehre vom Rechtsbegriff' (1987) 27 *Juristische Schulung* 181 at 184.

37 Alexy, above n 13 at 92–3.

38 *Ibid* at 93.

This discussion of legal certainty in Alexy's work can be generalised. If Alexy's non-positivism can give a satisfactory account of the essential dichotomy in the legal enterprise between legal certainty and justice, so can, by extension, other forms of non-positivism, and that without causing certainty to succumb to the claims of justice. In other terms, non-positivism can be comprehensive enough to account for the full range of basic values currently associated with the existence of law. Therefore, non-positivism is perfectly able to offer a solid alternative to legal positivism. But, a caveat is relevant here. In order to be an alternative to legal positivism that can be truly comprehensive, non-positivism must of necessity take seriously the social existence as well as the institutional component of legal practices. Whereas Alexy's theory is by no means the only non-positivist view to do so, it is certainly a serious attempt at upholding the connection thesis without thereby giving up on the attempt to explain the social and institutional components of law. As a consequence, it is a view worthy of careful investigation in and outside the non-positivist camp.

5

Two Concepts of Objectivity

GEORGE PAVLAKOS*

INTRODUCTION

THIS CHAPTER AIMS to juxtapose two of the most influential contemporary cognitivist theories in legal philosophy: Ronald Dworkin's interpretive theory of law and Robert Alexy's discourse theory of law. Despite the fact that both assess the possibility of right answers in law, the two accounts begin from premises that are prima facie hard to reconcile. On the face of it, a concern arises that the idea of a right answer might be just an illusion, for objective answers cannot be reached by applying conflicting criteria.[1]

The issue ramifies: far from representing co-equal alternatives for attaining the same objective, the two theories embody radically opposing metaphysical views with respect to the domain of law in particular and normativity more generally. While Dworkin's theory has evolved over the years to suggest that norms and values are mind-independent, in the sense

* I owe many thanks for comments and critical remarks to audiences in Belfast, Prague, Venice and Kiel. The writing of the final draft has been made possible by a two-week research fellowship at the EMA in Venice. For their hospitality at the academy I thank Professors Koen de Feyter and George Ulrich. A warm thank you, too, goes to Sean Coyle and Carsten Heidemann for having saved me from several philosophical blunders; for those remaining the responsibility is, of course, entirely mine. Bonnie Litschewski Paulson and Stanley L Paulson have made a number of valuable suggestions on content and language which led to considerable improvements.

[1] Lest it give rise to the suspicion of confusing the truth of a proposition with the means for reaching it, the above formulation should be understood as pointing out the difference in cognitive content between knowledge and various degrees of belief: in other words, while it is possible to utter a true proposition p ('this is a cat') by relying on false criteria of identification ('all creatures with tails are cats'), there remains still a failing as regards the speaker's cognitive content: he or she fails to know p. For the requirements of knowledge and its importance for legal philosophy, see G Pavlakos, 'Normative Knowledge and the Nature of Law' in S Coyle and G Pavlakos (eds), *Jurisprudence or Legal Science?* (Oxford and Portland, Hart Publishing, 2005) 89–125. I thank Sean Coyle for drawing my attention to the potential confusion.

of there being normative states of affairs that pre-exist our ways of talking and thinking,[2] Alexy's discursive conception assumes that law is constructed in thought, albeit according to criteria that function as objective constraints of the construction. To put it in a more disciplined language: whereas in Dworkin, normative propositions (those counterparts of our normative sentences that admit of truth-values) are individuated externally, that is independently of anything that bears on the language in which they are expressed, on the discursive account, legal propositions are individuated by the structure of the relevant sentences in which they are expressed. What is at stake here is nothing less than the meaningfulness and objectivity of legal (and broader evaluative) discourse. Depending on which of the two accounts is taken on board, very different things follow for the status of our normative statements: the possibility of being right or wrong with respect to them; the relation between truth and action; and finally the control we have over normative standards (in cognising, criticising and revising them).

The chapter opens with a discussion of the conditions of objectivity in interpretivism, as Dworkin's theory of law has come to be known in recent years. It is argued that interpretivism is saddled with a number of shortcomings that give rise to an insurmountable dilemma whose horns hold us hostage to either scepticism or metaphysical extravagance, with objectivity being undermined in either case. Subsequently, the source of the dilemma is located in a *shallow* understanding of legal practice, one that interpretivism shares with the legal philosophies it is supposed to take on. Conversely, a viable idea of objectivity requires that legal practice be ascribed a dimension of *depth*, which manages to steer clear of scepticism without importing strong metaphysical premises. The dimension of depth requires that we depart from a strong notion of objectivity that rests on some rigid determinants of truth and correctness and adopt, instead, a modest variant of objectivity which flows from the activity of following a rule. The last part of the chapter attempts to work out this conception by taking stock of the discourse theory of law. There it is argued that the rules of discourse constitute a *grammar*, which regulates the structure of normative sentences without relying on any external determinants of objectivity but, rather, on the continuity implicit in the activity of rule-following. Two features of discursive grammar are given special attention: on the one hand, its multilayered character: discursive grammar comprises

[2] This claim will be cast in three steps: first, by referring to Dworkin's claim that interpretive facts rely for their existence on (moral) values which are extraneous to the interpretive practice of any particular community; secondly, by showing that Dworkin's rejection of semantic analysis blocks the understanding of those values as depending on our linguistic practices; finally by arguing that, having ruled out a language-dependent explication of moral values, Dworkin turns to a robust essentialist theory for capturing their content. The three steps are addressed separately below.

rules that extend over multiple levels of abstraction, as a result of which it can account graphically for the depth of legal practice. On the other, in virtue of its being shared by all species of normative discourse, discursive grammar may account for the continuity between law and the other domains of practical reason (morality, ethics).

INTERPRETIVISM AND OBJECTIVITY

In Dworkin's work, the claim for objectivity is closely intertwined with what he takes to be law's interpretive nature. To put it in a nutshell, interpretive nature is marked by two elements. The first is the existence of a distinct category of facts which have a sui generis ontological status in virtue of their complexity (interpretive facts).[3] Complexity, in this context, is the result of a combination of the factual aspects of some social practice (say, the practice of courtesy) and the values pertaining to that practice, those values that constitute something like the *point* of the practice, to borrow a familiar Dworkinian term.[4] Consequently, an interpretive fact (say, about the obligation of courtesy to concede one's seat to elderly people) cannot be fully located in, or analysed to, either only descriptive or only evaluative components.[5] Even though some of the facts of the practice, as well as of the values that inform it, bear on the existence of the relevant interpretive fact (obligation of courtesy), neither of them is in a position fully to determine its existence. To put it in the language of propositions: the truth of an interpretive proposition[6] is not fully determinable by either descriptive or evaluative propositions, although it may

[3] N Stavropoulos, 'Interpretivist Theories of Law' in *The Stanford Encyclopaedia of Philosophy* (October 2003) htpp://plato.stanford.edu/archives/win2003/entries/law-interpretivist/ at s 1.

[4] One assumption that remains undiscussed by Dworkin is that the point of a practice can be characterised independently of the facts that constitute it. This assumption is not as self-evident as Dworkin might assume, for moral theories with a more naturalistic outlook might want to argue for the possibility of reducing points (or values) to facts. What raises further concern in this context is that Dworkin has in the past evoked supervenience in order to illustrate the relation between the point of a practice and the facts that constitute it (see his 'On Gaps in the Law' in P Amselek and N MacCormick (eds), *Controversies about Law's Ontology* (Edinburgh, Edinburgh University Press, 1991) 84n). Far from failing to corroborate the degree of independence between fact and value that Dworkin's idea of interpretive facts would require, supervenience rather represents amongst contemporary philosophers a more elegant way of expressing the reduction of values to facts.

[5] Another problem concerns values: are they also interpretive facts? Or does Dworkin assume a naturalistic explication of value?

[6] As 'interpretive proposition' would count any proposition in a judgement stating principles that are not part of formally instituted legal norms; eg, the proposition 'no one should profit from one's own wrong' in *Riggs v Palmer* (1889) 115 NY 506, see R Dworkin, *Law's Empire* (London, Fontana, 1986).

supervene[7] on both. The reason for this is that there is no mechanical formula for relating descriptive propositions to evaluative ones in a way that could establish a one-to-one correspondence between the members of the two sets of fact and value.[8] Another way to put it is to say that descriptive and evaluative facts are *asymmetric*, for it is possible that the facts of a practice support a greater number of values than those the point of the practice actually comprises, and vice versa: that, namely, the evaluative point of the practice excludes some of the latter's factual constituents.[9]

Complexity gives rise to the second element of interpretive nature, that of interpretation. Given that interpretive facts are neither readily available in the environment nor fully determined by either the descriptive or the evaluative facts of a practice, an account of their origin is called for. Interpretivism pictures the origination of interpretive facts as an instance of construction undertaken by an *interpretive theory* which puts forward interpretive judgements with respect to single interpretive facts. The judgements of interpretive theory generate interpretive facts by undertaking a 'creative' projection of the evaluative point of the relevant practice onto its factual constituents. Along these lines, an interpretive judgement that states what the law requires in a particular case undertakes an interpretation of the institutional facts of the relevant practice (be they political, legislative or adjudicative) in the light of the evaluative point of the practice. In addition, interpretations must satisfy the two criteria of fit

[7] For the notion of supervenience in general, see F Jackson, *From Metaphysics to Ethics* (Oxford, Clarendon Press, 1998); J Kim, *Supervenience and Mind: Selected Philosophical Essays* (Cambridge, Cambridge University Press, 1993); EE Savellos and ÜD Yalçin (eds), *Supervenience: New Essays* (Cambridge, Cambridge University Press, 1995); in moral philosophy, see RM Hare, *The Language of Morals* (Oxford, Clarendon Press, 1952) 80 and 153; *idem*, *Freedom and Reason* (Oxford, Clarendon Press, 1962) 19ff; Dworkin uses the concept of supervenience in his paper 'On Gaps in the Law', above n 4.

[8] Such correspondence would be necessary in order to circumscribe the problem of the *shapelessness* of normative properties. This term purports to account for the phenomenon that normative properties can be instantiated by infinite combinations of an infinite number of descriptive properties which, despite varying from context to context, give rise to the same normative property. Along these lines a descriptive proposition, however complete it may purport to be, will fail fully to determine a unique normative property, unless it is 'shaped' or 'constrained' by the property in question.

[9] It is important to notice that Dworkin's theory attempts to rule out an explication of interpretative facts as sums of pre-existing parts. On such a reading, an interpretive fact rests on a more basic layer of descriptive facts about a legal community which needs to be purged of all irrelevant facts through interpretation. For Dworkin, the existence of an interpretive fact is not gradual: it does not exist before its construction through interpretation, and anything else that pre-existed it is significant only as a raw-datum for the interpretation, but not as self-standing component of the forthcoming interpretive fact. To use an example: we cannot say that a legal obligation X (say to act as good faith requires) can be broken down to distinctive parts, some of which would be facts about legislation, others about adjudication, or even about the value of promises. Obligation X exists only after the interpretation has taken place.

and justification.[10] Fit refers to the requirement that any interpretation cohere with the institutional pedigree of the practice in question, to the effect that it still constitutes an interpretation of that practice as opposed to any other. Justification, on the other hand, purports to capture the evaluative dimension of the practice. An interpretation will be adequately justified only if it amounts to the morally best reconstruction of the factual components of the practice in the light of the values the practice serves. What confers upon an interpretation its moral quality is a rather obscure matter in Dworkin's theory. Although this is supposed to be judged against the values that together comprise the point of the practice, Dworkin seems to postulate an extra modicum of moral correctness that springs from a standpoint more universal in scope. The latter requires that the interpreter transcend the boundaries of the local practice and refer to moral values which extend beyond the point of any particular practice.[11]

The positioning of the moral values that account for the evaluative dimension of interpretive facts vis-à-vis the interpretive practice of a community is of key importance to an understanding of the nature of objectivity the interpretive theory solicits. If those values are placed within the practice of interpretation, then they require that an interpretive judgement come into existence. Conversely, if they are assumed to exist independently of such judgements then the importance of interpretivism is severely compromised, for what matters after all are entities that account for the truth of legal propositions independently of the practice of interpretation. In what follows I shall argue that Dworkin has come over the years to embrace the latter view. This development has been manifested through his ardent rejection of all accounts involving an analysis of the linguistic practice of a community (so-called semantic accounts). This rejection is underpinned by the view (mistaken, I believe) that any practice-dependent account of value fails to secure objectivity because it leads of necessity to a conception of legal practice that has no resources for accommodating law's normativity (*shallow practice*[12]). In contradistinction to semantic accounts, Dworkin attempts to retrieve a richer conception of practice by advancing a robust notion of practice-independent or

10 See R Dworkin, *Law's Empire* (London, Fontana Press, 1986) 65–8.

11 In *ibid* at 424–5, Dworkin argues that conceptions of justice transcend the boundaries of particular social practices and can serve as the basis for criticising other peoples' practices of justice; elsewhere he states that justice has a latent global reach, which exempts it from having to fit the practice of any particular community, see *ibid* at 425 and 'What Justice Isn't' in R Dworkin, *A Matter of Principle* (Oxford, Clarendon Press, 1986) 214–20 at 219; also the exchange between Dworkin and Walzer in the pages of the *New York Review of Books* (14 April 1983), where Dworkin rejects Walzer's suggestion that justice be explained along the lines of an interpretive account. On these points see also the discussion in G Sreenivasan, 'Interpretation and Reason' (1998) 27 *Philosophy and Public Affairs* 142, who attempts to extend the interpretive account to moral and ethical concepts.

12 See below.

a-contextual moral values. However, the combination between the rejection of all semantic accounts and the import of a robust notion of moral value can only with great difficulty be reconciled with the original intuitions of interpretivism. In contrast, I shall argue below that these intuitions are much better served by a discourse-theoretical explication of the legal practice, one that is capable of retaining a practice-immanent conception of normativity without resorting to a robust, practice-independent notion of values.

With the main parameters of interpretivism in position, it is time to enquire in a more sustained manner into the claims of objectivity that interpretivism raises. The subject of objectivity is vast and any attempt to take stock of the relevant philosophical discussion would, of course, exceed the limits of this chapter.[13] A simple way to capture the central intuition behind objectivity is to make room for a gap between what we think to be the case and what actually is the case. This gap is supposed to take into account the finiteness and imperfection of our cognitive capacities which make it possible that, although most of the time we do get things right, there are cases where we fail to do so. The likelihood of error suggests the existence of objective standards, which inform the content of our mental states and allow us to ascribe error to or affirm the truth of what we (or others) think and say. In so far as those standards determine the correctness not only of our mental states but also of the language we use and the thoughts we think, the issue of objectivity seems to touch upon more than one domain: our mental lives, perceptive powers, the language we use, the external world, as well as the relations between and among all the above. It is not out of place, therefore, to employ the vocabulary of *propositions* as a means of capturing the complexity of the demands of objectivity.[14]

Speaking generally, propositions are the 'objective' counterparts of sentences that enable communication between speakers independently of

[13] For a detailed discussion of objectivity, see R Nozick, *Invariances* (Cambridge, Mass, Harvard University Press, 2001); and in the domain of law, the seminal work of N Stavropoulos, *Objectivity in Law* (Oxford, Oxford University Press, 1996); also Stavropoulos's more recent paper 'Objectivity' in M Golding and W Edmundson (eds), *The Blackwell Guide to the Philosophy of Law and Legal Theory* (Oxford, Blackwell, 2005) 315–23. See also my discussion of objectivity with respect to legal knowledge in my 'Normative Knowledge and the Nature of Law', above n 1.

[14] I should guard against a possible misunderstanding that was drawn to my attention by Carsten Heidemann: talk of propositions usually evokes the suspicion of Platonism (ie the view that there is a realm comprising entities that are simultaneously non-physical and mind-independent). However, for the suspicion of Platonism to be substantiated, propositions need to be combined with a strong objectivist theory like the one I ascribe to Dworkin in this chapter. Conversely, if propositions are made entirely dependent upon linguistic usage, as I believe they are in the case of discourse theory, they are disarmed of their 'explosive' metaphysical load and may serve as useful means for addressing the complex nature of objectivity as suggested above.

the subjective features of speakers' utterances (such features include the particular language an utterance is made in). Given the function they fulfil, propositions are equipped with a hybrid nature that places them at the interface of language, mind and world. Leaving out a lot of detail, one of the most controversial issues regarding propositions concerns their individuation—or their existence. Contested as it may be, the issue of individuation is crucial as regards the degree and the foundations of objectivity solicited by a philosophical theory. As regards this matter, philosophical theories are traditionally classified in two large groups: on the one hand we have those theories that are realist in nature[15]: here criteria of individuation are fully located outside our practices of communication. The attractiveness of such a strong degree of objectivity notwithstanding, realist philosophies are vulnerable to sceptical arguments that call into question our ability to acquire the degree of certainty that realism requires. On the other hand, there are theories, call them in contradistinction non-realist, which suggest that propositions with respect to any domain be individuated intra-linguistically, that is, within the structures of sentences and the communicative practices of a linguistic community. Although such theories lack[16] the objectivist force of the realist ones, they may well turn out to be far more resistant to sceptical attacks, for they depart from claims that are less easy to undermine.

With these remarks in place we may distinguish between two possible understandings of the way interpretive theory casts criteria or grounds of individuation for legal propositions.[17] As for the first way, the weaker of

[15] I am referring here to the philosophical move of realism and not to what is usually characterised as 'realism' in legal theory. Notably, as regards their positions, the two movements should be deemed incompatible, for while philosophical realism builds on a strong notion of truth and objectivity, one that is independent from our contingent practices, realism in the legal context argues for the dependence of the truth of legal statements on the features of the societal formations within which those are advanced.

[16] To avoid any misunderstanding: non-realist philosophies are no less interested in the mind-independence and objectivity of the criteria of propositional individuation. The main difference between them and realist theories is that, while the latter solicit an objectivity that is independent of our conceptual scheme (ie, an objectivity that might remain forever elusive), the former argue for an objectivity that applies to our conceptual scheme, or the set of conditions for knowledge that is transparent to us. Many thanks to Sean Coyle who pointed out to me the possible misunderstanding here.

[17] Two seemingly appealing answers to the problem of individuation need to be summarily rebutted here: it will not help to tackle individuation through either interpretive facts or claims of fit and justification. Instead of determining the issue of individuation, these items themselves depend on a prior settlement of the issue. The answer to what is an interpretive fact may arise in a number of ways, depending on how we identify the grounds of legal propositions. The same applies to fit and justification. Which interpretation strikes the right balance between fit with past instances, on the one hand, and justification within the scheme of principle of a practice, on the other, presupposes that we have an answer with respect to the issue of individuation. It follows that an explanation of the issue of individuation of interpretive propositions which rests on either interpretive facts or claims fit and justification will be circular.

the two, criteria of individuation are determined internally to the practice of a legal community; conversely, the second, the stronger way, argues that interpretive theory has to refer to some special substance which pertains to legal phenomena and can be characterised independently of communal practice. Both understandings will be shown to be untenable on closer scrutiny. The weaker one may be rejected along the lines of the criticisms Dworkin has advanced against analytical positivism and, in any case, it is unavailable to him for that precise reason. For the stronger one to be rendered plausible, one must assume that legal concepts are *rigid designators* which depict some (mysterious) legal essences in the environment. Although at times Dworkin and some of his followers allude to the latter view, there are good philosophical reasons to render it unworkable. When taken conjointly, the two understandings give rise to a dilemma; it appears insurmountable, for it either leads to a total loss of objectivity if the weak understanding is adhered to; or it makes objectivity unattainable if the strong one is followed. However, the dilemma is far from compulsory. It arises only if a particular conception of legal (and broader communal) practice is adopted. Dworkin assumes that this conception, which I am going to refer to as shallow, counts among the burdens borne by the philosophy of analytical positivism. Nonetheless, I argue that it extends equally to the strong understanding of objectivity that Dworkin advances, the one that postulates grounds of individuation that are external to the practice of a community.

Weak Objectivity and Analytical Positivism

A weak understanding of objectivity suggests that the grounds of individuation of legal propositions be specified internally to the practice of a legal community. This means, roughly, that for an interpretive judgement to meet the requirements of fit and justification, it has to undertake a reconstruction of the evaluative point of a practice through reference to existing past and present instances of that practice and not to some item that is characterisable independently of the practice. Reconstruction of those instances amounts to stating criteria derivable from the behaviour of the participants of the practice, which are deemed relevant to the individuation of legal propositions. Under Dworkin's influential reading, Hart's analytical jurisprudence has come to be regarded as a paradigm case of this type of analysis.

Dworkin's reading of Hartian positivism adds a semantic flavour to it, which purports to capture the post-linguistic-turn spirit of Hart's method of analysis. Thus, instead of being concerned about just any practice-dependent criteria of individuation, Hart is alleged to be interested in semantic criteria (hence the characterisation of his theory as semantic[18]). In this case, what individuates propositions of law are criteria for the use of legal expressions which are made explicit through a systematic analysis of the linguistic behaviour of the community in question.[19] Through observation of a particular practice the legal theorist can infer 'implicit' rules that determine the use of legal language and specify a number of criteria which may be grouped together into a master definition of the concept 'law' (what Hart calls the 'rule of recognition' of a system). Subsequently, this definition functions as a litmus test for the existence of a proposition of law and the meaningfulness of the sentence in which it is expressed. In addition, any violation of the putative criteria by any of the members of the community is to be treated as an instance of misunderstanding rather than an act of meaningful disagreement. Anyone who fails to act upon them will be assumed to have failed correctly to apprehend the criteria and would have to have their content explained anew. On the face of it, by specifying the extension of the concept 'law', semantic analysis undertakes the seminal task of illustrating the kind of phenomenon law is, and demarcating it from other related normative phenomena (ethics, morality and so on).

Dworkin has criticised these views by putting forward the argument from the 'semantic sting', which attacks a conception of legal meaning based on semantic criteria specified by a rule of recognition. The gist of his criticism is that if one assumed a semantic theory of legal meaning, then any form of disagreement surrounding legal meaning would have to be deemed meaningless. This, however, would fly in the face of the actual fact of disagreement between lawyers. Dworkin convincingly shows that legal discourse very often consists of instances of passionate disagreement about the real nature of law or the true meaning of a legal precept, disagreement that stems from concrete cases and becomes pervasive in many instances of adjudication. Accordingly, disagreement ought to be shown to be more meaningful than any sheer logomachy over semantic criteria and definitions could suggest. This would happen, however, only if we assumed an object of disagreement that extended beyond the practice of disagreement itself (which is linguistically confined). Along these lines, Dworkin postulates the possibility of a strong notion of objectivity with respect to legal claims, one requiring that the essence or nature of law lie outside language, which might or might not succeed in capturing it. To see the significance of

[18] See Dworkin, above n 10 at chs 1 and 2. Dworkin's claim has been further explored in Stavropoulos' highly incisive 'Hart's Semantics' in J Coleman, *Hart's Postscript: Essays on the Postscript of the Concept of Law* (Oxford, Oxford University Press, 2001) 59–98.

[19] Stavropoulos, above n 18 at 69–79.

his ideas we need to revert, for a moment, to the vocabulary of propositions: following Dworkin's conception, propositions of law are individuated with respect to the real substance of legal entities, that is, prior to the way we use language within the boundaries of a practice. The full-blown version of this idea can be found in Dworkin's notorious claim that it is possible for a community to go wrong with respect to the true meaning of legal sentences. Why so? It is so because for Dworkin, it is always possible to have a proposition individuated by the essential properties of a case, which, as a result, escapes the semantic rules of the community: thus, there may be a true legal proposition lp despite the fact that the community has no place for it in its conceptual (or semantic) scheme. Meaning does not depend on what semantic rules tell us but on how things really are, legally speaking. Thus, proposition lp may be a proposition of law irrespective or even *in spite of* the criteria specified in a Hartian rule of recognition.[20] The moral Dworkin draws is that Hart should have done things in the reverse order: he should first have looked into the real essence of law and then specified rules that fix the meaning of legal sentences. Only then would it have been the case that the reality of law determines language and not vice versa.

A reading of Dworkin's rejection of semantic accounts in the light of his belief in practice-transcendent values helps one to anticipate the next move towards an account of those values. In rejecting semantic accounts, Dworkin blocks the path to all explanations that depart from the possibility of explaining values within a social practice as a cognitive process that is semantically articulated. No sooner has this block been set in place, however, than the precarious path to metaphysical extravagance begins to appear more appealing.

Strong Objectivity and Essentialism

Dworkin's criticisms target a conception of objectivity that exhausts itself in criteria immanent to legal practice. Conversely, the semantic sting shows that the source of objectivity regarding legal judgements must extend beyond the practice of a legal community; otherwise, no coherent account of the fact that lawyers engage in meaningful disagreement could be

[20] This seems to me to be a distortion of the semantic view, for semantic explications of propositions need not exhaust truth and falsity: they merely sketch the possible ontological combinations of the building blocks of the world. A semantic explication of ontology does not say when a proposition is true or false; it merely says which propositions are candidates for truth and falsity. Thus, even on a semantic explication, we can have a validly formulated sentence that still fails to correspond to anything in the world (say a sentence about Unicorns). Cf with the discussion of Hart's semantic analysis in G Pavlakos, 'Law as Recognition: HLA Hart and Analytical Positivism' in T Murphy (ed), *Western Jurisprudence* (Dublin, Round Hall, 2004).

offered. Even though Dworkin rejects semantic criteria, the idea of meaningful disagreement still requires that some amount of agreement prevail between disagreeing parties.[21] Such agreement, however, cannot rest on semantic criteria but, instead, needs to comply with the demands of strong objectivity as suggested by the argument from the semantic sting. Hence, it must hook up directly to the essence of law as opposed to any intermediary criteria linguistic in nature. What strong objectivity requires, in other words, is agreement in essence.[22]

Agreement in essence presupposes that it be possible to settle semantic issues, including those of agreement and disagreement, by linking up legal language with law's essential characteristics, those that are assumed to be non-linguistic and are, hence, independent of the practice of communication. This possibility becomes available only if the objective bearers of legal meaning, that is propositions of law, are individuated through direct reference to law's extra-linguistic nature. A theoretical model that allows for individuation along these lines can be traced back to recent work in the philosophy of mind and language.[23] In the late 1970s and early 1980s, a group of philosophers, in particular Hilary Putnam and Saul Kripke, forcefully argued that the meanings of our words are found 'not in our heads' but in the environment. Their argument was chiefly directed against internalist theories of meaning, then dominant in the philosophical landscape. Those theories took concepts to refer to whatever was stipulated by appropriate definitions that contained necessary and sufficient conditions and could be arrived at independently of the environment. It is not difficult to see some form of radical scepticism associated with such an idea: should meaning be rooted in speakers' heads, one would end up believing in the existence of a well-defined conceptual universe that has no bearing whatever on the actual environment.[24] Putnam and Kripke set out to

[21] See Dworkin's discussion of agreement as regards the so-called pre-interpretive stage in Dworkin, above n 10 at 46–9 and 65–8; also the discussion in K Kress, 'The Interpretive Turn' (1987) 97 *Ethics* 834 at 854–6.

[22] Kress (*ibid*) has suggested this option as a version of semantic theory that escapes Dworkin's attack on criterial theories and resolves, too, some of the problems that relate to Dworkin's explanation of a necessary degree of agreement through reference to the pre-interpretive stage. I shall assume, henceforth, that this kind of essentialist semantics, which Kress suggested in 1987 as a middle solution, was taken up later by Stavropoulos and made an integral part of Dworkinian interpretivism (Stavropoulos, *Objectivity*, above n 13). A question lingers as to whether this kind of essentialist semantics really differs from the (merely verbally) more robust version of moral essentialism endorsed by Michael Moore (cf his *Educating Oneself in Public* (Oxford, Oxford University Press, 2000)). To the extent that it does not, my criticism applies also to the latter.

[23] One may even speak here of a semantic theory, albeit one of a very different kind than those we have been discussing so far. This shows that Dworkin's real target is not semantic theories *tout court*, but only a particular kind thereof: those resting on criteria that are internal to a linguistic practice.

[24] This should be the case if the meaning of, say, 'water' should be determined by a linguistic convention as opposed to the actual stuff it refers to (H_2O). This is not an

undermine this particular understanding of meaning by demonstrating that the meaning of natural-kind concepts and name concepts is causally determined by the actual properties of the entities referred to, rather than any properties of our mental states.[25] On the face of it, the importance allocated to the *intension* (conventions of use or definitions) and the *extension* (actual referents) of (natural-kind) concepts is hereby reversed: conventions and definitions are rendered subordinate to actual referents. Moreover, conventions and definitions may retain their value as guidelines for speakers only to the extent that they remain open to revision in the light of new (empirical) discoveries vis-à-vis the environment. Thus, our language and the ways we employ it cease to be constitutive in our understanding of the environment, instead, the latter becomes the measure for a successful employment of language that leads to communication. This new explication of meaning makes it possible for a speaker correctly to employ a concept (say, 'water') without having a complete understanding of the conventions or the definitions that determine its use within a linguistic community, for stability in communication relies on the properties of the actual referent (the fact that it is H_2O) rather than any facts about the linguistic practice.

This notion of a standard of meaning that lies outside our practices opens up a gap between the practice and its referent, a gap that makes room for the possibility of error and, hence, for the idea of objectivity. Objectivity is intertwined with the possibility that we might be wrong in our understanding of the world precisely because the world may actually be different from what we take it to be. To put it in a different way, the world itself rather than our linguistic practices is what determines how the world is.

extravagant thought: just think of speakers in Classic Athens using 'water' without knowing much about its actual chemical composition. In their case it would be very easy to confuse water with some other stuff that superficially resembles it.

[25] Roughly speaking, Putnam's argument runs as follows: suppose there are two parallel universes: Earth and Twin-Earth. Two-thirds of Earth's surface is covered by some colourless and odourless liquid stuff whose chemical composition is H_2O. Equally, Twin Earth is covered for two-thirds of its surface by some superficially identical stuff, whose chemical composition is XYZ. Now the inhabitants of Earth use 'water' to depict H_2O whereas the inhabitants of Twin-Earth use 'water' to depict XYZ. Suppose also that both groups of speakers refer to the same definition or conventional rule when they use 'water' (ie, there is an identity of *intension*). Be that as it may, 'water' as employed by Earthians has a different reference (or *extension*) than 'water' as employed by Twin-Earthians. It follows that the difference in extension must give rise to some difference in meaning. Hence 'water' has a different meaning in each case, one that is determined by the actual stuff the concept depicts. See H Putnam, 'The Meaning of "Meaning"' in *idem, Mind, Language and Reality* (Cambridge, Cambridge University Press 1975) 215–71 and his more concise 'Meaning and Reference' reprinted in AW Moore (ed), *Meaning and Reference* (Oxford, Oxford University Press, 1993) 150–61.

It is not difficult to see why moral and legal philosophers were mesmerised by those ideas.[26] Considering that problems of scepticism and relativism are far more intense in the domain of evaluative (moral, legal or ethical) language, these philosophers were very happy to be given a new theory that set meaning free from conventions and definitions, with the latter two serving to substantiate efforts to make a case on behalf of relativism. By contrast, the new theory would allow an explication of normative meaning as depending on the actual properties of normative (moral, ethical or legal) kinds, properties that exist independently of a community's linguistic practices and the conventions they give rise to.

Tempting as the analogy with natural and name kinds may well strike one, it is in fact unworkable, the main reason being the different nature of the kinds depicted in each case. Normative kinds (rights, contracts, norms and so on) lack the essential underlying microstructural property[27] of natural kinds that made it possible for Putnam and Kripke to develop their theory of meaning.[28] The microstructural property of natural kinds (which can be discovered by science) is responsible for causally determining meaning from the outside, that is, independently of any convention or definition and irrespective of our knowledge of the microstructural property itself. This is, however, not the case with normative kinds. Unless one postulates something like an *underlying microstructural property* for normative kinds, the option of casual determination of normative meaning from the outside is not available. In other words, there is nothing in the environment that is essentially normative and is capable of causally determining the reference of our normative expressions irrespective of our knowledge of it. Be that as it may, Dworkin's theory (and other similar theories from the field of moral philosophy) seems to rely on such a microstructure and to look for entities of the appropriate kind. To that extent, and despite declarations to the contrary, what Dworkin sets out to discover are sui generis evaluative particles[29] that (causally?) determine the

[26] The way to such work in the area of normative philosophy was paved by the writings of Tyler Burge, who developed a sophisticated externalist theory of meaning for concepts that denote 'social' and 'artefact' kinds (eg 'arthritis' and 'sofa' respectively). See T Burge, 'Intellectual Norms and the Foundations of Mind' (1986) 83 *Journal of Philosophy* 697. And for an explicit reliance on Burge's work, see Stavropoulos, *Objectivity*, above n 13 esp at chs 2 and 6.

[27] The term connotes the fact that such kinds exist qua the elementary particles of matter (atoms and electrons).

[28] Similar criticism has been developed with respect to Tyler Burge's externalist theory of meaning for artefact kind concepts. See the recent discussions of J Brown, 'Critical Reasoning, Understanding and Self-Knowledge' (2000) LXI *Philosophy and Phenomenological Research* 659; Å M Wikforss, 'Externalism and Incomplete Understanding' (2004) 54 *The Philosophical Quarterly* 287.

[29] In the twentieth century, the first to postulate such entities was the Cambridge philosopher GE Moore, who argued that evaluative concepts are unanalysable because they refer to basic moral universals that can be perceived through intuition. Intuitionism, as

meaning of legal expressions.[30] How these properties are individuated and by which means we access them cognitively, must remain a mystery.[31]

What is more, the essentialist underpinning of objectivity entails a picture of legal meaning that fails on an additional ground. This takes on board the issue of normativity of meaning and is discussed by Wittgenstein in his *Philosophical Investigations* under the rubric of rule-following.[32] Leaving aside the plethora of interpretations that have been offered in regard to Wittgenstein's views, his remarks bear a high degree of relevance to the present discussion of objectivity, for Wittgenstein discusses rule-following with respect to standards that may create a match between mind, language and world. On his view, anything that purports to determine meaning in a conclusive way, by forming something like an ultra-criterion, is doomed to fail, for it will itself be in need of further criteria of application and so on until a hopeless regress of interpretations arises.[33] The deeper reason for this is that ultra-criteria tend to highlight one particular aspect or moment of a broader practice, cutting it off from the rest of the practice and freezing it into some kind of guideline that purports to determine conclusively the propositions we form as a result of our participation in that practice. This amounts to a rather *static* picture that cannot explain how and why a practice can be normative, in the sense of being capable of showing past and future instances thereof to fall within the same scheme of conduct. Conversely, the normative element behind any practice that is responsible for its continuity requires a dynamic reading of the criteria, one that prevents them from becoming privileged points of reference and shows them, instead, to be continuously amenable to the pattern of conduct that the practice realises (more will be said on the dynamic conception of criteria below). It would not be an exaggeration to say that through the prism of Wittgenstein's thoughts, both essentialist and semantic criteria, along the lines Dworkin takes Hart to employ, present us equally with a static conception, one that falls short of supporting a viable

Moore's theory came to be known, has been attacked in many occasions for its metaphysical extravagance, the most distinctive attack being the one by John Mackie who famously accused Moore's metaphysics of queerness. See J Mackie, *Ethics: Inventing Right and Wrong* (Hamondsworth, Penguin Press, 1977).

30 Many philosophers evoke the notion of supervenience in an attempt to avoid both the reduction of evaluative properties to physical properties, and the idea of some robust evaluative realm that is non-physical and whose perception would require that agents be equipped with some kind of sixth sense.

31 See Mackie's accusation of queerness in Mackie, above n 29.

32 See L Wittgenstein, *Philosophical Investigations*, 3rd edn (Oxford, Blackwell, 2001) paras 134–242.

33 *Ibid*. See also the discussion in S Kripke, *Wittgenstein: On Rules and Private Language* (Oxford, Blackwell, 1982) 7–54.

notion of objectivity. In fact, it is the static character rather than any semantic or practice-dependent quality of criteria that actually bears on the issue of objectivity.

If we confine our options within the weak and strong understandings of objectivity, we are then left with a devastating dilemma: either objectivity evaporates, if the interpretive theory is confined to the boundaries of communal practice. Or, if we expand the interpretive theory to include some kind of practice-independent essences, objectivity becomes so demanding that it is rendered unattainable. It seems, however, that both horns of the dilemma can be traced back to the same notion of criteria of the individuation of the propositions, the notion that was identified as static and was shown to succumb to Wittgenstein's critical remarks on meaning. The static conception of criteria is linked up with a particular picture of practice, one that will be referred to as *shallow*. Influential as the shallow conception of practice may be, it is far from compulsory. Instead, there is an alternative conception of practice, one that corresponds to the idea of dynamic criteria we introduced earlier, which for reasons of convenience will be labelled the *deep* conception of practice. Once the latter is adopted, the dilemma is avoided. No sooner is the deep conception taken on board than a new understanding of objectivity surfaces, one that is able to relate criteria of individuation with propositions and meaning in a fresh manner, a manner that prevents the handicaps associated with the shallow conception of practice from arising.

Shallow and Deep Practice

Practices can be conceived of as comprising a level of brute facts that mark the interaction between the participants of a practice as well as a level of normative patterns that regulate interaction in a manner that presents the various instances of the practice as a unified whole. Thus, for a fact to belong to a practice it must form part of a pattern of continuity that has normative force over the participants of the practice. Following the linguistic turn in philosophy, an influential way of capturing this requirement is to assume that any practice consists of external behaviour that complies with patterns of action that can be expressed as normative sentences—in this way neither of the two, language or fact, comes first. To this extent, the vocabulary of propositions that has been utilised all along in this chapter dovetails with the continuity between facts and norms, for propositions are items that allow for an integration of language (norms) with the world (facts). Although it is analytically possible to distinguish between these two aspects of practice, permitting too large a gap to open between them poses the threat of losing sight of the practice (as is the case when propositions are individuated through reference to only one of the aspects). Thus, depending on which of the two, language or fact, a theory places the emphasis on, we may distinguish between two conceptions of practice: a shallow and a deep one.

The shallow conception corresponds roughly to the ideas Dworkin reads into Hart's analysis of rules. In Dworkin's reading of Hart, a practice can be described in terms of the brute facts that mark the interaction of the participants. In fact, it is assumed that an analysis of rules, the normative constituents of the practice, can be given through a dispassionate description of the participants' behaviour in terms of neutral brute facts.[34] This (explanatory) prioritisation of behavioural facts interrupts the continuity of facts and norms that serves to guarantee normativity in a practice. The ensuing loss of normativity precludes the participants from grasping the practice as possessing normative depth or, in other words, the explanatory resources for representing past and future cases as partaking of the same rationale. Notably, in the case of a normative practice such as law, such loss of depth becomes intolerable, for it prevents participants from referring to genuine reasons that justify their actions by way of linking them up to a common scheme of normative purposes the practice serves. The loss of depth is not hard to understand: surface facts referring to the behaviour of legal participants are especially unsuitable for individuating propositions of law, for they present a typical instance of ultra-criteria, which fail to underpin the normative character of the relation between facts and norms within a practice (and not, as Dworkin would say, because they are practice-immanent or semantic). Ultra-interpretations, as Wittgenstein has taught us, are inept for determining meaning, for they are themselves in further need of interpretation in the sense explained earlier.

But postulating, along with Dworkin, other facts that lie outside the practice and are essentially normative, is not going to take us very far, either. In truth, such facts fall all the more into the domain of ultra-criteria castigated by Wittgenstein.[35] They constitute ultra-determinants, which purport to generate criteria of individuation for legal propositions, criteria that are supposed to be external to the practice of a legal community but, at the same time, are capable of capturing what is normative about the practice: namely the scheme of conduct that embeds into the practice what would otherwise appear as random events. As a result, Dworkin's strong notion of objectivity presupposes the shallow conception of practice every

[34] It is really a mystery why Dworkin, and more recently Stavropoulos in 'Hart's Semantics', above n 18, labels this method of analysis 'semantic'. Given that semantic analysis can be expanded to include far more (cf Pavlakos, above n 20), one can only assume that what these two authors really purport to attack is the criterial character of Hartian analysis. Kress agrees on this (above n 21).

[35] On an influential reading, they form just the second horn of a dilemma whose first horn comprises normatively inert brute facts that are in need of further interpretation. See J McDowell, 'Wittgenstein On Following a Rule' (1984) 58 *Synthese* 325.

bit as much as do those theories he targets.[36] It is, then, more accurate to say that what determines shallowness in this context is the character of criteria as ultra-determinants, rather than their positioning (internal-external) with respect to a practice. Ultra-determinants fail because they disrupt continuity between the scheme of conduct and the various instances of a practice, for they invest single facts with absolute power of determination (be they facts about the semantic behaviour of the participants of the practice or about law's 'real' essence).

Conversely, a deep explication of communal practice purports to bring out the continuity between facts and norms that represents the instances of any practice as being integrated into a coherent scheme of conduct. In exploring conditions of depth, I shall turn to Robert Alexy's discourse theory of law and argue that this theory manages successfully to substantiate the specified conditions for depth. To that extent, the discourse theory of law offers the optimum basis for objectivity. In fleshing out this claim, two conditions of depth will be considered: the first is the dynamic character of the criteria of individuation. In contrast to the shallow conception of practice and the static criteria it gives rise to, a dynamic conception of criteria requires that individuation of legal propositions be conceived of as an instance of rule-following. Here, criteria cease to be in the forefront, retreating to the background, for what determines individuation are rules or patterns that are not exhausted by any single instance of application but represent, instead, what is common between and among all instances. This ideal of individuation as rule-following will be linked up with a system of discourse rules—rules for the regulation of propositional content, which range over multiple levels of individuation: semantics, syntax, rationality and pragmatics. Owing to its forming a structure that imposes normative constraints on propositional content, the system of discourse rules will be referred to as *discursive grammar*. Finally, the first condition of depth purports to construct a more modest conception of objectivity that prevents it from breaking down along the lines of the two horns of the dilemma arising from the shallow conception of practice.

The second condition of depth purports to explain how it is possible for the deep conception of practice and the idea of rule-following that pertains to it to guarantee objectivity. Whereas the previous condition of depth is

[36] Dworkin in his early work defended a constructivist idea of objectivity, which in many ways was closer to analytical positivism than he would have wanted it to be. In this early phase criteria of individuation are spelled out in a constructive model of evaluative knowledge, one that rests on a method of reflective equilibrium rather than on any epistemic access to practice-transcendent normative universals, see R Dworkin, *Taking Rights Seriously* (London, Duckworth, 1977) 160l8; later, however, driven by the myopic view that shallowness derives from practice-immanence, he moved away from practice-dependent criteria to the essentialist idea of objectivity that one finds in *Law's Empire* and subsequent writings. Cf Kress, above n 21 at 854.

negative, in the sense that it tells us what is required in order *not* to arrive at the dilemma that stems form the shallow conception, the second condition purports positively to account for the potential of the idea of rule-following to deliver objectivity. The possible blocks that need to be set aside are two in number: first, how is it possible to extract any type of criterion from something that never ceases to flow (a rule or a pattern)? In other words, if the rule is never to be rendered frozen on pain of degeneration of objectivity, how is it possible to single out anything that can be used as a standard of correctness for our judgements and action? This ties up with the second issue. As the reader may recall, a central intuition about objectivity was that normative propositions are responsive to something that is external to our linguistic practices, for it is important that we are able to distinguish between right and wrong applications of the practice. Closely connected, any type of rule-following that is not reducible to anything external to it faces the following challenge: it almost always fails to determine the practice, for it can be seen as self-referential and self-reproducing. It will be argued that discursive grammar enables one to specify criteria and reasons that retain a certain distance from the practice, while remaining practice-dependent. Here, we shall see that it is possible actually to single out criteria that remain dynamic on the ground that they are part of a multilevelled discursive grammar. The multiple levels of discursive grammar represent graphically the condition of depth, which is indispensable to the possibility of objectivity.

Before turning to examine discursive grammar in more detail, a short comment is in order. One may claim that Dworkin's theory aims precisely at furnishing a deep conception of practice, in the sense explained above. This is not the case, for in order to endorse the line of reasoning exposed earlier, Dworkin would have to accept a mild form of Archimedeanism, or the view that there is a hierarchy between the linguistic practices (or language-games) we engage in. Hierarchy pertains to the dimension of depth, for the latter requires that there be a higher-order language-game (or practice) within which it is possible to refer to all other language-games (including the legal one). For discourse theory, this is the overarching language-game of communication[37]; in contrast, Dworkin, throughout his writings, has vehemently criticised references to any form of hierarchy between the various practices we engage in.[38]

[37] Cf n 40 below.

[38] For a recent restatement of his aversion to all forms of Archimedeanism, see R Dworkin, 'Hart's Postscript and the Character of Political Philosophy' (2004) 24 *Oxford Journal of Legal Studies* 1. The comment in this paragraph counts as a reaction to some highly incisive comments by Sean Coyle.

DISCURSIVE GRAMMAR AND OBJECTIVITY

In an early work from the 1970s, Alexy elaborated a system of rules that constitute a structure imposing normative constraints on the content of any normative proposition (discursive grammar).[39] Along with Apel and Habermas,[40] Alexy argues that every instance of evaluative or prescriptive speech aiming at communication must possess an argumentative or discursive structure. The necessity of the communicative aspect is demonstrated against the background of a transcendental argument whose task is to make explicit the rules which make up the discursive structure. These rules spell out a series of standards that regulate the happy employment of prescriptive utterances and ultimately bring about the elevation of prescriptive speech to discourse. Failing to live up to these requirements, a normative utterance will either fall short of qualifying as a norm or will be deemed faulty. Simplifying Alexy's own classification somewhat, one may distinguish among three kinds of rules of discursive grammar: rules of logic; rules of rationality; finally, pragmatic rules for the utterance of normative sentences. Whereas rules of the first and second categories address largely the level of semantics, those of the third category refer to the pragmatic relation between subjects who engage in normative communication. In addition, all three categories of rules are common to law and morality, for, as the transcendental argument purports to show, discursive grammar pertains to any prescriptive utterance.

Before turning to a look at how discursive grammar satisfies the requirements of depth, a brief comment on the notion of grammar is called for. The idea of grammar has been employed many a time in the twentieth century in order to offer an objective account of knowledge and meaning.[41] Roughly speaking, grammar-based accounts of propositional content identify some 'objective' logico-syntactical structure of sentences on the

39 I am referring in particular to transcendental-pragmatic reasoning and the long list of discourse rules that Robert Alexy identified as early as his PhD thesis, *Theorie der juristischen Argumentation* (Frankfurt am Main, Suhrkamp, 1978) and in English translation *A Theory of Legal Argumentation: The Theory of Rational Discourse as Theory of Legal Argumentation* (R Adler and N MacCormick (trans), Oxford, Clarendon Press, 1989); see also G Pavlakos, 'The Special Case Thesis. An Assessment of R Alexy's Discursive Theory of Law' (1998) 12 *Ratio Juris* 126; and C Roversi, 'Constitutionalism and Transcendental Arguments' forthcoming in (2008) 59 *Northern Ireland Legal Quarterly*.

40 See K-O Apel, *From a Transcendental-Semiotic Point of View* (Manchester, Manchester University Press, 1998); J Habermas, 'Discourse Ethics: Notes on a Program of Philosophical Justification' in *idem*, *Moral Consciousness and Communicative Action* (C Lenhardt and S Weber Nicholsen (trans), Cambridge Mass, MIT Press, 1992) 79.

41 Among the philosophers who employed it are the logical positivists and Wittgenstein in his early work. For an account of grammar in the context of legal and more general philosophical positivism see G Pavlakos, 'Positivism and the Construction of Law', paper given at IVR World Congress, Granada, Spain, 27 May 2005; a version of this paper survives as a part of chapter 2 in G Pavlakos, *Our Knowledge of the Law* (Oxford and Portland, Hart Publishing, 2007).

basis of which it is possible to reconstruct the world within language. The advantage of grammar is that it allows for the possibility of individuating concepts and propositions in a language-immanent way, albeit without succumbing to either psychologism or scepticism. Closely connected, the idea of grammar is receptive to an account of normative content without succumbing to the two horns of the dilemma arising from the shallow conception of practice. Still, having said that, it may be that the notion of grammar is not sufficient on its own to substantiate a deep conception of practice or the notion of dynamic criteria that derives from it. Many a time in the past, philosophers of grammar have taken rules of grammar to be dependent on some privileged segment of the environment that functions as an ultra-determinant.[42] Despite good intentions, such conceptions undermine what is most appealing in the project of a philosophical grammar, for they allow a gap to open between the rules of grammar and the criteria for their application, a gap that invites scepticism and indeterminacy along the lines explained earlier.

Conversely, discursive grammar steers clear of the defects associated with earlier conceptions of grammar, for it is capable of delivering objectivity without succumbing to either of the horns of the dilemma that the shallow conception of practice gives rise to. To buttress this claim, it will be shown that discursive grammar meets the two conditions of depth specified earlier: rule-following and possibility of objectification.

Discursive Grammar and Rule-following

The first condition of depth regarding a practice is rule-following. Far from conceiving criteria of individuation as isolated determinants, the possibility of objectivity requires that they be embedded into a single perspective, one that is kept open through the activity of rule-following. Before moving on to illustrate the links between rule-following and discursive individuation, it will be helpful to make a brief comment on the ability of rule-following to escape the problems pertaining to ultra-determinants and the shallow conception of practice fostering them.

According to an influential interpretation of the idea of rule-following,[43] the relation between the rule and its various instances ought to be

[42] For instance, Wittgenstein's picture theory of meaning in his early work, or Carnap's idea that all rules of grammar must be reducible to some simple propositions which make direct contact with elementary sensorial input from the environment (the notorious *Protokollsätze*).

[43] See eg GP Baker and PMS Hacker, *Wittgenstein: Rules, Grammar and Necessity; vol 2 of an Analytical Commentary on the Philosophical Investigations* (Oxford, Blackwell, 1988); McDowell, above n 35; and SL Hurley, *Consciousness in Action* (Cambridge Mass, Harvard University Press, 1998).

conceived of as *internal*, that is, as free from the need of any additional items that could play the role of the intermediary between the rule and its applications. Internality means that the rule and its applications make contact in grammar, as the two sides of the same coin, rather than standing in some hierarchical relation to one another. Were the latter the case then there would be a need for some intermediary to bridge the gap between the rule and its applications. It is precisely such intermediaries that purport to function as ultra-determinants (or static criteria) and trigger the sceptical regress of interpretations.[44]

Thus conceived, internality entails *implicitness*, namely the requirement that rules of grammar be followed without being 'discussed' or 'quoted' in each and every stance of their application.[45] Conversely, if rules were explicit, that is, if there were a moment when we could picture them before us, display them on a pedestal, then instances of rule-following would become external to the rule. Such a result would bring about the disengagement of the criteria of application from the rule, and the regress of interpretations that is pertinent to the static conception of criteria (or the shallow conception of practice) would arise anew.

The system of discourse rules takes seriously the idea of rule-following as a continuous activity that cannot be 'frozen' into any of its individual moments. In particular, two elements of discursive grammar need to be emphasised and expanded. First their implicitness: given the link between rule-following and implicitness, discourse rules must be deemed implicit. Conceiving of discourse rules as implicit serves to redeem the internality between the rule and the instances of its application, internality that is essential to a dynamic conception of the criteria of individuation of normative propositions. Nonetheless, the condition of internality appears to be at odds with another characteristic of discourse rules that Alexy deems seminal: their ability to function as justificatory reasons. The latter asks that rules be made explicit as reasons that speakers can refer to in order to justify their normative propositions. Even so, implicitness need not be in breach of this requirement; a rule that functions as a justificatory reason is not required to be explicit at all times, as it were diachronically, but only when necessary. What is more, to allow for some rule to function as an explicit justification, even for a short moment, one needs to follow some other rule, say, a semantic rule of objectification, which makes it possible to refer to the first rule albeit by remaining implicit.[46]

[44] See above n 33.

[45] Cf P Pettit, 'The Reality of Rule-Following' (1989) 99 *Mind* 1, where he argues for a dispositional account of rule-following by contrast with Kripke's influential reading of Wittgenstein (above n 33). I believe, however, that the properties Pettit says a rule ought to possess can be satisfied by the two conditions of depth without resorting to a dispositional account of rule-following.

[46] Cf with the discussion in the next section.

All in all, when regarded in its entirety, discursive grammar still satisfies the condition of implicitness, even though some of its rules are made explicit on certain occasions. Nonetheless, discourse theory needs to accommodate more explicitly this possibility and, on occasion, replace its rigid vocabulary, one that gives rise to the suspicion of treating discourse rules as static structures, with a more flexible one falling into place with the idea of rule-following. This theme will be further explored below, alongside the discussion of the second condition of depth, that is, the ability to 'objectify' criteria of individuation for normative propositions.

Discursive Grammar and Objectification

The condition of rule-following having been established, it is time to address the other prerequisite of depth: the possibility of objectification. Conceiving of criteria of individuation as generated by a rule or a pattern steers clear of the problems that the static conception of criteria gives rise to: criteria cease to be privileged points of reference—be they brute facts (Hart) or essentially normative entities (Dworkin)—of a kind that, sooner or later, are bound to perish in an incessant line of interpretations. Be that as it may, it should still be possible to refer to such criteria or the rules that generate them in a manner that makes them available for grounding or justifying our normative propositions. This need is even more pressing with respect to rules of discursive grammar, as their function is justificatory *par excellence*. Such rules (authors of discourse theory never fail to remind us) are to be used as standards of justification and correctness by those who aim at communication through normative speech. However, for any rule or pattern to function as a standard, the dynamic aspect of rule-following needs to be suspended, at least for a short while, and the rule be made explicit (or objectified).

Furthermore, objectification is desirable on another count: this is the minimal requirement entailed by any conception of objectivity, namely, that there be room for error between what we say or believe and what is actually the case. In other words, objectivity requires that criteria of individuation of propositional content do not collapse into what we actually happen to say or think; rather they retain a certain critical distance from our current practices.[47] Desirable as objectification may be, there is a serious handicap connected with it, one that calls for urgent action: it seems that any attempt to render implicit rules explicit would give rise anew to the regress of interpretations that Wittgenstein associates with

[47] From this it does not follow that criteria have to be language or practice-independent. It is precisely the thesis of discourse theory that it is possible to reconstruct a practice, even one that is in error, in such a way that we arrive at objective criteria.

ultra-determinants of the kind generated by the shallow conception of practice. A way out of this conundrum is to evoke the multilayered character of discursive grammar. Owing to it, it will be argued, it is possible to retain both the dynamic character of criteria and the condition of objectification. In addition, the illustration of the multiple levels will represent graphically the deep structure of practices.

What are the benefits of a multilayered grammar? And what is it that makes it capable of coping with both rule-following and objectification? In clarifying these points we need to divert briefly to the more general discussion that Wittgenstein offers in the *Philosophical Investigations*: depth in this context has to do with the way Wittgenstein connects rules of meaning with a practice. His particular construction makes rules implicit, or devoid of the need of justification, only to the extent they are embedded in a dynamic structure (practice) that does not allow any of the rules to dissolve into any kind of decisive or exhaustive criteria at any single moment. As such, our practices consist of many layers of different rules (or clusters of rules, often referred to as language-games) that are intertwined but also serve different functions. Be that as it may, the different layers are not insular; instead, it is possible to utilise one of them in order to refer to another (or others). It follows that, although when one follows a particular rule, say about counting, this rule remains implicit, it is still possible to refer to it by distancing oneself from the language-game of counting and switching to a different one, say, that of logic or syntax. Now 'add 5' is no longer a rule but some kind of object that one can name and, as a result, refer to. My uttering 'add 5' can now serve as justification for what I do even if only for a short moment—and only to the extent that it remains parasitic (or implicitly connected) to the practice of counting.[48]

To revert to discursive grammar, take for instance the discourse rule (DR): 'everyone who can speak may take part in discourse'.[49] Explicit reference to this rule requires that (DR) be inserted in a sentence of the form 'F is G'. When this takes place then (DR) ceases to be a rule and becomes an object in virtue of occupying a certain position in the logical structure of a sentence. In this case, too, we continue to engage in rule-following, yet rule-following found at a different level: the rule we follow now is no longer the initial rule (DR) but a semantic rule that

[48] In a similar way Frege proclaims that 'der Begriff "Pferd" ist kein Begriff' ('the concept "horse" is not a concept'). Absurdity in this context is avoided only if the sentence is interpreted as an attempt to capture ontological categories through the semantic structure (or the grammar) of the sentence. Thus, anything that occupies the space of the grammatical subject cannot be but an object (even if this is 'the concept "horse"'). See G Frege, 'Über Begriff und Gegenstand' in *idem* , *Funktion, Begriff, Bedeutung*, 4th edn (G Patzig (ed), Göttingen, Vandenhoeck & Ruprecht, 1994) 66 at 71.

[49] See Alexy's list of discourse rules in *A Theory of Legal Argumentation*, above n 39 at 187n.

determines the structure of a sentence of the form FG. Similarly in the domain of law; take legal norm (N): 'All thieves ought to be punished'. This is a norm that can be referred to by switching into discursive grammar. The latter ensures that N is objectified through the appropriate semantic-logical rules that determine the logical structure of sentences.

A consolidation of the multilevel structure of discursive grammar requires a closer relation between the system of discourse rules and various other normative language-games whose content is more local. Given the difference of levels between rules of different language-games, the individuation of normative propositions of a particular type (legal, ethical, etiquette-related, moral, and so on) needs to be considered in the normative context that is more appropriate to it. This by no means compromises the increased importance of the general rules of discourse, for it is they that carry out the fundamental function of objectification and, hence, of the exchange of reasons. It merely points to the need that the plurality of normative practices be reflected in the rules that specify criteria of correctness of normative propositions for each particular domain (law, morality, and so on). To that extent, discourse theory must make room for the more local or specific practices that effect normative communication.[50]

Before concluding, a short comment ought to be added on the relation between the different domains of practical reason. It seems that one of Dworkin's main intuitions for developing interpretivism has been the need to account for the continuity between legal and moral norms. Having seen that the main tenets of this theory trigger a breakdown of objectivity, it is natural to ask whether any other effort to account for continuity between law and morality would share the same fate; and the other way round: whether any account that succeeds on the level of objectivity would have to fail on the level of producing a unifying account of law and morality. The discourse theory of law demonstrates that it is possible to combine the two tasks. First of all, it shows that communication has a discursive or argumentative structure. This structure underpins any type of prescriptive speech that aims at communication and in doing so establishes common standards of correctness for normative propositions. Most important amongst them is the condition of universalisation, namely that every valid normative proposition should meet the agreement of all those who take part in a discourse. Universalisation becomes the common denominator between the various domains of practical reason, for it imposes a common constraint on what it is possible to think of as a valid normative

[50] This may be carried out by a theory of legal pluralism which is normatively sensitive and does not cut itself off from the fundamental premises of objectivity enshrined by the rules of discursive grammar. For a legal pluralism sensitive to the idea of normative correctness, indeed along the lines of discourse theory, see the original work of E Melissaris, 'Perspective, Critique, and Pluralism in Legal Theory' (2006) 57 *Northern Ireland legal Quarterly* 597.

proposition. Thus, it is possible to retain the notion of objectivity deriving from a dynamic conception of criteria without dropping the project of a unified account of the domain of practical reason.

In this context a legal norm like (N): 'All thieves ought to be punished' implies an interaction between different levels of practical correctness: as a matter of legal discourse the norm gives rise to a pattern of rule-following that involves Parliaments, officials, courts, sanctions, and so on; at this level, the norm remains more or less *implicit* while its verbal formulation serves merely the purpose of a cursory indication of the underlying practice. What determine its content are criteria internal to the pattern of rule-following corresponding to the norm. Once in a while, however, the need arises to make out of (N) an object of reference in order to justify a court judgment or some other action (say, an arrest by a police officer). This can be done only by ascending to the level of practical discourse. Now things look slightly different: (N) becomes the object of another practice, one that is demarcated by the rules of discursive grammar and whose purpose, as it were, is to make norms like (N) *explicit*. With this move, a shift in criteria of correctness takes place: the content of the norm is being subjected to the standards of the discourse, most notably the requirement of universalisation. Subjecting legal norms to universalisation brings about, furthermore, an interaction between legal and moral norms, for the content of universalisation cannot be specified independently of other norms that are universalisable. Here the norms of morality count above all. Thus, even though legal practice retains a relative autonomy vis à vis other domains of practical discourse, the possibility of referring objectively to legal norms through discursive grammar renders law a special case or *Sonderfall* of practical discourse.[51]

CONCLUDING REMARKS

I began by identifying an ostensible incompatibility between interpretivism's account of objectivity and that offered by the discourse theory of law. I then showed that the interpretive conception of objectivity is untenable, leading to an understanding of legal practice that lacks the resources to account for law's normativity. This understanding not only preserves the

[51] See R Alexy, *Theorie der juristischen Argumentation*, above n 39 at 263–72 and 349–59; *idem*, *Begriff und Geltung des Rechts* (Freiburg i Br and Munich, Alber, 1992) 126–36; *idem*, 'The Special Case Thesis' (1999) 12 *Ratio Juris* 374. For recent criticisms of the thesis, see A Engländer, 'Zur begrifflichen Möglichkeit des Rechtspositivismus. Eine Kritik des Richtigkeitsarguments von Robert Alexy' (1997) 28 *Rechtstheorie* 437; J Habermas, *Faktizität und Geltung*, 2nd edn (Frankfurt am Main, Suhrkamp, 1992) 283–91; K Günther, *Der Sinn für Angemessenheit. Anwendungsdiskurse in Moral und Recht* (Frankfurt am Main, Suhrkamp, 1988); *idem*, 'Critical Remarks on Robert Alexy's "Special-Case Thesis"' (1993) 6 *Ratio Juris* 143.

shortcomings of those theories interpretivism purports to refute, but also contradicts the initial intuition of interpretivism as an explication of legal practice that brings out its argumentative depth. Conversely, I suggested that such a deep conception of legal practice can be attained more faithfully by the notion of objectivity found in the philosophically more subtle idea of a discursive grammar of argumentation.

6

Discourse Ethics, Legal Positivism and the Law

PHILIPPOS C VASSILOYANNIS*

INTRODUCTION

EVER SINCE HIS seminal doctoral dissertation, Professor Robert Alexy has persuasively argued that legal argumentation constitutes a special case of moral argumentation.[1] Its peculiarity lies in the fact that the claim to correctness of legal argumentation can only be fulfilled within the institutional framework of an existing legal order; therefore, given that Alexy is by no means a proponent of a relativist conception of correctness, the fulfilment of that claim depends on the degree of correctness of positive law. If positive law were not correct (and setting aside whether it makes any sense to speak of extremely unjust law[2]), then the claim to correctness that is inherent in legal argumentation (as Alexy also persuasively argues) would remain unsubstantiated. But what does the correctness of propositions of positive law depend on?

Lacking a moral bridge that would take us from moral to legal argumentation (in other words, without a moral justification of the form of law), the discursive conception of legal argumentation cannot but reproduce the positivistic distinction between law and morality, and ends up a mere apology for legal discourse. Alexy rested content with a rather traditional choice of methodology, that of demonstrating (though not offering a moral justification for) the peculiarity of legal argumentation. He first traced the *genus proximum* to which it belongs, namely moral

* This project is co-funded by the European Social Fund and the National [Hellenic] Resources (EPEAEK II) PYTHAGORAS II.

1 R Alexy, *A Theory of Legal Argumentation* (R Adler and N McCormick (trans), Oxford, Oxford University Press, 1989).

2 See R Alexy, *The Argument from Injustice: A Reply to Legal Positivism* (SL Paulson and B Litschewski Paulson (trans), Oxford, Oxford University Press, 2002) esp 40.

argumentation, and then he identified its *differentia specifica*: the institutional constraints that render legal argumentation a special case of moral argumentation. The inevitable question that arises at this point, however, is whether legal argumentation just happens to be a special case of moral argumentation or whether its peculiarity, that is, the relevant legal constraints, can itself be derived from the discursive conception of legal argumentation, from discourse ethics, by virtue of purely moral reasons; in short, from a moral justification of the form of law.

Alexy justifies the necessity of law by invoking,[3] among others, the need for institutional settlement of the following problem: the process of (moral?) deliberation does not guarantee that only one (right?) answer will come out. The problem therefore arises of the knowledge of the law. This problem, argues Alexy, is solved by the authoritative enactment of the law, by political decisions reached through predetermined (legal?) processes and on the basis of majority rule. Anticipating a bit, one could wonder, following Rousseau's critique of Grotius[4]: doesn't majority rule presuppose unanimity at least once, when we unanimously establish majority rule as a decision-making principle that commands the adherence of the minority to the view of the majority? To avoid circularity, we ought to offer a moral justification for majority rule.

Failure to solve the problem of knowledge of the law leads—where else?—to anarchy. As is obvious, this argument does not establish the moral necessity of the law without further ado. Why wouldn't a legal positivist subscribe to this way of establishing the necessity of the law? It is not my purpose in this contribution to examine in a systematic way Alexy's theory of law.[5] I shall confine myself to arguing that legal positivism can only be anchored in a merely procedural conception of argumentation (as put forward by Habermas, for example), which is its worst version for both epistemological and, more importantly, moral reasons. This is why, in my view, Alexy, ought to have shifted his very interesting conception of the discursive justification of human rights in a more straightforward way toward a moral justification of the law.

One last introductory point: Kant himself and all Kantians are in a sense formalists. Their formalism, however, is based on moral reasons. The notorious unencumbered self, which has so often been criticised by various versions of both right and left communitarianism, is the outcome of a series of reasonable abstractions and, foremost, the manifestation of

[3] See his 'Discourse Theory and Human Rights' (1996) 9 *Ratio Juris* 209 at 220.

[4] JJ Rousseau, 'The Social Contract' in V Gourevitch (ed), *'The Social Contract' and Other Later Political Writings* (Cambridge, Cambridge University Press, 1997) 49.

[5] I have tried to raise some doubts about his theory in my short book review of *Theorie der Grundrechte* on the occasion of its translation into English (*A Theory of Constitutional Rights* (J Rivers (trans), Oxford, Oxford University Press, 2004)), see (2004) 55 *Northern Ireland Quarterly* 206.

respect to others: in order to take them all into consideration, without exclusion and *sub specie aeternitatis*, one must make certain relevant and even radical abstractions.[6] On the other hand, when it is not justified by appeal to moral reasons, a merely procedural claim to correctness, a formalistic legal discourse (quite independently of whether it can be conducted successfully or whether it serves any purpose), leads to a belated revival of *Begriffsjurisprudenz* (the distinctive type of German legal positivism of the nineteenth century) and to the so-called *juristische Methode*.

KANT'S MORAL PHILOSOPHY AND DISCOURSE ETHICS

No doubt, discourse ethics is a philosophical achievement. In effect, by elaborating discourse ethics Apel and Habermas have managed to overcome with considerable success on the one hand a traditional way of dealing with philosophical problems that ignores the linguistic turn in philosophy, and on the other the dominant meta-ethical preoccupation of moral philosophy after the Second World War that aspired to explicate morality in a morally neutral way, to explore moral language without making first-order commitments, without any moral prerequisites. Discourse ethics, at least in Apel's version, seeks to justify morality in essentially Kantian fashion. By this, I imply precisely that it is not Kant's own line of argument. Thus, it must be noted that, while the philosophical views that Kant primarily sets himself to refute are (to use anachronistic terminology) consequentialism and perfectionism, discourse ethics takes as its philosophical adversary a type of radical scepticism about the possibility of finding a foundation for morality. This fundamental choice of strategy is not without consequences. If the philosophical programme of discourse ethics misses the mark with regard to the philosophical evaluation of its discovery, it runs the risk that it might have very little to offer to moral philosophy.

To explain in outline the normative proximity of Kant's moral philosophy and discourse ethics, we could make the following remarks: (1) For Kant, the foundation of morality cannot be anything external to our subjectivity as beings with reason, but practical reason itself. For discourse ethics, the justification of moral judgements cannot be external to our subjectivity as discursive beings, that is, beings with a capacity to communicate, to give arguments and reasons. Our moral judgements cannot but be based on the best argument. (2) For Kant, morality cannot be based on self-love. For discourse ethics, morality cannot be monological. Or, put differently, both Kant and discourse ethics claim that of necessity morality cannot be a private matter. (3) For Kant, the supreme principle of morality

[6] Compare J Rawls, *Political Liberalism* (New York, Columbia University Press, 1993) 43.

is not a matter of the substantive content of our moral evaluations, or a matter of referring their content to a comprehensive moral ground principle (eg 'love thy neighbour as thyself'!). The moral agent is, according to Kant in the dark, if she follows prescriptions that have not been subjected to critical scrutiny. For discourse ethics, the supreme principle of morality stems from the recognition of the validity of certain inescapable procedural rules, the rules of argumentation. In short, in Kant's case the standard of scrutiny is the categorical imperative, in the case of discourse ethics it is the principle of discourse. To summarise, this principle states that only those norms are valid that are or can be the outcome of an argumentative procedure. As for the crucial test of universality (that is, the transcendence of individual or collective self-love or, likewise, monologue), whereas Kant argues that the moral agent is called upon to conceive of—at first solely—personal maxims as universal laws, according to discourse ethics she is called upon to follow those rules that would gain universal agreement in ideal deliberation: in unforced discourse governed solely by the best argument.

It is to be noted right from the outset that, like the concept of the categorical imperative, the concept of the principle of discourse is subject to interpretation and is understood differently by diverse (and maybe conflicting) conceptions. We can state the questions that set the challenge for different conceptions of that principle as follows:

(i) In the Kantian vein, discourse ethics sets itself to anchor the status of morality not in the substantive content of our moral judgements, whichever this may be, but in the procedural conditions of their validity. The first question then that different conceptions must face concerns whether this enterprise is epistemic or purely moral (or both by some happy coincidence: let me point out in passing that the parallel philosophical enterprise undertaken by Kant regarding the philosophical justification of the categorical imperative is primarily moral and has epistemological importance only in a derivative sense: any dependence of morality on substantive conceptions of the good would render it a mere means for the attainment of dubious purposes; what is more, even if there exists no uncertainty (or indeterminacy) in what is required of moral agents to attain their wellbeing, no doubt there exists a moral obligation to respect the pluralism of the conceptions they happen to endorse). Now, if the philosophical project of discourse ethics is taken to be epistemic, it reflects a crucial moral demand for certainty. However, the primordial and all-important issue at this point is not so much certainty as the very idea of moral correctness.

(ii) Discourse ethics aspires to provide a definitive and indeed silencing response to a radical sceptical challenge concerning the possibility of justifying our moral judgements. But what does this goal consist in? It may be taken to consist solely in the affirmation of the inescapable character of moral argumentation (merely procedural conception of the principle of discourse). But discourse ethics places all substantive moral issues beyond the scope of moral philosophy, confronting the sceptic with a critical dilemma: either he totally exempts himself from argumentation or he admits defeat and seriously participates in it. The relevant set of questions for discourse theorists is whether, how and to what extent we can argue about moral issues from the standpoint of moral discourse itself; and, more important for present purposes, how we can derive the moral necessity of the law, the form of law, from discourse ethics.

In what follows I shall stress, first, the moral significance of deliberation rather than the alleged significance of discourse for morality. I shall argue that discourse ethics can plausibly be regarded as a privileged entry point in the moral world, but only in so far as it truly, as Apel claims,[7] explicates in its own distinctive way the famous *fact of reason*, which Kant also invokes as proof of the moral law (instead of any other). But in order to succeed in this, I shall suggest, discourse ethics would have to show that rules of argumentation have primarily moral value. Now, before I proceed to the main argument, let me put to the test what I think is ultimately an unrealistic defence of discourse ethics.

According to Habermas (in his early work at least[8]) 'The criterion of the truth of propositions is the possibility of universal assent [*Zustimmung*] *to* an opinion, whereas the criterion of the rightness of a commendation or admonition is the possibility of universal agreement [*Übereinstimmung*] in an opinion'.[9] The successful performance of the relevant speech acts presupposes rules of fair discourse. It is these rules that make possible a well-founded consensus between participants in an argumentative procedure; that is, a consensus based on the best argument (which is achieved under conditions of ideal communication). According to this moral criterion (which Habermas would prefer to be meta-ethical), only those acts are right that conform to norms, the validity of which is based on the potential consensus of all those possibly affected under conditions of ideal communication.

Even at this preliminary stage we can raise a number of objections to this view. First, if we are to take discourse ethics seriously, how are we to know which argument is the best before the relevant argumentative procedure takes place? The best argument cannot be adopted before the conclusion of

[7] K-O Apel, 'Notwendigkeit, Schwierigkeit, und Möglichkeit einer philosophischen Begründung der Ethik im Zeitalter der Wissenschaft' in Αφιέρωμα στον Κωνσταντίνο Τσάτσο [*Studies Presented to Constantine Tsatsos*] (Athens, Νομικαί εκδόσεις Αντ. Ν. Σάκκουλα [Ant N Sakkoulas Law Publishers], 1980) 264.

[8] See J Habermas, *On the Pragmatics of Social Interaction: Preliminary Studies in the Theory of Communicative Action* (B Fultner (trans), Cambridge Mass, MIT Press, 2001) 85. I do not take into account subsequent elaborations of this idea by Habermas. The point I seek to make in the text is philosophical rather than biographical.

[9] *Ibid* at 92.

that procedure. One could invoke Rousseau's paradox here: in a voting process the will of an individual cannot be evaluated for its conformity with the *volonté generale* (and not just the *volonté des tous*), since the *volonté generale* will make itself manifest only in the result of the vote.[10] We agree in an opinion because it is true. No matter how you twist and turn this, a consensus theory of truth is still a bizarre theory of truth. To put it emphatically, any theory must have some monological correspondence to reality. Seen from a different angle, even if the idea of truth (or correctness) as consensus merely restates the so-called 'argument against private language', from a moral point of view it becomes utterly trivial. Correctness as consensus must acquire genuine moral significance by being related with some moral reasons.

JUSTIFICATION OF DISCOURSE RULES

Discourse ethics aims to discharge what is at first sight a reasonable burden of proof (which is imposed by the so-called 'Münchhausen's Trilemma'). That is, it must rebut the challenge that it is presumably impossible to ground our moral judgements in a fully rational way, because, to do this, we would have to invoke a higher-order moral norm, thus mounting on an infinite regress. Every norm we invoke we must in turn justify by appeal to a higher-order norm and so on.[11] This alleged infinite regress is blocked by a brilliant philosophical argument by Apel, which he labels transcendental-pragmatic: Whoever claims that the attempt to provide an ultimate justification for our moral judgements is pointless makes a performative contradiction. By his very participation in the argumentative process he ought to recognise as valid a minimum set of non-refutable moral norms that are necessary for any argumentative procedure,[12] even for the capacity to raise sceptical objections. So the radical sceptic refutes himself.

Habermas,[13] too, defends discourse rules as the unavoidable preconditions of discourse and not as mere conventions that happen to be accepted by participants. Take the sentence (1)*:

I told A a lie to convince him that p.

When the interlocutor in this situation asserts that p, he enters into a discourse and he thereby accepts the epistemic condition that one cannot,

[10] Rousseau, above n 4 at 124.

[11] See H Albert, *Treatise on Critical Reason* (M Varney Rorty (trans), Princeton, Princeton University Press, 1985) 16.

[12] Cf J Habermas, 'Discourse Ethics: Notes on a Program of Philosophical Justification' in *Moral Consciousness and Communicative Action* (C Lenhardt and S Weber Nicholsen (trans), Cambridge Mass, MIT Press, 1992) 79.

[13] Cf *ibid* at 89.

properly speaking, *convince* anyone by telling lies but at most, 'he can talk him into believing something to be true'. In order for the content of our moral judgements to be congruent with their inherent (tacit) claim to correctness, we must refrain from epistemic surprises and recognise the validity of the rule (1): Each speaker may only assert what he himself believes.[14] In the light of this rule the assertion in sentence (1)* is *discursively impossible.* Or consider the sentence (2)*:

> After excluding A, B and C from discourse (either by forcibly silencing them or by imposing on them our own views), we managed to convince ourselves that the norm x is valid.

Any attempt to justify the validity of x by appeal to the fact of our agreement involves a performative contradiction. For, on one hand our conduct violates the argumentative preconditions that govern the harmonisation of illocutionary and perlocutionary speech acts, namely that we address those speech acts to an unbounded communication community, and on the other we tacitly recognise the force of those preconditions when we argue for the correctness of norm x. From this normative situation we can derive the following discourse rules[15]: (2.1) Anyone who can speak may take part in discourse. (2.2) (a) Anyone may render any assertion problematic. (b) Anyone may introduce any assertion into the discourse. (c) Anyone may express his/her opinions, wishes and needs. (2.3) No speaker may prevented by constraint within or outside the discourse from making use of his/her rights established in (2.1) and (2.2). The justification of discourse rules is therefore transcendental, that is, it takes the following form: the assertion that p is possible, if and only if it is true that (1) (2.1) (2.2) (2.3). Therefore (1) (2.1) (2.2) (2.3).

THE TRANSCENDENTAL-PRAGMATIC ARGUMENT

Furthermore, according to Apel, 'whoever participates in argumentation has already confirmed *in actu* and acknowledged that *reason is practical*, that is, *responsible for human action*'.[16] He acknowledges, that is, that claims to correctness can only be fulfilled by means of exchange of argument. This means that 'the *ideal rules of argumentation*, in an in principle unbounded communication community of participants who mutually recognize one another as equal, constitute *normative conditions for the possibility of reaching a decision on claims to moral correctness by consensus*'. Hence, consensus must unavoidably be sought, regardless of

14 R Alexy, 'A Theory of Practical Discourse' in S Benhabib (ed), *The Communicative Ethics Controversy* (Cambridge Mass, MIT Press, 1990) 163.
15 *Ibid* at 166.
16 Apel, above n 7 at 264.

whether its attainment is in fact feasible. Here, too, we need to distinguish between ideal and actual consensus, since the impossibility of actual consensus does not foreclose the possibility of ideal consensus (an analogy can be made with Rawls' scheme of principles of justice to which parties in the original position would agree). The aforementioned fundamental moral rule is not, according to Apel, in need of (further) justification; to ask for such justification is to be guilty of *apaideusia* (lack of education)[17] as Aristotle puts it: 'it shows lack of education not to know of what we should require proof, and of what we should not'.[18]

Indeed, the validity of the transcendental-pragmatic presuppositions of argumentation is not dependent on the subjective taste of interlocutors. Whoever refuses to accept them thereby abdicates his status as a person and embarks on 'a pathological route, at the end of which there is "idiocy", that is, the loss of one's already discursively attained personal identity'.[19] We are free, argues Apel, to violate the transcendental-pragmatic rules of discourse, but not to deny their validity, for, otherwise we lose our capacity for communication and self-identification. (Even in a serious monologue, we are obliged to presuppose certain moral discourse rules; for example, do we have the right to lie to ourselves? This is why the ever-present objection of discourse ethics directed at traditional philosophy (including Kantian philosophy) that presumably it is monological is largely unwarranted. Strictly speaking, there can be no monologue, not even philosophical monologue, in the same way that there can be no private language.)

On the basis of the previous analysis, we can state the transcendental-pragmatic argument as follows[20]: (1) Whoever takes part in discourse of necessity enters into a game that is governed by binding rules. (2) Whoever does not take part in discourse, that is, lacks the capacity to give reasons, cannot take part even at an most elementary level in the distinctively 'human form of life'. Or, to formulate the argument for discourse ethics in terms akin to the Cartesian methodological enterprise: whoever puts in question discourse ethics is already taking part in argumentation; therefore, he recognises the moral character of argumentation *in actu*.

Summing up, to accept discourse rules means to be able to participate at an elementary level in the distinctively 'human form of life', because in every culture it is possible to raise the question 'why?', and therefore also to use certain *universalia*. But is it possible to justify in a similar way moral

[17] *Ibid* at 252.

[18] *Metaphysics*, 1006a 6–9 (Book I–IX, H Tredemnick (trans), Cambridge Mass, Harvard University Press, 1933) 162–3).

[19] Apel, above n 7 at 270.

[20] Compare R Alexy, 'Nachwort (1991): Antwort auf einige Kritiker' in *Theorie der juristischen Argumentation*, 2nd edn (Frankfurt am Main, Suhrkamp, 1991) 418.

and legal norms, like the moral norms enshrined in the constitutional guarantees of certain fundamental rights? In other words, is it possible to appeal to discourse ethics in order adequately to rebut not only sceptical but also relativist challenges?

PROCEDURAL AND SUBSTANTIVE MORALITY

The possibility of such a *direct* justification of moral and legal norms—even the most fundamental and self-evident ones—is denied by Habermas, especially in his later work, which is rather influenced by a certain version of legal positivism. There, Habermas[21] argues that discourse ethics, by justifying the principle of discourse, is cognitivist, as opposed to sceptical, because it demonstrates that it is possible to justify our moral judgements. It is also universalist, as opposed to relativist, because it demonstrates that all participants in a discourse can reach agreement on certain judgements about the validity of moral and legal norms, when their validity becomes the object of an actual discourse. However, Habermas continues, discourse ethics is also strictly formalist, in contrast with perfectionist substantive theories of wellbeing. The third characteristic listed above reflects the commitment of discourse ethics to the validity of certain universal rules of argumentation. On the other hand, though, by precluding any appeal to even a partially substantive deontological ethics, formalism also signals the strict methodological adherence of discourse ethics to proceduralism. 'Basic norms of law and morality', claims Habermas,[22] 'fall outside the jurisdiction of moral theory; they must be viewed as substantive principles to be justified in practical discourses'. The substantive norms of conduct, in short, our rights and duties, inevitably emerge from actual discourses:

> Since historical circumstances change, every epoch sheds its own light upon fundamental moral practical ideas. Nevertheless, in such discourses we always already make use of substantive normative rules of argumentation. It is *these rules* alone that transcendental pragmatics is in a position to derive.[23]

This quotation makes one wonder whether discourse rules have no further normative presuppositions and whether a discourse can produce any outcome.

To begin with, one can reasonably raise the following question: does a strictly procedural conception of discourse ethics have normative value? Let us explore the parallel issue whether there is normative value in a strictly procedural principle of justice, as conceptually distinct from

[21] See J Habermas, 'Moral Consciousness and Communicative Action' in *Moral Consciousness and Communicative Action*, above n 12 at 120.

[22] Habermas, above n 12 at 86.

[23] *Ibid.*

substantive questions of distributive justice. In his critique of Rawls' theory of justice, Habermas argues that Rawls was wrong not to have adhered to a strictly procedural conception of his theory, free from substantive assumptions.[24] By contrast, according to Habermas, discourse ethics 'focuses exclusively on the procedural aspects of the public use of reason and ... can leave more questions open because it entrusts more to the *process* of rational opinion and will formation'.[25] In his response, Rawls persuasively maintains that he sees no reason why discourse ethics should not be thought of as also substantive,[26] and quite plausibly puts forward a distinction between justice (or fairness) of a procedure and justice (or fairness) of its outcome. Both types of justice are employed to exemplify certain political values and are to be harmonised. The justice of a certain procedure is always based on the justice of its likely outcomes, that is, on substantive justice. Therefore, Rawls concludes, 'procedural and substantive justice are connected and not separate'.[27] From this we can infer that fair procedures are underlain by procedural values, e.g. the value of impartiality confers on all an equal chance to present their case publicly and in a fair manner.[28] For Rawls then, to take a view on these matters is not to choose between substantive and procedural justice, since all sides agree that procedural justice is also underlain by substantive justice, as is the case in the controversy between 'majoritarians' and 'constitutionalists'. The former do not claim that a democratic regime is merely procedural, but that it serves certain substantive values,[29] for instance, that majority rule (as well as the political compromises that are necessarily involved in order to ensure its institutional effectiveness) is a good thing because it guarantees the self-determination of at least most citizens.[30] Otherwise, they would not be in position to defend their cause against constitutionalists. Rawls points out that for Habermas, too, public deliberation can only produce reasonable outcomes, if it adequately upholds the conditions of ideal communication. That is, its rules must realise, so far as possible, equality, impartiality, openness and lack of coercion, so that as a result it is possible to generalise the interests of all participants. The outcome of the procedure is therefore substantive. This is something which—

[24] See J Habermas, 'Reconciliation through the Public Use of Reason: Remarks on John Rawls's Political Liberalism' (1995) 92 *Journal of Philosophy* 109, and also Rawls' reply, 'Reply to Habermas' (1995) 92 *Journal of Philosophy* 132.

[25] *Ibid* at 131.

[26] See Rawls, 'Reply to Habermas', above n 24 at 170.

[27] *Ibid.*

[28] *Ibid.*

[29] *Ibid* at 172.

[30] See H Kelsen, 'On the Essence and Value of Democracy' in AJ Jacobson and B Schlink (eds), *Weimar: A Jurisprudence Crisis* (California, University of California Press, 2002) 100.

remarkably—Habermas himself concedes, when he claims that 'the outcomes of political will formation are reasonable'.[31] His agreement can also be tacitly inferred from the fact that he does not claim that all substantive questions are open in actual discourse.[32]

The same can be said about moral discourse in general. One can reasonably distinguish procedural from substantive morality, the morality of procedure from the morality of its outcomes. Both types of morality exemplify certain moral values and must be harmonised. The morality of procedure always depends on the moral merit of its likely outcomes, that is, on substantive morality (not on good luck). Therefore, we can conclude following Rawls that procedural morality and substantive morality are connected and not separate.

DISCOURSE RULES AS MERE RULES OF SPEECH?

But let us suppose by contrast that Habermas contends that all substantive issues are open in discourse, in the sense that how they are resolved is a matter of political decision through and through. In this rendition of Habermas' claim, which can plausibly be attributed to him, discourse ethics has no resources to rebut the relativist challenges that will predictably be raised. At any rate, on this reading, discourse ethics retreats to the meta-ethical level, thus making itself vulnerable to a number of critical epistemological objections that also have direct moral relevance: How can we ever justify the distinction (let alone make the distinction practicable) of rule (2.1): Anyone who can speak may take part in discourse, and the semantically equivalent rule (2.1)': Anyone who can speak may take part in discourse, where the former only binds someone qua interlocutor, while the latter binds him qua moral agent, qua bearer of rights and duties toward others (for example, we can plausibly imagine rule (2.1)' summing up a provision guaranteeing the relevant right within the framework of an ideal and ecumenical political community)? In this regard Alexy insists that discourse rules are only rules of speech and, accordingly, that we cannot directly derive substantive norms of conduct from them.[33] What kind of impossibility is implied here? Alexy cannot possibly mean that it is a logical impossibility. But if it is not a logical impossibility, then, unless Alexy's claim is based on moral reasons, it is guilty of circularity. For a claim like his can only be substantiated by appeal to substantive moral reasons. (It would be worth exploring what these reasons would look like from the perspective of discourse ethics, because those reasons would

[31] Rawls, 'Reply to Habermas', above n 24 at 173.
[32] *Ibid* at 174.
[33] Alexy, above n 3 at 222.

presumably also justify the form of law and distinguish it from morality (in a strict sense), whose singularity, as we have seen, is established by means of a transcendental-pragmatic argument).

We can shed some light on the source of this persistence on meta-ethics by bringing out the correlation of procedure and correctness latent in discourse theory.[34] Alexy thinks that the one-right-answer thesis can only be epistemologically grounded in a theory of absolute correctness. He further distinguishes between discursive necessity, impossibility and possibility,[35] so that certain judgements come out discursively necessary or impossible and some merely discursively possible. We get to discursive necessity and impossibility by employing the rules of discourse as premises in our moral judgements. So, for instance, starting from the aforementioned rules (2.1), (2.2), and (2.3), we can offer a justification for certain considered moral convictions[36] as e.g. the moral demerit of social exclusion. This example suggests that by appeal to the idea of discursive necessity and impossibility, we are able to identify certain moral reasons that precede discourse; put differently, that by appeal to this idea, we truly seem to be able to establish rules of conduct from mere rules of speech. But is this conclusion compatible with a strictly procedural conception of the principle of discourse, whereby the sole requirement for the justification of moral judgements is the test of reason-giving?

From the point of view of speech act theory, on which the discursive conception of ethics by Habermas is largely based, the alleged distinction between rule (2.1) as mere rule of speech and the same rule as rule of conduct, is unwarranted; at any rate, it cannot be conceptual, because speech itself is performed through acts and not just words.[37] Conversely, we use words to perform various acts, like to declare, promise, threaten, insult, defame, praise, tell lies and so forth, and it is precisely through words that we consent. Here then is another suggestion. Maybe the thrust of the distinction under discussion is just that rules of discourse only bind us within a discourse but not necessarily without. But this kind of self-constraint does not seem to follow from or be compatible with the procedural (in Habermas' sense) conception of discourse ethics, since there surely are institutionalised discourses, as for example dispute resolution before a court. This is an instance of discourse in so far as it is also governed by the rules of discourse. Granted, there is a difference. In the case of court proceedings, the addressees of the rules of discourse are moral

[34] Cf Alexy, above n 20 at 410.

[35] Alexy, above n 3 at 177.

[36] See J Rawls, *A Theory of Justice*, rev edn (Oxford, Oxford University Press, 1999) 42.

[37] This is why the feminist critique against pornography, namely that it is not speech and is therefore not covered by freedom of speech, is not justified, not for this reason anyway; cf R Langton, 'Pornography, Speech Acts, and Silence' (1993) 22 *Philosophy and Public Affairs* 293.

agents (the various actors of the trial whose roles are defined by their procedural rights and duties, like the duty of sincerity). However, this difference is not sufficient to occasion a conceptual shift, a radical change in content of the rules themselves qua universal rules. Hence, I conclude that the distinction may only be moral in character.

Take the following example. The duty of sincerity, under the distinction in question, binds interlocutors in a discourse, but not bearers of the constitutional right to freedom of expression. Or, to put the same point from the first person perspective, as a participant in moral discourse I ought to be honest, otherwise I am led to refuting myself *in actu*. However, as a writer, politician or citizen I am entitled to dispute the Holocaust as a historical fact, even if I thereby consciously intend to deceive my audience. But why, generally speaking, do I have a right to lie by virtue of my freedom of expression? And, further, is it compatible with discourse ethics to say that having a right to lie is merely discursively possible; that is, to say that it is an open question whether it will be adopted as a legal norm?

DISCOURSE AS A FACT OF REASON

According to a strictly procedural conception of the principle of discourse, since moral theory does not offer us moral reasons—and ought not to, unless it is inspired by a Platonic ideal of 'philosopher-kings'—, but at most rules of reason-giving; since, furthermore, moral reasons must be justified by a process of actual discourse between real, flesh-and-blood citizens, regarded as free and equal, the need arises for a possibly democratic (though not necessarily the best judged from the perspective of the theory of democracy), but at any rate authoritative, institutional mechanism for the enactment, not the discovery or moral construction of law. Discourse ethics, like any moral theory, must be supplemented by a legal theory (as well as a legislator). Its legal theory is not necessarily legal positivism (nor is its legislator any given deliberative institution).

As we have seen, Habermas (as well as Alexy) denies that transcendental-pragmatically derived rules of discourse may bind us qua moral agents, whatever this qualification may be taken to imply. At this point, it is fair to ask whether by virtue of the transcendental-pragmatic justification of the rules of argumentation we acquire moral reasons to observe those rules, and further whether those moral reasons no longer apply in so far as a substantive rule of conduct (whatever the term 'substantive rule of conduct' is taken to mean) is not grounded in transcendental-pragmatic fashion. To begin with, performative contradictions in the conduct of moral agents are conceivable, a well-known fact in political philosophy. Consider the case of slavery. Abdication of one's own personality constitutes an extremely contradictory action, leading to one's self-refutation. Therefore, it cannot, strictly speaking, be a legally binding engagement.[38] The performative contradiction consists in the fact that the claim to correctness of the act of consent (which stems from the status of the consenting party as a rational being) contradicts the content of his expression of will. Likewise, from the standpoint of discourse theory, we cannot tolerate the so-called paradoxes of freedom, toleration and democracy. Consider the abolition of freedom as a result of its arbitrary exercise, non-interference with totalitarian practices in the name of the principle of toleration itself and the abolition of democracy decided by majority vote.[39] The principle of democracy, which is conceptually intertwined with the principle of discourse (as I shall attempt to argue below), shows those paradoxes to be no more than performative contradictions by free and equal citizens.

Apart from the conceptual objections rehearsed above, Habermas' version of discourse ethics ignores that the principle of discourse may be conceived of as a fact of reason (as Apel rightly suggests). To put it briefly, the principle of discourse as fact of reason means that, as reasonable beings that take part in argumentation, we are conscious of the moral law as the supremely authoritative and regulative law for us and we inescapably recognise it as such in our ordinary moral thought and judgements.[40] The fact of reason is not the moral law itself.[41] The performative contradictions of the sceptic that Habermas invokes have no moral edge. Indeed, according to a merely procedural conception of the principle of discourse, participants in discourse are required to recognise one another only as interlocutors, not as persons. But this evaluation of our normative commitments within the discourse misses the mark. As participants in discourse we are inescapably bound to recognise our interlocutors as persons. For otherwise how would we be able to distinguish a mere exchange of words from a deliberation? Discourse presupposes mutual respect between fellow-participants. But why do we respect our interlocutors? The fact that it so

[38] See C de Montesquieu, *The Spirit of the Laws* (AM Cohler, BC Miller and H Stone (trans), Cambridge, Cambridge University Press, 1989) 247; Rousseau, above n 4 at 48; I Kant, 'On the Common Saying: That May be True in Theory, but it is of No Use in Practice' in *Practical Philosophy* (MJ Gregor (trans), Cambridge, Cambridge University Press, 1991) 291, and *The Metaphysics of Morals*, in *Practical Philosophy* 431; GWF Hegel, *Elements of the Philosophy of Right* (HB Nisbet, Cambridge, Cambridge University Press, 1991) 97; and JS Mill, 'On Liberty' in '*On Liberty' and Other Writings* (Cambridge, Cambridge University Press, 1989) 103. Hegel is also invoked by K Marx in *Capital: A Critique of Political Economy*, vol 1 (B Fowkes (trans), London, Pelican Books, 1976) 150.

[39] See K Popper, *The Open Society and its Enemies*, vol 1, 5th edn (London, Routledge and Kegan Paul, 1963) 265, notes 4 and 6.

[40] Here I follow the restatement by J Rawls in B Herman (ed), *Lectures on the History of Moral Philosophy* (Cambridge, Cambridge University Press, 2000) 260.

[41] As Rawls puts it, *ibid*.

happens that we cannot but communicate with them (for reasons external to the discourse) is not in itself the moral basis of our respect for them.

THE IMPORT OF CONSENSUS

Going back to Alexy's theory, it is not sufficient that the peculiarity of the form of law, its conceptual connection with morality, be based on moral reasons. In addition, it must be based on reasons that flow from discourse ethics. I cannot embark on a full-scale analysis (it would take a book to do that), so I shall confine myself to a couple of remarks. Using Kantian terminology, we would say that the postulate of practical reason with regard to rights lies in the co-existence of a group of people in an organised society governed by legal institutions; in short, in the justification of the exercise of state force, state coercion. This postulate cannot be met, from the standpoint of discourse ethics, unless legal institutions incorporate respect for the reasonable (or rational[42]) consensus of moral agents as an intrinsic moral value.

On this view, consensus emerges as the key concept. Its normative function is similar to the one attributed to rights by Dworkin. That is, it operates as a trump card in collective decision-making.[43] Can we say anything more specific about the import of consensus? Here we need to distinguish two conceptions of consensus. According to the first conception, which is also the most popular, consensus is a pragmatic condition for certain things to come about. For instance, I cannot be held bound by a contract, unless I am a contracting party. But discourse ethics does not aim primarily at an actual consensus. For, according to it (whether in its procedural version or in some other), we are not only bound by the outcome of actual discourses, but also by the potential or necessary outcomes of ideal deliberation (otherwise the requirement of the best argument would be normatively inert). But if, as is reasonable, we accept that ideal discourse—unlike an actual discourse—has some necessary outcomes (for example, wouldn't it necessarily follow from ideal discourse that slavery is morally unacceptable?), then what does the invocation of consensus add to the argument? Isn't it in a sense superfluous, as is probably the invocation of the social contract in the establishment of the political community? Indeed, to stick to our example, if agents in the state of nature (or in the original position *pace* Rawls) have the features that they are assigned, then there seems to be no room left for any negotiation

[42] See D Parfit, 'What We Could Rationally Will?' (2004) 24 *Tanner Lectures on Human Values* 285.

[43] See R Dworkin, 'Rights as Trumps', in J Waldron (ed), *Theories of Rights* (Oxford, Oxford University Press, 1984) 153.

between them[44]: on those assumptions about the circumstances under which the social contract is supposed to be agreed upon, all agents as well as their interests are identical (it is about omnilogue, not dialogue). Or, since according to Kant, the law is in itself an end, the social contract that presumably establishes it is rather redundant. From the foregoing analysis it can be concluded that the second kind of normative significance of consensus lies in the fact that, regardless of whether a discourse is actually conducted, some moral judgements may be justified while some others are impossible. This means, in other words, that it is moral philosophy that tells us whether a moral judgement is discursively possible, impossible or necessary; hence there truly are moral theories of consensus. The problem then with a merely procedural conception of the principle of discourse, viewed as a moral theory of consensus, is that, without really or fully putting forward moral reasons for this choice, it privileges actual consensus, the consensus reached by participants in actual discourses.

There is a further problem with a procedural theory of consensus (if taken at face value). It not only fails its own test of correctness, but also proves itself to be non-consensual and therefore undermines itself. I will not go into much detail here. Let me just note that this self-undermining is produced by the inability of the procedural theory to subject itself to the test that it prescribes as the test of correctness. But why do I say it proves itself to be non-consensual? Let us suppose the opposite. Let us suppose it is consensual. This would mean either that it is the outcome of an actual discourse of all parties affected (or maybe just the moral philosophers), or that it cannot but be the outcome of an ideal deliberation, governed by the best argument. The first option is shown to be false by experience. The second option which Habermas is, of course, entitled to defend—is, as I have tried to show, proven wrong by the moral reasons that I elaborate in this chapter. If, finally, someone were to claim that this procedural conception has come about out of dialogue and confrontation with other philosophical views, he would no doubt be right, but only in a trivial sense: we can say the same thing about almost any theory, moral or otherwise. Hence, no moral theory need be consensual, literally speaking. Why then not adopt the counter-intuitive (to say the least) conclusion that all theories are for this reason equally true (or false)?

The crucial question is whether it is justifiable to use state force in order to impose moral norms, even if they are the outcome of ideal discourse, even if the recalcitrant person (as far as his conduct goes) himself consents to them (as far as communication goes). If we did that, then, evaluating our act from the viewpoint of the requisite consensus, we would be using

[44] With regard to the alleged contractarianism of Rawls's theory, see the objections raised in J Hampton, 'Contracts and Choices: Does Rawls have a Social Contract Theory?' (1980) 77 *Journal of Philosophy* 315.

the recalcitrant person as mere means for the goal of imposing true morality. Since morality cannot forcibly be exacted, we have a moral reason to distinguish it from the law. This is a liberal premise. Here, too, it is important to stress the moral relevance of Kant's distinctions of internal and external duties, and morality and legality (contrary to what new and old Hegelians accuse it of, Kantian morality is not vacuous). The discursive premise, which Alexy states as follows: Everyone has a right to judge for himself what is right and good, and to act accordingly,[45] corresponds to the Kantian principle of freedom (as constitutive of law),[46] from which individual liberties flow. Intimately connected with the enjoyment of individual liberties is the duty of respect on the part of all others, which in turn is the basis for a right to coerce invaders into respect. This premise corresponds to the Kantian principle of equality (as constitutive of law).[47] Lastly, from the same viewpoint, law's addressee cannot but be its creator. Hence, every citizen, besides being a bearer of political rights, must also be entitled to certain other primary goods (in Rawls' sense[48]). In this case, the enjoyment of individual liberties guarantees the authenticity of the popular will. This last premise corresponds to Kant's principle of independence (as constitutive of law).[49]

A crucial aspect of the point of view of law's addressee as its creator is *the public use of reason* (in Rawls's sense), the reciprocity that inheres in public reason. Within the institutional framework of free democratic discourse, participants are required to uphold only the inescapable preconditions of their discourse (especially the principles of freedom and equality, as they are institutionally specified), as well as its consensual outcomes when they do not conflict with the afore-mentioned preconditions. Anyone who wants to claim the allegiance of others must invoke reasons acceptable to them. In other words, someone who reasonably disagrees with the reason invoked cannot be bound. So we ought to look for another point of convergence. Throughout, our method must remain Socratic. When someone says: 'I disagree', he trumps the reason invoked. His disagreement then leads to the inadmissibility of that reason.[50] It is worth quoting a characteristic passage from Rawls at this point:

45 Alexy, above n 3 at 226.
46 See Kant, above n 38 at 291.
47 *Ibid* at 292.
48 See, eg *Political Liberalism*, above n 6 at 179.
49 See Kant, above n 38 at 294.
50 Speaking rather technically, self-refutation goes against narrow reflective equilibrium, which satisfies certain conditions of rationality (see J Rawls, 'The Independence of Moral Theory' in S Freeman (ed), *Collected Papers* (Cambridge Mass, Harvard University Press, 1999) 289), given the principles, whereas reciprocity is a manifestation of wide reflective equilibrium, in which the principles themselves are desiderata. Cf N Daniels, *Justice and Justification: Reflective Equilibrium in Theory and Practice* (Cambridge, Cambridge University Press, 1996) 1.

> [J]ustification is addressed to others who disagree with us … To justify our political judgments to others is to convince them by public reason, that is, by ways of reasoning and inference appropriate to fundamental political questions, and by appealing to beliefs, grounds, and political values it is reasonable for others to acknowledge. Public justification proceeds from some consensus: from premises all parties in disagreement, assumed to be free and equal and fully capable of reason, may reasonably be expected to share and freely endorse.[51]

Foundationalist moral theories that predictably run into a performative contradiction are committed to a linear argumentation. Discourse ethics seeks discursive (and not just monological) coherence. It has rightly been pointed out that coherence is like 'a puzzle with identically shaped pieces, say, one-inch squares, which must be arranged into a meaningful, coherent picture'.[52] If we misplace one cubicle, this affects the correct arrangement of all the rest. Transferring the metaphor in the context of our discussion, we might say that no free and equal citizen may have his convictions violated, without this affecting the correctness of the collective decision reached. This means that all decisions reached through democratic processes are in principle correct, on condition that our theory of democracy is also correct. When this condition is met, ideal democratic processes have intrinsic value, in which case their violation, that is, not paying due respect to every free and equal citizen, renders the collective decision reached unacceptable without further ado, without recourse to any external criteria of correctness.

From the same point of view, majority rule must be upheld, precisely because it is intertwined with the categorical principle of autonomy as consensus. It has been remarked that otherwise discourse ethics would not be in position to deal with the normative question of disagreement.[53] Given disagreement, insistence on unanimity would unavoidably lead either to the exclusion of some interlocutors from discourse or to some arguments being privileged for reasons external to the discourse and in violation of the rules of discourse.

OUTLINE OF A DISCURSIVE JUSTIFICATION

This is the first step toward an outline of a discursive justification of fundamental principles of the law, from which individual, political and social rights follow. As far as the rest of the law is concerned, it can be

[51] J Rawls, *Justice as Fairness: A Restatement* (Cambridge Mass, Belknap Press of Harvard University Press, 2001) 27.

[52] KJ Kress, 'Coherence' in D Patterson (ed), *A Companion to Philosophy of Law and Legal Theory* (Oxford, Blackwell Publishers, 1996) 535.

[53] Cf G Postema, 'Public Practical Reason: Political Practice' in I Shapiro and J Wagner deCew (eds), *Theory and Practice* (New York, New York University Press, 1995) 372.

grounded, as the principle of autonomy as consensus demands, in contracts by moral agents already equipped with rights in the competitive legal world. Hence, law as contract acquires all the distinctive features of a contract in general. It presupposes individual and political freedom, equality of allowance and consideration, and ignores the motives that led contracting parties to will formation, since what matters is for their wills to coincide, regardless of any further aims and goals they might have (which are usually intended to serve their wellbeing).

We can thus infer that Apel, as opposed to the reluctant Habermas, rightly pinpoints the inherent link between the principle of discourse and the political morality of the constitutional state:

> The meaning of moral argument could almost be expressed in the by no means novel principle that all human *needs*—as potential claims—i.e. which can be reconciled with the needs of all the others by argumentation, must be made the concern of the communication community.... [T]his outlines the basic principles of an ethics of communication, a principle which also represents the hitherto non-existent foundation for an ethics of the democratic formation of the will through *agreement* ('convention'). The basic norm ... acquires its binding character not merely through *factual acknowledgment* of those who reach an agreement ('contract model'). Rather, it commits all people who have acquired 'communicative competence' through the process of socialization to strive for an agreement for the purposes of the collective formation of the will in every matter that affects the *interests* (the potential *claims*) of others. Moreover, it is this basic norm—and not, for instance, the *fact* that a given agreement has been reached—that guarantees to individual norm conforming agreements their binding moral character.[54]

Law may be a contract, but it is not exhausted by the content of the contract; of necessity it encompasses its evaluative conditions and normative presuppositions. The content of the law, qua content of a contract, cannot be just anything. This is so for moral reasons, by virtue of its foundation, and not by virtue of the self-commitment of certain free agents (here I use 'freedom' in the Hobbesian sense).

CONCLUSION

A merely procedural conception of the principle of discourse proves itself to be non-Kantian on the crucial point about the existence of an essential connection between law and morality (although it ought to be Kantian). Nonetheless, it may prove itself Kantian with regard to the right to

[54] 'The a priori of the communication community and the foundation of ethics: the problem of a rational foundation of ethics in the scientific age' in *Towards a Transformation of Philosophy* (P Vandevelde, G Adey and D Fisby (trans), London, Routledge and Kegan Paul, 1980) 277.

resistance (although on this point it had better not be Kantian). The only form of disobedience to the sovereign compatible with law's form, according to Kant, lies in the right to a soft criticism, since the sovereign may have the monopoly of force but not the monopoly of knowledge: to the extent that he expresses the general will, he must pursue his enlightenment, otherwise he contradicts himself *in actu*.[55]

By disengaging the law from a deontological principle of discourse, the correct substantive outcome of moral discourse is merely brought to the attention of the sovereign (whoever the sovereign may be, especially the people-electorate). Therefore, the sovereign may do wrong, without a question of legality being raised by his action. For such a question to be raised, there needs to be a conceptual connection between law and morality; in short, a community that is in fact governed by principles of justice. However, even in such a community, respect for certain democratic decision-making processes does not pre-empt monological conscientious objection or civil disobedience, precisely because there are some individual and political liberties that cannot be violated in a democracy, since democratic will formation presupposes them. But to say as much is to go into a different topic.

[55] See Kant, above n 38 at 302.

Part III

Constitutional Rights

7

Political Liberalism and the Structure of Rights: On the Place and Limits of the Proportionality Requirement

MATTIAS KUMM

INTRODUCTION

WHAT DO YOU have in virtue of having a right? Are rights 'trumps' over competing considerations of policy?[1] Do they have priority over 'the good' in some strong sense?[2] Are rights 'firewalls' providing strong protections against demands made by the political community?[3] Even though there are interesting and significant differences between conceptions of rights in the liberal tradition, they generally[4] share the idea that something protected as a matter of right may not be overridden by ordinary considerations of policy. Circumstantial all-things-considered judgements on what is in the general welfare are generally insufficient grounds to justify infringements of rights. Reasons justifying an infringement of rights have to be of a special strength.

Yet this claim of a special priority of rights sits uneasily with a prominent feature of constitutional and human rights adjudication. As comparative constitutional scholars have pointed out, a general feature of

[1] R Dworkin, 'What Rights do We Have?' in *Taking Rights Seriously* (Oxford University Press, 1978) 266. See also R Dworkin, 'Principle, Policy, Procedure' in *A Matter of Principle* (Oxford University Press, 1985) 72.

[2] J Rawls, *Political Liberalism* (Columbia University Press, 1993) 173–211.

[3] J Habermas, *Faktizität und Geltung* (Suhrkamp, 1992) 315.

[4] Exceptions include J Raz, *The Morality of Freedom* (Oxford University Press, 1986) and R Alexy, *A Theory of Constitutional Rights* (Oxford University Press, 2002).

rights analysis all over the world is some version of a proportionality test.[5] Though proportionality analysis does have a role to play in US constitutional practice as well,[6] it is a more prominent and more explicitly embraced feature of rights reasoning under constitutions or treaties established after the Second Word War.[7] Proportionality is widely used as a test by judiciaries to determine the limit of a constitutionally guaranteed right. An act of a public authority that infringes the scope of a protected right can still be justified, if it can be shown to pursue legitimate purposes in a proportional way. Only acts by public authorities that are disproportionate will be struck down on the grounds that they violate an individual's right. But does the proportionality test provide an adequate structure for assessing rights claims? Can it do justice to the basic liberal intuition that rights enjoy some kind of special priority over considerations of public policy, and that reasons overriding rights must be of some special, compelling strength?

This chapter will proceed in two parts. The first will provide a brief description and further illustration of an account of rights that puts proportionality analysis front and centre. The purpose of this part is to provide a better understanding of the proportionality test and its connection to rights. This part will draw on Robert Alexy's influential theory of constitutional rights. The second part will assess whether and to what extent such a conception of rights can adequately accommodate basic commitments of Political Liberalism. Within the tradition of Political Liberalism there are three basic ideas that are connected to the idea of the special priority of rights, which I will refer to as antiperfectionism, anticollectivism and anticonsequentialism, respectively. The implications of each of these ideas for an adequate structure of rights will then be assessed. As will become clear, reasoning about rights has a more complex structure than the focus on proportionality analysis suggests. The proportionality structure is rightly a central feature of rights reasoning, but it is merely one of three distinct structural elements central to reasoning about rights as a

[5] D Beatty, *The Ultimate Rule of Law* (Oxford University Press, 2004); N Emilou, *The Principle of Proportionality in European Law* (Dordrecht, Kluwer, 1996); W Sadurski, *Rights Before Courts* (Springer, 2005) 266.

[6] TA Alenikoff, 'Constitutional Law in the Age of Balancing' (1987) 96 *Yale LJ* 943 at 967.

[7] For the claim that US constitutional rights jurisprudence is exceptional in its suspicion of proportionality, see L Weinrib, 'The Postwar Paradigm and American Exceptionality' in S Choudhry (ed), *The Migration of Constitutional Ideas* (Cambridge University Press, 2006). Explanations are provided by F Schauer, 'Freedom of Expression Adjudication in Europe and the United States: A Case Study in Comparative Constitutional Architecture' in G Nolte (ed), *European and US Constitutionalism* (Cambridge University Press, 2005); V Jackson, 'Ambivalence, Resistance and Comparative Constitutionalism: Opening up the Conversation on "Proportionality" Rights and Federalism' (1999) 1 *U Pa J Const L* 583. See also M Kumm, 'Whats' So Special about Constitutional Rights in Private Litigation?' in Sajo (ed), *The Constitution in Private Relations* (2005).

matter of political morality. Other structural features of rights discourse include the idea of excluded reasons and the prohibitions of certain means-ends relationships. Furthermore, there are institutional considerations that sometimes justify imposing additional requirements on the justification for an infringement of a right, requiring reasons of special strength. There is no one structural element that is the defining feature of rights reasoning. Rights reasoning, as it occurs in the practice of courts and tribunals worldwide, reflects the structural richness of reasoning about political morality.[8] The language of rights in human and constitutional rights practice merely provides a way to structure the assessment of policy choices as they relate to affected individuals. What you have in virtue of having a right is as strong or as weak as the proposition of political morality that the claim is grounded in.[9] Analysing the structure of rights reasoning helps provide a clearer understanding of the structural complexity of a liberal political morality. Additionally, it helps guard against a narrow understanding of rights that unconvincingly ties the very idea of rights to a particular moral structure.

RIGHTS AS OPTIMISATION REQUIREMENTS: PROPORTIONALITY

Not all constitutional or human rights listed in legal documents require proportionality analysis or any other discussion of limitations. The catalogues of rights contained in domestic constitutions and international human rights documents include norms that have a simple categorical, rule-like structure. They may stipulate such things as: 'No quartering of troops in private homes in peacetime'. 'The death penalty is abolished.' 'Every citizen has the right to be heard by a judge within 48 hours after his arrest.' Most specific rules of this kind are best understood as authoritative determinations made by the constitutional legislator about how all the relevant first-order considerations of morality and policy play out in the circumstances defined by the rule. Notwithstanding interpretative issues arising at the margins, the judicial enforcement of such rules is generally not subject to proportionality analysis or any other meaningful engagement with moral considerations.

But at the heart of modern constitutional rights practice are rights provisions of a different kind. Modern constitutions establish abstract requirements such as a right to freedom of speech, association and religion.

[8] What you have in virtue of having a right can be legally further complicated by legal tests reflecting institutional considerations of various kinds. For an overview of these tests in the context of US constitutional law see R Fallon, *Implementing the Constitution* (Oxford University Press, 2001) 76–101.

[9] For a similar view see J Raz, *The Morality of Freedom* (Oxford University Press, 1986) 193–216.

These rights, it seems, cannot plausibly have the same structure as categorical, rule-like rights provisions. Clearly there must be limitations on such rights. There is no right to falsely shout fire in a crowded cinema or to organise a spontaneous mass demonstration in the middle of Times Square during rush hour. How should these limits be determined?

Constitutional texts provide some illumination as to how those limits ought to be conceived. As a matter of textual architecture[10] it is helpful to distinguish between three different approaches to the limits of rights.

The first textual approach is to say nothing at all about limits. In the United States, the First Amendment, for example, simply states that 'Congress shall make no laws ... abridging the freedom of speech ... [or] ... the free exercise of religion'.[11] Here the text suggests that all the interpretative work needs to be done when assessing what is to count as 'speech' under this provision. The absence of any kind of limitation clause seems to invite the argument that there are no limitations. Not surprisingly, it remains a unique and feature of US constitutional rights culture to insist on defining rights narrowly, so that there are as few exceptions as possible to them.[12] Arguments about rights are generally focused on the question whether the behaviour in question is protected as a right. Conversely, focus of rights discourse is generally not on whether there are good reasons under the circumstances, for restricting that right.

The second approach is characteristic of human rights treaties and constitutions enacted in the period following the Second World War. These generally adopt a bifurcated approach. The first part of a provision defines the scope of the right. The second describes the limits of the right by defining the conditions under which an infringement can be justified.

Article 10 of the European Convention on Human Rights, for example, states:

> 1. Everyone has the right to freedom of expression ...
>
> 2. The exercise of these freedoms ...may be subject to such formalities, conditions, restrictions or penalties as prescribed by law and are necessary in a democratic society, in the interest of national security, territorial integrity or public safety ... .

Similiarly, Article 2, para I of the German Basic Law states:

> Every person has the right to the free development of their personality, to the extent they do not infringe on the rights of others or offend against the constitutional order or the rights of public morals.

[10] This formulation derives from Schauer, above n 7.

[11] First Amendment of US Constitution.

[12] Schauer, above n 7. See also C Fried, *Right and Wrong* (Oxford University Press, 1978).

The first part defines the scope of the interests to be protected—here: all those interests that relate respectively to 'freedom of expression' or 'the free development of the personality'. The second part establishes the conditions under which infringements of these interests can be justified: 'restrictions ... necessary in a democratic society in the interests of ...' and 'when the limitation serves to protect the rights of others, the constitutional order or public morals'. The first step of constitutional analysis typically consists in determining whether an act infringes the scope of a right. If it does, a prima facie violation of a right has occurred. The second step consists in determining whether that infringement can be justified under the limitations clause. Only if it cannot is there a *definitive* violation of the right.

Even though the term proportionality is not generally used in constitutional limitation clauses immediately after the Second World War, over time courts have practically uniformly interpreted these kinds of limitation clauses as requiring proportionality analysis. Besides the requirement of legality—any limitations suffered by the individual must be prescribed by law—the proportionality requirement lies at the heart of determining whether an infringement of the scope of a right is justified.

The third approach, typical of more recent rights codifications, often recognises and embraces this development by substituting general default limitation clauses for rights-specific limitation clauses.[13] Article II-112 of the recently negotiated European Charter of Fundamental Rights, for example, states:

> Subject to the principle of proportionality, limitations may be made only if they are necessary and genuinely meet the objectives of general interest recognized by the Union or the need to protect the rights and freedoms of others.

A number of criticisms have been directed against an understanding of rights in which the real work in the deciding of concrete cases is done within the framework of proportionality analysis. Some have claimed that there are no rational standards available that allow for distinguishing between measures that are proportional from those that are not. Others have insisted that even if there are such standards, their specific content is likely to be subject to considerable disagreement, either abstractly or in application. To the extent that is the case, it is not clear why courts, rather

[13] The Canadian Charter prescribes in s 1 that rights may be subject to 'such reasonable limits prescribed by law as can demonstrably be justified in a free and democratic society'. Section 36 of the South African Constitution states that rights may be limited by a 'law of general application to the extent that the limitation is reasonable and justifiable in an open and democratic society based on human dignity, equality and freedom, taking into account all relevant factors, including: a. the nature of the right; b. the importance of the purpose of the limitation; c. the nature and extent of the limitation; d. the relation between the limitation and its purpose; and e. less restrictive means to achieve the purpose.

than politically accountable actors, should have a comparative institutional advantage in assessing the proportionality of publicly endorsed policies. Still others have lamented that rights guarantees subjected to proportionality limitations are insufficiently specific to provide either citizens or legislatures with much guidance.

While these questions are important, I will ignore them here and focus on a different concern. I address the question whether a structure of rights that puts proportionality analysis front and centre can adequately reflect the commitments central to Political Liberalism and the idea of a special priority for rights. Whatever additional function rights may have, human and constitutional rights as they are understood in post-Second World War legal documents are first and foremost an attempt to legally institutionalise basic moral prerogatives ultimately grounded in the enlightenment tradition of Political Liberalism and its commitment to human dignity and autonomy.[14] Can such an attempt succeed, if the rights that are legally guaranteed provide little more protection than the proportionality test provides?

This requires further examination of how proportionality is connected to the idea of rights and how it actually operates as a test to assess the limits of rights. The connection between rights and proportionality analysis has been subjected to a rigorous analysis by Robert Alexy. Alexy's theory of constitutional rights was developed as a reconstructive account of the practice of the German Constitutional Court, but has been widely recognised as a theory that helps to shed light on human and constitutional rights practice more generally.[15]

According to Alexy, the abstract rights characteristically listed in constitutional catalogues are principles. Principles, as Alexy understands them, are optimisation requirements. They require the realisation of something to the greatest extent possible, given countervailing concerns. As optimisation requirements, principles are structurally equivalent to values. Statements of value can be reformulated as statements of principle and vice versa. We can say that privacy is a value or that privacy is a principle. Saying that something is a value does not yet say anything about the relative priority of that value over another value, either abstractly or in a specific context.

[14] This link is established specifically in the UN Declaration of Human Rights, GA Res 217 (III 1948). Article 1 states the basic premises of the enlightenment liberal tradition: 'All human beings are born free and equal in dignity and rights. They are endowed with reason and conscience and should act towards one another in a spirit of brotherhood'. The Preamble of the European Convention on Human Rights in turn refers to the UN Declaration. The German Constitution in Art 1 para 1 provides: 'The dignity of human persons is inviolable. To respect and protect it is the duty of all state powers. 2: The German People therefore professes its allegiance to inviolable human rights as the basis of all human communities, peace and justice in the world'.

[15] See eg, AJ Menendez and E Eriksen (eds), *Fundamental Rights Through Discourse* (Arena report no 9, Oslo, 2004).

Statements of principle, express an 'ideal ought'. Like statements of value, they are not yet 'related to possibilities of the factual and normative world'.[16] Whenever there is a conflict between a principle and countervailing concerns, the proportionality test provides the criteria to determine which concerns take precedence under the circumstances. In order to assess what individual principles require in particular circumstances, a proportionality test needs to be applied.[17] The proportionality test provides an analytical structure for assessing whether limits imposed on the realisation of a principle in a particular context are justified.

Whereas the language of proportionality, necessity and balancing abounds in constitutional adjudication across jurisdictions, the specific structure of the proportionality test is not always clear.[18] According to Alexy, and indeed according to the German Constitutional Court, the proportionality test has four prongs. Two prongs—suitability and necessity—focus on empirical concerns. They express the requirement that principles be realised to the greatest possible extent relative to what is factually possible. The other two—legitimate ends and balancing—are normative and express the requirement that principles be realised to the greatest extent possible given countervailing normative concerns.

The link between constitutional rights as principles and proportionality thus conceived is *not* one of institutional convenience, but conceptual necessity. The fact that principles are optimisation requirements *means* that their application requires proportionality analysis. The proportionality test is not merely a convenient pragmatic tool that helps provide a doctrinal structure for the purpose of legal analysis. If rights are optimisation requirements, the proportionality structure provides an analytical framework to assess the necessary and sufficient conditions under which a right takes precedence over competing considerations as a matter of first-order political morality.

An example drawn from the European Court of Human Rights (ECtHR) illustrates how proportionality analysis operates in the adjudication of rights claims. In *Lustig-Prean and Beckett v United Kingdom*,[19] the applicants complained that the investigations into their sexual orientation and their discharge from the Royal Navy on the sole ground that they were gay violated Article 8 of the European Convention on Human Rights (ECHR). Article 8, in so far as is relevant, reads as follows:

[16] Alexy, above n 4 at 58.

[17] *Ibid* at 66. See also the discussion of structural discretion in *ibid* at 394–414.

[18] See J Rivers discussing the case law of the European Convention on Human Rights and in Canada in the 'Introduction' in *ibid* at xxxii. For the United States see Aleinikoff, 'Constitutional Law in the Age of Balancing' (1987) 96 *Yale LJ* 943.

[19] *Lustig-Prean and Beckett v United Kingdom* [1999] ECHR 71 (31417/96;32377/96, 27 September 1999).

> 1. Everyone has the right to respect for his private ... life ...
>
> 2. There shall be no interference by a public authority with the exercise of this right except such as is in accordance with the law and is necessary in a democratic society ... in the interest of national security, ... for the prevention of disorder.

Since the government had accepted that there had been interferences with the applicants' right to respect for their private life—a violation of a prima facie right had occurred—the only question was whether the interferences were justified or whether the interference amounted to a *definitive* violation of the right. Since the actions of the government were in compliance with domestic statutes and applicable European Community law, and thus fulfilled the requirement of having been 'in accordance with the law', the question was whether the law authorising the government's actions qualified as 'necessary in a democratic society'. The ECtHR had essentially interpreted that requirement as stipulating a proportionality test. The following is a reconstructed and summarised account of the court's reasoning.

The first question the ECtHR addressed concerns the existence of a *legitimate aim*. This prong is relatively easy to satisfy in cases where the constitutional provision does not specifically restrict the kind of aims that count as legitimate for justifying an interference with a specific right. In this case the constitutional provision limits the kind of aims that count as legitimate for the purpose of justifying an infringement of privacy. Here, the United Kingdom offered the maintenance of morale, fighting power and operational effectiveness of the armed forces, a purpose clearly related to national security, as its justification to prohibit homosexuals from serving in its armed forces.

The next question then was whether disallowing homosexuals from serving in the armed forces is a *suitable means to further the legitimate policy goal*. This is an empirical question. A means is suitable if it actually furthers the declared policy goal of the government. In this case a government commissioned study had shown that integration problems would be posed to the military system if open homosexuals were to serve in the army. Even though the ECtHR remained sceptical with regard to the severity of these problems, it accepted that there would be *some* integration problems if homosexuals were allowed to serve in the armed forces. Given this state of affairs there was no question that, as an empirical matter, these problems could be significantly mitigated, if not completely eliminated, by excluding homosexuals from the ranks of the armed forces.

A more difficult question was whether the prohibition of homosexuals serving in the armed forces is necessary. A measure is necessary only if there is no less restrictive but equally effective measure available to achieve the intended policy goal. This test is reflected in the requirement known to

US constitutional lawyers that a measure be narrowly tailored towards achieving substantial policy goals. In this case the issue was whether a code of conduct backed by disciplinary measures—clearly a less intrusive measure—could be regarded as equally effective. Ultimately, the court held that even though a code of conduct backed by disciplinary measures would go quite some way to address problems of integration, the government had plausible reasons to believe that it would not go so far as to qualify as an *equally* effective alternative to the blanket prohibition.

Finally, the ECtHR had to assess whether the measure was proportional in the narrow sense by applying the so-called balancing test, which involves applying what Alexy calls the 'law of balancing': 'The greater the degree of non-satisfaction of, or detriment to, one principle, the greater must be the importance of satisfying the other'.[20]

The decisive question in this case was whether on balance the increase in the morale, fighting force and operational effectiveness achieved by prohibiting homosexuals from serving in the armed forces justified the degree of interference in the applicant's privacy, or whether it was instead disproportionate. On the one hand, the court invoked the seriousness of the infringement of the soldiers' privacy, given that sexual orientation concerns the most intimate aspect of the individual's private life. On the other hand, the degree of disruption to the armed forces absent such policies was predicted to be relatively minor. The court pointed to the experiences in other European armies that had recently opened their armed forces to homosexuals, the successful co-operation of the UK army with allied NATO units which included homosexuals, the availability of codes of conduct and disciplinary measures to prevent inappropriate conduct, as well as the experience of successfully admitting women and racial minorities into the armed forces, which had caused only modest disruptions. On balance, the UK measures were held to be sufficiently disproportionate to fall outside the government's margin of appreciation and the court held the United Kingdom to have violated Article 8 of the ECHR.

This example illustrates two characteristic features of rights reasoning: first, a rights-holder does not have very much in virtue of having a right. More specifically, the fact that a rights-holder has a prima facie right does not imply that he holds a position that gives him any kind of priority over countervailing considerations of policy. An infringement of the scope of a right merely serves as a trigger to initiate an assessment of whether the infringement is justified. But the fact that rights are not trumps in this sense does not mean that they provide no effective protection. The example

[20] Alexy, above n 4 at 102. Alexy illustrates the 'law of balancing' using indifference curves, a device used by economists as a means of representing a relation of substitution between interests. Such a device is useful to illustrate the analogy between the law of balancing and the law of diminishing marginal utility.

demonstrates that, in practice, even without such priority, rights can be formidable weapons. The second characteristic feature of rights reasoning is the flipside of the first. Since comparatively little is decided by acknowledging that a measure infringes a right, the focus of rights adjudication is generally on the reasons that justify the infringement. Furthermore, the four-prong structure of proportionality analysis provides little more than a structure which functions as a checklist for the individually necessary and collectively sufficient conditions that determine whether the reasons that can be marshalled to justify an infringement of a right are good reasons under the circumstances. Assessing the justification for rights infringements is, at least in the many cases where the constitution provides no specific further guidance, largely an exercise of general practical reasoning, without many of the constraining features that otherwise characterise legal reasoning. Rights reasoning under this model, then, shares important structural features with rational policy assessment.[21]

Conceiving rights in this way also helps explain another widespread feature of contemporary human and constitutional rights practice that can only be briefly pointed to here. If all you have in virtue of having a right is a position whose strength in any particular context is determined by proportionality analysis, there are no obvious reasons for narrowly defining the scope of interests protected as a right. Shouldn't all acts by public authorities affecting individuals meet the proportionality requirement? Does the proportionality test not provide a general purpose test for ensuring that public institutions take seriously individuals and their interests and act only for good reasons? Not surprisingly, one of the corollary features of a proportionality-oriented human and constitutional rights practice is its remarkable scope. Interests protected as rights are not restricted to the classical catalogue of rights such as freedom of speech, association, religion and privacy, narrowly conceived. Instead, with the spread of proportionality analysis, there is a tendency to include all kinds of liberty interests within the domain of interests that enjoy prima facie protection as a right. The European Court of Justice, for example, recognises a right freely to pursue a profession as part of the common constitutional heritage of Member States of the European Union, thus enabling it to subject a considerable amount of social and economic

[21] That does not mean that the two are identical. There are at least four differences between substantive rights analysis and general policy assessments. First, courts are not faced with generating and evaluating competing policy proposals, but merely assessing whether the choices made by other institutional actors is justified. Secondly, they only assess the merit of these policy decisions in so far they affect the scope of a right. Thirdly, specific constitutional rules concerning limits to constitutional rights or judicial precedence establishing rules that fix conditional relations of preference frequently exist. Fourthly, proportionality analysis leaves space for deference to be accorded to other institutional actors. The ECtHR refers to this as the 'margin of appreciation'.

regulation to proportionality review. The ECtHR has adopted an expansive understanding of privacy guaranteed under Article 8 ECHR, and the German Constitutional Court regards any liberty interest whatsoever as enjoying prima facie protection as a right. In Germany, the right to the 'free development of the personality' is interpreted as a general right to liberty understood as the right to do or not do whatever you please. It has been held by the Constitutional Court to include such mundane things as a right to ride horses through public woods,[22] feed pigeons in public squares,[23] smoke marihuana[24] and bring a particular breed of dogs into the country.[25] In this way the language of human and constitutional rights is used to subject practically all acts of public authorities that affect the interests of individuals to proportionality review.

POLITICAL LIBERALISM AND THE STRUCTURE OF RIGHTS

But does such a weak conception of rights do justice to the commitment of Political Liberalism? Does a liberal political morality, appropriately conceived, exhibit an optimisation structure of the sort that the linkage between principles and proportionality analysis suggests? Here there seems to be cause for serious doubt. Liberal political rights are widely perceived as having special weight when competing with policy goals. The idea is expressed, for example, by Ronald Dworkin's conception of rights as trumps and the corollary distinction between principles and policies,[26] or by what Rawls calls the 'priority of the right over the good',[27] or by Habermas' description of rights as firewalls.[28] Ultimately these ideas can be traced back to a theory, perhaps most fully developed by Immanuel

[22] BVerfGE 80,137. (BVerfGE refers to the official collection of the judgments of the Federal Constitutional Court. The first number refers to the volume, the second refers to the page number on which the decision begins. A bracketed third number refers to the exact page on which a particular citation can be found. Particularly well-known cases are conventionally named either after the complainant or the core subject matter addressed by the decision.)

[23] BVerfGE 59, 158.

[24] BVerfGE 90, 145.

[25] BVerfGE 110, 149, holding that when the legislator has reasonable grounds to assume that certain breeds of dogs pose a particular danger to people, a prohibition of the breeding and importation of certain breeds of dogs does not constitute a disproportional infringement of a general right to liberty, equality or the right to freely pursue your business of breeding and importation. The FCC insisted, however, that the legislator was under a duty to keep up with scientific findings relating to the issue. This concerns scientific insights relating to the extent to which the aggression of dogs is genetically determined or a feature of the conditions under which the dog is held, as well as studies relating to the relative aggression of various species of dogs that may undermine the inclusion or exclusion of a particular breed of dog on the list of prohibited breeds.

[26] R Dworkin, *Taking Rights Seriously* (Oxford University Press, 1977) and *A Matter of Principle* (Oxford University Press, 1985).

[27] J Rawls, *Political Liberalism* (Colarado University Press, 1993) 173.

[28] J Habermas, *Between Facts and Norms* (Oxford University Press, 1996) 254.

Kant, grounded in the twin ideals of human dignity and autonomy viewed as side-constraints on the pursuit of the collective good. Yet nothing in the account of rights as principles prioritises rights. Rights and policies compete on the same plane within the context of proportionality analysis.[29] The question is whether a conception of constitutional rights that does not capture the priority of rights is deficient in some way.

To address this issue, I distinguish three distinct ideas underlying the 'priority of rights' thesis. The first concerns the relationship between justice and perfectionist ideals. Here the basic liberal idea is that rights protect individuals from strong paternalist impositions relating to how they should live their lives, in particular with regard to dominant religious practices. Questions relating to what it means to aspire to be the best person you can—to instantiate an example of human perfection—is not the proper subject matter of political decision-making and legal coercion. This expresses well the idea of the priority of the right over the good. The second idea concerns taking the individual seriously, and is anticollectivistic. Here, the basic idea is that ind ividual rights are believed to enjoy priority over the 'general interest' or the 'collective good' in some way. The third idea concerns the anticonsequentialist or deontological nature of rights as side-constraints. Here the claim is that cost-benefit analysis along the lines suggested by 'balancing' is unable to take into account strong prohibitions on using persons as a means to achieve some desirable end. Using people as a means—sacrificing them for some greater good—is subject to significantly stronger constraints. Each of these ideas is internally complex and subject to considerable dispute. My purpose here is not primarily to uncover their complexity, or engage in these disputes. Even though it will be impossible to avoid contentious territory, my core purpose here is to focus on the implications of each of these ideas for the structure of rights.

Antiperfectionism and 'Rights as Trumps': Excluded Reasons

An integral part of most liberal conceptions of political justice is some form of a prohibition on imposing upon the individual a particular conception of the good life through the coercive means of the law. It is not within the jurisdiction of public authorities to prescribe what the ultimate orientations and commitments of an individual should be. In the tradition of Political Liberalism this idea finds its expression, for example, in Article 4 of the Declaration of Human and Citizens' Rights of 1789, which

[29] In the United States, Richard Fallon in 'Individual Rights and the Powers of Government' (1993) 27 *Ga L Rev* 343 has argued that rights and consequential interests are part of the same decisional calculus.

prescribes: 'Liberty consists in doing whatever does not harm another: In this way the exercise of natural rights of each person has no limits except for those limitations, that assure the exercise of the same rights by other members of society'. In a similar vain Kant writes: 'Freedom ... in so far as it can coexist with the freedom of any other member of society under a general law is a right that every individual has'.[30] John Stuart Mill's 'harm' principle expresses a similar idea. These formulations all insist that the class of reasons that can legitimately be used to limit individual liberty are limited. They are more limited than the class of reasons that are of interest to someone trying to seek orientation and meaning in her life. One way to interpret this idea is to insist that reasons relating to the realisation of demanding perfectionist ideals of any kind, may not be used to justify infringements of individual liberty. Such reasons are off limits for the purpose of justifying limitations of individual liberty.

To illustrate the point, imagine a public authority prescribing that the school day in public schools should begin with a common prayer, such as the Apostolic Profession of Faith. Legislative history and public debates reveal that there are three kinds of reasons invoked in support of this legislation. For some, the purpose of the legislation is to further a general commitment to a Christian way of life and help craft souls in the community that are worthy of salvation. Others invoke the importance of religion for themselves and their children and stress the importance of connecting something as basic an experience as public school education with their religious life in order to sustain and nourish it. Still others make claims about the instrumental usefulness of religion for general policy purposes, and point to the connection between religion in schools and low crime rates, low teenage pregnancy rates, and lower drop-out rates. The law passes after vigorous debate and protest by the minority of agnostics, atheists, Jews and Muslims.

How would a constitutional court called upon to assess whether an individual's right to religious freedom was violated rule? There is no doubt that the right to religious freedom is infringed by such a prayer requirement. The question is whether it can be justified. It is unlikely that a court in a liberal constitutional democracy would address the theological and philosophical questions relating to whether compulsory school prayers of this kind are in fact suitable and necessary to help craft souls worthy of salvation. Nor would courts assess, whether, all things considered, the purpose of crafting souls worthy of salvation justified the significant infringement of an individual's freedom of religion. Instead, there is little doubt that any court in a liberal constitutional democracy would insist that any reasons that depend on the premise that a Christian way of life is the

[30] I Kant, *Metaphysics of Morals* (Cambridge, Cambridge University Press, 1996) 63.

right way of life are simply irrelevant to the issue. Furthering a Christian way of life—or, for that matter, furthering any other perfectionist commitment—would not count as a legitimate government purpose. In US constitutional practice the idea that the purpose of a government action has to be secular[31] captures much of the non-perfectionist commitment of Political Liberalism, though the idea of 'secular purposes' would have to be interpreted to also exclude secular perfectionist ideals.

But, of course, there are other potentially legitimate purposes in play. One possible justification for school prayer could be that the equal right to freely exercise religion requires respect for the majority's parental interests in having their children connect their educational experience with their religious commitments in order to sustain and nourish it. Here, the central question would be whether such an exercise of religious liberty by the majority imposes a disproportionate burden on those parents and children who do not share that belief. Framed in this way, the issue becomes one of delimitating respective spheres of liberty between equal right-bearers. Public authorities have to be neutral in the sense that they are required to respect and take equal account of the competing interests in play and strike an appropriate balance between them. Here, the proportionality framework and the idea of balancing in particular clearly provides a helpful structure for assessing the competing claims.

What this means for the resolution of the issue would, of course, depend on the particular features of the social world to which it applies. To the extent that no opt-outs are provided for those who do not share a belief, it is difficult to imagine a context in which compulsory common prayer would not impose a disproportionate burden on the minority. The issue becomes more complex once real opt-outs are provided and a general background culture of tolerance and inclusion minimises the pressure on the non-believing minority to conform. Furthermore, arguments within the balancing exercise relating to beneficial secondary effects would also come into play. On one side, these could include, for example, lower drop-out and teen pregnancy rates, if duly supported by empirical evidence. On the other side of the equation, general policy concerns about keeping life in public institutions free from religious entanglement may have significant weight in a strongly pluralistic and deeply divided society.[32] Clearly, then, much of how this issue would be resolved would depend on contingent features of the social world, which would have to be assessed within the proportionality framework.[33] But even within proportionality analysis, the

[31] This is the first prong of the so-called '*Lemon* test', see *Lemon v Kurtzbach*, 403 U.S. 602, 612–13 (1971).

[32] In the United States this requirement is the third prong of the *Lemon* test, see *ibid*.

[33] It follows that even such basic questions as whether a constitution should erect a wall between religion and the state or whether it should allow for the establishment of an official

truth or falsity of religious beliefs and the desirability of a life that derives an ultimate purpose and meaning from religious revelation would not provide reasons that are part of the balancing equation.

Reasons related to the furtherance of specific perfectionist ideals, then, are excluded both at the first prong of the proportionality test, since they are not a legitimate purpose that can justify infringements of individual liberty, and at the level of balancing, since furthering a particular perfectionist ideal is not a reason to weigh when assessing the proportionality of a measure furthering some other legitimate purpose. To the extent that Political Liberalism is understood as incorporating an antiperfectionist commitment, the idea of excluded reasons can help operationalise such a commitment within the context of the proportionality test.

The idea of excluded reasons as a structural feature of human and constitutional rights analysis has a central role to play in human and constitutional rights analysis beyond the operationalisation of antiperfectionist commitments.[34] The idea of excluded reasons is, for example, also central to the right of freedom of speech and freedom of association. Generally, a law may not prohibit demonstrations or speech in favour of a wrongheaded cause defended by bad arguments. Reasons that discriminate between views on the basis of plausibility or correctness, are excluded as reasons that are capable of limiting the freedom of speech or association. The justification for infringements of speech has to be neutral with regard to the question whether the speakers claims are true or false. Proponents of a flat tax may be deeply mistaken that their reform proposals would further justice. The right view may well be that relatively aggressive progressive taxation is a considerably more just way to raise revenue, all other things being equal. Yet whether or not the views of flat tax proponents are right or wrong is completely irrelevant to the question of whether or not they should be able to articulate and defend them. Freedom of speech is not balanced against the harm done by proposing false ideas.

Whether or not there are limits to the idea of content neutrality is subject to disagreement both within and across liberal constitutional democracies. Proponents of militant democracy,[35] for example, defend the idea that

church is not a question that principles of Political Liberalism provide an a priori answer to. Instead, an answer to that question depends on contingent features of the political community to which the constitutional rules are to apply. This explains why in the United States, the Establishment Clause has long been interpreted to erect a wall between churches and the state, whereas in Scandinavian countries there are established state churches, notwithstanding the guarantee to freedom of religion.

[34] For the relevance of the idea of excluded reasons in US constitutional law see R Pildes, 'Avoiding Balancing: The Role of Exclusionary Reasons in Constitutional Law' (1993/94) 45 *Hastings L J*. See also R Pildes, 'The Structural Conception of Rights and Judicial Balancing' (2002) 6 *Review of Constitutional Studies,* 179.

[35] For a discussion of militant democracy in a variety of institutional contexts, see A Sajo (ed), *Militant Democracy* (Eleven, 2004).

content neutrality has its limits when speech questions the very foundations of liberal constitutional democracy. Fascists, communists, theocrats, advocates of presidential dictatorship, those advocating terrorism as a means of political change, may have their speech limited in some liberal constitutional democracies. Clearly, then, the domain over which a class of reasons should be excluded is to some extent a matter of constitutional debate. The resolution of the question of whether and where these limits should be drawn depends on a host of complex empirical and moral assessments.[36] But just as clearly, the idea of content neutrality, and therefore the idea of excluded reasons, must have some purchase in the context of a right to freedom of speech and association.

Furthermore, even in the case of homosexuals in the military, as discussed by the ECtHR, the idea of excluded reasons can plausibly help throw light on what many would claim is the central feature of that decision. The fact that the court analysed in some depth whether the prohibition of homosexuals in the military was justified by reference to the legitimate purpose of furthering morale, fighting power and operational effectiveness of the armed forces should not cover up the fact that justifications more directly linked to homophobic sentiments in the army were *not* considered as reasons justifying the prohibition. The reasoning of the court clearly suggests, for example, that arguments relating to homophobic traditions (we have a long tradition of not tolerating deviant sexual orientation in the military!), conventions (this is the way we do things here!) or preferences (our soldiers generally dislike homos!) are irrelevant to the justification of excluding homosexuals from the military.[37] They are, therefore, not discussed. Furthermore, it is not unlikely that exactly because the problems relating to 'operational effectiveness' etc were the side-effects of illiberal homophobic sentiments, that the Strasbourg court felt emboldened enough to claim that a question pertaining to the make-up of the national military, which involved complex empirical assessments, did not fall under a state's margin of appreciation. Any justification relating to consequences of the existence of illiberal homophobic sentiments, the court could have said, should presumptively not affect the rights of homosexuals and will receive extensive scrutiny. The idea of excluded reasons, then, helps throw light on some core structural features of liberal constitutional practice, features that the focus on proportionality alone tend to obscure.

But acknowledging that the idea of excluded reasons is central to an understanding of rights in liberal constitutional democracies does not mean

[36] An interesting second order question is whether the proportionality framework provides an adequate structure for discussing the domain over which a class of reasons ought to be excluded.

[37] For a similar point relating to 'other-regarding' interests more generally, see R Dworkin, 'Liberty and Liberalism' in *Taking Rights Seriously*, above n 26 at 263.

the idea of excluded reasons can serve as a *substitute* for the idea of proportionality. Instead, proportionality and excluded reasons are complementary structural features of rights in liberal constitutional democracies. To illustrate the point: it is possible to understand the claim that rights are trumps as a claim that the idea of excluded reasons, rather than proportionality, is the defining feature of rights. Under such an approach, the scope of a right is defined by the reasons it excludes. The right to freedom of speech could be conceived as the absolute right not to be constrained in one's speech on grounds relating to the content of the speech act. The right to privacy is an absolute right not to be subjected to limitations justified by reference to other-regarding preferences. The free exercise of religion is an absolute right not to be subjected to measures that have the purpose of furthering a particular religion. Rights conceived in this way leave no space for proportionality analysis.[38]

However, such a conception of rights would suffer from serious deficiencies. Those deficiencies are all related to the fact that rights conceived in this way would not protect against a core concern that rights are generally believed to protect against. Human and constitutional rights not only protect against public authorities acting on reasons that are inappropriate. At the very least, they also protect against measures that are enacted for relevant reasons, when those reasons are massively disproportionate in relationship to the seriousness of an infringement of individual liberty. To illustrate the point: A is sentenced to several years of prison without parole for having run a traffic light. Assume that there was no traffic and no one was endangered. The reason for prosecuting and sentencing A are related to general and individual deterrence. A, as well as potential other offenders, should know that running a traffic light may have serious consequences. Ultimately, the criminalisation of such traffic offences has the purpose to increase road safety. Clearly the government is acting for relevant reasons, when it decides to sanction traffic offenders by locking them away for a number of years. Yet it is equally clear that the nature of the infringement of a violator's liberty does not stand in a reasonable relationship to the relative increase of road safety achieved by the imposition of such draconian sanctions. A conception of constitutional and human rights that does not also protect citizens against these kinds of manifestly disproportional measures is deficient.

It is not surprising therefore, that in practice proportionality analysis complements the idea of excluded reasons. In US constitutional practice, for example, it may be true that the idea of content neutrality has a central

[38] There are some suggestions in the writing of R Dworkin of such an approach. See eg, R Dworkin, 'Is There a Right to Pornography' in *A Matter of Principle*, above n 26 at 335 and 'Freedom of Speech' in *Freedom's Laws* (1996). See also R Dworkin, 'What Rights Do We Have?' in *Taking Rights Seriously*, above n 26 at 271.

role to play in the area of free speech. But even when the government acts for reasons that are neutral, for example by establishing time, place and manner restrictions to ensure public order, these restrictions have to meet a version of the proportionality requirement.[39] Furthermore, in important areas of the law, such as the Eighth Amendment's prohibition of cruel and unusual punishment, the Sixth Amendment's prohibition of unreasonable searches and seizures, the Supreme Court's analysis is strongly informed by proportionality-related considerations, rather than the idea of excluded reasons. The idea of excluded reasons complements, but does not replace, proportionality as central to the understanding of constitutional and human rights.

Anticollectivism and 'Rights as Shields': Reasons of a Special Strength

A second way rights are believed to enjoy priority is in relationship to collective goods or 'the general interest'. Here the priority is clearly not of a categorical nature. If a collective good (public safety) is invoked as a justification for an infringement of a liberty interest (the over-the-counter sale and purchase of land-to-air missiles is prohibited), it is clear that under any plausible account of rights the liberty interest will have to yield at some point. Here the priority of rights can only mean that individual rights should not be treated lightly, but be given the weight they deserve as a general conception of political justice grounded in the basic ideas of dignity and autonomy. This is an understanding of the priority of rights that proportionality analysis can easily incorporate. The application of the 'balancing' test is guided by the idea that the greater the degree of infringement, the greater the importance of the reasons supporting the infringement must be. Such a test provides a formal structure for the reasoned assessment of the competing concerns at stake. Whether or not a particular infringement is serious, requires an understanding of what it is about the particular interest at stake that matters morally, and what is lost when it is infringed. The same is true for assessing the importance of reasons that support a contested measure. The metaphor of 'balancing' should not obscure the fact that the last prong of the proportionality test will in many cases require the decision-maker to engage in theoretically informed practical reasoning, and not just in intuition-based classificatory labelling. At the level of evaluating the relative importance of the general interest in relation to the liberty interest at stake, the weights can be assigned and priorities established as required by the correct substantive

[39] In *United States v O'Brien*, 391 U.S. 367 (1968), the United States first established the canonical formula that such restrictions 'must further an important or substantial government interest and must be no greater than is essential for the furtherance of that interest'.

theory of justice. The last prong of the proportionality test then provides a space for the reasoned incorporation of an understanding of liberties that expresses whatever priority over collective goods is substantively justified. The fact that proportionality analysis does not prioritise individual rights over collective goods on the structural level, then, does not mean that such a priority cannot be given adequate expression within that structure.

Furthermore, it is not clear what a more attractive competing structural account—one which better captures the priority of individual rights over collective interests—would look like. There is a competing structural account of rights according to which what you have in virtue of having a right is less than a trump, but more than what is required by the proportionality test. According to this intermediate conception of rights, only reasons that have a special kind of force are sufficient to override the position protected by the right.[40] To illustrate the point, and provide some context, compare the following provisions of the German and US constitutions respectively.

Article 2, para 1 of the Basic Law states:

> Every person has the right to the free development of their personality, to the extent that they do not infringe on the rights of others or offend against the constitutional order or public morals.

The Fifth and Fourteenth Amendments of the US Constitution state:

> No person ... shall be deprived of liberty ... without due process of law.

When confronted with texts of this kind two questions present themselves. The first focuses on the scope of the right. How narrowly should it be conceived? What is meant by the free development of personality? What is meant by liberty? The second focuses on the broad or narrow understanding of the constitutional limitations of such a right. The texts mention 'the rights of others, offences against the constitutional order or public morals' and 'due process of law' respectively. What does this mean for the purposes of articulating a judicially administrable test for acts by public authorities subject to constitutional litigation?

There are two kinds of answers that courts have given to these questions. The first has been to interpret broadly both the scope of rights and the scope of limitations permitted on that right. The German Federal Constitutional Court (FCC), for example, was quick to dismiss narrow conceptions of the 'free development of personality' that limited the scope of the right to 'expressions of true human nature as understood in western

[40] See F Schauer, 'A Comment on the Structure of Rights' (1993) 27 *Georgia Law Review* 415. See also F. Schauer, 'Rights as Rules' (1987) 5 *Law and Philosophy* 115 and F Schauer, 'Exceptions' (1991) 58 *University of Chicago Law Review*.

culture', as had been suggested by influential commentaries.[41] Instead, the FCC opted for an interpretation under which the right guaranteeing the free development of the personality should be read as guaranteeing general freedom of action understood as the right to do or not do as one pleases.[42] This means that the scope of a general right to liberty encompasses such mundane things as the prima facie right to ride horses in public woods[43] and feed pigeons in public squares.[44] If public authorities prohibit such actions they would infringe the general right to liberty. As a corollary to the wide scope of the right, the FCC has opted for a broad interpretation of the limits of the right. Any infringement of the right is justified if it follows appropriate legal procedures and is not disproportionate. The three requirements stipulated by Article 2, para 1 (rights of others, constitutional order, public morals) in the jurisprudence of the FCC translate into the requirements of legality and proportionality. Here again it is important to point out that even though the substantive limit of proportionality is broad, it does have bite. It is not adequately compared to the analysis—or as many would claim, lack of it—that generally characterises the application of the 'rational basis' test in cases involving non-fundamental liberty interests.[45]

Another approach is to define narrowly both the scope and the permissible limitations of the rights. This has been the approach of the US Supreme Court, which insists that only particularly qualified liberty interests—liberty interests that are deemed to be sufficiently fundamental—enjoy meaningful protection under the Due Process Clause. When an interest is deemed to be sufficiently fundamental, the limitations that apply are narrow too. They are narrow in the sense that the requirements that must be fulfilled to infringe a protected interest are demanding. Only 'compelling interests' are sufficient to justify infringements of the right.

It is not obvious how to understand the 'compelling interest' test. On one interpretation, the test translates into nothing more than a proportionality requirement. Given the initial determination of the importance of the interests at stake—it must be 'fundamental' to qualify as a right—the 'compelling interest' requirement can be understood as merely pointing to the fact that the only reasons that are proportional under the circumstances are reasons so weighty to be appropriately classified as 'compelling'. The conception of rights as shields would amount to little more than

[41] For further references see Alexy, above n 4 at 224 n 5.

[42] BVerfGE 6, 32 (Elfes).

[43] BVerfGE 39, 1, BVerfGE 88, 203.

[44] BVerfGE 54, 143 (147).

[45] See L Tribe, *American Constitutional Law*, vol 1, 3rd edn (Foundation Press, 2000) 1362.

the application of a conception of weak proportionality-limited rights to interests deemed sufficiently fundamental.[46]

A different interpretation of the 'compelling interest' test is structurally more interesting, but problematic from the point of view of substantive political justice. The test could suggest that a right really does provide protection against infringement beyond what proportionality requires. Under this interpretation, the 'compelling interest' test loads the dice in favour of the protected right and raises the bar for justifying infringements when compared to the requirements of proportionality. A measure may be proportional, but not meet the 'compelling interest' test. Rights could be thought of as exhibiting a rule-like structure. They would only be overridden and inapplicable in cases where it is immediately apparent that countervailing concerns have significantly greater importance than the protected interest. Such a conception would clearly be distinct from rights as principles. It is this conception that, following Fred Schauer, I will refer to as 'rights as shields'.[47]

The question is whether such a structure for determining the limits of rights is morally attractive. If proportionality analysis taken seriously means that all relevant considerations must be taken into account and attributed the weight they deserve, then what could justify protecting an interest beyond what proportionality requires? If constitutional rights overprotect certain interests relative to what political justice requires, then there can be no justification for such a conception of rights on the level of political justice. As a matter of political morality, then, neither a conception of 'rights as trumps' or a conception of 'rights as shields' provide a more attractive account of the structure of a right than 'rights as principles'.

But there is still a way to make sense of the 'rights as shields' conception. Even if 'rights as shields' is not a plausible conception of rights for the purposes of a first-order account of moral rights, it could still be the best account of judicially enforced legal rights. It is by no means obvious that the best structural understanding of legal rights simply mirrors the structure of rights as requirements of political morality. Institutional considerations may suggest that requirements of political morality are likely to be realised to a greater extent, all things considered, if constitutional rights are conceived as exhibiting a rule-like structure as described by a conception of rights as shields.[48] Just as the archer aims at a point above the target, it may well be the case that a court ought to design doctrines so as

[46] This seems to be Fallons understanding of the test, above n 8.

[47] See Schauer, 'A Comment on the Structure of Rights', 'Rights as Rules' and 'Exceptions', above n 40.

[48] See Schauer, 'A Comment on the Structure of Rights', above n 40.

to overenforce some rights (and perhaps underenforce others). Constitutional texts and doctrinal structures are not merely embodiments of what constitutional legislators or courts deem political morality to require. To some extent they also reflect institutional considerations relating, for example, to biases of courts and other institutions or the guidance function of courts.

Some version of a 'compelling interest' test may, for example, helpfully complement the idea of excluded reasons in some instances: there is a temptation to undermine the idea of excluded reasons by exaggerating secondary effects of practices enjoying prima facie strong protection. The case involving homosexuals in the military may again help illustrate the point: even though homophobic traditions, conventions and preferences are excluded as valid reasons justifying disadvantaging homosexuals, secondary effects relating to operational effectiveness emerge as reasons that, at least prima facie, provide respectable support for the legal entrenchment of antihomosexual measures. In the real world it is often the case that reasons relating to secondary effects of protected activities serve as an intellectually respectable cover for attitudes that in fact deny the rights-holder his rightful position. That does not mean that reasons relating to secondary effects should not be regarded as relevant. They obviously are relevant. But in order for them to succeed, the requirement that they be of a special strength could serve to focus the attention of the court on whether these empirical claims are in fact true. The requirement for these reasons to be of a special strength helps counteract the epistemic biases in favour of finding such effects with regard to suspect activities of unpopular groups.

Furthermore, in many situations any real secondary effects produced by such protected activities are likely to be temporary and tend to decrease, or even disappear altogether, once the wider public has become accustomed to them. As the ECtHR rightly pointed out, any disruption relating to the integration into the military of traditionally excluded persons based on race, ethnic identity or gender has tended to decrease over time. Similarly, an open engagement with even the most atrocious political ideology over time may well function to lessen, rather than increase, its attractiveness. If these kinds of dynamics over time are characteristic of secondary effects, and if it is true that courts have the tendency to underestimate such dynamics, this would provide another reason for insisting on a 'compelling interest' test rather than proportionality analysis. Raising the bar by requiring reasons related to secondary effects to be 'compelling', rather than just proportional, may well be a helpful doctrinal tool to institutionally ensure that rights are adequately protected.

The idea of 'rights as shields', then, points to a structure of rights reasoning—the requirements of reasons of a special strength—that may well deserve its place as part of a structurally complex institutional practice of rights adjudication. But to the extent that such a structure is appropriate in some contexts, it is appropriate not because it reflects first-order requirements of political morality, but because it reflects second-order concerns relating to institutional design.

Anticonsequentialism and Rights as Deontological Constraints: on the Relevance of Means-Ends Relationships

A further reason why the proportionality structure is inadequate is that it imposes a structure on rights reasoning that is consequentialist. As a consequentialist structure, it is unable to reflect the deontological nature of at least some rights. There is considerable disagreement over the nature of deontological constraints. But the basic idea is that there are restrictions connected to the idea of the inviolability of persons that impose constraints on actors seeking to bring about desirable consequences. Saving three lives does not necessarily justify sacrificing one, and significant gains for many cannot necessarily be justified by losses imposed on the few. At least one of the functions of human and constitutional rights is to reflect these deontological constraints. Yet the proportionality structure is unable to do so.

In order to gain a better understanding of the relationship between proportionality analysis and deontological constraints, the trolley problem may provide a helpful, if not particularly original,[49] point of entry. Consider the following two scenarios:

1. A runaway trolley will kill five people if a bystander does not divert it onto another track, where, he foresees, it will kill one person.

2. A runaway trolley will kill five people if a bystander does not push a fat man standing close by on to the track to stop the trolley. The fat man will foreseeably die in the process.

In both cases the intervention by the bystander foreseeably leads to the death of one person in order to save five. Yet it is a widely shared view that in the first case the bystander may divert the trolley, thereby killing one person (let us call him 'V' for victim), whereas in the second case he may not. There is something puzzling about this result. Why isn't it the case that what really matters morally is that in both scenarios V dies and five are saved? Would it not be more consistent either to allow the bystander to

[49] The problem was first introduced by Phillipa Foot in 'The Problem of Abortion and the Doctrine of Double Effect' in *Virtues and Vices* (1978). For further illuminating discussions of the issue see J Jarvis Thompson, 'The Trolley Problem' (1985) 94 *Yale L J* 1395 and FM Kamm, *Morality, Mortality*, vol II (Oxford University Press, 1996) 143–71. See also T Nagel, *The View from Nowhere* (1986).

save the five in both cases if you are a consequentialist, or insist that the life of V cannot be traded off against another life, whatever the circumstances, if you believe in the existence of deontological constraints? There is considerable debate on what justifies making a distinction between these cases. The following can do no more than briefly present one central idea, without doing justice to the various facets and permutations of the debate.

A significant difference between the cases is that in the first the death of the one person is merely a contingent side-effect of the bystander's course of action. There is no doubt that it would be permissible for the bystander to divert the trolley if V did not exist. In the second example the fat man is being *used as a means* to bring about the end of saving the five. His being pushed and the trolley ramming into his body is a necessary condition for the success of saving the five. Without V's involvement there would be no rescue action to describe.

The reason why this difference is morally relevant lies in the different strength of the claims that V can make in these cases. Here the distinction between V as a *disabler* and as an *enabler* is central.[50] The claim of a disabler is considerably weaker than the claim of the enabler. In the first scenario V makes a claim that his being harmed is a reason to disable the otherwise permitted and desirable rescue action of the bystander. In the second scenario V makes a claim that he should not be used as a means to enable the rescue of others. Only the claims of the disabler are susceptible to proportionality analysis. The claims of the enabler impose significantly stronger restrictions.[51] No one can be forced to be a hero and sacrifice their life for others.

This is not the place to probe more deeply into the nature of deontological constraints. But if an account along these lines can make sense of the trolley problem and deontological constraints more generally, there are constraints that cannot be captured by consequentialist accounts of morality. At the same time, it has become clear that consequentialist reasoning does have a central role to play, even in situations where the lives of individuals or similarly fundamental concerns are in play. The relevant question is not so much whether there are deontological constraints, but to identify the situations in which they are in play and distinguish them from situations in which they are not.

[50] Here I follow A Walen, 'Doing, Allowing and Disabling: Some Principles Governing Deontological Restrictions' (1995) 80 *Philosophical Studies* 183.

[51] It is disputed whether these kinds of deontological constraints are absolute or not. Can you push the fat man to save 1,000 people, a million, the world? According to Kant, even the existence of the world would not provide a good reason to overcome deontological restrictions (*fiat iustitia pereat mundus*!). According to Nozick, deontological constraints are overcome in exceptional circumstances to prevent 'catastrophic moral horrors'; R Nozick, *Anarchy, State and Utopia* (1974) 29.

With regard to the structure of human and constitutional rights, the question remains whether situations involving deontological constraints are sufficiently ubiquitous to be of relevance for an understanding of human and constitutional rights. It may well be that the proportionality structure is inadequate as a universal approach for the assessment of moral issues. But in the world of human and constitutional rights adjudication it is not just that trolley problems rarely arise. It also seems to be evident that the daily work of courts rarely concerns moral conflicts involving deontological restrictions. It does not follow, however, that there are no constellations in which deontological constraints have a central role to play.[52] The following provides a sampling of some topical legal and political issues, in which deontological constraints are implicated. To illustrate how pervasive questions relating to deontological constraints are, all examples are narrowly drawn from topical debates loosely related to contemporary preoccupations with terrorism and responses to it.

(1) The first example concerns a recent decision by the German Federal Constitutional Court, striking down a law enacted in the wake of September 11th currently before the German Constitutional Court.[53] The Air Security Act[54] allows for a passenger plane to be shot down by the German Airforce if this is the only way to avert a clear and present danger to human life and it is not disproportionate.[55] The FCC held that the law was unconstitutional in part[56] because the authorisation to shoot down a plane necessarily constitutes a violation of the passengers' right to life. The argument is that even under circumstances in which shooting down the plane is the only suitable and necessary means to save a large number of persons, and even if the number of persons saved is considerably larger than the number of persons in the plane, such an action would still be unconstitutional. Saving many lives does not justify the killing of other innocent people. Shooting down the plane means treating innocent passengers and crew members 'as mere objects of the state's rescue operation for the protection of others. Such a treatment ignores the status of the persons affected as subjects endowed with dignity and inalienable rights'. Being used as a means to save others, they are treated as objects and at the same time deprived of their rights. With their lives being disposed of unilaterally

[52] For such a claim see T Nagel, *Equality and Impartiality* (1991) 141.

[53] See judgment of 15 February 2006, 1 BvR 357/05.

[54] Gesetz zur Neureglung von Luftsicherheitsaufgaben, 11 January 2005, BGBl 2005I Nr3, 77 (Air Security Act or ASE).

[55] See Art 14 ss 2 and 3 ASE.

[56] The FCC also held the law to be unconstitutional on the grounds that the federal government lacked the competencies, and that, more specifically Art. 35 of the Basic Law is not a sufficient legal basis to enact legislation authorising an operational mission of the armed forces with specifically military weapons for either the control of natural disasters or 'grave accidents'.

by the state, the persons on board the aircraft, who, as victims, are themselves in need of protection, are denied the value which is due to a human being for his or her own sake'.[57]

The case nicely exemplifies how arguments relating to deontological constraints can be misunderstood. It is true that the government may not require that a few be sacrificed for the many, if this implies using those few as a means, as enablers. But the claims made by the innocent passengers in the hijacked plane are not the strong claims of enablers. Theirs are the weaker claims of disablers. It seems clear that a hijacked plane about to be used as a weapon or as a platform from which a weapon is launched could be shot down if there was no one or only the hijackers on board. The claim by the passengers is that the fact that they are on board should disable the government from doing what otherwise it would be permitted to do. Claims of disablers, however, are subject to proportionality analysis and nothing stronger. A law that provides adequate procedural safeguards to rule out mistakes and ensures that authorisation will only occur when a commensurate number of lives are saved does not violate the right to life.[58]

(2) Questions relating to deontological restrictions are also in play as nations struggle to agree on an appropriate definition of terrorism. The disputes on the appropriate definition are in part a dispute over whether the prohibition of terrorism is supported by strong deontological reasons or merely general policy concerns. Definitions informed exclusively by consequentialist considerations tend to focus on the illegality of a violent act and its harm to the state and its institutions.[59] Its core concerns are policy concerns related to upholding public order and security. A consequentialist justification of this kind is insufficient to plausibly support a *categorical* prohibition of terrorism. What if the public order is corrupt and the terrorists are freedom fighters seeking to establish a just order and carefully selecting their targets to ensure their actions are both effective

[57] The position taken by the court was widely shared by the literature, see eg Wolfram Höfling and Steffan Augsberg, 'Luftsicherheit, Grundrechtsregime und Ausnahmezustand' (2005) 22 *Juristenzeitung* 1080 at 1081.

[58] There is a further complication to the case, but it concerns the question whether the plane could be shot down even if the numbers saved by that act would be smaller than the number of people killed. In cases where the plane is used as a weapon to crash into buildings or similar scenarios, those killed by being shot down would also have died if events had taken their course and the plane had flown into a building. It has been suggested that under those circumstances the number of lives lost by shooting down a plane whose passengers would have died anyway should count for zero, thus making it proportional to shoot down the plane even if only a handful of people on the ground are threatened. On the other side the argument is made that the future life-span of those that are killed is an irrelevant consideration for the question whether taking of a life is justified.

[59] The League of Nations Convention, drafted in 1937 but never coming into force, eg defined 'terrorism' as 'all criminal acts directed against a state and intended or calculated to create a state of terror in the minds of particular persons or a group of persons or the general public'.

and do not cause disproportionate harm? Of course in the real world there is likely to be disagreement over whether the old order is really that corrupt and whether the 'just cause' is just another brutal ideology. There also may be disagreement about empirical questions relating to the effectiveness of terrorist methods and the balancing of the advantages of having some kind of public order versus the real possibility of a civil war. But in principle here, the saying that one man's terrorist is another man's freedom fighter, applies: whether an act of violence against the state is justified depends on an assessment of the purpose it serves and the extent to which terrorism is an effective, necessary and proportionate measure of furthering it. This is one of the reasons why peoples who have known suppression may well believe that they are right to venerate the heroes of their respective liberation movement, even if their methods included terrorism. It is also the reason why categorical prohibitions of terrorism that do not make exceptions relating to liberation struggles are difficult to get agreement on.

But there is a very different, and in my view more convincing understanding of terrorism. According to this view, the central characteristic of terrorist acts is the particular nature of the means-ends relationship.[60] Such an approach is reflected in the 'draft outcome document' of the UN World Summit held in September 2005. It included the following statement:

> we declare that any action intended to cause death or serious bodily harm to civilians or non-combatants, when the purpose of such an act, by its nature of context, is to intimidate a population or to compel a Government or an international organization to carry out or abstain from any act cannot be justified on any grounds and constitutes terrorism.[61]

The core idea underlying this categorical prohibition of terrorism is that it is never justified to use civilians and non-combatants *as a means*—as enablers—for the purpose of making the government or other people do or abstain from doing something.[62] The particular evil of terrorism lies not in

[60] For a focus on the means-end relationship in the discussion of terrorism, see J Waldron, 'Terrorism and the Uses of Terror' (2004) 8 *Journal of Ethics* 5.

[61] See A/59/HLPM/CRP.1/Rev.2, 5 August 2005, at recital 65. The United States pushed aggressively, but, it seems, ultimately unsuccessfully for such a definition. This definition is not included in the final Document adopted by the General Assembly, see A/60/L.1, 20 September 2005, recitals 81–92 (discussing terrorism issues).

[62] Note how under this definition of terrorism it is not evident that the September 11th attacks on the Pentagon constitute terrorist acts, even though the attacks on the World Trade Center clearly are paradigm examples. Note, furthermore, that once the idea of civilians and non-combatants is not understood as a reference to legally defined categories of persons, but more loosely as 'those who are innocent in the sense of not actively participating in the enterprise of violent suppression', then Trotzky's arguments about the absence of innocent persons in the context of modern oppression have the effect to undermine this definition. See Leon Trotsky, 'Terrorism and Communism' in RG Frey and C Morris (eds), *Violence, Terrorism and Justice* (Cambridge University Press, 1991).

undermining public order and security, though that would be bad enough in most cases, but rather in violating individuals as persons by treating them as a means to achieve political purposes. No one has the right to treat other persons the way that terrorists treat them: killing or seriously harming them as a means to bring about certain effects in others in order to bring about political changes. The legitimacy of the purpose pursued by terrorists does not matter. Nor does it matter whether terrorists have any plausible alternative means to effectively fight oppression (terrorism is typically the weapon of the weak and there may not be other plausible options), or whether the actions are proportional. Even if all these requirements are met terrorism would remain a morally prohibited means of achieving legitimate ends. If such an understanding of deontological constraints is closely connected to commitments of Political Liberalism, it should not be surprising that there have been few liberal movements that have endorsed terrorism. Liberalism is a fighting faith and does not eschew the use of violence and revolution as a means of political struggle.[63] But the methods of terrorism, narrowly conceived, tend to be methods used by political movements whose understanding of the individual person is informed by ideologies that exhibit a more teleological, consequentialist structure.

One of the historically more prominent forms of state-sponsored terrorisms that even liberal democracies have succumbed to is terror-bombing. Terror-bombing, as opposed to strategic bombing, fulfils all the requirements of the above definition. In case of strategic bombing, the purpose of the bombing is to destroy military targets. Non-combatant deaths that are the side-effect of such bombings—'collateral damage'—do not render such bombings impermissible, if those deaths are not disproportionate to the objectives pursued.[64] Terror-bombing, on the other hand, the purpose of which is to terrorise and demoralise the population in order to increase pressure on the political leadership to bring an end to the war, is impermissible. Victims of terror-bombing are right to complain that their rights have been violated, and international criminal law rightly sanctions it. Victims of strategic bombing may suffer equally, but they are unable to make a similar claim.

(3) The final example illustrating the relevance of deontological constraints for contemporary rights debates concerns the protection against

[63] This is a point rightly insisted upon by Stephen Homes in *The Anatomy of Antiliberalism* (1993).

[64] Note that with the development of weapons technology, the necessity prong of the proportionality test gains importance. Whereas carpet-bombing by B-52 bombers of industrial areas of major cities may have been permissible in the Second World War, it is unlikely to be permissible today. The general availability of satellite technology (think of Google World) in conjunction with technology ensuring the 'surgical' accuracy of targeting, significantly decreases the extent to which 'collateral damage' is acceptable.

and prohibition of torture. On the one hand, international and domestic law in most countries categorically prohibits torture without exception. On the other hand, in the context of the current 'war on terrorism' (but not only in that context[65]), it has become respectable to discuss whether or not torture is acceptable, at least in some situations.

The United Nations Convention against Torture and Other Cruel and Inhuman or Degrading Treatment or Punishment defines torture as:

> any act by which severe pain or suffering, whether physical or mental, is intentionally inflicted on a person for such purposes as obtaining from him or a third person information or a confession ... when such pain or suffering is inflicted by or at the instigation of or consent or acquiescence of a public official or other person acting in an official capacity.[66]

The reasons why torture is condemned so widely are in many respects obvious. There are strong consequentialist reasons to insist on a general prohibition of torture. Torture involves the infliction of severe pain and suffering on persons who are in the custody of public authorities and at the mercy of public officials. Besides the immediate pain and fear, these experiences often leave deep psychological marks that make it difficult for the victim ever to engage in ordinary human relationships. The infringement of the tortured person's interests is thus extremely severe. Furthermore, there is always the possibility that the authorities are wrong to believe that the individual has the knowledge they seek. The information gained through torture is often unreliable. The possibilities of abuse, as well as the psychological corruption of the torturer, are very real, and the possibility of institutionalising effective controls to cabin or limit torture may prove difficult to administer.

Under such circumstances, there may be good institutional reasons to insist on an overinclusive blanket prohibition of torture, even if, from a perspective of political morality, there may be specific instances in which torture is justified. There may even be a good case for establishing a general public taboo on the discussion of moral justifications for torture on these grounds, given that the public discussion of possible exceptions to a prohibition on torture may obscure and colour the perception of clearly unjustified patterns of torture that occur in the real world.

[65] This concerns the discussion of the Daschner case which created something of a stir in the German media in the second half of 2004. Daschner is a senior police official who had threatened the use of torture against a kidnapper in order to find the whereabouts of the kidnapped victim. The kidnapper confessed to the deed and informed the police of the whereabouts of the (already dead) victim. Daschner was criminally prosecuted and convicted. But he received an extremely lenient sentence and suffered no further professional disciplinary proceedings or sanctions.

[66] Article 1 of the UN Convention against Torture and Other Cruel, Inhuman or Degrading Treatment or Punishment, GA res 39/46 (annex, 39 UN GAOR Supp (No 51) at 197, UN Doc A/39/51 (1984)) entered into force 26 June 1987.

But there are good grounds to be sceptical of any prohibition of torture grounded exclusively in consequentialist concerns. Those who insist that the prohibition of torture be grounded in stronger, deontological constraints can point to two features of torture. First, people are not tortured because they are dangerous. Even the most dangerous criminal is no longer a threat once he is effectively in custody.[67] Even the most unruly prisoner can be put in chains and locked away. Assuming a captive is not simply tortured for the perverse delectations of sadistic officials, a captive is tortured because he refuses to co-operate with the authorities. He is tortured because he refuses to *enable* public authorities to draw on what he knows to more effectively realise their goals. Torture has the purpose to make the victim a 'willing' means to the ends pursued by officials. Secondly, torture is a particularly invidious way to make an individual a means in the service of others. It does so in a way that betrays the very idea that the individual is an end in himself. As Sussman has recently argued:

> torture forces its victim into the position of colluding against himself through his own affects and emotions, so that he experiences himself as simultaneously powerless and yet actively complicit in his own violation. So construed, torture turns out to be not just an extreme form of cruelty, but the pre-eminent instance of a forced self-betrayel, more akin to rape than other kinds of violence characteristic of warfare or police action.[68]

Together these features seem to provide a good case that torture is prohibited by something stronger than just consequentialist concerns.

Consequentialists tend to challenge the idea of a more deontologically grounded prohibition of torture by pointing to some version of the 'ticking bomb' hypothetical: imagine a terrorist hides a bomb powerful enough to kill hundreds in a crowded metropolitan area. Having achieved his life plan, he then decides that he wants to savour his victory by being a witness to official helplessness. He thus walks into a police station and informs the police what he has done and that the bomb will detonate in three hours. He will not, however, tell the police where it is or how to defuse it. I share the view of consequentialists that in such a case the terrorist does not suffer injustice when he is tortured for the purpose of finding out where the bomb is located. But the example does not succeed in undermining the idea that the prohibition on torture is grounded in more than just consequentialist concerns. Instead the hypothetical's insistence on the large number of victims unhelpfully obfuscates the real point. Two alternative hypotheticals may help to get a better understanding how deontological constraints

[67] H Shue, 'Torture' (1978) 7 *Philosophy and Public Affairs* 124 (arguing that the prohibition against an assault on the defenseless is what makes torture so morally reprehensible, and worse, for example, than killing someone in combat).

[68] D Sussman, 'What's Wrong with Torture?' (2005) 33 *Philosophy and Public Affairs* 1 at 4.

function in the context of torture. It is not the large number of victims that is doing the work in this hypothetical.

Instead of a terrorist that has hidden a powerful explosive device endangering hundreds, imagine a kidnapper of a sole child who was caught picking up the ransom money.[69] He admits to having buried the child alive making it foreseeable that the child will die by suffocation in a matter of hours if not rescued. The kidnapper refuses to reveal the whereabouts of the child. Even in this situation, where only one other life is at stake, it seems to me that torture is morally permitted as a last resort. A policeman that threatens or engages in torture may violate legal prohibitions that have been established for good institutional reasons. But he is not violating a moral right of the person he tortures. The point is, however, that the reasons for torture being permissible in this case do not lie exclusively in the fact that a life can be saved. The consequences alone are insufficient to justify torture. Saving a life may be a necessary condition,[70] but it is certainly not a sufficient condition to justify torture. The reason why torture may be morally permitted in this case lies in the *special relationship* between the kidnapper and his victim. The kidnapper is responsible for creating a life-threatening situation for the child and refuses to remove it. Structurally, the torture of the kidnapper is comparable to an act of third party self-defence. Torture is permitted, if it is a necessary and proportional means to fend off an ongoing attack on the life of the child by the kidnapper. The kidnapper is *personally responsible* for the *specific threat* that the victim faces. Any refusal to co-operate with authorities to do what is necessary and proper to rescue the child in effect perpetuates an attack against the child. Such a refusal to co-operate can be addressed by whatever measures are necessary and proportionate to save the child. The specific link between the personal responsibility of the person to protect others from the imminent danger he has created and the purpose of torture neutralises deontological constraints both in this case and in the case of the terrorist planting a bomb. Measures aimed at ensuring that a person complies with special duties of this kind are only subject to proportionality analysis. Under the circumstances, the concrete danger of the loss of one life seems to outweigh whatever suffering the tortured kidnapper may have to go through. From a moral point of view, the prohibition of torture under these kinds of circumstances is relatively weak.

Now go back to the terrorist who has planted a bomb that threatens many hundreds of people. Imagine the terrorist turns out to be resistant to

[69] This scenario closely reflects the Daschner case, above n 65. In that case the kidnapper had not yet admitted, however, that he was in fact the kidnapper. Furthermore the police had merely threatened torture.

[70] Torture would not be justified, eg, to coerce a thief who refuses to reveal where he has hidden the loot.

torture. Nothing can be done to make him reveal the hiding place of the bomb. But it turns out he has a seven-year old-daughter, whom he loves dearly. Is it permissible to torture her, in order to force the terrorist to reveal the whereabouts of the bomb, if this is the only serious option to prevent the deaths of many hundred people? I think not. Here, it seems to me, the full force of deontological restrictions kick in. Unlike the previous cases, the child has no special obligation to those endangered by the terrorist acts grounded in her previous actions. She is not the attacker. The self-defence analogy does not apply. Here, the prohibition against torture is of a more categorical nature. Even if the lives of many are at stake, the moral rights of the victim would be violated if she were tortured.

This suggests that in the 'ticking bomb' example, the fact that a considerable number of people are threatened is not the decisive moral feature of the situation that explains why many believe that torture is permitted. Torture is permitted only because its purpose is to make the tortured person comply with his special obligation towards those whose lives he is threatening.

Implications for the structure of rights: the purpose of the above discussions was not to provide a comprehensive account of any of the issues involved. It merely touched the surface of some contemporary debates highlighting their structural features. The discussion illustrates two points. First, it shows how deontological considerations are in play in the discussion of a number of contemporary legal and political issues closely connected to the protection of human and constitutional rights.[71] The issues underlying the trolley problem are sufficiently ubiquitous to be of significance for an adequate account of the structure of human and constitutional rights. Secondly, it is not enough to be aware of the existence of deontological constraints. The task is to identify the situations in which they are relevant from situations in which they are not. What then does this suggest for an adequate account of the structure of rights?

The idea of deontological constraints cannot be appropriately captured within the proportionality structure. The reasons why proportionality analysis and the balancing test in particular is insufficient to capture these concerns is that it systematically filters out means-ends relationships that are central to the understanding of deontological constraints. When balancing, the decision-maker first loads up the scales on one side, focusing on the intensity of the infringement. Then he loads up the other side of the scales by focusing on the consequences of the act and assessing the benefits realised by it. Balancing systematically filters out questions concerning means-ends relationships. Yet the nature of the means-ends relationship

[71] Other rights-sensitive contemporary debates in which the existence of categorical constraints is rightly or wrongly believed to be in play concern stem-cell research, cloning and abortion.

can be key. Whether the claims made by the rights-bearer against the acting authority are made as an enabler or a disabler, whether public authorities are making use of a person as a means, or whether they are merely disregarding the claim to take into account his interests as a constraining factor in an otherwise permissible endeavour, are often morally decisive features of the situation. These questions only come into view once the structure of the means-ends relationship becomes the focus of a separate inquiry.

Furthermore it would be a mistake to think of the structural features of the situation as merely a factor to be taken into account within an overall balancing exercise. Whether the infringed person is an enabler or a disabler is not only relevant in the weak sense that it provides additional reasons to be put on the scale when balancing. Rather, the distinction between enablers and disablers completely changes the baseline to be used to assess rights infringements. In the case of torture and terrorist killing, baseline change implies something close to a categorical prohibition against coercively sacrificing an individual's life or integrity as a means to further a political purpose. It does not matter how legitimate the political purpose is and that such a sacrifice may be necessary to furthering that purpose.

This does not mean, of course, that there is a categorical prohibition against using people as a means—as enablers—to further a desirable purpose. We generally use people as a means to further our purposes all the time. For the most part, however, we do so with their consent. Even absent consent, there is no categorical prohibition on using people as a means. Provisions of tort law and criminal law that require a passer-by to suffer minor inconveniences to come to the aid of another person in serious distress, for example, raise no serious moral concerns. There is no general categorical prohibition on requiring people to make themselves available as a means to serve the needs of other people or the larger community. The point is merely that the baseline used to discuss these issues is very different from the baseline used in cases where individual citizens are not the instruments used to realise political purposes.

This leads to a final point. The proportionality test may be helpfully employed also to assess state measures in which individuals are used as a means. It still makes perfect sense to require that when individuals are drafted into the service of the community these impositions have to meet proportionality requirements. The individual may be used as a means by public authorities only if it is necessary to further a legitimate public purpose and is not disproportionate. The different moral baseline merely means that, on application, what counts as proportionate is very different from what counts as proportionate in situations where the individual person is not used as an enabler. It is central to the assessment of a government act whether it uses individuals as a means, that is, whether the individual is an enabler or a disabler. Once this agent-relative feature of the situation is included in the description of the infringing act, proportionality analysis applies. But the *substantive evaluation* of the competing concerns changes radically. More specifically, on application it suggests that the ultimate sacrifice of a citizen's life or integrity is never, or nearly never,[72] justifiable. The citizens imagined as part of the social contract, those whose reasonable consent is hypothesised, did not sign on to a pact that includes provisions authorising their sacrifice.

CONCLUSION: THE STRUCTURE OF RIGHTS

At the heart of the antiperfectionist and anticonsequentialist commitments of Political Liberalism is the basic idea that public institutions may not use their coercive powers to force citizens to become either saints or heroes.[73] From the perspective of Political Liberalism, what saints strive to be and heroes do is superogatory. The obligations they respond to and the acts they perform are not part of what we can claim from each other as free and equals. Public institutions may not enact legislation on the ground that a particular conception of the good is the right one, and they may not sacrifice the life of an individual for the community, even if this were to enhance the general welfare. If the argument presented here is correct, these central commitments of the tradition of Political Liberalism are not adequately reflected in a structure of rights that is exclusively focused on proportionality to determine the limits of rights. Instead, the antiperfectionist aspect of Political Liberalism is appropriately operationalised by the structural idea of *excluded reasons*. The anticonsequentialist aspect of Political Liberalism finds its expression in sensibilities to *means-ends relationships* and the distinction between claims of *enablers and disablers*. The anticollectivist aspect of Political Liberalism, on the other hand, is appropriately reflected in the proportionality structure. If there is a justification for something like a 'compelling interest' test that imposes stronger requirements than the proportionality test, it must be a justification grounded in institutional concerns. The claim would have to be that

[72] There is disagreement over what happens in truly catastrophic situations. According to Nozick, eg, in case of 'catastrophic moral horrors' exceptions can be made. According to Kant, sacrificing an individual would not be justified even if it meant that the world must perish (*fiat iustitia pereat mundus*).

[73] It may be conceptually and practically impossible for legislation to coerce sainthood, though in the case of heroism coercion can plausibly play a greater role. Sainthood is too closely connected with inner struggles and conscience to be meaningfully and predictably responsive to anything that can be coerced. 'Profess your sins, change your life and commit yourself to God who is love or you'll be shot' may give rise to all kinds of pretensions and hypocrisies, but not a saintly life. On the other hand, you can be a hero by fighting heroically as a soldier, even if the only reason you are fighting heroically is that you expect to be shot if you attempt to desert and you expect to be killed by the enemy if you do not do the same to him first.

ultimately the enforcement of rights as defined by the proportionality test is better achieved by way of an institutional division of labour between courts and other institutions that requires courts to insist on reasons of a special strength to override certain protected interests.

Furthermore, the discussion has made clear that the structural features of rights reasoning that reflect antiperfectionist and anticonsequentialist commitments are a relatively pervasive feature of moral reasoning. The idea of excluded reasons and concerns about means-ends relationships have a pervasive influence on the discussion of political and legal issues framed in terms of human and constitutional rights.

This does not mean, however, that proportionality analysis is not central to reasoning about rights. It clearly is. But it should not detract from central features of rights reasoning that exhibit a different structure. Awareness of the idea of excluded reasons and the relevance of means-ends relationship in the assessment of rights claims help sharpen rights analysis. They help understand, for example, why the Strasbourg court was so strict in its scrutiny of the 'combat effectiveness' arguments in *Lustig-Prean and Beckett*. Combat effectiveness may matter for the purpose of justifying the exclusion of homosexuals from the military, but the homophobic resentments that give rise to these problems do not. Furthermore, an understanding of the nature of deontological restrictions would also help the German Constitutional Court address the issue of the constitutionality of the Air Security Act. It would help the court to distinguish between cases in which one life may not be sacrificed for the benefit of others from situations where the loss of a few lives may be justified when it is necessary to save many. A better understanding of the structures of political morality should help focus and improve the discussion of competing claims in the context of rights analysis.

Finally the discussion showed that it is a mistake to connect the idea of rights with the strength of a rights claim. Rights are not optimisation requirements, but nor are they trumps or shields. Rights can serve as all of those things but should not be identified as or reduced to either. Rights are not the non-consequentialist component of morality. In many contexts a right can be overridden by general policy considerations. But in some contexts—when the policy considerations are related to excluded reasons or involve using the rights-bearer as a means—rights provide stronger protections. What you have in virtue of having a position guaranteed as a right depends on the reasons that support that position in a particular context. These reasons are not only of different strengths in different contexts, they exhibit a variety of structures. A conception of human and constitutional rights that tries to make sense of and reconstruct the kind of judicial practice that has arisen after the Second World War in constitutional democracies worldwide would do well to give up trying to establish an analytical connection between the strength of a rights claim and its status as a rights claim.

There are two conclusions to be drawn from this. First, there is no plausible way to constitutionalise the protection of rights that reflect the commitments of a liberal political morality that excludes proportionality analysis as an important feature of rights adjudication. And secondly, rights analysis has a more complex structure than the exclusive focus on proportionality suggests.

8

Proportionality, Discretion and the Second Law of Balancing

JULIAN RIVERS

INTRODUCTION

IN THE POSTSCRIPT to *A Theory of Constitutional Rights*,[1] Robert Alexy seeks to position the *Theory* between two competing critical perspectives. On the one hand, there are those who suspect that the technique of balancing is too 'soft', permitting judges to undermine the hard edges requisite to a workable theory of rights. It destroys an important 'firewall'. On the other hand, others fear that the theory is too rigid, supposing that the entire substantive content of law can be derived by a rational process from first principles.[2] A similar tension between competing conceptions of rights can be found in the theoretical human rights literature.[3] Alexy meets these concerns by demonstrating that the theory of principles is compatible with discretion on the part of other branches of government, but that this discretion is not unlimited. The doctrine of proportionality does deliver a set of limits to legislative action. Both criticisms are therefore unfounded.

The concerns expressed by Alexy's critics have a common source in the problem of institutional competence and legitimacy. Habermas' concern can be equally well understood as a fear that the specific judicial role of protecting rights might be jeopardised by the possibility of justifying any level of legislative incursion into rights in pursuit of other public interests. Böckenförde's critique can be understood as a demand that constitutional

1 R Alexy, *A Theory of Constitutional Rights* (J Rivers (trans), Oxford, Oxford University Press, 2002).

2 *Ibid* at 388–90.

3 See A McHarg, 'Reconciling Human Rights and the Public Interest: Conceptual Problems and Doctrinal Uncertainty in the Jurisprudence of the European Court of Human Rights' (1999) 62 *Modern Law Review* 671.

review should not supplant the proper contribution of legislative and executive bodies to the process of public decision-taking. Both, then, presuppose a distinctive judicial function within the well-ordered constitution which appears under threat from the *Theory*.

This reaction is understandable. *A Theory of Constitutional Rights* presents itself simultaneously as a rational substantive theory of normative decision-taking and a legal theory of constitutional review. If the doctrine of proportionality is the rational way of optimising the enjoyment of competing interests, and if the judiciary are tasked with ensuring that all state action is proportionate, the impression is easily created that the constitutional court should become a committee of Platonic philosopher-kings. This impression is only given greater strength by the equanimity with which Alexy countenances broad conceptions of prima facie rights to liberty and equality,[4] constitutional rights to protection, process and positive state action,[5] as well as a radiating effect of the constitution on all law.[6]

At least at first sight, a purely rational theory of legal decision-taking would presumably be institutionally neutral, in the sense that it would only address *how* decisions are taken, without implications as to *who* should take them. A clear example of a tendency to institutional neutrality in the Theory can be found in the nature of the public interests which may justify a limitation of rights. These are presented as principles, or optimisation requirements.[7] But they cannot be optimisation requirements in the same sense as rights, since legislatures are under no obligation to optimise them or even pursue them at all. One could accept that they are unenforceable optimisation requirements on account of a lack of a relevant cause of action. But even under constitutional systems which permit legal actions to ensure the general constitutionality of a measure,[8] courts never consider whether legislatures have pursued the public interest to the greatest possible extent. Thus, public interests have to be construed as optimisation permissions, and principles must be redefined as optimisation requirements or permissions. Only rights correlate to optimisation requirements in the strict sense. This necessary modification already adds an element of institutional differentiation into the theory of principles.

However, it would not be correct to assume that *A Theory of Constitutional Rights* is purely a rational theory of legal decision-taking. It also takes account of formal principles which restrict the power of courts. For

4 Alexy, above n 1 at chs 7 and 8.
5 *Ibid* at ch 9.
6 *Ibid* at 351–65.
7 *Ibid* at 65.
8 The German legal system clearly does permit forms of 'objective' review, whereas the English system requires the infringement of a subjective right.

example, the general form of a definitive social constitutional right is that of an entitlement required by the principle of factual freedom after taking due account of 'the formal principles of the decision-taking competence of the democratically legitimated legislature and the separation of powers, as well as substantive principles relating above all to the legal liberty of others, but also to other social constitutional rights as well as collective goods'.[9] This shows that the *Theory* begins to move from a rational substantive theory of legal decision-taking to a theory of constitutional review by way of a reference to formal principles.

Constitutional courts are not simply tasked with ensuring the rationality of all state action; their legal responsibility is structured by formal principles as well. A substantive doctrine of proportionality constructed on the basis of the theory of principles needs combining with a formal doctrine of institutional competence and legitimacy before it can function as a legal device for testing the constitutionality of limitations of rights. The question is whether the account of discretion in the Postscript adequately accounts for the relevance and impact of formal principles in this respect.

Alexy starts by drawing attention to an important distinction between structural and epistemic discretion. Structural discretion is the more familiar form of discretion as a choice between different legally permissible options. The argument is that the doctrine of proportionality leaves other state organs with a choice: it neither dissolves all limits nor does it require one right answer. Epistemic discretion arises on account of the fact that we suffer relative ignorance about the world, so we do not always know to what extent policies will be successful or how significant a particular breach of rights is. In spite of such relative ignorance we still need to decide what to do. It may be appropriate to risk a breach of rights for the chance of a greater gain to the public interest. To the extent that legislatures may pass measures in spite of the risk of disproportionality, they enjoy epistemic discretion.

The distinction between structural and epistemic discretion is not always clear. This becomes apparent in the case of normative epistemic discretion. Imagine two similar states of legal regulation which we are trying to evaluate. We find it impossible to distinguish between them in terms of their infringement of a principle, so we are free to choose either. This may be because there is no distinction between them, or it may because although there is a distinction we are unable to perceive it. The former possibility is ontological and thus related to structure; the latter possibility is epistemological and thus any discretion granted is properly termed epistemic. We are likely to categorise the discretion according to prior

[9] Alexy, above n 1 at 343.

metaphysical commitments in respect of the status of norms. But it does not matter in practice which view one takes.

In the course of the Postscript, Alexy introduces the 'second law of balancing'. This is based on a formal principle and regulates who is to take the decision in a case of empirical doubt. The first law of balancing states that the more serious an infringement of rights is, the more important must be the public interest to outweigh it.[10] It is implicit in the idea of principles as optimisation requirements. Our problem is that we are often ignorant about the level of realisation of the public interest, its factual basis and how to quantify the values at stake. This doubt could be resolved against the legislature and in favour of rights, but for the existence of a formal principle stating that the legislature should be able to take important decisions. In cases of uncertainty this indicates a sliding scale of competence according to the second law of balancing: the more intensive an interference in a constitutional right is, the greater must be the certainty of its underlying premises.[11]

The argument of this chapter is that this formulation of the second law of balancing is incomplete. Some forms of discretion enjoyed by legislatures identified in the Postscript are already implicit in the first law of balancing and are compatible with review by a constitutional court for correctness. They require no formal principle for their existence. However, Alexy does not account for other forms of discretion which are more obviously in the control of the courts. Thus, while the second law of balancing as formulated in the Postscript is correct in presupposing a judicial institutional competence to act as the guardian of rights, it betrays a tendency to downplay the significance of formal principles. The second law of balancing requires reformulation to take full account of these principles.

STRUCTURAL DISCRETION

The discussion of structural discretion in the Postscript proceeds by identifying discretion at each stage of the doctrine of proportionality. Thus it is pointed out that legislatures have discretion to select the end to be pursued, the means to be adopted and the level of realisation of the public interest. Much of the discussion is devoted to demonstrating that proportionality in the narrow sense identifies a set of states of legal regulation all of which are 'balanced'. Legislative bodies therefore have a choice from that set. They may select a policy that balances a high level of rights

[10] *Ibid* at 102–9.
[11] *Ibid* at 418–19.

protection with minimal attainment of the public interest, or they may select a policy that pursues the public interest to a large extent but at a greater cost to rights.[12]

It is suggested that this argument alone does not show the existence of policy-choice discretion. Rather, such discretion depends upon the relationship between all the stages of the proportionality doctrine, and in particular the relationship between the test of necessity *and* the test of balancing. Legislatures are free to select from policies that are capable of pursuing legitimate aims by means that are the least intrusive necessary and are balanced. We should not assume that each stage of proportionality narrows down the field of choices left open by the previous stages.

The first two stages of proportionality (pursuit of a legitimate aim by capable means) set threshold conditions, presupposed by the final two stages. Thus, any necessary policy will, by definition, be capable of achieving its aim, and any proportionate policy will, by definition, be in pursuit of a legitimate aim in the first place. These two stages will always be satisfied by necessary and proportionate measures.

The same cannot be said for the relationship between proportionality and necessity. The test of necessity requires that there be no avoidable fundamental rights sacrifices. If a particular end could be equally well achieved by less intrusive means, then the decision-taker is obligated to select those less intrusive means. A number of features of necessity are significant. First, it does not rule out any level of achievement of any legitimate end. For example, it works even in the case of a legislature seeking near-perfect protection for national security, simply asking, *given* this level of national security, is freedom of expression restricted to the least extent possible? Thus, it still leaves as much discretion as a legislature could reasonably want. It allows every level of achievement of every permissible end. Secondly, it does not require a comparative evaluation of the competing principles. In the example given, we do not need to know how to relate freedom of expression to national security. All we need to be able to do is to rank states of legal regulation according to whether they are more or less restrictive of one value. Undoubtedly, this gives rise to some problems of relative evaluation within one value, and to difficulties of prognosis and empirical evidence about the impact of norms on society. For example, we might need to know of two alternative policy options whether one will actually achieve as much national security as the other. These problems give rise to other types of discretion considered below. For now, it is worth noting that the test of necessity does not require us to balance competing principles.

12 *Ibid* at 394–414.

In the light of what is to follow, it is worth trying to illustrate necessity graphically. The idea of necessity is none other than that of efficiency or Pareto-optimality applied to the realisation of different amounts of two competing principles.[13] Picture an x-y axis with the degree of realisation of Pi represented by increasing values of x and degree of realisation of Pj represented by increasing values of y. The world being what it is, it will not be possible to have high levels of realisation of both Pi and Pj, but we can avoid small levels of both. They will have to be played off against each other. As we would expect with an efficiency graph, this results in a convex curve of some nature, such as $x^2+y^2 = c^2$. As one moves up the graph, so one also has to move in. The field within the curve represents the domain of possible realisations of both principles, and the field outside the curve represents the domain of impossible realisations. The boundary line is the line of necessity because it is the maximum possible realisation. Note that the normative element of the rule that limitations of principle are only acceptable if they are the least intrusive means to achieve a given level of some other good is *external* to the graph, which simply represents a set of efficient states of regulation. The graph should make clear that the rule of necessity taken by itself does not prevent a total loss of freedom of expression if that is what it takes to achieve a certain level of national security, or vice versa. This is shown in Figure 8.1.

The final stage of proportionality requires a principle to be optimised relative to another principle, which means that costs to one principle must be adequately offset by gains to the other. This in turn means that balancing also admits of a range of possible options, ie those in which the cost to one principle is offset by the gain to another. The line of acceptable substitutions of principles can be represented by an indifference curve going through a set of states of legal regulation in which the degree of achievement of one principle is inversely proportional to the degree of achievement of the other.[14] This can be equally well expressed to match more closely the way lawyers tend to speak: balancing requires the extent of satisfaction of one principle to be directly proportional to the degree of infringement of another. It does not matter which way round one looks at it.

Thus, the test of balancing can be graphically represented on the same x-y axis as before by an indifference curve. This time, the curve represents the set of states of affairs in which the cost to one principle (or its relative lack of realisation) is acceptably offset by the gain to another principle. Mathematically this can be expressed by the formula $xy= c^2$. The fact that the curve shoots off to infinity for very low values of either principle

[13] *Ibid* at 105 n 222 and 398–9.
[14] *Ibid* at 103–5, 410.

Figure 8.1 Necessity

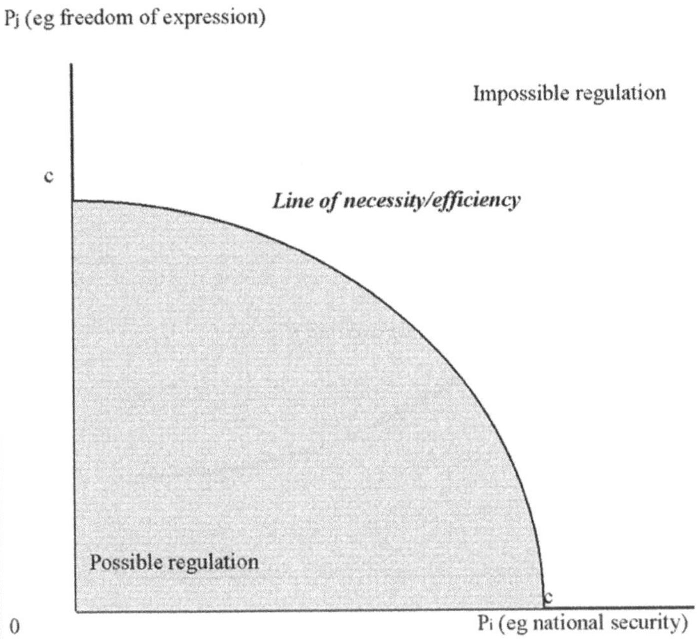

Increasing realisation of Pi (eg national security) is represented on the x-axis; increasing realisation of Pj (eg freedom of expression) is represented on the y-axis. States of legal regulation are points on the graph.

The shaded area represents all possible states of legal regulation, and its limit, the convex curve, is the Pareto-optimal set of states of legal regulation in which no gain to one principle can be made without cost to the other. The test of suitability/capability requires one to select a point in the shaded area, and the test of necessity requires one to choose the least intrusive state of legal regulation possible for any given level of realisation of the other principle, ie one must select a point on the convex curve.

expresses the idea that the more a principle is interfered with, the more *proportionately* the justification must increase. The normative component is here *internal* to the graph, because what is represented are normatively acceptable balances of two principles. This can be seen in Figure 8.2.

It is of the first importance to see that necessity curves are convex (efficient) but balancing curves are concave (indifferent). The significance of this is as follows: states of legal regulation which achieve moderate levels of one principle are likely to be balanced in respect of some other competing principle, so long as that other principle is limited to the least necessary extent to achieve the moderate level of realisation of the first principle. However, at the extremes of realisation of a principle, even the least necessary infringements are likely to be unbalanced. Imagine a state

Figure 8.2 Balance or proportionality in the narrow sense

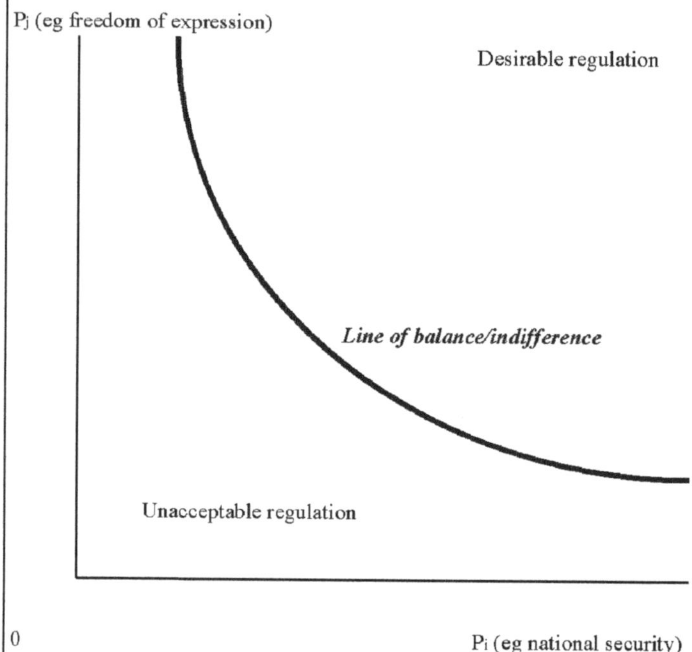

The solid thick line represents an indifference curve representing states of legal regulation in which we would be happy to trade off losses and gains of one principle for the other. It is concave, on account of the fact that the less one has of one principle, the correspondingly more one requires of the other to accept the cost-benefit trade-off. Points on or above this line outside the shaded area are desirable; points below the line are unacceptable.

of affairs in which there are already high levels of national security and low levels of freedom of expression. People being what they are, more draconian restrictions on freedom of expression are unlikely to add much more to the level of national security; leaks and illegal speech will take care of that. By getting still closer to the axis virtually nothing will be added to the already high value of national security. The curve is concave. However, from the normative perspective of balancing, given the already high levels of national security and low levels of freedom of speech, further restrictions on freedom of expression would require a remarkable and substantial improvement in national security. One can only draw closer to the axis if the value increases dramatically. The curve is concave.

The doctrine of proportionality thus requires us to compare these two sets of states of legal regulation. The first set is Pareto-optimally efficient and represents the least possible intrusion on one principle given a full range of realisations of the other. The second set represents the relative value of two principles along an indifference curve, ensuring that the product is constant. Policy-choice discretion arises when potential policies satisfy both tests, in other words for those points on the necessity curve and on or above the balance curve.

The key to structural policy-choice discretion lies in the relationship between the two curves. There are three possibilities in the relationship between the two sets of states of legal regulation. On the first possibility, the indifference curve lies wholly above the efficiency curve. This expresses the idea that no possible satisfaction of both principles is normatively acceptable. It is the utopian position that seeks to enjoy every value to the fullest extent. It would strike down every decision as unacceptable and even castigate a failure to act. It is wholly unrealistic. The second possibility is that the indifference curve lies wholly (or, rather, almost wholly) below the efficiency curve. Here almost every balanced solution is possible. We could call it the pragmatic position that asserts that every realisation of every value must be possible, whatever it costs, so long as it costs as little as possible. It removes the test of balancing from the field of useful controls.

The third possibility is that the two curves intersect. Within this there are two sub-possibilities. One is that the intersection takes place at just one point, where the two curves are tangential to each other. This corresponds to the one right answer thesis, namely that there is only one state of legal regulation which is simultaneously the least intrusive means to a given end and which correctly balances the competing principles. The other is that there are two points of intersection, in which case the options open to the decision-taker lie along the line of necessity (which may or may not also be the line of proportionality) between the two points of intersection.

The idea that the indifference curve is adjustable relative to the necessity curve can be expressed by introducing another variable into the equation. Thus $xy = nc^2$. By adjusting the value of n one can move the indifference curve relative to the efficiency curve $x^2+y^2 = c^2$. $N>0.5$ is the utopian position whereby no necessary play-off is acceptable. $N=0.5$ is the one right answer approach. The curves intersect at $x=y=c/\sqrt{2}$. For $0<n<0.5$ there will be two points of intersection, and this represents the normal state of affairs in which a range of decisions are proportionate, but in which there are also limits. This is represented graphically in Figure 8.3.

The variability of the relationship between balance and necessity suggests that the doctrine of proportionality by itself does not guarantee any policy-choice discretion on the part of other bodies. Courts could take the view that their role is to ensure that legislative and executive bodies select the one policy represented by the intersection of what is necessary and the highest practical optimisation of interests. In practice, of course, courts do not adopt such a position. Rather the final stage of proportionality is cast

Figure 8.3 Policy-choice discretion

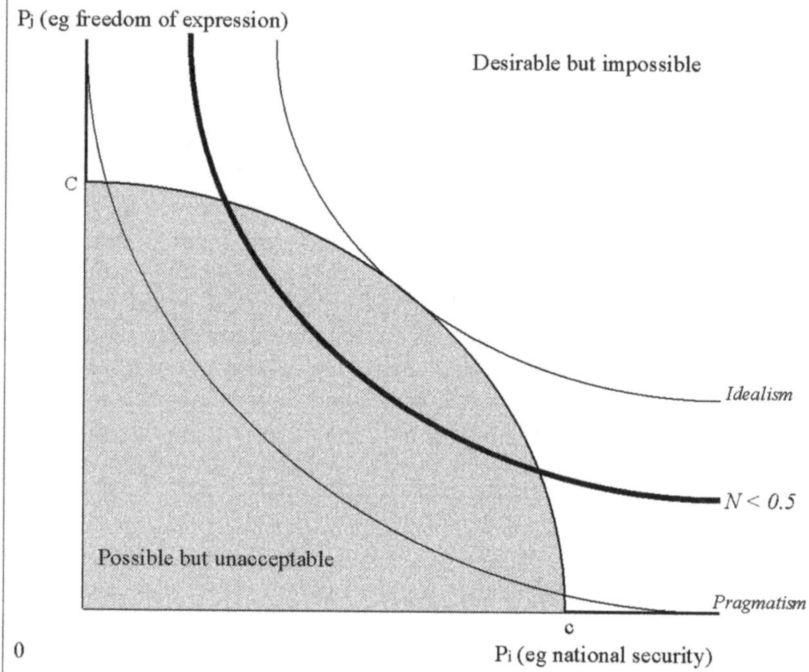

Increasing realisation of Pi (eg national security) is represented on the x-axis; increasing realisation of Pj (eg freedom of expression) is represented on the y-axis. States of legal regulation are points on the graph.

The shaded area represents all possible states of legal regulation, and its limit, the convex curve $x^2+y^2 = c^2$, is the Pareto-optimal set of states of legal regulation in which no gain to one principle can be made without cost to the other. The test of suitability/capability requires one to select a point in the shaded area, and the test of necessity requires one to choose the least intrusive state of affairs possible for any given level of realisation of the other principle, ie one must select a point on the convex curve.

The solid thick line is an indifference curve representing states of legal regulation in which we would be happy to trade off losses and gains of one principle for the other. It is concave, on account of the fact that the less one has of one principle, the correspondingly more one requires of the other to accept the cost-benefit trade-off. It corresponds to the formula $xy=nc^2$. Points on or above this line outside the shaded area are desirable but impossible to realise. Points below the line are unacceptable.

The two thin solid lines represent two alternative approaches by a court. In the case of pragmatism, all, or practically all, necessary measures are acceptable (n is very small). In the case of idealism (n=0.5), only one necessary measure is acceptable. This corresponds to the 'one right answer' thesis.

One feature of this diagram is counter-intuitive. This is the idea that a necessary state of legal regulation may be 'better than optimal' in the sense that the product of the relevant principles is greater than required for an acceptable trade-off. The concave indifference curve dips below the convex Pareto-optimality curve. In practice, courts have no need to draw attention to this feature, since they are only interested at the last stage in *disproportionality*, in other words they are only interested in those points on the necessity curve that are *below* the balance curve.

as a duty to avoid disproportionate policies, which indicates a set of limits represented by the intersections of curves representing a less idealistic approach.

The variability of balancing as against necessity has great explanatory power. For example, it explains how the doctrine of proportionality can function as a heuristic for correct answers on the part of primary decision-takers, while remaining open to a range of solutions from the perspective of the court. In a typical case of new legislation limiting rights, the legislature perceives a threat to a legitimate state aim which needs addressing. It recognises that the proposed legislation will have costs to rights as well as gains, but considers that the future state of legal regulation will be better all things considered than the current state. In other words, it considers that the current state of legal regulation is below the indifference curve. However, from the perspective of court reviewing and approving the new legislation, both the old and the new states of legal regulation are constitutionally legitimate: there is no obligation to act, but nor is there a prohibition on acting. Both states of legal regulation are on the indifference curve. Effectively, the two bodies are working with two different indifference curves, and the court's is less demanding.

However, we are left with the question: what is to guide the court in determining how pragmatic or idealistic to be? The answer to that question will determine the extent of the legislature's structural discretion.

EPISTEMIC DISCRETIONS

Alexy's discussion of epistemic discretion is rooted in the problem of ignorance and divides it up into empirical and normative discretion. Empirical epistemic discretion arises from our ignorance of fact. We may not know to what extent a particular aim will be realised. We know that if the aim will only be realised to a small extent the limitation of rights will not be justified, but that if the aim is realised to a large extent, the limitation will be justified. But we cannot tell which it is. Suppose that in spite of this ignorance we permit the limitation. We will have accepted the existence of discretion (to risk an unjustifiable rights-infringement) on account of empirical epistemic ignorance.

Normative epistemic discretion arises from the fact that even when we know all the relevant factual background we may still be uncertain how serious a limitation of a right actually is. As we have seen, this problem may in fact be structural—breaches of rights may only exist as discrete points on a relatively small scale, or it may be epistemic—differences exist but they are not perceivable. In practice, it does not matter how one understands the difference. More important is the observation that normative doubt may arise in three different respects. First, we may be unsure how to rank ordinally different infringements or realisations of a single principle. For example, we might find it hard to rank according to relative seriousness a prohibition of published writing and a prohibition of oral speech. Secondly, we may be unsure as to the relative abstract weight of values. Abstract weight is always relative, because it compares one value with another, identifying one as less or more important in general than the other. For example, we might agree that life is (in general) more important than liberty, but we may not know by how much. Again, we may not know how to relate liberty and privacy. Thirdly, we may be unsure as to the relative concrete weight of values. We might know how serious a particular infringement of rights is relative to other possible infringements of the same right, and we might know how important the right is in general relative to some other principle, and we might know how important this particular realisation of that other principle is, but we may still be unsure how the two scales correlate to each other. These considerations give rise to three distinct types of discretion: cultural, evidential and scalar discretion.

Cultural Discretion

Policy-choice discretion is the most significant form of structural discretion in the domestic context. The theory of principles also offers a way of understanding an allied discretionary doctrine within international and European law: the 'margin of appreciation'.[15] This doctrine is not fully coherent, in that it performs a number of functions including a preservation of the subsidiary nature of international adjudication and the reliance of international courts on domestic fact-finding processes. However, the margin of appreciation is also the means by which cultural diversity is accommodated. In this role it can be distinguished from forms of discretion in domestic contexts.

Of course, the admission of an element of cultural diversity into 'universal' international and European human rights protection is controversial. Some argue that the standards should be fixed in all detail for all. But the argument that political communities should be permitted to establish their own hierarchies of value within the relatively open texture of human rights instruments is at least plausible, and the theory of principles is able to account for this.

The level of satisfaction or infringement of a principle is a function both of the specific degree to which it is affected on the facts of the case and the abstract value of the principle. Abstract values may be identical, but they

[15] See J Rivers, 'Proportionality and Discretion in International and European Law' in N Tsagourias (ed), *Transnational Constitutionalism: International and European Perspectives* (Cambridge, Cambridge University Press, 2006).

may also vary relative to each other. We tend to assume, broadly speaking, that life is more important than physical integrity, which is more important than liberty, which is more important than property. The meaning and location of privacy and equality in the ranking are more controversial. What 'more important' means is given by the relationship of the ranked set of limitations of one right to the ranked set in respect of another right. One right is more important in the abstract than another right when the first of every pair of situations ranked equally on an ordinal basis in the context of a single value is more important than the second. Different political communities differ from each other in their abstract rankings. For example, the United States tends to favour liberty more highly than privacy relative to European states. North and South Europeans differ over the claims of equality. It is not at all obvious that it is the function of international courts to ensure the adoption of a uniform political culture in the sense of an identical hierarchy of the different values expressed in human rights instruments. Thus, political communities may choose within limits what abstract weight to accord to the different values at stake.

It is important to note that cultural discretion can only affect the test of proportionality in the narrow sense; it cannot affect necessity. The reason for this is, first, that necessity does not compare two different values. It simply requires the avoidance of unnecessary human rights costs given any level of realisation of a public interest. Abstract weight cannot affect the ordinal ranking of states of affairs relative to any single value. Secondly, necessity depends on the world as it is factually constituted. The least intrusive means of achieving some end is set by the way people and societies are. Rather, the effect of cultural discretion is to accept as balanced laws which at first sight might appear to be unbalanced, on account of the abstract weight of the principles involved. The effect is to widen the scope of structural policy-choice discretion, by pushing the boundaries of the range of balanced necessary measures outwards.

The question is once again, how much cultural discretion an international court should permit to a domestic system. In form, this question is very similar to that of policy-choice discretion, since the court is asking what range of necessary rights-limitations it will also accept as balanced. This time though, instead of the court being faced with a range of positions from pragmatism to idealism, it is faced with a range from relativism to absolutism. A relativist court could argue that there is no right answer to the relative abstract values of principles; since objectively speaking, the values are incommensurable, virtually any scheme of values is plausible, so long as it does not deny the minimum basis of human rights instruments that the values represented there must count for something. An absolutist international court will not permit any cultural variation to the scheme of abstract values it adopts.

The problem of cultural discretion is therefore very similar to that of policy-choice discretion, in that they both concern the adoption of less demanding balance curves by a reviewing court. This should not surprise us, in that cultural discretion is the main form of normative epistemic discretion, which as we have seen can equally well be represented as a structural discretion.

Evidential Discretion

In the Postscript, Alexy solves the problem of empirical epistemic doubt by reference to a formal or procedural principle: namely the principle that the democratically-elected legislature should take as many decisions as possible. This means that uncertainty is not necessarily to be resolved in favour of rights protection. Rather, it indicates the existence of a second law of balancing which runs as follows: the more intensive an interference in a constitutional right is, the greater must be the certainty of its underlying premises.

He exemplifies this by reference to the 'co-determination judgement' with its triadic scale of intensity of review.[16] Where limitations of rights are minor, the court need only be satisfied that the empirical basis is not evidently false, ie that there was some basis for the empirical judgement. Where limitations of rights are moderate, the court should ensure that the factual prognosis is at least plausible. Where limitations of rights are serious, there must be an intensive review of content.

This seems to conflate several questions, and it is not immediately clear whether this represents a desirable simplification or the glossing over of important distinctions. First, there is the 'objective' question of the chance of realising a particular outcome. In practice, this question is made more complicated by the fact that there will be a range of outcomes, with some minor effects very likely and some highly desirable gains extremely unlikely.[17] Let us assume however that this complexity can be reduced to a single chance-factored level of outcome. Secondly, there is the procedural question of what the legislature has done, and should do, in order to ground its assessment of the chance of a gain. At one extreme, the policy may be based on intuition and 'common knowledge'; at the other extreme, the policy may have been preceded by extensive research and consultation. This does not affect the chance of the outcome (which is a function of the world as it is), but it does affect the reliability of the legislature's judgement of that chance. Thirdly, there is the question of what the court should do

[16] BVerfGE 50, 290 at 333.

[17] Carlos Bernal Pulido, 'On Alexy's Weight Formula' in Agustín J Menéndez and Erik O Eriksen (eds), *Fundamental Rights through Discourse* (ARENA Report 9/2004, Oslo, 2004).

when faced with a dispute about a matter of factual prognosis. Typically, the legislature will maintain that enough has been done for its judgement of the chance of policy success to be sufficiently reliable. The complainant, on the other hand, will allege either that not enough has been done to be sure or that the chance of policy success has been unjustifiably inflated. Assuming that the court does not have its own resources for carrying out the relevant empirical research, whom should the court believe?

The first observation to make is that uncertainty can affect either side of the balancing equation. The degree to which a right is infringed could be uncertain, as could the extent of any realisation of a competing interest. We should therefore at least reformulate the second law of balancing as follows: the greater the chance that one principle may be seriously infringed, the greater must be the chance that another principle is realised to a high degree. In other words, a certainty factor must appear on both sides of the weight equation.[18] The second law of balancing as it is formulated in the Postscript is only a specific instance, namely the case in which the degree of infringement of a right is certain but the degree of achievement of a competing social goal is uncertain.

In practice, that specific instance is entirely normal. If we imagine a challenge to a ban on certain forms of expression for national security purposes, it will be no answer for the government to point out that people will say things anyway in spite of the prohibition, and that prosecutions will be rare, so the effect of the ban on freedom of expression is not so great. They must assume that what is legally prohibited will not happen. By contrast, the same type of argument (the ban is unenforceable, etc) is good in the mouth of the aggrieved individual as a way of demonstrating that the gain to national security is illusory. This is not sleight-of-hand. The cost to freedom of expression is directly related to the prohibition; the gain to national security is only indirectly related; the government cannot rationally care about people being prohibited from talking as such; what they care about is military secrets getting into the hands of those who could use them to undermine the security of the state. But whereas the government must assume obedience to law in its restrictions on rights, it cannot assume obedience to law in its gains to policies. Uncertainty about the effect of a policy on the enjoyment of rights is only appropriate in circumstances where the state is not directly responsible for rights violations, as typically in cases of horizontal effect or repatriation of an individual into the jurisdiction of another state.

Evidential asymmetry is thus normal in fundamental rights cases, and it means that in practice uncertainty usually plagues the extent to which

[18] Alexy's more recent formulation of the second law of balancing recognises this: 'On Balancing and Subsumption: A Structural Comparison' (2003) 16 *Ratio Juris* 433 at 446.

desirable social goals will be achieved, but not the extent to which rights are limited. It follows that evidential problems will play no part in a clash of rights. If an individual is given a new private law cause of action (eg a right under a tort of privacy) we can assume that they will do what they are permitted to do, and that individual liberties will be constrained as a result. In this context we are considering states of legal regulation rather than states of affairs.

However, the recognition that uncertainty could afflict either side of the proportionality equation casts doubt on the suggestion that formal principles necessarily have a role to play. The function of proportionality is to optimise the enjoyment of relevant principles, and optimisation is secured when certainty is factored into the degree of infringement or realisation of a principle. The duty of any decision-taking body is to optimise in the light of what is known, taking due account of the relevant risks and uncertainties. If a decision-taker only acted on the basis of certainty, it would not optimise over time. It follows from this that the more serious an infringement of rights being considered, the greater must be the chance of realising a weighty public interest—and both the weight of the public interest and the chance of realising it are relevant to this equation. This is independent of any procedural question of what must be done in order to be certain about that chance, or any formal principle governing the role of courts reviewing legislative action. If the Postscript is ambiguous on this point, subsequent writings have clarified it.[19]

Courts cannot engage in empirical research themselves; they are in practice reliant on the other branches of government. However, they can insist that the other branches take sufficient steps to ensure that their judgement of the chance of outcome is not merely subjectively persuasive, but objectively binding on the court. It is suggested that this is the purpose of the discussion in the co-determination judgement of intensity of review. Courts will only accept limitations of rights if the empirical judgements underlying the policy in question are sufficiently *reliable* that they may adopt them as their own. Reliability here means something quite different from probability. A judgement is reliable if courts ought to accept it as correct.

This indicates that the second law of balancing could be understood in one of two ways. It could be interpreted as follows:

> (probability formulation) the more serious a violation of rights is, the greater must be the objective chance of realising some competing interest to a sufficiently great extent.

Or as follows:

[19] 'On Balancing and Subsumption', above n 18, combines the first and second laws of balancing into a 'complete' weight formula.

(reliability formulation) the more serious a violation of rights is, the greater must be the reliability of the legislature's assessment that a competing interest will be realised to a sufficiently great extent.

The first interpretation is implicit in the first law of balancing and does not require separate elucidation. The second interpretation is truly dependent on formal principles and is worth identifying.

Is there any practical difference between these two formulations? It is undoubtedly the case that courts often do not distinguish probability from reliability. A policy may be found disproportionate on the basis of a combination of concerns embracing both the chance of realisation and the trustworthiness of the legislature's prognosis. Alexy's preference for the probability formulation may be another example of the tendency already noted to downplay the significance of formal principles and to seek to understand the legal doctrine of proportionality as a purely substantive device.

The main objection to the probability formulation is that it construes the problem of evidential discretion as requiring us to presuppose a formal principle that the legislature has the right to take 'important decisions', ie a right to take chances. This is, presumably, pitted against a right on the part of the court to review for proportionality. But it is not clear why this should give rise to variable review in accordance with the seriousness of the limitation of rights. It would not be unreasonable to suppose that a decision is more important if it infringes rights seriously. To explain the co determination judgement we need a formal principle stating that courts should care more about checking that serious limitations of rights are indeed proportionate. This must balanced with another formal principle stating that legislatures should identify and evaluate the factual basis for their proposed policies.

In short, the problem of empirical epistemic (or evidential) discretion concerns the reliability of the legislature's factual prognoses. Its extent is governed by two competing formal principles, namely the principle that it is the proper role of the legislature to make the relevant factual prognosis and the principle that the courts are the guardians of rights. It follows that as a limitation of rights becomes more serious, the reliability of the factual prognosis must rise, in the sense that the court may demand that the legislature put more procedural resources into establishing the factual basis, before it will accept the prognosis as correct.

Scalar Discretion

The final form of discretion is the leeway left to legislatures when the court adopts a certain scale of value realisations.

If the court were to adopt a two-point scale, all infringements of principles would be equal. The court would only be able to identify the existence (or not) of an infringement of a right and the existence (or not) of a legitimate aim. This corresponds to a situation of maximal discretion. However, once one is prepared to recognise the possibility of greater or lesser infringements or realisations, the possibility of carrying out the necessity and the balancing test is also given.

Alexy sets up a three-point[20] scale of light, moderate and serious. As he rightly points out, we need not adopt a three-point scale; it could be nine-point or indeed anything. The interesting point for us is that the 'thickness' of the curves representing necessity and proportionality will be affected by the fineness of the scale. On his three-point scale, one-third of the possible states of legal regulation will overvalue one principle relative to the other; one-third will undervalue them and one-third will have them balanced. Since in the context of constitutional review it will normally be adequate to show that the level of achievement of the public interest is at least great enough to outweigh the cost to rights, two-thirds of the possible situations will be constitutionally acceptable. However, if we adopt a nine-point scale, four-ninths of the possible states of regulation will overvalue one principle, four-ninths undervalue them and only one-ninth will get them balanced. Five-ninths of possible states of affairs will be constitutionally acceptable. The general lesson is clear: on an n-point scale of value, only 1/nth of the possible states of legal regulation will be balanced, and (n+1)/2n will be constitutionally permissible.[21] As n increases this figure tends to 50 per cent.

To put all this in (tolerably) plain English, the extent of discretion of a decision-taker is inversely proportional to the ability of a court to assess degrees of realisation of the relevant competing principles. Let us call this discretion, 'scalar discretion'. Its scope is determined by the number of points on the scale.

One feature of the effect of fineness of scale on possible states of legal regulation should be noted and distinguished. On an n-point scale, the chance of the nth most serious violation of rights being constitutionally acceptable is 1/n. The chance of the (n-1)th most serious violation of rights

[20] Strictly speaking, this is four-point scale on account of the possibility that there is no infringement of rights at all.

[21] On an n-point scale, there will be n^2 possible pairs of levels of rights infringements and interest realisations. N/n^2 of these will be balanced. $(n^2-n)/n^2$ will therefore be unbalanced, half of these with the rights infringement weightier than the interest realisation (ie typically constitutionally unacceptable) and half of these with the rights infringement less significant than the interest realisation (ie typically constitutionally permissible). In total, therefore, $n/n^2 + (n^2-n)/2n^2$ will be constitutionally acceptable, being either balanced or with an interest realisation outweighing the cost to rights. This reduces to $(n+n^2)/2n^2$ or $(1+n)/2n$. I am grateful to Robert Alexy for clarifying this point.

being constitutionally acceptable is 2/n, etc. 'Chance' is to be understood in this context as the pre-argumentative probability of discovering something to be the case. The point is that the chance of constitutional acceptability reduces *both* as the limitation of rights becomes more serious *and* as the scale that the court adopts becomes more fine. The first of these is simply an outworking of the first law of balancing. The second raises the possibility that courts may control the scope of discretion by adopting more or less fine scales.

Problems of normative epistemic doubt in cases of concrete evaluations arise in two different circumstances. When considering necessity, courts are required to ask of hypothetical alternative policies (a) whether they achieve the legitimate aim to the same extent and (b) whether they infringe rights to a lesser extent. This does not require commensuration, but simply ordinal ranking within a single value. As a consequence, very fine distinctions are easy to draw. In practice, courts struggle with the fact that the distinctions they seem capable of drawing are too fine. It is often very easy to identify slight improvements in the level of rights enjoyment without any discernable loss to the legitimate aim. Strictly speaking, the policy under review has been exposed as unnecessary in some respect, although in the case of trivial modifications to policy, courts resist this conclusion.

By contrast, when considering proportionality in the narrow sense (balance), the identification of a rights limitation as light, moderate or serious is cardinal, in that 'light' means 'justifiable by reference to a small gain in the public interest'. It assumes the possibility of commensurability. At this point, courts often struggle to work with fine-grained scales, and it may well be the case that even the nine-point scale suggested in the Postscript is ambitious.

The important point to note is that courts have some control over the fineness of the scales they choose to work with. In respect of necessity they have the power to ignore improvements in rights enjoyment that are too trivial. In respect of proportionality in the narrow sense, they can demand better reasons for accepting that the gain to the legitimate aim is at least as great as the cost to rights. It is at this point that we need some principle to guide the court in assessing how fine a scale to choose.

THE SECOND LAW OF BALANCING

It is worth summarising the argument so far. Alexy introduces the second law of balancing as a solution to problems of epistemic uncertainty: the more serious a violation of rights, the more certain the underlying premises must be. We have seen that on one interpretation, such a maxim is already implicit in the first law of balancing. It does not require the adoption of any formal principle governing the relationship between court and legislature. Given that our knowledge is limited, it will inevitably be the case that a serious limitation of rights will not be outweighed by risky attempts to achieve our aims, whereas a moderate limitation of rights may or may not be outweighed by the chance of a major gain, depending on the size of the chance. It is also implicit in the first law of balancing that the more serious a limitation of rights is being contemplated, the less the likelihood is at a pre-argumentative stage of there being sufficient gains to justify the limitation being contemplated.

However, we have also seen that in reviewing for proportionality, courts are faced with a series of further questions: (1) How idealistic should courts be in seeking to maximise the balance of rights and the public interest and thus constrain policy choice? (2) To what extent should international courts permit cultural variation in abstract conceptions of rights? (3) In what circumstances should courts demand that primary decision-takers put more procedural resources into establishing matters of empirical fact? (4) When may the court ignore trivial gains to rights in the context of necessity review? (5) How insistent should courts be that they hear all the arguments for and against the policy in question? In all five ways courts have the power to control the discretion of primary decision-takers when reviewing for proportionality.

These questions cannot all be answered in the same way. For example, the question about cultural discretion must be answered systemically. It would make nonsense of the idea of a permissible range of abstract weightings to argue that where the limitation of rights is serious, the range is small. International courts must simply take a position on how much variation they will permit and then act consistently.

The other questions do admit of degree, but not the same type of degree. Policy-choice discretion cannot vary with the seriousness of the limitation of rights, because it is concerned to identify a range of permissible policies which themselves vary from low cost, low gain to high cost, high gain. However, the discretion could vary with the abstract seriousness of the right. Thus, one could take the view that policies which limit the enjoyment of very important rights admit of a smaller range of permissible options than those which limit the enjoyment of less important rights. The concept of importance in this context could take account both of substantive importance (eg the right to life) and procedural importance in relation to the competence of courts (eg criminal process).

There is some evidence that courts reviewing the limitation of more important rights admit a smaller degree of policy-choice discretion than when reviewing the limitation of less important rights. Moreover, this model can explain the limiting case of policy-choice discretion, ie the situation in which there is just one point of intersection between the set of necessary policies and the set of balanced policies. According to the law of competing principles, we would expect the most serious rights to admit only of a single set of rule-based exceptions. This is what we regularly find in the case of the right to life, for example.

This leaves us with evidential and scalar discretion. These do admit of degree according both to the seriousness of the limitation on the facts at hand and to the abstract weight of the relevant right.

It is suggested that the proper role of the second law of balancing is to guide the courts in determining the intensity of review, wherever the court has the power to review more or less intensively. It can be expressed generally as follows: the more serious a limitation of rights is, the more intense should be the review engaged in by the court.

As applied to the three variable discretions identified above this means that:

- the more weighty a right is engaged, the less will be the scope of structural discretion;
- the more serious a limitation of rights is, the more procedural resources must be devoted to establishing the factual basis of the policy under review;
- the more serious a limitation of rights is, the more concerned the court will be to identify slight gains to rights enjoyment at no cost to the policy and the more willing it will be to differentiate the level of policy achievement from the level of rights limitation.

It is suggested that the second law of balancing thus formulated represents a formal counterpart to the substantive first law of balancing. It is based upon the formal principle that the court is the guardian of rights. Just as greater infringements of rights require more weighty realisations of the public interest to justify the infringment, so too greater infringements of rights require more heightened scrutiny by the courts.[22]

CONCLUSION

The account of discretion in the Postscript, like much of the *Theory* itself, shows tendencies towards institutional neutrality. An institutionally neutral account of discretion would make the extent of discretion co-extensive with the extent of proportionality. Since the doctrine of proportionality leaves us with a range of possible rational courses of action, courts can enforce proportionality to the fullest extent and still leave legislatures with a range of possibilities.

[22] An attempt to apply this in the British context can be found in J Rivers, 'Proportionality and Variable Intensity of Review' (2006) 65 *Cambridge Law Journal* 174.

However, it is suggested that the problem of discretion cannot be solved by application of substantive theory alone. Legislative discretion is unavoidably related to questions of competence and legitimacy, and is thus institutionally aware. It requires the recognition of formal principles, not least the principle that the judiciary are the guardians of rights.

This indicates that the first law of balancing underlying the doctrine of proportionality must be supplemented by a second, formal, law. This states that: the more serious a limitation of rights is, the more intense should be the review engaged in by the court.

'Intensity of review' relates to a number of features of constitutional rights adjudication over which the court has control. It refers to the size of the range of proportionate decisions a legislature may take, as well as the requirements for ensuring the reliability of empirical prognoses and the fineness of the scales of evaluation adopted.

9

Human Rights and the Claim to Correctness in the Theory of Robert Alexy

JAN-R SIECKMANN*

INTRODUCTION

THE THESIS THAT people necessarily lay claim to truth or correctness in practical argumentation and are therefore committed to the idea of moral truth or correctness constitutes a central element in Robert Alexy's discourse theory of law. It not only provides a basis for the justification of rules of discourse[1] and of the thesis that juridical discourse is a special case of practical discourse,[2] but also provides a link between the procedural theory of discourse and certain substantial conclusions, namely, the thesis of a necessary connection between law and morality[3] as well as a discourse theoretical justification of human rights.[4]

* I am greatly indebted to Bonnie Litschewski Paulson for corrections and improvements in the English of my text.

[1] R Alexy, 'Diskurstheorie und Menschenrechte' in R Alexy, *Recht, Vernunft, Diskurs* (Frankfurt am Main, Suhrkamp, 1995) 127 (English translation: 'Discourse Theory and Human Rights' (1996) 9 *Ratio Juris* 209); cf also the justification of discursive rights in J Habermas, *Die Einbeziehung des Anderen* (Frankfurt am Main, Suhrkamp, 1996) 62.

[2] R Alexy, *Theorie der juristischen Argumentation*, 2nd edn (Frankfurt am Main, Suhrkamp, 1991) (English translation of the 1st edn, *Theory of Legal Argumentation* (Oxford, Clarendon Press, 1989)); R Alexy, 'The Special Case Thesis' (1999) 12 *Ratio Juris* 374.

[3] R Alexy, *Begriff und Geltung des Rechts*, 2nd edn (Freiburg/München, Alber, 1994) (English translation: *The Argument from Injustice: A Reply to Positivism* (Oxford, Clarendon Press, 2002)); R Alexy, 'Law and Correctness' (1998) 51 *Current Legal Problems* 205. For a discussion of this thesis, cf E Bulygin, 'Alexy's Thesis of the Necessary Connection between Law and Morality' (2000) 13 *Ratio Juris* 133; R Alexy, 'On the Thesis of a Necessary Connection between Law and Morality: Bulygin's Critique' (2000) 13 *Ratio Juris* 138; C Heidemann, 'Law's Claim to Correctness' in S Coyle and G Pavlakos (eds), *Jurisprudence or Legal Science?* (Oxford and Portland/Oregon, Hart Publishing, 2005) 127.

[4] Alexy, above n 1 at 132.

The latter issue is the subject of this chapter. Alexy bases his defence of the existence of universal human rights on the thesis of the necessity of a claim to correctness in practical discourse. The attractiveness of this approach is that if one can show that people necessarily claim correctness in their argumentation, one can refer to this claim in arguing for the validity of certain rights. Hence, one would not need a substantial justification of human rights, but could refer to what all people presuppose in their argumentation.

I will discuss the argument of the claim to correctness in Alexy's theory and its use within his discursive justification of human rights. After outlining his theory, I comment critically on it. Finally, I suggest an alternative conception of a claim to correctness in normative argumentation.

ALEXY'S CONCEPTION OF A NECESSARY CLAIM TO CORRECTNESS

The basis of Alexy's thesis of the necessity of a claim to correctness is an analysis of the presuppositions of discourse. This type of argument is typical for discourse theories. According to Karl-Otto Apel's theory of communicative ethics, everyone taking part in communication must make certain transcendental-pragmatic presuppositions.[5] According to Jürgen Habermas' discourse theory, communicative action includes certain universal-pragmatic presuppositions, in particular the principle of discourse, according to which norms are justified if and only if they can gain the consent of all participants in an ideal discourse.[6]

According to Alexy, the necessity of a claim to correctness forms part of a transcendental-pragmatic argument establishing the universal validity of the rules of discourse. He elaborates on this argument by analysing the speech act of assertion, assuming the transcendental necessity of making assertions, and pursues the argument by extending the discursive claim to correctness to the necessity of accepting the principle of autonomy, which forms the basis of the recognition of human rights.

Justification of the Rules of Discourse

Alexy's basic thesis is:

(1) Whoever asserts something lays claim to truth or correctness.[7]

[5] K-O Apel, *Transformation der Philosophie*, vol 2 (Frankfurt am Main, Suhrkamp, 1973) 414.

[6] J Habermas, *Faktizität und Geltung*, 4th edn (Frankfurt am Main, Suhrkamp, 1994).

[7] Alexy, above n 1 at 135.

According to Alexy, denying this claim to truth would amount to a performative contradiction. A performative contradiction results when, with a particular speech act someone presupposes something denied by the content of that very speech act. Alexy's second thesis is:

(2) The claim to truth or correctness implies a claim to justifiability *(Begründbarkeit)*.[8]

The claim to justifiability requires that a reason can be given for an assertion. The claim requires neither that the reasons given be good reasons nor that in every case a reason must be given. However, if a reason is asked for and there is no warrant for refusing to give a reason an obligation to give a reason exists. As a consequence, Alexy offers as a third thesis:

(3) The claim to justifiability implies a prima facie obligation to give a reason for an assertion when a reason is asked for.

Moreover, making an assertion means entering into discourse, and from this act follow further presuppositions with normative content. When participating in discourse, one must presuppose that certain requirements are met.[9] In Alexy's theory, these normative presuppositions of participation in discourse are included in a fourth thesis:

(4) Giving a justification implies, at least with respect to the argumentation itself, the claims to equal rights, freedom from coercion and universality.[10]

From this are inferred the right of everybody to participate in a discourse and the rights of equality and liberty within a discourse. Thus, certain rights within a discourse are established. Alexy himself emphasises, however, that the argument so far does not suffice to justify any norms or moral rights outside a discourse.[11]

The next step of the argument is to establish the necessity of the claim to correctness. Alexy suggests that the stated claims connected with assertions are not based on a mere definition of what an assertion is, but that making assertions of this kind is necessary. This is the basis of a transcendental argument.[12] Alexy's thesis is:

(5) Whoever in his whole life makes no assertion in the sense defined by theses (1) to (3) and gives no justification in the sense of thesis (4) does not take part in the most general form of human life.

[8] *Ibid* at 136.

[9] In Habermas' theory, these requirements consist of the right to take part in the discourse with equal chances for everybody who has to make a relevant contribution; the sincerity of the participants; the absence of coercion, cf Habermas, above n 1 at 62. These presuppositions are supposed to justify the principle of discourse D, that only those norms can claim validity that can gain the consent of all participants in a practical discourse: *ibid* at 49.

[10] Alexy, above n 1 at 138.

[11] *Ibid* at 147; Habermas, above n 1 at 62.

[12] Alexy, above n 1 at 139.

Alexy considers it to be practically impossible not to take part in argumentation as the most general form of human life. Such universal elements of argumentation as described in the rules of discourse belong to all forms of human life.[13] He concedes, however, that the capacity to resolve conflicts by means of argumentation does not necessarily imply making use of this capacity. Argumentation plays this role only if human beings have an overriding interest in resolving conflicts in the correct way, in the sense of a just resolution.[14]

At this point, Alexy distinguishes between the ideal and the real validity of the rules of discourse. These rules are valid ideally or hypothetically only if correctness is considered from an ideal point of view. This validity is factually limited,[15] so Alexy supplements his transcendental argument by positing that human beings have an interest in correctness sufficiently strong to override other interests. He does not assume that everybody actually has such an interest in correctness, but instead he distinguishes between subjective and objective validity. Subjective validity refers to motivation, objective validity to external behaviour.[16] According to Alexy, objective recognition of the rules of discourse is necessary because in the long run that would be advantageous in maximising utility. One must expect that at least some people have an interest in correctness and it would be advantageous therefore at least to pretend an interest in correctness.[17]

Discursive Justification of Human Rights

Alexy points out two issues with regard to the justification of human rights: the problem of form, that is, why it is necessary that human rights take the form of positive law, and the problem of content, that is, which human rights must be recognised.[18] I will confine my discussion to the problem of content. In this context, Alexy distinguishes between direct and indirect justification of human rights. A direct justification must show that certain rights are discursively necessary, independently of any actual discourse, while an indirect justification stems from a political procedure that meets discourse theoretical requirements. Alexy addresses only a direct justification of human rights.[19] He denies the possibility of directly deriving human rights from the rules of discourse, for these are merely

13 *Ibid* at 140.
14 *Ibid* at 141.
15 *Ibid* at 142.
16 *Ibid* at 143.
17 *Ibid* at 143, 144.
18 *Ibid* at 144.
19 *Ibid* at 147.

rules of speech, which do not have implications for the realm of action. Further premises are needed, therefore, which must be discursively necessary. Alexy suggests three independent but mutually supportive arguments: the argument from autonomy, the argument from consensus and the argument from democracy.[20] I will discuss only the argument from autonomy, for it is here that the claim to correctness plays a role.

According to the argument from autonomy, every serious participant in a discourse must presuppose the autonomy of the other participants, and this rules out the denial of certain human rights.[21] To participate seriously in a discourse is to aim at resolving social conflicts by means of agreements discursively generated and governed.[22] It implies the exclusion of coercion and the recognition of the right of the other participants to follow only those principles that they consider, upon sufficient deliberation, to be correct and valid. Because these requirements protect autonomous decision-making, the interest in correctness implies an interest in autonomy.[23] Someone with a fully developed interest in moral correctness, thus combining the interest in moral correctness with an interest in autonomy, is called a 'genuine participant' in discourse.[24]

Alexy concedes that a justification based on such interests is hypothetical in that it holds only for those who acknowledge the principle of autonomy. Just as the rules of discourse cannot be established as subjectively valid by means of a transcendental argument, so likewise the subjective or motivational validity of the principle of autonomy cannot be so established. According to Alexy, however, the objective or institutional validity of the principle of autonomy can be justified on the basis of a long-term interest in maximising utility, just as the rules of discourse can be so justified.[25] Along the lines of Machiavelli, Alexy argues that even a dictator must at least pretend to follow the rules of discourse and the principle of autonomy if he wants to maximise utility for himself in the long run.

Alexy infers from the above argument a general right to autonomy—ie the right to judge freely what is obligatory and good and to act accordingly—as well as specific rights that follow from the general right of autonomy analytically or by means of teleological reasoning.[26]

20 *Ibid*.

21 *Ibid* at 148, referring to CS Nino, *The Ethics of Human Rights* (Oxford, Clarendon Press, 1991) 138.

22 Alexy, above n 1 at 149.

23 *Ibid* at 150.

24 *Ibid* at 151.

25 *Ibid* at 152.

26 *Ibid* at 154. The argument from consensus is that the legitimacy of the law depends on the recognition of basic rights, which citizens must mutually grant to each other if they want to regulate their common life legitimately by means of positive law (*ibid* at 155, referring to Habermas, above n 6 at 151). This argument supplements the principle of autonomy, according to Alexy, with elements of universality in the form of equality and impartiality

CRITIQUE

There are problems with Alexy's characterisation of the claim to correctness as well as with its foundation and its application to the justification of human rights. These problems stem from Alexy's primary focus on assertions as elements of discourse, the ambiguity of the term 'correctness', the various aspects of claiming correctness, the necessity of making such a claim, and the relevance of such claims in justifying discursive requirements like equal discursive rights, freedom from coercion and universality, as well as in justifying human rights.

Assertions in Normative Discourse

Alexy's argument for the necessity of a claim to correctness refers to making assertions in discourse. This speech act is said to be of primary importance in rational discourse, alongside the acts of asking questions and offering justifications. The assumption that assertions (or assertoric sentences) constitute the elements of argumentation seems almost to be common ground in epistemology and the theory of argumentation. Arguments are usually understood as sets of sentences that yield a particular conclusion.[27] This understanding, however, creates problems when applied within a discursive or, in general, a procedural theory of justification.

Problems arise because assertions contain propositions of what is, ie, assertions purport to state facts. For example, 'one shall not hurt other people', when used as a normative proposition, means that a norm exists that prohibits hurting other people. It is because of the existence of a corresponding fact that a proposition claims to be true or correct. This is not to say that facts can be identified independently of such statements and can therefore be used as a criterion for the truth of such statements. But propositions and facts go hand in hand, and one cannot separate a

(Alexy, above n 1 at 156). The argument from democracy is that whoever is interested in correctness and legitimacy must be interested in democracy, and whoever is interested in democracy must be interested in basic and human rights (*ibid* at 163). This argument is based on the assumptions that the principle of discourse requires an institutionalisation by democratic procedures according to which discursive requirements are approximately met, that such procedures require the recognition of human rights and equal opportunity to enjoy them, and that the possibility of enjoying such human rights requires the recognition of some non-political rights, like life, a minimum level of subsistence, and a certain level of education.

[27] D Buchwald, *Der Begriff der rationalen juristischen Begründung* (Baden-Baden, Nomos, 1990) 86, 88; H Wohlrapp, 'Über nicht-deduktive Argumente' in P Klein (ed), *Praktische Logik* (Göttingen, Vandenhoeck, 1990) 232; H Prakken, *Logical Tools for Modelling Legal Argument* (Dordrecht, Kluwer, 1997) 203.

proposition from the presupposition that a corresponding fact exists. At least, one cannot separate them without undermining the common understanding of assertions.[28]

The problem with assuming that arguments in a procedural theory of justification have the structure of propositions is the problem of how a statement of a normative fact, which might be the result of discourse, can be made at the beginning of a justificatory procedure. Arguments, which start or continue a procedure, are not statements of the result of a procedure. If it were possible to state the result of a justificatory procedure, there would be no need to go through with the procedure. Assertions or statements made at the beginning of a justificatory procedure presuppose something to be true or existent that one cannot yet know to be true or existent—or, if one could know, the justificatory procedure would be redundant.[29] The first problem with Alexy's conception of a necessary claim to correctness is that by focusing on assertions he seems to render a procedural justification redundant.

Conceptions of Correctness

The second problem is with the concept of correctness. Various uses of the term 'correctness' can be found in Alexy's writings. A first interpretation is correctness in the sense of the truth of a statement or of something analogous to truth in the case of a normative judgement.[30] Secondly, correctness is defined as discursive possibility.[31] Thirdly, correctness is used to indicate the use of the highest-level criterion for evaluation, for example, the use of truth to evaluate sentences, or the use of justice to evaluate the

[28] An interpretation of assertions without reference to facts is suggested by D Patterson, *Law and Truth* (Oxford and New York, Oxford University Press, 1996).

[29] Even more radically, one might doubt whether rational discourse can be an instrument of normative justification if moral truth exists, as normative assertions claim. For moral truth would be independent of discourse. Discourse could only be a heuristic device for finding the correct solution, whose correctness would be independent of rational discourse. If, by contrast, there were no criteria of moral truth, the conception of correctness as discursive possibility would be problematic. For then there could be different normative solutions able to gain (though not necessarily gaining) the consent of all participants in a discourse. If different normative solutions are possible, it seems too strong an inference to claim validity for any of them.

[30] R Alexy, 'Probleme der Diskurstheorie' in Alexy, *Recht, Vernunft, Diskurs*, above n 1 at 118 (English translation: 'Problems of Discourse Theory' (1988) 20 *Crítica* 43). Cf also Alexy, above n 2. A problem with this view is whether normative statements or arguments can be said to be true. Cf P Holländer, *Rechtsnorm, Logik und Wahrheitswerte* (Baden-Baden, Nomos, 1993) 16. Alexy leaves open the question of whether correctness is to be interpreted as truth. Some authors try to avoid the concept of truth in normative theories, talking instead of the correctness of norms: Habermas, above n 1 at 54. But this does not seem to be necessary as long as truth is used merely in a semantic sense necessarily connected with statements.

[31] Alexy, 'Probleme der Diskurstheorie', above n 30 at 121.

distribution of goods.[32] Fourthly, correctness is understood as moral correctness in discussions of the interest in correctness and its necessity.[33]

The various uses of the term 'correctness' may be interpreted as instances of a general concept of correctness that signifies accordance with certain requirements. For example, assertions should be true, and hence they are correct if they conform to this requirement. The results of discourse should be in accordance with the rules of discourse and hence should be discursively possible. Distribution of goods should conform to the norms of justice. Actions should conform to moral norms. In this interpretation, correctness is a relational concept expressing the conformity of something to a set of requirements.

One may question whether this conception of correctness is adequate. A central problem is that interpretations of correctness as truth or something like truth and as discursive possibility do not fit well together. Moreover, both are inadequate to a theory of procedural justification.

Defining correctness in practical discourse as discursive possibility is a special feature of Alexy's theory of discourse.[34] A judgement is said to be correct if it might be the result of ideal discourse.[35] This interpretation of correctness, however, seems to be implausible. First, assessing an action as correct usually means more than its mere admissibility. For example, if the issue is whether to have a cup of tea or a cup of coffee, both actions would be admissible, but it would be odd to say that it is correct to take the cup of tea. One might say, though, that it is correct to give money back that one has found. The evaluation as correct here has, beyond the mere admissibility of the act, the connotation that one is doing the right thing, ie, something required or obligatory.

Moreover, the interpretation of correctness as discursive possibility seems to be incompatible with the interpretation of correctness as something like truth. The truth of one judgement excludes the possibility that incompatible judgements are also and at the same time true. But according to the definition of correctness as mere discursive possibility, incompatible judgements could be simultaneously true. Alexy has reacted to this

[32] R Alexy, 'Gerechtigkeit als Richtigkeit', unpublished manuscript; cf also R Alexy, 'My Philosophy of Law: The Institutiona-lisa-ti-on of Reason' in L Wintgens (ed), *The Law in Philosophical Perspectives* (Dordrecht, Kluwer, 1999) 24.

[33] Alexy, 'Diskurstheorie und Menschenrechte', above n 1 at 141.

[34] Alexy, above n 2 at 357, 413; R Alexy, 'Die Idee einer prozeduralen Theorie der juristischen Argumentation' in Alexy, *Recht, Vernunft, Diskurs*, above n 1 at 110.

[35] Cf also J Habermas, 'Richtigkeit vs. Wahrheit' in Habermas, *Wahrheit und Rechtfertigung* (Frankfurt am Main, Suhrkamp, 1999) 285, who defines 'correct' (*richtig*) as 'ideally justified acceptability' (*ideal gerechtfertigte Akzeptabilität*).

problem by distinguishing between a relative procedural concept of correctness, which admits various possible solutions, and an absolute non-procedural concept of correctness, which everyone must use individually.[36] An individual cannot, according to Alexy, accept incompatible answers, but must claim that his answer is the only correct one.[37] Alexy describes this as a regulative idea of correctness, which requires trying to find the single correct answer. However, it follows neither from this regulative idea nor from anything else that, within a discursive conception of justification, one could as an individual claim to find the single correct answer. That would amount to claiming that rational discourse is redundant as an instrument of justification. The distinction between a relative procedural concept of correctness and an absolute non-procedural concept of correctness does not solve this problem. Rather, it leads to the conclusion that an individual cannot use in his reasoning a procedural conception of justification and therefore cannot base his normative justifications on discourse theory.

Alexy's conception of correctness does not conform then, to a conception of discursive justification. This does not imply that a conception of correctness cannot be developed that is adequate to discourse theory. The most plausible alternative seems to be the interpretation of correctness as something required. A position is correct if it must be accepted. This interpretation of correctness fits well with the procedural character of justification in discourse theory, for justifying norms or decisions within a procedural conception of justification requires performing the procedural acts of offering and accepting arguments. So it is plausible that the correct result is one that must be accepted. Correctness in this interpretation consists in the requirement of acceptance. It should be made clear, however, that this is not Alexy's conception of correctness.

Complexity of a Claim to Correctness

A further ambiguity is involved in the conception of making a claim. Alexy presents an explication of what is meant by laying claim to correctness, including, as elements, the assertion of correctness and therefore of justifiability, the guarantee of justifiability, and the expectation of acceptance:

> [Legal acts] are always connected to the non-institutional act of *asserting* that the legal act is substantially and procedurally correct ... Correctness implies justifiability. Therefore, in raising a claim to correctness, law also raises one to

36 Alexy, above n 2 at 413.
37 *Ibid* at 414.

> justifiability. In recognising this claim it does not only accept a general obligation to justification in principle; it also maintains that this obligation is complied with or can be met. The claim to correctness therefore includes not only a mere assertion of correctness but a *guarantee* of justifiability. Moreover, there is a third element besides assertion and guarantee. It is the *expectation* that all addressees of the claim will accept the legal act as correct as long as they take the standpoint of the respective legal system and so long as they are reasonable.[38]

The problematic elements of this conception of a claim to correctness are the guarantee of justifiability and the expectation of acceptance.[39] First, it is not clear what 'justifiability' means. Assertions claim to be true, and justifying such an assertion might be understood as proving it to be true, which implies that it is the only correct solution. A weaker claim might be that the assertion cannot be defeated, that is, cannot be proven to be wrong. This, however, would neither support the claim to truth of the assertion nor justify the expectation that everyone will accept or should reasonably be required to accept the assertion, for if different solutions are justifiable, other agents might well hold different views. If one takes the idea of discourse seriously, one cannot be sure that one's own view will turn out to be the result of discourse, and so one cannot reasonably guarantee that one's own position will not be defeated in rational discourse. Another and even weaker option would be to claim that one can give an argument for one's assertion, though perhaps merely a defeasible one.[40] This might be the sense of the claim to justifiability in Alexy's thesis (3), stating a prima facie obligation to give a reason for an assertion when a reason is asked for. It would be misleading, however, to call such a defeasible claim a 'guarantee' of justifiability. And the 'expectation' that the asserted claim will be accepted as correct cannot be supported in this way.

A guarantee of justifiability seems to imply, then, not just that reasons can be given but that these reasons are sound and finally must be accepted. The guarantee of justifiability refers to the result of rational discourse, but one cannot know in advance what the result of discourse will be or, if one

[38] R Alexy, 'Law and Correctness' (1998) 51 *Current Legal Problems* 206; R Alexy, 'Recht und Richtigkeit' in W Krawietz (ed), *The Reasonable as Rational?, Festschrift Aarnio* (Berlin, Duncker & Humblot, 2000) 3.

[39] Moreover, these claims are ambiguous owing to the unclear meaning of a claim to correctness. If only legal correctness in the sense of compatibility with the legal norm is meant, then only justification and acceptance of a decision as legally correct would be required. This, however, would not suffice to establish a claim to moral correctness. If a claim to moral correctness and, accordingly, the normative implications of such a claim are to be proven necessary, a stronger concept of correctness must be used.

[40] On the concept of defeasibility cf P Wang, *Defeasibility in der juristischen Begründung* (Baden-Baden, Nomos, 2003); J Hage, *Reasoning with Rules* (Dordrecht, Kluwer, 1997); Prakken, above n 27.

could know, discourse would be unnecessary and redundant as an instrument of justification. Alexy himself emphasises in another context that there cannot be a guarantee that discourse will lead to consensus.[41] But if there cannot be a guarantee of consensus and, according to discourse theory, consensus is the criterion for justification, then one cannot guarantee that one's own position is justifiable.

Moreover, one cannot expect that the other participants in discourse will accept one's own position even if they adopt the legal point of view and are reasonable. For just as reasonable people may disagree on normative issues, they may well have different opinions. Alexy himself emphasises that different positions may be discursively possible and therefore correct.[42] Accordingly, it would be unreasonable to expect—in either an empirical or a normative sense—that all other agents will agree to one's own position. Such an expectation would be unfounded and cannot be part of a necessary claim to correctness. One might expect, though, that one's argument is accepted as not being faulty and in this weak sense correct. If, however, one concedes that reasonable disagreement is possible and that there may be valid arguments for contrary views, one cannot expect that all other agents will accept one's own argument. If, by contrast, one assumes that there is a single correct solution to a disputed issue, one might well expect that one's own assertion will be met with general acceptance. Indeed, Alexy assumes that an agent must claim from his own point of view that his position is the only correct one. From this, an individual's point of view, however, practical discourse can have only a heuristic, not a justificatory function. The dilemma is that connecting assertions to a guarantee of justifiability and an expectation of acceptance renders practical discourse redundant as a justificatory device, while taking discourse seriously, conceding that one's own position will not necessarily coincide with the result of discourse, excludes a guarantee of justifiability and an expectation of the acceptance of one's own position.

Necessity of a Claim to Correctness

The critique of Alexy's conception of a claim to correctness implies that such a claim cannot be supposed to be necessary. One might concede that the justifiability of one's own position cannot be guaranteed, that one's own view may not be accepted by other agents as the result of discourse, and that contrary views can be correctly held. One might wish therefore to avoid making assertions and to look for other forms of argument, forms that do not entail the claim to correctness as characterised by Alexy. Even

[41] Alexy, above n 2 at 412.
[42] *Ibid* at 413.

if there were a practice for making normative assertions, it does not follow that this practice would be correct or that such a practice could not be changed.

As to the latter point, John Mackie has suggested that the use of normative statements rests on a mistake.[43] The grammar of such statements implies an assertion of the existence of a corresponding norm, but, according to Mackie, this assertion is erroneous, and the structure of normative language should be changed. If Mackie is right, it cannot be necessary to make assertoric claim of the correctness of normative statements. Of course, one may question Mackie's 'error thesis', but Alexy's thesis of the necessity of a claim to correctness offers nothing that could refute Mackie. Thus, one cannot hold that it is necessary to make normative statements that lay claim to correctness.

General Implications of a Claim to Correctness

A further problem is what follows from the necessity of laying claim to correctness. Having rejected Alexy's thesis of the necessity of a claim to correctness as well as his conception of the claim, one has no basis for accepting the implications he attributes to the claim. But one might ask whether the suggested implications do hold within Alexy's theory.

The problem here is what follows from an assertoric claim to truth. A statement that p implies an assertion that this statement is true. If someone were to assert 'p' but to deny that p is true it could hardly be said that a statement of p was made at all. The thesis that statements are necessarily connected to a claim to truth seems to be true for semantic reasons.[44] This does not, however, seem to have implications for the justification of norms or rights.

Truth is usually taken to be independent of what people think of or accept as true. But if a statement is true independently of people's beliefs, there seems to be no reason, if a statement is claimed to be true, for implicitly acknowledging the norms or rights of those people. If the statement is true, it is true independently of the recognition of certain norms or rights. The semantic claim to truth, therefore, does not suffice for any normative conclusions.

Discourse theory might try to solve this problem by assuming that a statement is true if it would be accepted as a result of ideal discourse, which would have to involve the recognition of certain rights as well as the paying of due respect to arguments. But this does not measure up as an

[43] J Mackie, *Ethics: Inventing Right and Wrong* (London, Penguin, 1980) 58.

[44] J Sieckmann, 'Semantischer Normbegriff und Normbegründung' (1994) 80 *Archiv fur Rechts und Sozialphilosophie* 229. Cf also Heidemann, above n 3 at 132.

analysis of truth because truth is different from ideal consensus or rational acceptability.[45] A claim to correctness implying the recognition of certain norms or rights might be based on the claim that something is the result of a correct discursive procedure in which certain discursive rights have been respected. But the recognition of certain rights cannot be based simply on the claim to truth included in assertions. Accordingly, if the justification of discursive rights is to succeed, it must be based directly on a theory of procedural justification. And if the theory of discursive justification is to be correct, it must be presupposed. But its correctness cannot be based on the presuppositions of assertions.

Justification of Human Rights

Alexy presents the justification of human rights as an attempt to justify norms not only in the sphere of discourse but also in the sphere of action.[46] Although one might expect, then, that my critique of his conception of a necessary claim to correctness will bear on his justification of human rights, this is not entirely clear. The claim to correctness made with assertions does not figure directly in Alexy's justification of human rights, where his argument is based on an interest in resolving conflicts by means of discursively governed agreements. This requires the recognition of certain rules and rights, in particular the right of the other agents to autonomy. The reference to discursively governed agreements does not invoke the conception of correctness based on the claim to truth of assertions. Agreements and assertions have different foundations. In fact, Alexy's argument for the necessity of recognising discursive rights and individual autonomy is compatible with the critique here, which emphasises the tension between assertoric claims to correctness and discursive justification. The part of the critique that remains standing is that Alexy neither distinguishes between these different claims to correctness nor offers a conception of a claim to correctness that is not based on the presuppositions of assertions.

There is another problem with Alexy's justification of human rights. His argument begins as a transcendental argument and ends up referring to the long-term interests of dictators. This is unsatisfactory, for his argument rests in the end on empirical interests and, what is more, on the interests of dictators and not of those whose human rights should be protected. Thus, Alexy's attempt to justify human rights by means of a transcendental argument seems to fail. One must note, however, that the final stage of Alexy's argument, with its reference to dictators' interests, is an attempt to

[45] Cf also Habermas, above n 1 at 53.
[46] Alexy, 'Diskurstheorie und Menschenrechte', above n 1 at 144.

extend the core argument in order to make it universal. The core argument turns on the necessary claim to correctness of genuine participants in a discourse and its implications. Extending the argument to show that an 'objective' interest in correctness serves the long-term interests even of dictators is meant to show that *every* rational being will accept a claim to correctness and, consequently, some human rights. The problem is whether such an extension of the argument is sound.

The air of paradox that colours justifying human rights by appeal to dictators' interests suggests that the extension is not sound, but this does not rule out the justification of human rights. The problem is that rational justification must be distinguished from moral justification. Human rights, as a type of moral right, require moral justification, in particular the claim that human rights are morally valid and therefore binding. The justification of this claim must show that making the claim is correct in the sense of being legitimate. It is the task of moral theory, not to be discussed here, to elaborate on the criteria that such a justification must meet.

The crucial point is that moral justification does not depend on showing that any rational being must accept the suggested right because of his long-term self-interest. Although a strong philosophical tradition tries to reduce moral to rational justification, this approach must be rejected. It bases moral claims on irrelevant premises. Moral justification must be based on normative judgements and cannot be based directly on interests. Interests may be a relevant factor, but moral judgements must comply with the requirements for moral justification, which go beyond empirical interests. Interests are relevant only in so far as they comport with the theory of moral justification, and the interests of dictators usually do not. This, of course, does not undermine the validity of a moral justification of human rights.

The difference between rational and moral justification implies that moral justification need not be universal among rational beings. It is not necessary for moral justification that any rational person agrees with it. Indeed, it is possible that someone rationally holds a view contrary to what is morally justified. Universality of moral justification must therefore have a different meaning. A moral justification is universal if there is no alternative to it among the range of acceptable moral theories. Everyone who aims to make a moral argument must argue in accordance with this theory alone. Someone holding a different view cannot justify his view morally and so cannot claim that it is normative in the strict sense of being morally valid.

Accordingly, one cannot expect a moral justification to show that everybody must accept it on merely rational grounds. A characteristic of norms is that they are not necessarily complied with, and this is also the case with norms for moral justification. So, too, people may argue in a way that does not conform to the requirements for moral justification. But non-compliance with norms does not affect their validity, and the same holds for the requirements for moral justification.

AN ALTERNATIVE: THE CLAIM TO CORRECTNESS OF JUGDEMENTS REACHED BY BALANCING PRINCIPLES

Alexy's argument based on a necessary claim to correctness of legal reasoning and law has been found defective, in particular because a semantics that is restricted to assertions and propositions is indequate to a conception of discursive justification. The claim to correctness made within assertions appears inappropriate within a conception of discursive justification because assertions include epistemic claims about something that cannot be known at the beginning of a justificatory procedure. This points toward a general problem with a procedural justification of norms. If such a procedure is based on valid arguments that lead to a certain result, the procedure seems irrelevant for the justification of the result. If, by contrast, there are no arguments for this result, it can hardly be said to be normatively justified.

An alternative approach seems possible, an approach based on the model of principles and the methodology of balancing normative arguments. The model of principles has been discussed by various authors, including Alexy himself.[47] The balancing of principles is missing, however, in Alexy's analysis of the claim to correctness. Moreover, the conception suggested here is different from Alexy's.

A characteristic feature of the model of principles is the method of balancing principles. This method implies distinguishing two levels of reasoning and two types of norms, namely, principles as normative arguments to be balanced against each other and definitive norms as the result of balancing. The 'strict separation thesis' suggests that principles and definitive norms have different logical structures.[48] It is a matter of dispute whether there is such a logical difference and if so just what it is.[49] An adequate analysis of the distinction, however, is key to reconstructing the claim to correctness of normative argumentation.

The distinctive feature of the model of principles used here is that principles are conceived of as normative arguments having the structure of

[47] R Alexy, *Theorie der Grundrechte* (Baden-Baden, Nomos, 1985) (English translation: *A Theory of Constitutional Rights* (Oxford, Oxford University Press, 2002).

[48] Cf R Alexy, 'Zum Begriff des Rechtsprinzips' in Alexy, *Recht, Vernunft, Diskurs*, above n 1 at 177 *passim*.

[49] Cf eg M Atienza and J Ruiz Manero, *A Theory of Legal Sentences* (Dordrecht, Kluwer 1997).

requirements for the definitive validity of norms.[50] Principles therefore express claims regarding the result of balancing. In this sense, the principle of protecting health includes the claim that certain norms protecting health shall definitively be valid, eg, that smoking in public places shall definitively be prohibited. Someone demanding that smoking in public places should be prohibited for reasons of the protection of health does not state that this norm is definitively valid, but is arguing that such a norm should be accepted as the result of argumentation and therefore as definitively valid. Normative arguments do not make an epistemic claim of what the correct result is, but make a normative claim as to which result should be accepted. The justification for the claim is that making such claims is legitimate for autonomous agents. Also, the relation between arguments and result is a normative relation, not an inferential one. The result is accepted because it is required by stronger reasons, that is, the reasons the agent holds to be stronger. With this conception of normative arguments, the cognitive presuppositions of an epistemic claim to correctness are avoided.

The claim to correctness of a judgement reached by balancing consists in the claim that this judgement is required by stronger reasons. Whatever the agent decides, he must hold the view that his judgement is based on and required by stronger reasons. In addition to this normative claim to correctness, there will be claims to correctness regarding the formal requirements for balancing and the correctness of the empirical premises relevant to balancing. The peculiar feature of the model of principles, however, is the normative character of the claim to correctness of judgements reached by balancing.

The structure of the balancing of normative arguments affects the structure of the justification of norms and normative judgements,[51] in particular the justification of human rights.[52] An elaboration on this conception is beyond the scope of this chapter.

Summing up, I sketch the main points of my critique of Alexy's discursive justification of human rights, based on his argument for the necessity of making claims of correctness. Alexy's conception of a claim to

[50] Cf J Sieckmann, 'Logische Eigenschaften von Prinzipien' (1994) 25 *Rechtstheorie* 227. The conception of reiterated requirements for validity is rejected by R Alexy, 'On the Structure of Legal Principles' (2000) 13 *Ratio Juris* 294. However, his representation of this conception as an 'oscillation' between definitively valid norms and norms in a purely semantic sense replaces an infinite structure with two finite structures and therefore misses the point. Cf J Sieckmann, 'Principles as Normative Arguments' in C Dahlman and W Krawietz (eds), *Values, Rights and Duties in Legal and Philosophical Discourse* (2005) 21 *Rechtstheorie* (Suppl. vol) 206.

[51] Cf J Sieckmann, 'On the Tension between Moral Autonomy and the Rational Justification of Norms' (2003) 16 *Ratio Juris* 105.

[52] Cf J Sieckmann, 'Cultural Pluralism and the Idea of Human Rights' in A Soeteman (ed), *Pluralism and Law* (Dordrecht, Kluwer, 2001) 235.

correctness, by focusing on assertions, is inadequate to a conception of discursive justification. His justification of human rights uses but does not elaborate on a different conception of the claim to correctness. And his attempt to show that every rational agent must at least pretend an interest in correctness aims to prove too much and is not necessary for a moral justification of human rights. An alternative to Alexy's account might be a model of principles that defines the structure of sound normative reasoning, including a structure for the justification of human rights.

10

Three-Person Justification

JONATHAN GORMAN*

ROBERT ALEXY TELLS us in his *A Theory of Constitutional Rights*, 'substantive theories of morality giving precisely one answer to every moral question with intersubjectively binding certainty are not possible'.[1] His reasoning is that normative claims are not self-justifying: they 'do not refer to any kind of non-empirical object, characteristic, or relation as is assumed by intuitionism, nor are they reducible to empirical expressions as is claimed by naturalism'.[2] Moreover, any attempt to justify normative claims requires reference to further normative claims which will also need justifying, and this involves an infinite regress. This 'Münchhausen Trilemma'[3] can be avoided (up to a point) by specifying requirements—pragmatic rules of rational discussion, following Habermas—which govern the procedure of justification.[4] Yet this procedural theory of rational practical discourse, while limiting the possible substantive outcomes, does not determine a single outcome: 'there is always a wide space for the discursively merely possible'.[5] Moral theory has to be combined with a procedural model in the theory of law to determine a decision in the way we require.

* This is a development of a paper with the same title given to the Forum for Law and Philosophy's Workshop on Law and (the Possibility of) Discourse at Queen's University Belfast in June 2004, an occasion supported by The British Academy, by Manchester School of Law, and by Queen's University. I am most grateful to George Pavlakos for continuing discussion of Robert Alexy's legal theory and to him, Robert Alexy, Emilios Christodoulidis, Maeve Cook, David Evans, Emmanuel Melissaris, Giovanni Sartor and others at the Workshop, for their comments on the paper.

[1] R Alexy, *A Theory of Constitutional Rights* (Oxford, Oxford University Press, 2002) 370.

[2] R Alexy, *A Theory of Legal Argumentation* (Oxford, Clarendon Press, 1989) 177.

[3] Alexy, above n 2 at 179, referring to H Albert's description.

[4] Alexy, above n 2 at 179.

[5] Alexy, above n 1 at 370.

INTERSUBJECTIVELY BINDING CERTAINTY

What is 'intersubjectively binding certainty'? We can attempt to see what Alexy means here by examining his reasoning for the claimed *impossibility* of 'intersubjectively binding certainty'. His reasons are those which are commonly offered by a sceptic in respect of more general philosophical issues: there is no knowable 'object' in some moral realm, whether to be accessed a priori or by experience, which either explains the truth of our moral claims or enables us to bring to an end the series of justifications which we offer in supporting those claims. We can always ask, 'why?' Typically, we seek to decide on the basis of an objectively true principle, and in the face of a general scepticism that calls on us to justify the truth of what we claim. It is a familiar, if arguably empty, victory on the part of the sceptic that such 'objective certainty' is not possible.

This reasoning, however, is irrelevant to what has to be an essential point of Alexy's argument. Alexy's 'intersubjectively binding certainty' is not plausibly to be understood as 'objective certainty', if 'objective certainty' is read in a realist way as meaning what it does in typical sceptical arguments. We should distinguish in this context subjective from objective justification.[6] Justification of some position or belief may be held to be 'subjective' in so far as its function is held to consist in ensuring acceptance of the position or belief, or in the removal of relevant doubt, on the part of those to whom the justification is addressed. Reception by an audience or readership is an essential feature of such justification. Notice that this refers to 'those' to whom the justification is addressed: 'subjective' here is typically plural rather than singular in its reference and involves no essential commitment to being understood in terms of individualist psychology as opposed to some social criterion; further analysis is nevertheless still required, and will be given below. We may now contrast this 'subjective' justification with 'objective' justification by holding that justification is 'objective' in so far as it achieves a correct and truthful and determinate proof of the position or belief, a truth which is independent of subjective acceptance. No audience or readership is required for objective truth to be what it is, and similarly no audience or readership is required for the justification of that truth to be successful.

[6] Here I draw on a more detailed explanation in my 'The Truth of Legal Analysis' in S Coyle and G Pavlakos (eds), *Jurisprudence or Legal Science?: A Debate about the Nature of Legal Theory* (Oxford and Portland, Oregon, Hart Publishing, 2005) 33–49. There the material is expressed in terms of 'understanding'. Here it is expressed in terms of *justification.* I have expressed similar views elsewhere, in particular in 'Kellner on Language and Historical Representation' (1991) 30 *History and Theory* 356 and in 'From History to Justice' in Aleksander Jokic (ed), *Essays in Honor of Burleigh Wilkins: From History to Justice* (New York, Peter Lang, 2001) 19–69.

But how is this 'objective truth' to be understood? A realist, in holding that there is an eternal reality or truth independent of what we believe it to be, faces a difficulty: that there is an unknowable metaphysical something which is, despite its mystery and unknowability, an indubitable touchstone for truth as we know it, seems impossible. 'Truth', 'reality', 'objectivity', 'justification' and the like are ordinary words—*our* words—which have the meanings they do in so far as we understand them in our public discussions, and they cannot be tied to such mystery and unknowability. Two reasons for the sceptic's success in persuading us that we do not and cannot know the truth is that 'truth' here is so often given a realist interpretation and 'know' here is so often interpreted as requiring the same degree of certainty as does knowledge of necessary truth. These realist standards of objectivity and certainty are apparent in the above quotations from Alexy's arguments relating to the impossibility of 'intersubjectively binding certainty'.

Should we seek such 'objective' justification in legal decisions? Should we seek 'objective' legal truth? It is clear that, in the sense now described, we should not. One important advantage in dispensing with unnecessarily metaphysical versions of 'objectivity' is that, in seeking to justify decisions and thereby seeking to remove doubt in the minds of the parties to the case, we avoid the need to address a general scepticism. We nevertheless still need to reflect the everyday sense that human rights and other moral and legal values, and indeed the decisions of the courts themselves, have some kind of non-metaphysical independence or objectivity which gives them the authority which we commonly believe—or need to believe—that they have. Alexy's concept of 'intersubjectively binding certainty', properly understood, will help us to do this.

If 'intersubjectively binding certainty' means 'objective' in the realist sense now explained, then Alexy's reasoning here, while no doubt sound in removing this mysterious metaphysical option, is not relevant to his main point. But it is better not to understand 'intersubjectively binding certainty' in this way. 'Intersubjectively binding certainty' is more plausibly to be understood as relating to *our* world rather than some unknowable world beyond our own, and so understood it both avoids Alexy's realist-based metaphysical and epistemological pessimism (so inappropriate to his overall theory) and also helps us towards understanding how to make possible the determination of moral and legal decisions. Attending, then, to our own world, we should note the meaning of *our* words in Alexy's expression 'intersubjectively binding certainty'. We should observe first that 'intersubjective justification' is a more helpfully relevant expression in the present context than 'subjective justification', because 'subjective', as noted above, can be interpreted as ambiguously covering both the individual and the group, whereas we, while not ignoring individual acceptance, need to understand our world, and particularly our legal world, primarily in terms of a *plurality of people* whose *shared* acceptance is crucial both to the truthful status of some assertion and to its justification.

How big is this plurality of people? Our argument here is not an argument against metaphysical realism and its associated ideas. In contrasting 'intersubjective binding certainty' with 'objective certainty', and concentrating on the former, we leave open the question whether the latter has any epistemological or metaphysical merit. While obiter, it may nevertheless be helpful to observe that an antirealist approach might support the claim that 'objectivity' is itself best understood as 'intersubjective binding certainty'. Antirealist positions such as this are commonly regarded as only plausible if 'intersubjective' is read as referring to the *universality* of people. We may then imagine 'objectivity', understood antirealistically in terms of 'intersubjectively binding certainty', as depending on some kind of 'world-wide inter-community commonality of standard or acceptance which is neutral with respect to different communities or individuals and which makes sense of the possibility of translation between different communities of belief and also makes sense of the possibility of external judgement of the approaches of particular communities or individuals'.[7]

Understanding objectivity in this antirealist way, we have no obvious reason to accept the sceptical view that an intersubjectively binding answer to every moral question is *impossible*; indeed, we might require just this of an ideal legal system. We might wrongly take the 'ideality' of such a legal system to imply its unreality, but the 'unreal' nature of such an ideal legal system would consist rather in the unlikelihood or impracticality of its achievement rather than in its a priori impossibility. Nevertheless, complete impracticality, if such be the case, is not an objection: just as we can consistently aim to achieve perfect health, which our mortality ensures is a practically unrealisable goal, we can consistently imagine that a legal system involving an intersubjectively binding answer to every moral question may still be the right standard for us to adopt.

Yet such matters are remarked on here only in passing: our concern here is not with realism, objectivity or even the practical possibility of universal agreement. There is no reason to think that appealing to 'intersubjective binding certainty' in legal contexts necessitates reference to acceptance by the entire human race. There is, to be sure, a *universality* which is, following Kant, often assumed to be essential to what it is to be moral. That assumption is disputable, but our concern here is with the legal. Most striking in a legal context is the traditional view in common law systems that judges should speak to the particular case rather than to the universal. We can agree with the relevant part of a 2003 judgement of Lord Hutton,

[7] Or so I expressed the matter in 'The Truth of Legal Analysis', above n 6 at 40.

that 'it is not the function of the courts to decide hypothetical questions which do not impact on the parties before them'.[8] While by no means the only issue in practical legal decisions, 'impact on the parties' is central, and whether it is only the parties concerned or some wider grouping, the number involved in appealing to a 'plurality of people' is plainly a *contingency*. I shall not deal here with the question of which criteria should determine the proper readership or audience, although related considerations will be dealt with below. In any event, who counts as needing to accept a justification will vary in practice and certainly need not require the overturning of a general philosophical scepticism. This justifies Alexy's approach, which uses *pragmatic* rules of rational discourse. Legal justifications are not there to appease the sceptic. If we are called upon to judge between two people with conflicting demands, it is primarily they, rather than a general sceptic, to whom we have to provide our justification.

What counts as sufficient justification will also vary in practice, and again need not require the overturning of a general philosophical scepticism. Here we need to analyse the 'binding certainty' which Alexy asserts to be involved in intersubjective acceptance. Certainty is a contingently felt psychological state which can vary from one individual or group to another, and of course uncertainty is always logically possible. Felt psychological certainty constrains one's choices about what to believe. I may wonder whether a particular action is wrong, and my state of wondering is also a state of *indecision* about whether it is wrong. When my decision is finally made, whatever may have led to that decision,[9] I am then *certain* about the matter, and my state of certainty means that there is for me no longer a choice about the matter. In this way the presence of certainty implies the absence of choice. The justification—again, whatever that is—which leads to the decision is also accepted by me in so far as it 'leaves me no choice' what to believe. But then, suppose I decide that X must be guilty because he is poor. I simply recognise no alternative (poverty, to me, is sufficient justification), and I am quite certain. You, by contrast, are not; you may have listened to the evidence.

Justification in terms of 'binding certainty' cannot leave the situation like this, relying as it does on what might be a random distribution of inappropriately achieved particular psychological states. 'Binding' certainty implies, not just acceptance (with its hint of free choice followed by

[8] In *R v Attorney-General, ex parte Rusbridger and another*, House of Lords, 26 June 2003, referring to Lord Justice Clerk Thomson in *Macnaughton v Macnaughton's Trustees* [1953] SC 387 at 392.

[9] This does not imply that it is up to me to decide what is right or wrong. The 'whatever' might involve my reasoning the matter through for myself, but I may for example be *told* the answer, and choose to believe; similarly, I may decide to obey an order.

perhaps arbitrary psychological closure), but also some measure of *obligation*: a justification which can certainly be ignored or disobeyed but which nevertheless has some *authority*. Just as Kant argued that 'love, as an affection, cannot be commanded' but practical love—'beneficence for duty's sake'—may,[10] it is clear that we cannot wholly understand 'binding certainty' as a particular psychological state which a group of particular individuals are each required separately to *feel*. It has to cover that which in some way they *ought* to feel. Yet we should not move too quickly to the further view that what matters here is what people 'rationally' ought to feel, for our external measure need not be in terms of reason at all. Thus we might hold that a person ought to feel an appropriate degree of pity, say, at some tragic situation and are straightforwardly blameworthy if they do not; their capacity for reason might have nothing to do with it. Whatever the basis ought to be, it cannot be determined by the chancy contingencies of individual psychological states which would indeed merely leave 'wide space for the discursively merely possible'.[11]

Rather, such 'certainty' must be *shared*. It must be achieved 'intersubjectively' if it is to be binding on each, and this means that we must adopt a multiperson *procedure*, a procedure which involves external check on the achievement of certainty, a procedure which blocks decision and psychological closure or individual certainty until the appropriate justification is explicit and thereby shared, a procedure which is effective and determinate despite the wide range of grounds on which decisions might possibly be made. In part this requires that the parties to the judgement can recognise that the justification for the judgement is also a justification for them to accept the judgement. Adopting with Alexy a procedural theory of rational practical discourse involving such justification rightly limits the size of the audience which we need in practice to satisfy, and makes possible the determination of a final decision by using a procedural model of legal process.

WEIGHING, INCONSISTENCY AND DEADLOCK

To make determinate the 'discursively merely possible', the myriad grounds available here have to be 'weighed'. Consider Ronald Dworkin's presentation of the 1889 case of *Riggs v Palmer*.[12] A man murdered his grandfather. The grandfather's will named him as heir. Should he inherit? The

[10] I Kant, *Fundamental Principles of the Metaphysic of Ethics* (Thomas Kingsmill Abbott (trans), London, Longman, 1962 [1785]) s 1.

[11] Alexy, above n 1 at 370.

[12] RM Dworkin, 'Is Law a System of Rules?' in *idem* (ed), *The Philosophy of Law* (London, Oxford University Press, 1977) 38 at 44. I have summarised this material in a similar way in J Gorman, *Rights and Reason* (Chesham, Acumen, 2003) mainly in ch 10.

court had to enforce laws and contracts, and the grandfather's valid will was clear. Yet the court had also to ensure that common law maxims are followed, and no one is thereby permitted to profit from his own wrong. In fact the murderer was not permitted to inherit. Dworkin presented the reasoning in the case as a way of permitting laws to be 'controlled': 'all laws as well as all contracts may be controlled in their operation and effect by general, fundamental maxims of the common law'.[13] Part of what Dworkin wished to achieve with this example was an explanation of a distinction between laws as rules and laws as principles.

Principles were presented by him as controlling mere laws or contracts, yet we are not to think that principles always have controlling force. 'We say that our law respects the principle that no man may profit from his own wrong, but we do not mean that the law never permits a man to profit from the wrongs he commits.'[14] On the contrary, we are not to treat 'no man may profit from his own wrong' as a rule, which, where it conflicts with other rules, either permanently overrides them or is permanently overridden by them. Rules are different from principles. By regarding this expression as a principle, Dworkin is saying that its force within a situation of conflict is not fixed, and is a matter which has to be weighed on a particular occasion. Moreover, it is plain that for Dworkin it is not that principles have to be 'weighed' when they conflict with statutes or contracts (or with similar legal entities which are supposed to have the status of rules). What is the principle (that no man may profit from his own wrong) being weighed against in *Riggs v Palmer*? One might think that it could be the will itself; and yet Dworkin later says 'principles have a dimension that rules do not—the dimension of weight or importance'.[15] One cannot weigh a principle against something which has no such dimension. Dworkin's point is that principles have to be 'weighed' when they conflict with each other. In fact the principle is being weighed against another principle such as this: that courts should enforce wills or contracts. Whether and how far rules may be distinguished from principles has been much discussed,[16] and the matter will not be addressed here. The idea here derived from Dworkin's point is that principles are to be understood as lying on some legal or moral shelf, ready to be taken down as occasion demands and applied to particular cases. It is in the nature of their application to particular cases that they may conflict. A decision in a particular case will resolve the conflict, following the 'weighing' of the

13 Dworkin, above n 12 at 44.

14 *Ibid* at 46.

15 *Ibid* at 47.

16 See eg, a summary of the issues in H Davies and D Holdcroft (eds), *Jurisprudence: Texts and Commentary* (London, Butterworths, 1991) particularly 83. 'Principles' and 'rules' may be distinguished by their pedigree, even if their logical status is not clearly distinct.

principles and the subordination of one for the particular occasion, and so remove the inconsistency. The principles are then returned to the shelf after use, where they remain of equal force until the next occasion for 'weighing'. Yet what is on the shelf is the legal reality, the authoritative source of legal truth, and here we find inconsistent principles, principles which are inconsistent with each other just because they purport to apply to all cases and cannot do so without such inconsistency. They cannot all be realised at once.

It should not be supposed that this situation is different for rights, for it is not. In *Riggs v Palmer*, the grandson may have a right under his grandfather's will to inherit, while other possible inheritors may at the same time have a right that he should not, given that he murdered the grandfather. Only one of these rights can be enforced in a particular case, but both exist. Similarly, and typically, human rights conflict with each other just in so far as they can conflict in particular cases. So, similarly and typically, can the rights granted under constitutions, and it is at this level that Alexy directs his own arguments. Conflict is a widespread feature of many fundamental legal and moral concepts, and these have to be resolved for particular cases. A metaphor such as 'weighing' does not take us very far. We need a pragmatic 'theory of justice' to determine which rights take priority in specific conflict situations, and such a theory would not be a general ranking order such as Rawls might offer, but at most a localisable general procedure for resolving jointly unperformable specific conflicting actions or claims.[17] Alexy's use of discourse theory seems promising here. As noted earlier, such localising of procedures justifies the view that judges should, as they traditionally do, speak to the particular case rather than to the universal principle.

Even if not universalisable to all cases, we still seem to need some metric, some criterion, by which we might rank principles and rights in particular cases and come to determinate conclusions.[18] Yet we are not short of such criteria: there are many grounds on which we might base our ranking of principles. The trouble is that these too conflict. Consider the following point which Grotius saw clearly (and as summarised by JB Schneewind): in international law, 'if the nations in a dispute are as widely divided on the particulars of religion as the Protestant Dutch and the Catholic Portuguese and Spanish, then no appeal to the Bible or to specific Christian doctrines will help. Each side interprets the Bible in its own way'.[19] Note also Grotius' solution:

[17] Or so I argued at the end of *Rights and Reason*, above n 13 at 192.

[18] There are different ways of being, or failing to be, universal, which need further investigation.

[19] JB Schneewind, *The Invention of Autonomy* (Cambridge, Cambridge University Press, 1998) 71.

> Just as, in fact, there are many ways of living, one being better than another, and out of so many ways of living each is free to select that which he prefers, so also a people can select the form of government it wishes; and the extent of its legal right in the matter is not to be measured by the superior excellence of this or that form of government, in regard to which different men hold different views, but by its free choice.[20]

Appealing to truth, appealing to the Bible, does not resolve the dispute. Each side does perhaps interpret the Bible in its own way, but it does not follow that we ought to set about discovering who has the true interpretation. We cannot find out where the ultimate truth lies, and the problem is to do justice in the state of ignorance in which we find ourselves. We should not, however, see this problem as if it had essentially to do with our state of ignorance. The realist commitment to some theological truth which lies behind this example is only accidentally there, so far as our present difficulty is concerned. The essential point is that the Protestant Dutch and the Catholic Portuguese and Spanish dispute with each other, and share no ground for the resolution of the dispute. The situation is deadlocked: as Hillel Steiner rightly characterises deadlock, there is no prospect of (ie, the situation has no resources for) eliminating the disagreement, and we have 'obstinately adversarial customers'.[21] It is in such a situation that we resort to justice, and Steiner argues that justice succeeds in removing deadlock (while saving the disagreement[22]) by appealing to rights.

But which rights will do this? First we should note that, if rights are to resolve deadlock situations, then according to Steiner:

> the general content of such rights is not determined by any of the aims/priorities motivating the disagreement between the adversarial parties. For, *ex hypothesi*, they've already been down the road of searching for a consensus on these aims or priorities, and have returned empty-handed. ...So ... the general content of those rights has to be (in some sense) independent of the content of adversaries' competing objectives.[23]

We cannot allow a specification of rights to implicate 'some moral code which, if acceptable to the adversarial parties, would belie their adversarial situation'.[24] Again, 'The problem, as far as impartiality is concerned, is how to get a set of answers which are untainted by any particular set of

[20] Quoted from Grotius' *De Jure Belli ac Pacis* (1625) by Schneewind, above n 19 at 73.
[21] H Steiner, *An Essay on Rights* (Oxford, Blackwell, 1994) 193.
[22] 'The distinctive function of [rights] thinking is to secure the elimination of deadlocks *without* eliminating the disagreements that generate them. Rights supply adversaries with reasons to back off from interference when they have no other reason to allow the performance of the actions they're interfering with.' H Steiner, 'Working Rights' in M Kramer, NE Simmonds and H Steiner (eds), *A Debate Over Rights: Philosophical Enquiries* (Oxford, Clarendon Press, 1998) 237–8.
[23] Steiner, above n 22 at 238.
[24] Steiner, above n 21 at 215.

values ... that don't belie your adversarial situation'.[25] Moreover, to avoid further deadlock over rights themselves:

> the rights rule has to be such that, in any conceivable deadlock, only one of the parties is within his/her rights. And the way in which this is guaranteed is by having a rights rule that generates only rights which are compossible.[26]

Steiner's requirements of substantive moral emptiness and compossibility lead him to follow Grotius and particularly Kant to a solution in which it is a formal demand for freedom without moral content which justifies where the right lies.

Yet rights—even human rights—we know to conflict. I have argued elsewhere against the necessary compossibility of rights,[27] and I have argued also that it is plausible to claim that 'rights' is an essentially contested concept. If this approach is correct, we cannot appeal to compossible rights or to a balance of freedoms correlated with those rights in order to remove deadlocks. Where we have 'obstinately adversarial customers'[28] we no doubt have to resort to justice to decide between them, but that is the start of the problem, not the end. Yet we can conclude something about the content of the criteria which are appropriate to solve the problem. Steiner put the relevant point as follows: 'the general content of those rights has to be (in some sense) independent of the content of adversaries' competing objectives'.[29]

The logic of this is too narrowly expressed. We can generalise the point to its limit by expressing it in terms of a problem of truth.[30] Suppose we have two deadlocked contestants disagreeing about what is true. Each has reasons justifying (ie, subjectively justifying, and sufficiently for each) the claim made. Each, that is, uses his own criteria for truth centred on his own position as a contestant. We—as outsiders to the contest, perhaps as judges—cannot appeal to any contestant-centred criteria for truth in asking which of the opposing beliefs of the contestants is true, for that begs the question as to which criteria are to be used. The criteria we as judges use here will have to be different from the criteria which are in dispute. We cannot determine what these judge-centred criteria are a priori, since we do not know a priori which criteria are in dispute between the parties. Pragmatically, of course, we could find out what was in dispute, and then (in theory) use other criteria for the judgement. Yet these judge-centred criteria will be in general indeterminate, since they will vary from case to

[25] *Ibid* at 217.
[26] *Ibid* at 201–2.
[27] Gorman, above n 12 at ch 10.
[28] Steiner, above n 21 at 193.
[29] Steiner, above n 22 at 238.
[30] I expressed a similar argument, but in terms of reality rather than truth, in *Rights and Reason*, above n 12 at 129.

case. It is plausible then to say that there cannot be an external judge-centred set of criteria for truth, because any such set could in any particular case be the criteria disputed by one of the parties. There would then be no justification 'beyond dispute'. (Note that we have earlier excluded the objective justification of truth for any particular case, if there were such a thing.)

How, then, to decide? Must it be the case that *any* set of judicial criteria could in some particular case be the very criteria disputed by one of the parties? The judge could toss a coin. This answer is not as bad as it might look. We seek here a justification for the judge's choice. A fair toss can be a justification, of course, given that it is impartial between the parties. Note that one feature of this answer is that the judge is using a justification (if such it be) which is different from the justifications offered by either of the parties to the dispute. Justifications of other kinds are also available. Thus the judge might have the *authority* to decide a case, and select further justification on a whim. Superficially the justification used in such a decision might appear identical to the justification offered by one of the contestants for his own claim. But this would not be the real situation, for the judge's justification, fully understood, includes the judge's justifying authority which, *ex hypothesi*, both of the parties lack. We can imagine that the judge's justifying authority is mere power, and derives from being backed by the force of the state. Or we can imagine that the judge's justifying authority derives from agreement by the contestants to defer to his decision (which in constitutional terms would amount to the enforcement of a social contract). Tossing a coin might be a justified solution, with or without such backgrounds.

We might wonder what ground for complaint there could be against these imagined solutions, if the parties are willing to accept them and only subjective justification is possible. The difficulty is that they fail to meet the point made earlier, that our legal theory needs to reflect the sense that fundamental moral and legal values and the decisions of the courts themselves have some kind of non-metaphysical independence or 'objectivity' which gives them the authority which we commonly believe that they have. It is not a mere contingency that we seek a *reasoned* justification for our decisions.[31] While we may note, for example, the considerable variation in length and detail of reasoning which is reported of different jurisdictions which come under the umbrella of the European Court of Human Rights, we can still hope to make better sense than this example

31 Earlier I said that we might hold that people ought to feel an appropriate degree of pity at some tragic situation and are straightforwardly blameworthy if they do not, and 'reason' might have nothing to do with our justification. There is no contradiction between the present point and this earlier one: that a person did not feel pity would simply be the 'reason' for our blame.

suggests of the structure of a reasoned justification in the context of intersubjective justification. For the judge's decision, we seek a reasoned justification which has an internal justificatory quality which does not import bias or beg the question by being identical with the justifications used by either of the parties. Moreover, we additionally need a justifying authority which justifies the solution actually reached—that the judge has the agreement of the parties or the force of the state to justify the status of the decision is compatible with the judge making a completely arbitrary decision in rational terms, and this will not do. The only solution can be determining principles or rules which the judge uses in justification which cannot be available to the contestants or used in their own justifications. Thus we need an external judge-centred criterion for decision, but this criterion cannot have the content of any contestant-centred criteria, and therefore it seems that it must be empty of content. It is an argument of this kind which drives Grotius, Kant and Steiner to their final question for justice, namely, where does the freedom lie? A determinate outcome seems arbitrary.

THREE-PERSON JUSTIFICATION

Earlier I argued that we need to understand our legal world primarily in terms of a plurality of people whose shared acceptance is crucial, and I also argued against the view that we needed to see this 'plurality' as universal, as the whole of humanity. Pragmatically, we can bring our audience-addressing problems of justification down to a manageable size. But how small can we get? Could there be a solipsistic answer, with only one person in the world? It is a consideration of Wittgenstein's view against a private language which blocks this position and which helps our argument forward, and this is so whether one is for or against Wittgenstein on this: 'it is fairly generally agreed that the existence of a language involves the following of rules in some sense or other'; 'it requires that the same word be used regularly for the same thing'; 'it is agreed that rule-following presupposes the possibility of checking on the application of words, thereby making sure that the rule is being correctly followed'.[32] Our own position, in making sense of 'intersubjectively binding certainty', argued that we must adopt a multiperson procedure which blocks decision until the appropriate justification is explicit and shared. An essential feature of this is that it involves *external* check on the achievement of justified

[32] OR Jones, 'Editor's Introduction' in *idem* (ed), *The Private Language Argument* (London, Macmillan, 1971) 17. How it is possible for someone else to check on the correctness of the supposed application to myself by myself of a word like 'pain', and the implications of the answer for our understanding of the mind, is an important issue which is not our concern here.

certainty on the part of any one individual and it is in part this that makes it 'binding'. To engage in this process just is to engage in a rule-following process: Alexy's procedural model in the theory of law just has to be a rule-following model. As such it *must* involve an external check on the developing achievement of justified certainty and there *must* then be at least two people involved. It cannot be a 'private' process. It seems, at first sight, that the pragmatic principles of rational discourse are an ideal model and source for understanding this process, and Alexy's approach is available for this.

Yet the pragmatic principles of rational discourse derived from Habermas—Alexy's *Sonderfallthese* claims that legal discourse involves the *exchange* of formal practical arguments—are typically two-person principles and these are to be used in what are in practical legal terms multiperson situations. At first sight this may seem unproblematic: it might seem plausible to hold that legal decision processes can use two-person principles because they are only *contingently* multiperson situations. That, however, is wrong: the examples used above require legal decision processes that recognise that they are minimally *three*-person situations: two parties and a judge. One cannot set up the problem situations described above without specifying these three. But even that point does not prove a difficulty: in general there is no reason to suppose that a two-person set of pragmatic principles will not apply to a three-person situation, even if that is *necessarily* a three-person situation. But there is still a difficulty which needs to be noted: certain concepts which are necessary for us to understand legal decisions are essentially concepts applicable only in three(or more)-person situations and cannot be derived from essentially two-person principles of discourse. They are concepts the applicability and checking of which require at least three-person situations.

We can illustrate this if we consider the contrast between *puzzlement* and *disagreement*.[33] Stipulating to a very small extent for clarity, moral or legal puzzlement should be understood as existing within some particular individual, where the clash or conflict between different beliefs or attitudes lies within his or her own deliberation, in his or her own 'internal space'. The conflict and any necessary resolution of it are internal. Moral or legal disagreement, by contrast, should be understood as a feature of a relationship between two or more individuals, and the clash or conflict between different beliefs or attitudes then exists in what is often, and well, called 'public space'. The conflict and any necessary resolution of it are external.

Puzzlement exists in, for example, me, with regard to two beliefs or attitudes, when I am uncertain which I ought to adopt. By contrast,

[33] The argument appearing here appears also in my 'Convergence to Agreement' (2004) 43 *History and Theory* 114.

disagreement exists with two opposing people and not just two opposing views. Our disagreement in such a case exists in so far as neither of us defers to the other: here each of us claims more certainty about the acceptability of our own belief or attitude than of the other's belief or attitude.

Surely the resolution of intrapersonal moral/legal puzzlement must be analogous in philosophical structure to the resolution of interpersonal moral/legal disagreement? No: moral/legal puzzlement and disagreement are different in this regard. This is because, for any two inconsistent beliefs or attitudes, the need for their resolution, and the form that resolution should take, differ between the two cases. Briefly, and to illustrate, moral/legal disagreement raises at least the moral problem of toleration, but there is no analogue for this within puzzlement. In the case of puzzlement, the internal moral/legal deliberation is imagined to issue (in accordance with whatever moral/legal method or criterion or justification may be appropriate) in a moral/legal outcome. Yet in the case of disagreement a further moral/legal value exists in addition to whatever may arise in the case of puzzlement: this is the value of toleration, which points out that it may not be morally or legally right to use the outcome of the deliberation which removed the puzzlement because of the actual disagreement with that outcome on the part of another person. (Perhaps there should be negotiation or agreement to differ.)

Cannot puzzlement include this issue in its deliberation? No. Disagreement is not a special case of puzzlement, for puzzlement is understood as essentially internal. The difference between puzzlement and disagreement lies in the contingency of the latter: the mere happenstance that another person disagrees. The reality of this disagreement forces an external moral constraint on the outcome of internal deliberation which does not exist in the abstract consideration of merely possible disagreement which may arise in puzzlement.

To say all this is not to say that we ought to tolerate moral or legal differences. It is merely to say that the problem of toleration arises, and arises in such a way as to allow considerations of tolerance to constrain the outcome of any private deliberation, no matter what the principles used in that deliberation—even principles of tolerance! We do think that it is open to us to disagree about how far the different moral or legal views of others should be tolerated. Respect for such differences, and weighing that more highly than the resolution of the difference, is a respect which derives from the respect for other people as different, and, in the absence of more 'objective' moral or legal truth, as equally authoritative as oneself in the supply of beliefs.

If we understand law as there to keep the peace, then the reasons which justify legal decisions should do the same, and this seems to require that justifications be in a form which is, other things being equal, acceptable to the parties. This means that they can recognise that the reasons or justification for the judgement are also reasons or justification for them to accept the judgement. We only ensure peace if the reasons justifying the judge's position are also reasons for the losing party to tolerate the opponent's position. So force will not do. Moreover, it is essential to a legal determination that the losing party should tolerate the outcome, even if keeping the peace is not the primary purpose of law. This appears to operate against Steiner, for in his view justice succeeds in removing deadlock (while saving the disagreement) by appealing to rights, whereas it is toleration which better performs this task. To put the same point slightly differently, toleration is more centrally involved in justice than is an appeal to rights. Toleration, as a concept, has the three-person justification situation essentially built into it, since an accurate specification of the applicability of the concept minimally requires three separate moral or legal codes (by which I mean lists of principles; they can be very short lists): the code of one of the parties, the ex hypothesi conflicting code of the other party, and the code of the judge, which as earlier argued must differ in an essential part of its content from the other two.

Earlier we noted a difficulty following Steiner's reasoning: must it be the case that *any* set of judicial criteria could in some particular case be the very criteria disputed by one of the parties? There needed to be determining principles or rules for the judge to use in justification which could not be available to the contestants or used in their own justifications. These criteria could not have the content of any contestant-centred criteria, and therefore it seemed that they must be empty of content. But we can now see that they need not be empty of content, for they can be expressed in concepts which are essentially three-person concepts, concepts which are not properly available for use in the justifications offered by the contending parties.

It will be apparent that the argument has barely begun. In general, some judicial decisions are a special case of three-person justificatory discourse and the conditions for conversational discourse in general, which may be typically two-person, are not sufficient for our understanding here. Notice that this three-person understanding will also give us additional conceptual resources to evaluate those judicial situations which are currently of a two-person kind: for example, we might think of criminal cases as two-person, as involving the state (including the judge; an inquisitorial system might illustrate this) versus the criminal, or we might think of them as three-person, with judge-jury, prosecutor and criminal. The nature of the justificatory discourse in the three-person case may well illuminate the discourse in the two-person case, whether to its advantage or its disadvantage, so that we have resources enabling us to argue for conceiving criminal cases in one or other way. We need to understand more about the roles of concepts like 'justice' and 'toleration'—both seemingly minimally three-person concepts—in legal and moral justification, and understand their contrast with concepts like 'good', 'ought' and 'rights' which may have a different status. Our procedural model of legal decision must involve three-person justification.

Part IV

Discourse and Argumentation

11

Law's Claim to Correctness

MAEVE COOKE

THE THESIS THAT the law is open to criticism, not just from the outside but from within the system of law itself, is central to the discourse theories of law proposed by Robert Alexy and Jürgen Habermas. In inserting the critical dimension on the inside of the system of law they distance themselves from legal positivism in all its forms, be it the separation of law and morality advocated by HLA Hart or the view of law as a closed circuit of communication advanced by the systems theory of Niklas Luhmann.[1]

Alexy and Habermas start from the thesis, common to positivists and non-positivists alike, that law has a reference to validity built into it. Alexy calls this law's 'claim to correctness' (*Richtigkeitsanspruch*). Habermas refers to it either as law's claim to correctness or 'claim to legitimacy'.[2] (In the following, I adopt the term 'claim to correctness' for the sake of convenience.[3]) For positivists, this claim can be justified only through

[1] See HLA Hart, *The Concept of Law* (Oxford, Oxford University Press, 1972); N Luhmann, *Law as A Social System* (KA Ziegler (trans), F Kastner (ed), Oxford, Oxford University Press, 2004). In distancing himself from legal positivism Alexy often mentions Hart's theory, whereas Habermas tends to cite Luhmann's theory as an example of a positivist view that allows for no internal criticism of law from the point of view of the right or the good. However, it should be noted that Habermas does not just reject the systems-theoretic approach to law, he rejects legal positivism more generally: see J Habermas, *Between Facts and Norms* (W Rehg (trans), Cambridge, Mass, MIT Press, 1996) 202–3 and J Habermas, 'Introduction' to 'A Discursive Foundation for Law and Legal Practice: A Seminar on Jürgen Habermas' Philosophy of Law' (1999) 12(4) *Ratio Juris* 329 at 330.

[2] Habermas appears to use the two terms interchangeably: see eg, Habermas, *Between Facts and Norms*, above n 1 at 194–7. The English translation uses the word 'rightness' instead of 'correctness': both are acceptable translations of the German word '*Richtigkeit*'.

[3] The terms do have different connotations. By using the term 'correctness' (*Richtigkeit*), Alexy could be read as highlighting the similarity between the claim to validity raised for legal norms and decisions and the claim raised for moral norms. By using the term 'legitimacy' Habermas could be read as highlighting the difference between the claims to validity raised in both cases (but see above n 2). As the following discussion makes clear, I think both positions are partially correct. Thus, for my present purposes, nothing substantive turns on my adoption of 'correctness': it is merely a matter of convenience.

reference to the standards of legal validity already established in the prevailing system of positive law. For non-positivists, justifying the claim to correctness calls for a reference point that goes beyond what is justifiable within the prevailing legal system. In other words, non-positivists attribute a *context-transcending* component to the claim to correctness raised for legal norms and decisions.[4] Alexy and Habermas pursue this non-positivist line. Moreover, both link legal validity to discourse, understood as a form of intersubjective public deliberation in which participants are guided by idealising suppositions regarding the proper conduct of argumentation and are concerned to reach agreement as to the right (correct) answer. However, notwithstanding their agreement on these and other points, Alexy and Habermas disagree as to how the context-transcending component of law's claim to correctness should be understood. Alexy interprets it as a claim to *moral* validity that is universalist in reach and in content. For Alexy, as for Habermas, moral norms are universal in reach—their validity extends to all human beings, everywhere, at all times.[5] Their universal validity goes together with a claim to the universalisability of their content: its equal acceptability to everyone.[6] Alexy accounts for the validity of the context-transcending component of legal norms and decisions through reference to this universalist model of moral validity. This enables him to assert a conceptual connection, not just between law and context-transcending validity, but between law and a universalist morality. Habermas rejects Alexy's interpretation of the context-transcending component of legal validity, criticising it as an assimilation of the legitimacy of legal decisions to the validity of moral norms, thereby denying the independent logic of law and morality. He argues that Alexy's approach calls legal validity as such into question by construing it, in the end, as a form of moral validity. He insists that legal decisions are not correct in a context-transcending

[4] I use the word 'context-transcending' to characterise the component of law's claim to correctness that opens the system of law to criticism from the inside. I use it deliberately in order to leave open the question of whether this component should be understood in moral terms. This question is the subject of the debate between Alexy, Habermas and myself that I conduct in the following.

[5] Alexy and Habermas do not merely assert that the validity of moral norms extends to all human beings, everywhere, at all times, in the sense that their validity would have to be recognised by everyone who had the requisite insight; they assert, in addition, that moral norms are valid for all human beings qua human beings, whereby their validity for everyone rests on the universalisability of their content. The distinction between validity that is universal in reach and validity that is universalist in content will be important in the following. I make a comparable distinction in M Cooke, 'Realizing the Post-Conventional Self' (1994) 20(1–2) *Philosophy and Social Criticism* 87.

[6] R Alexy, 'Die Institutionalisierung der Menschenrechte im demokratischen Verfassungsstaat' in S Gosepath und G Lohmann, *Philosophie der Menschenrechte* (Frankfurt am Main, Suhrkamp, 1998) 244 at 249; R Alexy, 'Menschenrechte ohne Metaphysik' (2004) 52(1) *Deutsche Zeitschrift für Philosophie* 15 at 16.

sense in the same way as moral judgements: they are valid in a context-transcending sense not because they are justified by moral reasons but because they are justified by a bundle of moral, pragmatic and ethical reasons.

In the following I look more closely at this point of dispute, taking issue with both Alexy and Habermas with regard to their account of law's claim to correctness. My aim in doing so is to support their thesis that the law is open to criticism from the inside: that a potential for context-transcending criticism is built into the system of law itself. However, as they stand, I find neither Habermas' nor Alexy's accounts of the context-transcending component of law's claim to correctness convincing. Alexy's account gives an overly universalist interpretation to the content of legal norms and decisions: by interpreting the context-transcending component of law's claim to correctness as a moral claim, he fails to do justice to law's concern with particularity and expediency; nonetheless, he is right to emphasise the universal reach of the claim to correctness. By contrast, Habermas' account is overly contextualist: to all appearances, at least, he curtails the context-transcending power of law's claim to correctness by restricting its validity to the inhabitants of a particular democratic order; nonetheless, he is right to emphasise the difference between the content of moral judgements and the content of the context-transcending component of legal decisions. Against Alexy I suggest an interpretation of this component that replaces a concern for the universalisablity of the content of the claim to correctness with a concern to find a balance between the demands of universalisablity, particularity and expediency. Against Habermas I suggest an interpretation of the context-transcending component of law's claim to correctness that attributes to it a universal validity. This raises the question of the universality of non-moral claims to correctness: the question of how claims that do not have a universalisable content can be universal in reach. In the final section I address this question.

ALEXY'S CLAIM TO CORRECTNESS

The thesis of a necessary connection between law and correctness is at the core of Alexy's legal theory. By 'claim to correctness' he means a claim on the part of those 'subjects who act for and in law by creating, interpreting, using and enforcing it'.[7] Such a claim is not a private matter; rather, it is necessarily connected to the role of a participant in the legal system. According to Alexy, its non-private—'objective'—character is most evident in the case of the judge who raises the claim to correctness as a

[7] R Alexy, 'Law and Correctness' in MDA Freeman (ed), *Legal Theory at the End of the Millenium* (Oxford, Oxford University Press, 1998) 205–21 at 206.

representative of the legal system. The claim to correctness is directed not merely towards the addressees of particular legal acts (for example, the parties in a particular trial); it includes everyone who takes the point of view of a participant in the legal system in question.[8] As described so far, the thesis of a necessary connection between law and correctness is acceptable to both positivists and non-positivists. We have seen that the distinguishing mark of the non-positivist position is its interpretation of the claim to correctness as a claim to context-transcending validity. In Alexy's account, the connection between law and a context-transcending claim to correctness is held to be conceptual: the context-transcending component is made part of the concept of law itself.[9] His thesis of a conceptual connection between law and a context-transcending claim to correctness takes the open texture of law as its starting point.

Alexy stresses that this is something on which positivists and non-positivists agree. Law has an inherently open texture that results from factors such as the unavoidable vagueness of legal language, the possibility of conflicts between norms and the gaps in actually existing law.[10] Consequently, there will always be certain 'hard cases' concerning which decisions have to be made that cannot simply appeal to existing positive law. On what basis should decisions be made in hard cases? From a positivist point of view, no normative basis is available; since positivists deny the availability of a normative viewpoint other than that established by positive law, they are obliged to see decisions in hard cases as expressions of power or of personal preference.[11] In consequence, decisions in such cases cannot be regarded as motivated by considerations of correctness: they are held to be either a matter of strategy or a matter of decision. For positivists, in short, the claim to correctness is meaningless in hard cases. Non-positivists disagree. This calls on them to posit reasons for the correctness of a legal decision that go beyond those available within the prevailing legal system. Such reasons may be construed as moral reasons (this is Alexy's position) or as a bundle of moral, ethical and pragmatic reasons (this is Habermas' position). In each case, however, they can be said to claim validity in a sense that transcends the existing system of positive law.

It may be noted that the context-transcending validity of the reasons offered for legal decisions in hard cases can be justified in a variety of ways, for example, through appeal to the authority of God, to custom and

[8] *Ibid* at 207.

[9] *Ibid* at 209–12.

[10] See *ibid* at 215–16.

[11] R Alexy, 'Law and Morality: A Continental-European Perspective' in NJ Smelter and PE Baltes (eds), *International Encyclopedia of the Social and Behavioral Sciences*, vol 12 (Amsterdam/New York/Paris, Elsevier, 2001) 8465–7.

tradition, to natural or historical necessity or to the expertise and wisdom of the judge. Alexy, like Habermas, rejects these kinds of justification. Like Habermas, he proposes instead a discursive justification, which he understands as an intersubjective process of justification guided by norms of freedom and equality in which the participants see themselves and each other as autonomous agents. Autonomous agents are those who act according to norms and principles that they accept as correct on the basis of their own rational reflection.[12] Thus, for Alexy, justification of the reasons for legal decisions in hard cases is a matter of rational deliberation in discourse on the part of autonomous human agents.

Taking his lead from Habermas' distinction between various types of practical discourses, Alexy maintains that correctness has a different meaning in different discursive contexts.[13] Whereas in each case the point of discourse is to find the correct answer, what counts as correct in moral discourses is different to what counts as correct in ethical discourses, both of which are different again to what counts as correct in pragmatic discourses. In moral discourses, as indicated, the correctness of decisions is assessed from the point of view of universalisablity. In ethical discourses, correctness is assessed from the point of view of individual and collective ideas of the good for human beings; since ideas of the good depend on particular, individual and collective, self-understandings, ethical discourses have a fundamental concern with particularity that is absent from moral discourses. In pragmatic discourses, correctness is assessed from the point of view of expediency.[14] Whereas Habermas at times presents the various forms of practical discourse as independent modes of deliberation specialising in just one particular validity claim,[15] Alexy introduces the category of general practical discourse to cover modes of deliberation in which moral, ethical and pragmatic reasons are connected.[16] Alexy insists, moreover, that these different types of reasons are joined in a complex interrelationship that in concrete cases of practical judgement makes it impossible to disentangle one from the other.[17] In the actual democratic

[12] Alexy, 'Menschenrechte ohne Metaphysik', above n 6 at 20.

[13] R Alexy, 'The Special Case Thesis' (1999) 12(4) *Ratio Juris* 374–8. Cf J Habermas, 'On the Pragmatic, the Ethical, and the Moral Employments of Practical Reason' in *idem*, *Justification and Application*, (C Cronin (trans), Cambridge, Mass, MIT Press, 1993) 1–17.

[14] Alexy, above n 13 at 378–9.

[15] See Habermas, *Between Facts and Norms*, above n 1 at 167–68. However, in his 'Postscript', Habermas acknowledges that the schema presented here is misleading (*Between Facts and Norms*, 'Postscript', at 565 n 3). Moreover, even in the main text, certain formulations suggest that he does not view the various forms of practical discourse as separate from one another; this is particularly clear in his rejoinder to Alexy in which he writes that, in legal discourses, pragmatic, ethical and moral claims are bundled together (*Between Facts and Norms*, at 230).

[16] Alexy, 'The Special Case Thesis, above n 13 at 378.

[17] *Ibid* at 378–9.

process, as he puts it, '[t]he just is permeated with the good' (and, we might add, with the expedient).[18] He points out that if one conceives of justice as comprising all questions of distribution and retribution, then problems such as the welfare state and punishment have to be treated as matters of justice. Deliberation on such problems involves moral reasons (eg, reasons appealing to human rights), ethical reasons (eg, reasons appealing to collective self-understandings) and pragmatic reasons (eg, reasons appealing to the resources available in the given circumstances or in the foreseeable future). Thus, for Alexy, general practical discourse is not a simple combination of moral, ethical and pragmatic reasons but 'a systematically necessary connection expressing the substantial unity of practical reason'.[19]

Alexy argues that legal discourse is a special case of general practical discourse.[20] Since this argument contains a move that has crucial implications for his account of the context-transcending aspect of law's claim to correctness, it merits closer consideration.

ALEXY'S SPECIAL CASE THESIS

The three key components of Alexy's special case thesis are the claims, first, that law essentially involves the exercise of practical reason; secondly, that legal argumentation, like general practical argumentation, raises a claim to correctness and, thirdly, that legal discourse has special features that distinguish it from other forms of practical argumentation. Regarding the first, his claim is that practical reason justifies the existence of the legal system. As he puts it, practical reason 'has to be vivid in the procedures of democratic opinion and will-formation if their results are to be legitimate, and it must be employed in legal argumentation in order to fulfil the claim to correctness that is raised in it'.[21] Regarding the second, his claim is that legal reasoning, like practical reasoning in general, has an ideal or context-transcending moment, necessitated by the open texture of law.[22] Regarding the third, his claim is that general practical arguments are non-institutional arguments. By contrast, legal arguments have an institutional character that marks them off as a special case: '[w]hat is correct in

[18] *Ibid* at 379.
[19] *Ibid* at 379.
[20] *Ibid.*
[21] *Ibid* at 383–4.
[22] *Ibid* at 375.

a legal system essentially depends on what is authoritatively or institutionally fixed and what fits into it'.[23] In short, institutional reasons like statute and precedent are constitutive for legal discourse but for general practical discourse they are not.[24]

Closer consideration shows that the dependency of legal discourses on institutional reasons does not only distinguish them from general practical discourses; it also *connects* them with such discourses via the democratic decision-making process. For, in modern legal systems, the institution of law is tied to the democratic process in which ethical, pragmatic and moral reasons count as valid reasons. The relationship is one of mutual influence: the decisions and norms of institutionalised positive law impact on the employment of practical reason in the democratic decision-making process and this process, in turn, is not only historically important with regard to the formulation and justification of statutes, it plays a determining role in the formation of legal judgements in hard cases. If this is so, Alexy's assertion that legal discourses are not 'concerned with what is absolutely correct but with what is correct within the framework and on the basis of a validly prevailing legal order' is incomplete.[25] If the institution of law stands in a feedback relation with the democratic process, then legal discourses are not simply concerned with what is correct from the point of view of the institutionalised legal system, they are also concerned with what is correct from the point of view of a non-institutionalised idea of practical reason in which moral, ethical and pragmatic reasons interpenetrate.

To be sure, Alexy acknowledges the incompleteness of his remark on the non-absolute character of law with the qualification that it refers only to the first of two aspects of law's claim to correctness.[26] The first—positive—aspect is the claim that a given legal decision is correctly substantiated if it meets the standards set by the established law; the second—ideal or context-transcending—aspect is the claim that the established law on which the decision is based is just and reasonable. At this point, however, Alexy makes a surprising move. In light of his acknowledgement that deliberation on questions of justice involves moral, ethical and pragmatic reasons, one would expect him to locate the context-transcending aspect of the claim to correctness in the *substantial unity* of practical reason. Instead, surprisingly, he locates it in the *moral* component of practical reason: in its reference to what is just and reasonable from the point of view of what is equally in everyone's interests. His jump from the argument that legal discourse is a special case of general practical discourse to the

23 *Ibid* at 375.
24 *Ibid* at 378.
25 *Ibid* at 375.
26 *Ibid* at 381–2.

argument that there is a necessary connection between law and a universalistic morality[27] is not just surprising; it is also ill-advised. This is so for at least two reasons.

The first reason is that, in singling out the moral component of general practical discourse as the context-transcending component of law's claim to correctness, Alexy undermines his own insistence that general practical discourse displays the substantial unity of the moments of practical reason. Since, in my view, Alexy's account of general practical discourse captures an important feature of public deliberation on matters of justice in modern democracies, any move that would oblige him to abandon it is a mistake. Admittedly, Alexy does attempt to show the priority of the moral component of general practical discourse over the ethical and pragmatic components. However, even leaving aside the difficulties involved in demonstrating, in particular, the priority of the just over the good, this priority is a priority only on an abstract level. As Alexy himself recognises, priority is a simple matter only when what is ordered is clearly separated one from the other.[28] This is not the case in general practical discourse in which the various moments of practical reason are systematically interconnected. Thus, the argument that, on an abstract level, the just has priority over the good and the expedient provides insufficient grounds for disregarding ethical and pragmatic considerations in favour of purely moral ones in concrete contexts of democratic deliberation.

The second reason is that, by connecting law solely with the moral component of general practical discourses, Alexy undermines the most plausible explanation of the connection between the positive and context-transcending aspects of law's claim to correctness: the explanation that institutionalised positive law stands in a feedback relation with the democratic process. For, if the context-transcending aspect of law is interpreted in purely moral terms, it is no longer evident how it is fed into the system of law by way of the democratic process, the concerns of which are not exclusively moral.

In my view, Alexy would be better advised to interpret the context-transcending aspect of law's claim to correctness not in moral terms but in terms of the substantial unity of practical reason in the democratic process. His moral interpretation means that the context-transcending component of law's claim to correctness is construed as a claim to have reached decisions that are universally valid by virtue of their universalisable content. I propose, instead, an account of law's claim to correctness that construes it as a claim to have reached decisions that achieve the correct

[27] This jump is particularly evident in R Alexy, 'On Necessary Relations between Law and Morality' (1989) 2 *Ratio Juris* 167–80.

[28] Alexy, 'The Special Case Thesis', above n 13 at 378–9.

balance between considerations of universalisablity, particularity and expediency. On my alternative account, law's claim to correctness would be formulated along the following lines: a legal decision is correct if it is acceptable to everyone affected by it by virtue of the balance it achieves between the requirements of universalisablity, particularity and expediency and if it takes adequate consideration of the established system of positive law. An account of this kind is not only better able to do justice to the complex unity of practical reason as it operates in legal discourse; it is also better able to explain the connection between the two aspects of the claim to correctness, for it conceives of them as always mutually implicated.

I suspect that Alexy's reluctance to interpret the claim to correctness along the lines I propose can be traced back to two elements of his theory. The first is his view that the context-transcending component of the claim to correctness implies universality of reach: the correctness claimed for legal norms and principles extends to everyone, everywhere, at all times. This view of what context-transcendence entails seems to me correct. The second is his view that, among the claims of practical reason, only claims to moral validity are universal in reach. This seems to me incorrect. In the concluding part of my discussion I outline a model of practical reasoning that gives a universalist interpretation to other kinds of practical validity claims as well. Before doing so, however, I want to look at Habermas' interpretation of law's claim to correctness. Since, as indicated, his interpretation overlaps with Alexy's in a number of important respects, it will be sufficient to examine the point at which the two accounts diverge. Their divergence can be seen in Habermas' criticism of Alexy's special case thesis.

HABERMAS' CRITICISM OF ALEXY'S SPECIAL CASE THESIS

The main criticism that Habermas directs against Alexy's special case thesis is that it denies the differences between legal discourse and moral discourse and, in the end, construes the claim to legal validity as a claim to moral validity.[29] It is important to note that Habermas' criticism here is not based on the perception that Alexy denies the institutional character of legal discourse—our discussion has shown that this would be a misperception. Rather, it is based on the thesis that, since moral, ethical and pragmatic arguments are bundled together in legal discourse, legal discourse is not selective enough to generate the 'single right answer' which, in Habermas' view, is a requirement of moral validity.[30] For this reason, Habermas

[29] Habermas, *Between Facts and Norms*, above n 1 at 230–2

[30] *Ibid* at 230–1. It may be noted that Habermas' assertion that moral, ethical and pragmatic claims are bundled together in legal discourse is at odds with the schema he presents at 167–8 (see above n 15).

rejects Alexy's thesis of a conceptual connection between law and a universalist morality, asserting instead a conceptual connection between law and practical reason as a complex unity of moral, ethical and pragmatic moments. Thus, Habermas points in the direction of an interpretation of law's claim to correctness along the lines I have just proposed. However, if Alexy takes an ill-advised leap from the connection between legal discourse and general practical discourse to the connection between law and a universalist morality, Habermas makes a move that is equally misguided. Despite his insight into the connection between law and the complex unity of practical reason in the democratic process, he offers an account of democratic politics that threatens to undermine the context-transcending aspect of law's claim to correctness. The threat arises because he fails to provide an account of democratic validity in a context-transcending sense. Lacking such an account of democratic validity, his theory of law and politics seems to posit the community of citizens in a particular democratic order as the ultimate reference point for the validity of democratic decisions. One of the unwelcome consequences of this, as we shall see, is that it seriously curtails the context-transcending power he attributes to legal validity.

Habermas' Contextualist Understanding of the Validity of Democratic Decision-making

In his earlier work on discourse ethics Habermas was criticised for failing to discriminate adequately between the kinds of claims to validity raised in moral discourses, on the one hand, and discourses in the domains of law and politics, on the other.[31] In *Between Facts and Norms* he makes good this weakness, acknowledging a number of significant differences between moral validity, on the one hand, and legal validity and political validity, on the other. To be sure, Habermas does not distinguish carefully between legal and political validity, often referring to legal validity in the broad sense of "legal/political" validity or "democratic validity". It is clear, nonetheless, that certain sections of the book are concerned with legal validity in the narrower sense. This is true, for example, of his critique of Alexy and also of the 'Postscript', where he refers *inter alia* to the more

[31] See eg, A Wellmer, 'Ethics and Dialogue' in *idem,The Persistence of Modernity* (D Midgley (trans), Cambridge, MIT Press, 1991) 113–23; S Benhabib, *Critique, Norm, and Utopia* (New York, Columbia University Press, 1986).

restricted scope of claims to legal validity: they do not claim to apply to everyone, everywhere, at all times but only to the inhabitants of particular legal systems.[32]

How does this reference to the more restricted scope of claims to legal validity square with his non-positivist interpretation of law's claim to correctness? One way of making sense of the apparent discrepancy is to see claims to legal validity in the narrower sense as embedded in a broader process of democratic deliberation. Seen in this way, claims to legal validity have a context-transcending power precisely because they can be challenged and revised by way of the exchange of arguments in the democratic public sphere. (This is the feedback relation between institutionalised positive law and the democratic process that I emphasised in my discussion of Alexy.) However, this kind of non-positivist interpretation of legal validity claims merely shifts the question of context-transcending validity from the legal system in the narrower sense to the democratic process itself. For, if the context-transcending power of legal validity claims (in the narrower sense) is dependent on democratic processes of public deliberation, a great deal turns on whether the claims to validity raised in democratic deliberation have themselves a context-transcending power. Habermas gives no satisfactory answer to this question. In the absence of a convincing account of the sense in which claims to legal/political validity are context-transcending, we seem obliged to conclude that they are not. This implies, in turn, that claims to legal validity are context-transcending only in a limited sense, in that their force does not extend beyond the boundaries of a particular democratic order.This difficulty arises due to the distinction Habermas makes in *Between Facts and Norms* between moral discourses and legal/political (democratic) discourses. This distinction comes at a certain cost. For, by introducing this distinction, Habermas loses the internal connection between discourse and universal validity that was part of his earlier conception. In his earlier work Habermas made the claim to the universal validity of the outcomes of deliberation an indispensable component of the idea of discourse. Only theoretical discourses (those concerned with truth) and moral discourses (those concerned with justice) were held to satisfy this requirement.[33] As already indicated, in the case of moral discourses, the requirement of universality of reach is accompanied by the requirement of universalisability of content: moral

[32] Habermas, 'Postscript', *Between Facts and Norms*, above n 1 at 451–2. In his 'Introduction' to 'A Discursive Foundation for Law and Legal Practice', above n 1, too, he seems to refer to legal validity claims in the narrower sense when he speaks of their concern with the distribution of individual liberties rather than with the identification of moral duties: legal norms are concerned less with telling us what we *ought* to do than with delimiting a private sphere where everyone is free to do whatever she or he wishes.

[33] See J Habermas, *The Theory of Communicative Action*, vol 1 (T McCarthy, Boston, Beacon Press, 1984) 42.

norms and principles are not just acceptable as valid by everyone, everywhere, at all times; they have a content that could be accepted by everyone as equally in everyone's interests. Habermas subsequently dropped the requirements of universal validity and universalisability, opening up the category of discourse to include, on the practical side, pragmatic and ethical deliberations, neither of which were held to be connected with validity claims that are universal in reach and in content.[34] In *Between Facts and Norms* this shift in Habermas' understanding of the category of discourse is reflected in his introduction of a general discourse principle, which takes on a different meaning in legal/political and in moral discourses.[35] Whereas the moral principle stipulates that only those norms are valid that could be accepted by all participants for moral reasons, that is, on the grounds that the norms in question give equal consideration to the interests of all those possibly affected by them, the discourse principle stipulates that only those norms are valid that could be accepted by all participants for a mixture of pragmatic, ethical and moral reasons.[36] Evidently, however, this allows for agreements that are limited to the inhabitants of a particular democratic order and for agreements that are the result of a process of deliberation or negotiation in which particular value-orientations and interests are taken into account. This raises the question of what makes agreements reached in legal/political discourses valid. In the earlier version of his discourse theory, Habermas favoured an answer that combined procedural validity with epistemic validity: he held that public deliberation that satisfies the procedural requirements of discourse (mainly, inclusiveness, equality and openness in the conduct of deliberation) contributes constructively to the quality of its outcomes, which are also assessed according to epistemic standards of validity.[37] In this initial version, the principle of universalisability was held to constitute the relevant epistemic standard of validity for both moral and legal/political discourses, since Habermas did not distinguish between the two categories. The problem with his new account of democratic deliberation is that no equivalent epistemic standard of validity seems to be available.[38] Since the moral principle is no longer operative in legal/political discourses, general acceptability in a given context appears to replace universalisability as the criterion of epistemic correctness. However, making general acceptability in a given context the criterion of correctness gives rise to a difficulty analogous to that arising in hard cases in law. In a manner

[34] See Habermas, above n 13.

[35] Habermas, *Between Facts and Norms*, above n 1 at 107–8.

[36] *Ibid* at 107.

[37] See M Cooke, 'Five Arguments for Deliberative Democracy' (2000) 48(5) *Political Studies* 947 (esp at 952–4) for a discussion of this kind of argument.

[38] *Ibid* at 953. The only standards that appear to be available are procedural ones.

analogous to what happens in law, democratic deliberation is confronted with hard cases when the standards of validity prevailing in the given democratic order are called into question, eg, as a result of intercultural encounters, technological innovations, new ecological situations or social developments. And, like hard cases in law, hard cases in the democratic process call for rational decisions that cannot be substantiated through reference to the prevailing standards of rational acceptability. If divine authority, custom and tradition, historical or natural necessity or the expertise and wisdom of the judge are ruled out as possible normative reference points for decision-making in such cases, then democratic theory must find some other kind of context-transcending viewpoint from which the rationality of democratic decisions could be judged. But Habermas' democratic theory as presented in, and subsequent to, *Between Facts and Norms* makes no attempt to do so. In his conception as it stands, the claim to correctness that is raised in legal/political discourses for the content of democratic decisions lacks the context-transcending component he attributes to moral and, ostensibly at least, to legal claims. Without this, he ends up with a contextualist understanding of democratic deliberation.

Habermas is unlikely to feel happy about the contextualist implications of his account of democratic deliberation since it undermines his commitment to the context-transcending power of communicative reason. As understood by Habermas, the context-transcending power of communicative reason is universalist: it refers to the power of reason to transcend the standards of validity operative in every local context and to claim a kind of validity for propositions or norms that is not restricted to a local circle of addressees in a particular place at a particular time, but is held to obtain for everyone, everywhere, always.[39] As he puts it: 'the validity claimed for propositions and norms transcends spaces and times'.[40] His account of democratic deliberation is at odds with this universalist interpretation of communicative reason for it seems to reduce reason to what is generally acceptable in a particular democratic context. Rather than seeking to resolve this tension, however, either by attributing a context-transcending aspect to democratic deliberation or by modifying his universalist interpretation of communicative reason, up to now he has tended to ignore it. To be sure, he highlights the difficulty in question when discussing the work of other theorists, as his critique of the contextualist aspect of John Rawls' theory of political liberalism illustrates. For, one of Habermas' principal

[39] Habermas' failure to distinguish adequately between validity that is universal in reach and validity that is universalist in content is especially evident in passages such as these. See above n 5.

[40] J Habermas, 'The Unity of Reason in the Diversity of its Voices' in *idem*, *Postmetaphysical Thinking* (WM Hohengarten (trans), Cambridge, Mass, MIT Press, 1992) 139. For a discussion of Habermas' idea of communicative reason see M Cooke, *Language and Reason* (Cambridge, Mass, MIT Press, 1994).

objections to the constructivist strategy Rawls pursues in *Political Liberalism*[41] is that it purchases 'the neutrality of [Rawls'] conception of justice at the cost of forsaking its cognitive validity claim'.[42] However, until he clarifies the cognitive content of the claim to correctness implicit in his account of democratic deliberation, his own political theory is open to the same objection. So far, he has not acknowledged this.

As I see it, Habermas' democratic theory since *Between Facts and Norms* displays a deep ambivalence about the context-transcending, universalist aspect of the claim to democratic validity. On the one hand, he insists on the difference between the democratic principle and the moral principle. (The main difference, we will recall, is the restricted scope of claims to democratic validity, which he attributes to their reliance on ethical and pragmatic as well as moral reasons.) On the other hand, there are a number of indications that he does wish to attribute a context-transcending force to claims to democratic validity. One example here is his distinction between legal/political discourses and fair bargaining processes,[43] another example is his claim that majority rule bears an internal relation to truth[44] and a third example is his characterisation of democratic deliberation as a process of not just will-formation but also *opinion*-formation, by which he means that it serves the cognitive function of forming valid judgements.[45]

In sum, by contrast with his account of the system of law, which he opens to context-transcending criticism by virtue of its feedback relation with the democratic process, Habermas allows for no comparable criticism of the democratic process itself. Thus, the results of legal/political discourses cannot claim to be correct in a context-transcending sense. As indicated, this has significant implications for the context-transcending component of law's claim to correctness: if this component is justified through reference to an idea of democratic validity that does not itself make any claim to correctness in a context-transcending sense, its own context-transcending power is undermined. In this conception, we might say, law's claim to correctness is not context-transcending in a universalist sense: its claim to a validity that transcends spaces and times is cut short at the border of the historically specific democratic order in which it operates and is harnessed to the standards of validity prevailing in that order. As such, it is not genuinely context-transcending: it does not transcend *all*

[41] J Rawls, *Political Liberalism* (New York, Columbia University Press, (1993).

[42] J Habermas, 'Reconciliation through the Public Use of Reason: Remarks on John Rawls's Political Liberalism' (1995) XCII(3) *Journal of Philosophy* 109 at 110.

[43] Habermas, *Between Facts and Norms*, above n 1 at 164–7.

[44] *Ibid* at 179.

[45] In *Between Facts and Norms*, Habermas consistently refers to democratic deliberation as a process of both will-formation and opinion-formation. His point is particularly clear at 460.

particular contexts but only the particular context of legal deliberation. As we shall see, a genuinely context-transcending conception of validity requires not just universality but also a *dynamic* understanding of universality: the postulate of an ineliminable gap between the idea of universality and all actual claims to instantiate it.

I want to suggest that if Habermas is to rescue the context-transcending component of democratic deliberation, he must adopt a justificatory strategy along the lines I outline below. Doing so requires him to give up the view, which he shares with Alexy, that, among the claims to practical reason, only claims to moral validity are context-transcending in a universalist sense. This view appears to be at the root of the problems I identified in Alexy's and Habermas' accounts of law's claim to correctness: it leads Alexy to equate the context-transcending component of law's claim to correctness with a claim to moral validity and it leads Habermas to curtail the context-transcending component of law's claim to correctness and, ultimately, to undermine it.

JUSTIFYING THE CLAIM TO CORRECTNESS

Habermas' and Alexy's view that, in the domain of practical reason only ideas of correctness that have a universalisable content may claim universal validity, is due in part to a conception of justification that construes it as a matter of showing the *necessity* of certain principles and procedures, and of the ideas on which they are based. Necessity, in the sense of unavoidability, implies universality when it is attributed to features of human life in general. Up to recently, at least, both theorists subscribed to this kind of conception of justification. In his efforts to justify the universal validity of the principle of universalisability, Habermas pursued what he calls a reconstructive strategy of justification, reconstructing the unavoidable presuppositions relating to argumentation that he claims are implicit in all natural languages; ie, his programme of formal pragmatics.[46] For the same purpose, Alexy pursued what he calls an explicative strategy;[47] this is similar to Habermas' reconstructive approach in its concern to identify the idealising suppositions necessarily presupposed by participants in argumentation; however, it differs from Habermas' strategy by adopting a

[46] J Habermas, 'What is Universal Pragmatics?' in *idem*, *On the Pragmatics of Communication* (M Cooke (ed), Cambridge, Mass, MIT Press, 1998) 21–103. Cf Cooke, above n 40, for a detailed discussion of his formal-pragmatic justificatory programme.

[47] Alexy, 'Menschenrechte ohne Metaphysik', above n 6 at 19–20. In his earlier work Alexy seemed happy to use Habermas' earlier term 'universal pragmatics' to describe the kind of justification he endorsed (see R Alexy, 'A Theory of Practical Discourse' in S Benhabib and F Dallmayr (eds), *The Communicative Ethics Controversy* (Cambridge, Mass, MIT Press, 1990) 151–90 (esp at 160–1)).

transcendental rather than empirical mode of inquiry. The theorists agree that analysis of the unavoidable presuppositions of argumentation can have relevance for the claim to correctness only when this is given a universalisable, and hence formal and abstract, content. For, substantive, concrete ideas of correctness could be extracted from the necessary features of argumentation in general only by smuggling normative ideas into the concept of argumentation that have a specific historical and social-cultural index.

In Habermas' theory an additional reason for defining moral correctness formally and abstractly is prominent. This is his thesis that a discursively reached consensus is constitutive of moral validity.[48] Initially, at least, Habermas insisted that consensus must be reached in actual discourses. Since in modern democratic orders, value orientations are diverse and often intractable, arriving at consensus in discourse demands a high level of abstraction;[49] this rules out claims to correctness that refer to particular identities and value orientations and to particular interests in particular situations.

It is for reasons such as these that the theorists hold that the unavoidable presuppositions built into argumentation provide the basis only for a procedural ethics governed by the idea of universalisability.[50] Such an ethics confines itself to stipulating the procedure that must be adopted, and the formal rule that must be applied, if the validity of claims to correctness in a moral sense is to be established. It seems, therefore, that Habermas' and Alexy's pursuit of justificatory strategies that rely on the theory of argumentation leads them to restrict universal validity to ideas of correctness that are construed formally and abstractly and have a universalisable content and to reject the claim to universal validity of ideas of correctness that refer to particular value orientations and interests and to the exigencies of particular situations.

However, even in the case of the idea of universalisability, appeal to the theory of argumentation has proven problematic. Habermas' strategy is open to the objection that it can justify the principle of universalisability as the rule for establishing moral validity only by appealing to presuppositions of argumentation that are not in fact universal but specific to the

[48] Even in his most recent writings on moral validity, Habermas continues to insist that a discursively reached agreement is constitutive of the validity of moral norms and principles. See J Habermas, 'Rightness versus Truth: On the Sense of Normative Validity in Moral Judgments and Norms' in *idem*, *Truth and Justification* (B Fultner (trans), Cambridge, Mass, MIT Press, 2004) 237–6.

[49] J Habermas, 'Remarks on Discourse Ethics' in *Justification and Application*, above n 13 at 90–1).

[50] Alexy, above n 27 at 180; J Habermas, 'Discourse Ethics: Notes on A Program of Philosophical Justification' in *idem*, *Moral Consciousness and Communicative Action* (C Lenhardt and S Weber Nicholsen (trans), Cambridge, Polity Press, 1992) 42–115.

socio-cultural contexts of Western modernity.[51] Alexy's justificatory strategy does seem to appeal only to presuppositions of argumentation in general, but is open to the objection that the resulting conception of argumentation is too weak to justify the principle of universalisability.[52]

Their mistake, I suggest, is the attempt to construe the justification of the universal validity of the claim to correctness as a matter of demonstrating its necessity. This not only opens their justificatory strategies to objections of the kind just mentioned; it also leads to a model of justification that is fixated on correctness in the sense of universalisability and leaves no room for the justification of ideas of correctness of the kind involved in general practical discourse in which, as we have seen, moral, ethical and pragmatic elements form a substantial unity.

Of the two theorists, Alexy comes closest to acknowledging this. Even in his earliest writings, he drew attention to the insufficiency of an explicative theory of argumentation for the purposes of justifying the principle of universalisability.[53] At the same time, he seemed to think that it might one day be possible to produce something like a 'statute book of practical reason', in which the rules and forms of rational practical argumentation would be summarised and explicitly formulated.[54] Recently, however, he appears to have moved away from the position that justifying the principle of universalisability is a matter of explicating necessary rules to one that recognises the reliance of justification on rationally backed, normative decisions. This is indicated by his introduction of the category of 'existential justification' in which he highlights the importance of an interest in correctness that he sees as ultimately a matter of decision as to whether we want to be 'discursive creatures'.[55] Although I find it more helpful to speak of normative commitments than decisions, I consider this a move in the right direction.

While Habermas, too, has always acknowledged the need to supplement his formal-pragmatic strategy with other forms of justification, for the most part these other forms of justification are supposed to fulfil the function of indirect validation.[56] At least on occasion, however, he seems willing to admit that formal pragmatics is incomplete as a justificatory strategy since it requires the assistance of a theory of the development of collective and individual moral competence. Although in his essay on

[51] See S Benhabib, *Situating the Self* (New York and London, Routledge, 1992) at 32–3.

[52] As indicated below, Alexy himself acknowledges the need for supplementary justificatory strategies.

[53] Alexy, above n 47at 161.

[54] *Ibid* at 163.

[55] Alexy, 'Menschenrechte ohne Metaphysik?', above n 6 at 21.

[56] See J Habermas, 'Moral Consciousness and Communicative Action' in *idem*, *Moral Consciousness and Communicative Action*, above n 50 at 116–118.

discourse ethics he asserts unequivocally that 'the principle of universalization ... is implied by the presuppositions of argumentation in general',[57] this assertion is compatible with the view that certain of the idealising suppositions required in order to justify the principle of universalisability (in particular, those relating to inclusiveness and universal equality) are the result of socio-cultural learning processes in which the inherent logic of the universal presuppositions of argumentation are developed.[58] This reading is supported by his acknowledgement in his most recent writings that the principle of universalisability cannot be justified solely on the basis of the normative content of the presuppositions of argumentation.[59] However, even on this reading, Habermas can be seen to appeal to a conception of justification that construes it as a matter of demonstrating necessity. For, though he insists that it is a matter of historical contingency whether or not the normative intuitions built into argumentation develop along universalistic lines, he construes their development along these lines as the unfolding of an inherent logic.[60] In other words, he attributes no historical necessity to the dynamics of development—to the *unfolding* of the inherent logic of the normative intuitions on which discourse ethics depends; at the same time, he asserts the *necessity* of the lines along which they must develop, if they do.

Against this, I want to propose a model of justification that construes it, not as a matter of demonstrating the unavoidability of certain presuppositions, but as a matter of reasoning among autonomous human agents in practices of argumentation that are guided by certain idealising suppositions regarding the proper conduct of the discussion and in which participants seek the single correct answer in a context-transcending sense. This model of justification has a number of key features.[61] To begin with, it self-consciously acknowledges its reliance on certain assumptions, in particular, on the assumption that the postulate of correctness in a context-transcending sense is necessary in order to allow for the rationality of practical judgements in hard cases, be these in the areas of law or democratic deliberation; this assumption is itself held to be a matter for intersubjective deliberation in processes of argumentation. Its commitment to correctness in a context-transcending sense accounts for a second key

[57] Habermas, 'Discourse Ethics: Notes on A Program of Philosophical Justification' above n 50 at 86.

[58] See J Habermas, 'Historical Materialism and the Development of Normative Structures' in *idem*, *Communication and the Evolution of Society* (T McCarthy (ed and trans), London, Heinemann, 1979) 95–129.

[59] J Habermas, *Zwischen Naturalismus und Religion* (Frankfurt am Main, Suhrkamp, 2005) 94–6.

[60] Habermas, *Communication and the Evolution of Society*, above n 58 at 98.

[61] The following is an abbreviated account of the model of practical reasoning I outline in M Cooke, *Re-Presenting the Good Society* (Cambridge, Mass, MIT Press, 2006) ch 6.

feature of the proposed model. This is its postulate of an ineliminable gap between correctness qua transcendent object of enquiry and all actual articulations of this object.[62] For, commitment to the context-transcending power of reason not only calls for a universalist conception of context-transcendence; it requires, in addition, a *dynamic* conception of universality that construes it as never commensurate with its historically specific articulations. This dynamic quality can be contrasted with the static quality of claims to universal validity that posit the possibility of an end point of reason. When construed statically, claims to universal validity allege that the realisation of reason in history is possible: they allege, for example, that a world in which every human subject would be granted the full respect that is due to them or in which human subjects would live in perfect harmony with each other or in which human subjects would have full insight into their own subjectivities, is an attainable condition for human beings. In positing the attainability of a fully rational world, however, they deny the finitude of human knowledge and understanding, the creativity of human free will and the openness of the historical process. By contrast, a dynamic understanding of claims to universal validity acknowledges human finitude and creativity and keeps open the process of history. Although claims are raised for the correctness of certain normative ideas across socio-cultural contexts and historical epochs, there is an accompanying awareness that there is an insurmountable gap between universal validity and all actual claims to instantiate it. The claim to universality, in other words, is construed as inherently context-transcending. This dynamic understanding of universal validity and, by extension, of correctness, accounts for the third feature of the proposed model of justification: its view of judgements of validity as comparative and contestable. For, if there is an ineliminable gap between correctness and all actual articulations of it, judgements of validity must be regarded as comparative rather than absolute and as contestable rather than final. According to this model of justification, the aim of argumentation is not to establish that some position is correct absolutely but rather that some position is superior to other ones. Accordingly, practical rationality is mainly concerned with comparative propositions and with showing that the transition from one position to another constitutes an epistemic gain. At the same time, claims to the effect that a given position constitutes an epistemic gain are held to be contestable; moreover, it is acknowledged that such disputes can never be settled once and for all through appeal to fixed and given criteria. Whether or not something constitutes an epistemic gain

[62] Habermas' revised theory of truth (as opposed to moral validity) allows for such a gap. See M Cooke, 'The Weaknesses of Strong Intersubjectivism: Habermas's Conception of Justice' (2003) 2(3) *European Journal of Political Theory* 281. See also Cooke, above n 61 at ch 5.

is held to be in principle a contested matter, the subject of open-ended discussions in which multiple kinds of empirical, theoretical and normative arguments are brought to bear. It may be noted, finally, that on this dynamic, comparative and contestable understanding of the rationality of justification, the presupposition of concern for the single correct answer is not interpreted as a concern for consensus that is held to be constitutive of moral validity. According to the proposed conception, concern for the single correct answer is indeed an idealising supposition built into argumentation. It is argued, moreover, that this concern should be understood as a concern to reach consensus.[63] In contrast to Habermas, however, who makes it constitutive of moral validity, discursively reached consensus is held to be a regulative idea that guides participants in argumentation in their search for correctness.[64] Qua *regulative* idea, it orients human beings in their deliberations on matters of validity. Qua *idea*, it is a representation of correctness as opposed to correctness itself. In other words, regulative ideas, too, are conceived of as articulations of a transcendent object ('correctness') that are never commensurate with it. If discursively reached consensus is understood as a regulative idea rather than a criterion of validity, the search for consensus takes on a different kind of importance. Whereas, in Habermas' theory, actually achieving consensus in discourse is necessary in order to establish moral validity, in the proposed conception, searching for consensus in valid procedures of decision-making is one articulation of what it means to seek a single correct answer and of the point of legal and political deliberation. To be sure, the proposed conception acknowledges the need for rules of decision-making that reflect this orientation towards consensus. At the same time, however, it recognises that the concrete shape of these rules depends on the deliberative context: in some contexts majority rule, for example, may be held to be appropriate, in others, the principle of unanimity. Consequently, it understands these decision-making rules as institutional rules that have only a weak epistemic status: they do not *determine* the truth content of the norms and principles under discussion; rather, they mark a caesura in the search for

[63] The search for the single correct answer does not have to be interpreted as the search for consensus. If it *is* interpreted in this way, a stronger and weaker position may be adopted. According to the strong position, the validity of norms and principles is constituted by an argumentatively reached consensus. Habermas holds a constructivist view of this kind in the case of moral validity. I criticise it in Cooke, above n 62. According to the weaker position, the validity of norms and principles is conceptually tied to argumentatively reached agreement that they are valid. I suggest that there are good reasons based on the development of the modern Western social imaginary for understanding the concept of validity as tied to argumentation in this weaker sense (see Cooke, above n 61at ch 6).

[64] I set out my understanding of regulative ideas in Cooke, above n 61, esp chs 5, 6 and 7.

truth.[65] If we distinguish in this way between the orientation towards consensus and the institutional rules that testify to that orientation, the importance of actually arriving at consensus can be seen as a contextual question that will be answered in different ways in different decision-making contexts. This impacts, in turn, on the question of particularity. In Habermas' account of moral validity, as we have seen, the requirement of actually reaching consensus means that in societies with a plurality of conflicting value orientations, deliberations have to be conducted at a highly abstract level. An account of justification that drops this requirement opens the door for processes of practical reasoning in which not just considerations of universalisability but also considerations relating to particular identities and particular value orientations, and to particular interests in particular situations, are brought into play.

For our present purposes, this is the main advantage of the proposed model of justification: its ability to accommodate claims to correctness that assert universal validity but to which no universalisable content is assigned, for, by doing so, it allows for the context-transcending power of the claims to correctness raised in general practical discourse. In the models proposed by Habermas and Alexy, the theory of argumentation sets limits to the content assigned to correctness, since analysis of its necessary presuppositions seems to call for articulations of correctness that have a universalisable content; this is reinforced, in Habermas' case, by a view of moral validity as constructed by discursively reached agreement. In the model I propose, by contrast, no such limits are set. Correctness in a context-transcending sense is not extracted from unavoidable presuppositions but is an idealising supposition based on the need to allow for rational decisions in hard cases. Since, for this purpose, context-transcendence has to be understood in a universalist and dynamic way, no articulation of the content of correctness is commensurate with correctness itself: correctness is construed as a transcendent object that always exceeds its particular articulations. This holds for claims to correctness that appeal to the principle of universalisability as much as for claims that appeal to the principle of the right balance between considerations of universalisability, particularity and expediency; thus it holds for judgements of validity arrived at in moral discourses as much as for the judgements of validity arrived at in legal/political discourses qua general practical discourses, and in legal discourses as a sub-set of these. Furthermore, since discursively reached consensus is not constitutive of validity but a regulative idea, the pursuit of correctness in a context-transcending sense does not demand a high degree of abstraction (which would be necessary for the purposes of

[65] Habermas uses this phrase to describe the internal connection between the principle of majority rule and the search for truth. See Habermas, *Between Facts and Norms*, above n 1 at 179.

actually achieving consensus) but allows for consideration of matters of a particular, contextual and pragmatic nature. In sum, a model of rational justification of the proposed kind clears the way for an account of the context-transcending component of law's claim to correctness that acknowledges its connection with the substantial unity of practical reason in the democratic process; at the same time, it interprets the claim to correctness in a universalist, dynamic way that permits interrogation of the judgements of validity that are arrived at in processes of decision-making in existing legal and democratic orders.

CONCLUSION

In the foregoing I have endeavoured to strengthen Alexy's and Habermas' non-positivist view of law's claim to correctness: their view that law is open to a mode of criticism from the inside that is rational in a context-transcending sense. Against Alexy, but in the spirit of his account of practical rationality, I have argued that the context-transcending power of the claim to correctness should not be interpreted in purely moral terms; instead it should be seen as a complex interplay of moral, ethical and pragmatic elements. Against Habermas, but in the spirit of his account of communicative reason, I have argued for a universalist understanding of the context-transcending power of democratic reason that does not cut it short at the borders of a historically specific democratic order but sets it free to traverse spaces and times. For these purposes, I proposed a model of justification that, by construing the rationality of claims to correctness as comparative and contestable, and by making consensus a regulative idea rather than constitutive of validity, is able to accommodate claims to correctness that involve considerations of particularity and expediency as well as of universalisability. The proposed model of justification assigns a rationality to the claims to correctness raised in legal deliberations, and in the practical deliberations of the democratic process more generally, that has a context-transcending power. In this conception, accordingly, both legal and legal/political deliberations have a built-in orientation towards correctness that points, like a vector, beyond the standards of validity prevailing in any legal and political order, anywhere, at any time.

The proposed conception seeks to capture an intuition that it sees at the heart of Alexy's and Habermas' non-positivist accounts of law: the intuition that hard cases are the occasion for collective learning processes in which practical reasoning sparks off an internal, rational transformation of the existing legal order. It endorses their view that practical reasoning must take place in processes of argumentation guided by idealising suppositions relating to the procedure of deliberation and to its outcome. However, it diverges from either of their accounts of legal deliberation in one significant respect. It proposes a model of practical reasoning in which considerations of universalisablity, particularity and expediency lead to new legal judgements and decisions that claim neither moral validity (Alexy) nor general acceptability in a given democratic order (Habermas) but *practical rationality*, correctness in a context-transcending sense that is a complex interplay of moral, ethical and pragmatic elements.

12

A Teleological Approach to Legal Dialogues

GIOVANNI SARTOR*

INTRODUCTION

ROBERT ALEXY HAS dedicated a particular and persistent attention to both dialogues and teleological reasoning, and his work on both subjects has strongly influenced the legal-theoretical debate of the last decades.

Dialogues have been a central concern for Alexy since the very beginning of his inquiries. In 1978 he delivered his *Theory of Legal Argumentation*[1] where he provided an account of legal reasoning as a dialectical argumentation,[2] to be viewed as a special case of moral argumentation. Building upon Habermas' theory of discourse,[3] Alexy defined an abstract dialectical protocol—a set of rules governing the interaction of the participants in a dialogue—for carrying out moral discourse, and then identified what specific additions and refinements to such rules are required for dealing with legal issues. Moreover he showed how the resulting model of legal reasoning could be coherent with, and provide a justification for, many aspects of legal practice (such as constrained deference to legislation, precedent and legal doctrine). The importance of Alexy's work on legal

* Supported by the EU projects ONE-LEX (Marie Curie Chair) and ALIS (IST-2004-027968).

[1] R Alexy, *A Theory of Legal Argumentation* (Oxford, Clarendon Press, 1989) (1st edn in German, 1978).

[2] I shall always use the word *dialectical* in the sense of *dialogical*, namely, as pertaining to linguistic exchanges between two or more people. I shall not take into account the further and different senses this word (or the cognate noun *dialectics*) has been given in the philosophical tradition (eg, by Kant, Hegel or Marx).

[3] J Habermas, *The Theory of Communicative Action* (Boston, Beacon, 1985) (1st edn in German, 1981).

argumentation can hardly be underestimated: his analysis of legal dialectics represents one of the most significant and fruitful contributions to current legal theory.

Besides dialogues, also teleological reasoning has been an important concern for Alexy.[4] This is shown in particular by Alexy's theory of legal principles (developed in particular in his *Theorie der Grundrechte*),[5] which connects principles to values: for Alexy a principle is indeed the prescription to optimise the realisation of a certain value (taking into account the need to optimise also the satisfaction of other, possibly conflicting values). This approach puts teleological reasoning at the very core of legal thinking, if we understand teleological reasoning in a sufficiently wide sense, namely, as including all of the following: (a) the identification of the relevant values, namely, the *teloi* (goals, ends or purposes) that are to be pursued in politics and law; (b) the assessment of their relative importance, in different contexts; and (c) the determination of how (through what decisions, norms, institutions) the realisation of such multiple goals or values can best be achieved. And Alexy indeed has tried to provide some techniques for simplifying and facilitating this kind of reasoning in the circumstances of legal decision-making.[6]

There is a potential tension between these two aspects of Alexy's analysis of legal reasoning.

From a dialectical perspective, it seems that dialogues (or discourses, namely, dialogues carried out according to certain standards aimed at ensuring their fairness and rationality) should come first: it should be up to dialogues to determine what goals have to be pursued in law and politics, and how they should be pursued.

From a teleological perspective, on the contrary, it seems that values should come first: it should be up to teleological reasoning to determine what kinds of dialectical interaction we should practise, as the most appropriate for optimising the achievement of certain legal and political values.

Moreover, there is a kind of entanglement between the two aspects just considered. On the one hand, if dialectical rules have to aim at ensuring

[4] Alexy's recognition of teleology marks a significant difference between his conception of legal reasoning and that of Habermas, who, besides in general downplaying the significance of instrumental (means-end) reasoning (on instrumental reasoning as the core of rationality, see R Nozick, *The Nature of Rationality,* Princeton NJ, Princeton University Press,1993), also downplays the rational significance of the lawyers' effort toward achieving a balanced satisfaction of competing values, arguing that 'weighing takes place either arbitrarily or unreflectingly, according to customary standards and hierarchies' (J Habermas, *Between Facts and Norms* (Cambridge, Mass, MIT Press, 1999) 259 (1st edn in German, 1992.)).

[5] R Alexy, *Theorie der Grundrechte* (Frankfurt am Main, Suhrkamp, 1985).

[6] R Alexy, 'On Balancing and Subsumption: A Structural Comparison' (2002) 16 *Ratio Juris* 33.

fairness and rationality—epistemically intended as truth- or knowledge-conduciveness—of dialectical interactions (and possibly at realising other values as well), then their determination or at least their specification becomes a subject matter for teleological reasoning: we can view fairness and rationality as goals to be achieved and the rules governing a dialectical exchange as means (instruments) for achieving such goals. On the other end, teleological reasoning as well can be performed through dialogues, namely, though dialectical interaction aimed at identifying, and agreeing upon, what values are to be collectively pursued and how such values are to be realised.

This entanglement can be avoided only if certain strong assumptions are made. For achieving the independence of dialogues from teleological reasoning we need to assume that the structure of dialogues (or at least of certain kinds of them) is fixed in advance, that it precedes and constrains the formation of our beliefs and opinions (and that it survives any change on such beliefs and opinions): it is the immutable transcendental framework which necessarily binds all language users (or which is necessarily presupposed in every language use). On the other hand, for achieving the independence of legal and political values from dialectical interactions, we need to assume that only individual rationality or intuition, or the aggregation of individual rationalities and intuitions (as expressed eg, in voting) can identify such values and the best ways to achieve them, and correspondingly can guide legal and political action, regardless of inquiries carried out through dialectical exchanges and of agreements brought about through dialectical deliberation.

In this chapter, I shall make none of these assumptions, but I shall rather develop a teleological analysis of legally relevant dialogues. This means that I shall view different dialectical patterns as different institutions, having specific social functions (social effects justifying their continued practice) constituting their social purposes, namely, their embedded values. I shall distinguish the purposes of a dialectical institution (eg, civil proceedings) from the goals pursued by the parties to a corresponding dialogue (eg, the parties in a civil case): the institution's purposes are not necessarily endorsed by the parties to the dialogue as their own goals. And the goals of the parties may be collective goals they are co-operatively pursuing, or they may be individual goals they are pursuing independently or even competitively.

Thus, while some dialogues appear usually to be co-operative games, others appear as non-co-operative games, or even as adversarial zero-sum games, where the achievement of the goal of one party means defeat for the other (as it is often the case for legal proceedings). And the parties may have at the same time co-operative and competing goals (as when they exchange their view in front of an arbitrator they have chosen, sharing the goal to settle their dispute in this way, but having different goals with regard to what the arbitrator's decision should be).

Most legal dialogues will take place under strong resource constraints. The continuation of dialogue not only has direct costs for the parties (in terms of time, lawyers' fees, taxes on proceedings, and so on), but it also entails delaying the production of the outcome of the dialogue, and thus delaying the solution of the problem which originated the dialogue. While the dialogue goes on, such a problem can get worse (and produce further negative impacts on the parties and on others) and the implementation of the outcome of the dialogue can become more difficult and costly, or even impossible.

Thus, typical legal dialogues will generally be very different from the kinds of dialogues on which discourse theory usually focuses, namely, dialogues that only consist of 'communicative actions'[7] and that can go on indefinitely, until an agreed solution is found. However, also with regard to the law there is the opportunity, I shall argue, for developing co-operative dialogues, where each one gives his or her contribution for the collective purpose of increasing shared knowledge, and possibly coming to a shared opinion or even a binding agreement. Moreover, the diversity of legal dialogues, and of the goals at issue, does not exclude that we can view rational consent and co-operative debate as values (or regulative ideas) which should inspire legal reasoning and the design of legal institutions, as claimed by the advocates of deliberative democracy.[8] In many cases, however, they cannot be assumed to be the goals of the parties in legal interactions, or the direct purpose of the dialectical institutions governing such interactions.

DIALOGUES AND DIALECTICAL SYSTEMS

To understand how legal interactions are structured and to evaluate their merit, I refer to the idea of a *dialectical system*, an idea originally introduced by Hamblin.[9] In general, a dialectical system is an:

[7] As characterised by Habermas, namely, as the kind of interaction which is aimed toward agreement or consent, 'in which all participants harmonize their individual plans of action with one another and thus pursue their illocutionary aims without reservation': (Habermas, above n 3). For a critical discussion of Habermas's approach to communication, see R Tuomela, 'Collective Goals and Communicative Action' (2002) 22 *Journal of Philosophical Research* 29.

[8] See G Postema, 'Public Practical Reason: Political Practice' in I Shapiro and J Wagner De Crew (eds), *Nomos XXXVII: Theory and Practice* (New York, New York University Press, 1995).

[9] C Hamblin, *Fallacies* (London, Methuen, 1970).

> organised conversation where two parties (in the simplest case) speak in turn, by asking questions and giving replies (perhaps including other types of locutions) in an orderly way, taking into account, at any particular turn, what occurred previously in the dialogue.[10]

Dialectical procedures can be very different, in particular according to the following oppositions:

- The first is the opposition between *formal* and *informal protocols*, which concerns the language and the precision through which a dialectical system is specified. It opposes specification through natural language and specification through logical and mathematical formalisms.
- The second is the distinction between *description* and *design*, which concerns the purpose of the specification of a dialectical system. It opposes the aim of describing existing dialectical systems (the systems which are currently practised by the parties of certain dialogues) and the aim of designing new (or partially new) dialectical systems (as ways to improve dialectical interactions in certain contexts).

These oppositions are continuous dimensions, and define a two-dimensional space in which we can try to locate particular dialogue protocols, according to the extent to which they are more or less formal, and to which they reproduce practised protocols or innovate them.

All dialectical systems, regardless of their being formal or informal, and their aiming at description or design, are normative in the sense of including rules specifying how dialogues are to be carried out (if they are to respect the requirements of the dialectical system). However, designed dialogues are also normative in a different sense, concerning the choice of rules rather than their implementation: they suggest what rules ought to be adopted for certain purposes and in certain contexts.

When approaching dialectical systems we need to specify the idea of a *dialectical protocol*, by which is usually meant the rules governing the interaction of the parties in the corresponding dialogues. Here we will use this notion in a broader sense. We view the protocol of a dialectical system as a *practical theory*, that is, as the whole set of assumptions that may provide appropriate guidance to the implementation of the dialectical system in actual dialogues.[11] Thus, a protocol for a dialectical system does not include only rules, but also specifications of values and goals to be achieved, and information concerning opportunities and risks related to the implementation of the dialectical system.

[10] DN Walton and E Krabbe, *Commitment in Dialogue: Basic Concepts of Interpersonal Reasoning* (Albany, NY, State University of New York Press, 1995) 5.

[11] On this notion, G Sartor, *Legal Reasoning: A Cognitive Approach to the Law*, vol 5 of *Treatise on Legal Philosophy and General Jurisprudence* (Berlin, Springer, 2005) 78.

Dialectical systems can frequently be characterised as *games* in a strict sense, ie, according to game theory: the parties have certain *possible moves* (locution types) at their disposal, and under certain conditions the dialogue will *terminate* with certain outputs. Since the parties may assign different values to these outputs, somebody will then *win* or possibly *lose*.

The game-theoretical approach emphasises the *strategic* dimension of dialectical interactions: each party intends to achieve as much as possible (with regard to his or her goals), but this depends on the other party's moves. Therefore each party, besides respecting the rules of the game, must develop a strategy, and must do this by anticipating the other party's strategy. This does not mean that the parties need always to act one against the other. Some dialogues can indeed be qualified as *non-co-operative games*, where for each winner there is a loser, but others represent *co-operative games*, where parties win or lose together, according to their ability to co-ordinate their actions. And while in some co-operative games the parties have complementary individual goals (so that the same combination of their actions leads to satisfying at the same time their separate goals), in other cases they share a common collective goal, possibly agreed between them so as to generate a binding joint commitment.[12]

One of the most interesting features of the theory of dialectical systems is that it allows for the characterisation of infinite varieties of dialectical systems. At the descriptive level, this enables us to define dialectical systems that can approximate the concrete structure of different kinds of social interaction, taking into account the peculiarities of each of these kinds of interaction. At the design level, it allows us to specify what kinds of interaction would be more appropriate for achieving different purposes, in different contexts. Thus, a design characterisation of an interaction need not be an idealisation, to wit, it need not describe what might happen in circumstances that are not to be found in the real world. On the contrary, a dialectical system can be adapted to the concretely available possibilities and to the limitations (in knowledge, competence, time, and so on) characterising its likely parties, so as to provide rules that the parties are capable of respecting.

The features of the theory of dialectical systems we have presented so far make it a useful tool for the study of legal procedures. Legal processes are indeed dialectical interactions, in which different parties play different roles. These interactions are governed by rules establishing what kinds of locutions are allowed to each party, in what circumstances, and to what effects. There is much at stake, and there will usually be winners and losers, so that the parties will often develop a strategic interaction, each one anticipating the other's moves. There are various goals to be achieved,

[12] Tuomela, above n 7.

which will, and must, be reflected in the complexities of the rules of the game. The players are real persons acting under stringent resource constraints.

How to Characterise Dialectical Systems

A key aspect on the characterisation of a dialogue system consists in a set of rules. However, rules are not enough: they make sense only if we adopt a purposive, or functional perspective.

By the *function of a dialectical system*, we mean those outcomes of the practice of such a system which explain and justify its being practised. This function does not need to be the aim of all participants in the dialogue. Often, the function of a dialogue will rather be achieved through the institutional machinery governing the dialogue, even if the participants only aim at different particular purposes, corresponding to their individual interests.

For instance, in the typical legal proceedings in civil matters, the parties aim at opposite outcomes: each one wants to win the case, getting an advantageous outcome at the expense of the other. However, in pursuing their conflicting objectives the parties contribute to a different institutional purpose, that is, achieving a fair and informed justice while putting an end to their litigation. This difference—between the aims of the participants in a dialogue on the one hand and the function of the dialogue on the other hand—does not necessarily imply hypocrisy or self-deception: lawyers defending, legally and loyally, their clients, aim at winning their cases, but at the same time they may correctly believe that they are contributing to justice.

Viewing dialogues from a functional perspective enables us to understand the aim of each rule, that is, its contribution to the dialogue's general purposes. This allows us to move from the pure description of the dialogue's rules to an *immanent critique*, and ultimately enables us to move to from description to design: we wonder whether the current rules of the dialogue enable it to perform its function in the best way, and what different rules would improve the functioning of the dialogue.

Beside the function of a dialectical system and the goals of its participants, we also need to identify the side-effects it may have, distinguishing the positive and the negative ones, both when the dialogue achieves its end and when it fails.

To characterise dialogues, we start from the classification schema in Table 12.1 where we distinguish eight kinds of dialogue: persuasion, negotiation, deliberation, information-seeking, epistemic inquiry, practical inquiry, eristic, reconciliation.[13]

We shall not provide here a detailed comment of our schema, nor claim its exhaustiveness and adequacy. We will rather use it as a tentative pattern for identifying certain features of legal interactions, and thus to emphasise certain similarities and differences between them:

- making a contract or achieving a settled solution to a dispute can be classified as kinds of negotiation;
- parliamentary discussion falls under the headings of persuasion and negotiation, or sometimes of eristic (sometimes there is also an element of inquiry);
- doctrinal exchanges are instances of epistemic or practical inquiry (sometimes also of persuasion);
- judicial proceedings contain elements of persuasion, information-seeking, negotiation, and possibly of inquiry and reconciliation.

Structure of Dialectical Systems

Let us now move from a teleological perspective to a structural analysis, and consider the different types of rules that define the structure of dialogues.

A dialogue may be viewed as a succession of moves, each of which consists in performing a speech act. Performing one move has certain effects on the dialogue, and in particular on the *commitments* of the parties, that is, on the positions a party is bound to sustain (until the party can validly withdraw them, paying the penalties that are possibly linked to withdrawal). We may say that one party's commitments are those propositions the party is bound to recognise (eg, if I affirm something, I am bound to stick to it), unless the conditions for retraction are satisfied.

My analysis will be based on the model of Walton and Krabbe,[14] which distinguish the following types of dialogue rules:

- locution rules, establishing what moves are available to the parties;
- structural rules, indicating when the available moves can be performed;

[13] This is a revised version of the model proposed by DN Walton and E Krabbe, *Commitment in Dialogue: Basic Concepts of Interpersonal Reasoning* (Albany, NY, State University of New York Press, 1995) 66, which I have modified in two regards: I have added two new types of dialogues, practical inquiry and reconciliation, and also a description of the dangers ensuing from failure.

[14] *Ibid.*

Type	Sub-types	Initial situation	Main goal	Participants' aims	Beneficial side-effects	Implications of main goal	Dangers related to failure	Psychological disposition required
Persuasion	Dispute; discussion of proposals	One party's position not shared	Get to a shared position	Persuade the other(s)	Develop and reveal positions	Opponent commits to the persuader's thesis	Resent lack of understanding	Accept merit of arguments by others
Negotiation	Bargain; make a package deal	Need of co-operation; conflicting interests	Make a deal, possibly stable and fair	Make a deal convenient for oneself	Co-operate; recognise others' interests	All commit to the agreed deal	Resent greed; implement threats	Disposition to keep promises
Deliberation	Board meeting; political decision-making	Need to adopt a (rational) group-position	Good and effective decisions; participation	Favour a decision one views as better	Co-operation	Shared commitment to the decided result	Distrust, un-co-ordinated action, conflict	Disposition to work for the common good
Information-seeking	Interrogation; expert consultation	Interviewer needs to know; interviewee putatively knows	Spread knowledge; reveal positions	Gain or pass personal knowledge	Agreement; co-operation; prestige	Interviewee commits to statement		Sincerity
Epistemic inquiry	Scientific investigation; examination	General ignorance	Progress in epistemic knowledge	Find proofs or destroy them	Agreement; co-operation; prestige	Technological ability		Curiosity; passion for reason
Practical inquiry	Moral, political or doctrinal discussion	Uncertainty of what should be done	Progress in practical knowledge	Find arguments or destroy them	Agreement, co-operation, prestige	Ability to act correctly		Curiosity; passion for reason
Eristic	Quarrel; eristic discussion	Conflict; distrust	Reach provisional accommodation	Strike and defeat the other	Vent emotions; reveal positions	Reciprocal recognition	Physical violence; refusal to interact	Combativeness; resilience
Reconciliation	Peace-making; restorative justice	Past conflicts; distrust	Build trust; prepare co-operation	Repentance; forgiveness	Shared understanding of the past	Shared commitment to acceptance and co-operation	More struggle and distrust	Recognition; trust; sincerity

- commitment rules, specifying what effects moves have on commitments of the parties;
- termination rule, stating when the dialogue terminates and with what results.

Persuasion Dialogue: Structure

To illustrate the notions introduced in the previous paragraph, let us analyse the structure of the most studied type of dialectical system, the *persuasion dialogue*, of which I shall provide an elementary account. First we characterise the parties:

- there are two parties, let us call them Proponent and Opponent;
- Proponent is going to try to persuade Opponent and Opponent will resist persuasion.

Let us now consider locution rules and commitment rules (here we combine the two for simplicity) for the persuasion dialogue: we identify what speech acts are available to the parties and specify what effects these acts have on the commitments of the parties. The set of available moves can accordingly be described as follows:

(1) Claiming a proposition ϕ. This commits the speaker to ϕ. For instance, Proponent says: 'I claim that you have to compensate me for the damage to my crops'.
(2) Challenging a claimed proposition ϕ. This obliges[15] the hearer to give grounds for ϕ. For instance, Opponent says: 'I challenge your statement that I have to compensate you for the damage to your crops'. This obliges Proponent to give grounds that support the conclusion that Opponent has to compensate the damage.
(3) Conceding a proposition ϕ that was claimed by the other party. This commits the speaker to ϕ. For instance, Opponent says: 'I concede that the damage to your crops was caused by my cows'.

[15] The ideal of a dialectical obligation has two sides. On the one hand, it may express the notion of a *burden* or a *technical ought*: unless the participant does the 'obligatory' action, the participant will fail to achieve his or her dialectical goals. For instance, if the party in a legal dispute fails to support the proposition she is claiming, that party will probably lose (and the other party will not complain about this). On the other hand, a dialectical obligation may also express the notion of proper *deontic obligation*. This is when the goal to be achieved though the fulfilment of the obligation is a collective goal of the participants or a goal of another participant, and the obligation concerns giving one's contribution to achieve that goal. For instance, if in an academic discussion I keep for myself some information that is relevant to the subject matter and interesting for others, avoiding sharing it with my fellows, they can complain that I have failed to contribute to the discussion as I was supposed to do. Similarly, if I am questioned, I know the answer, and I fail to provide it, my partner can complain that I have violated a dialectical rule of the information-seeking dialogue (where one is supposed to give an answer, if one knows it).

(4) Claiming proposition ϕ as a complete reason supporting a previously claimed proposition ϕ. This commits the speaker to ϕ. For instance, assume that Proponent says: 'You have to compensate me for the damage to my crops, since (a) you own the cows that caused the damage, (b) cows are animals, and (c) owners are under the obligation to compensate others for damage caused by their animals'. (The claimed proposition is the conjunction of a, b, and c).
(5) Claiming proposition ϕ as a partial reason supporting a previously claimed proposition ϕ. Commits the speaker both to ϕ, and to the assumption that ϕ can be expanded into a complete reason for ϕ. For instance, Proponent, rather than stating the complete reason indicated in (4), can only provide a part of it, by saying: 'You have to compensate me for the damage to my crops, since you own the cows that caused the damage'.
(6) Challenging partial reason ϕ (in reply to move (5)). Obliges the hearer to complement ϕ with further partial reasons. For instance, Opponent says: 'I challenge your statement that the fact that I own the cows entails that I have to compensate you for the damage to your crops'.

Let us consider the structural rules, which indicate when the moves we have just described can legitimately be performed:

- The dialogue starts with an initial claim of Proponent, after which the parties take moves in turn.
- Opponent may attack (challenge) one of Proponent's previous statements, or accept it (concede).
- Proponent may defend (by giving grounds) the attacked statement.
- Those Proponent's statements that Opponent has not explicitly attacked count as being conceded, until they are explicitly attacked.

Finally, here are the termination rules:

- The dialogue terminates in favour of Proponent when, after a move by Opponent, the statements implicitly or explicitly conceded by Opponent form a valid argument supporting Proponent's claim.
- The dialogue terminates in favour of Opponent, when, after a Proponent's move, the statements conceded by Opponent or yet unchallenged do not form such a valid argument.

The latter rules, in other terms, say that Proponent wins if Opponent has explicitly or implicitly (ie, by not contesting) conceded all statements of an argument supporting Proponent's initial claim. On the contrary, Opponent wins if she has challenged all arguments so far proposed by Proponent and the latter does not put forward any further arguments supporting his claim.

Let us consider, eg, the following dialogue, where Proponent performs P-labelled statements, and Opponent, the O-labelled ones:

P1: I claim that you have to compensate me for the damage to my crops.
O1: I challenge your claim.
P2: You have to compensate me for the damage to my crops, since you own the cows that caused the damage.
O2: I concede that I own the cows that caused the damage to your crops, but I challenge that this entails that I have to compensate you for such damage.
P3: I claim that owners are under the obligation to compensate others for damage caused by their animals (and that cows are animals).
O3: I concede that owners are under the obligation to compensate others for damages caused by their animals.

Proponent wins the dialogue since Proponent concedes (explicitly or implicitly) premises that are sufficient to support Proponent's request for compensation. The winning argument is shown in Figure 1, which also indicates the dialectical status of each proposition.

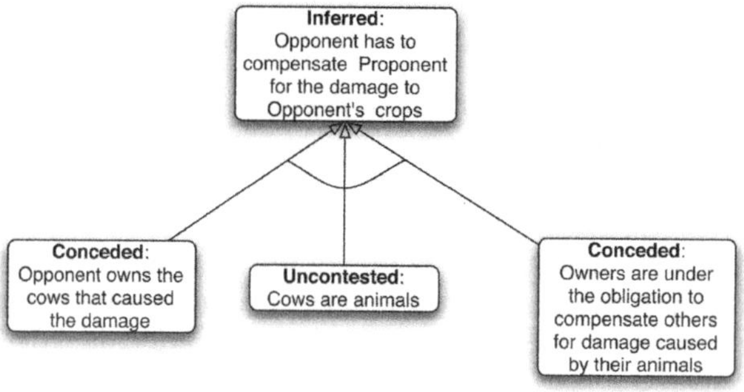

Persuasion Dialogue: Position of the Parties

In a persuasion dialogue the proponent tries to push the opponent into a situation where the opponent will be forced either to fall in a contradiction (or in an unsustainable position) or to concede elements sufficient to establish the claim of the proponent. Thus, in principle the opponent enjoys an advantaged position: she may avoid losing just by challenging whatever statement the proponent puts forward and never committing to anything. If the opponent adopts this strategy, she will be sure that she will never fall in a contradiction (and the proponent in the end will have to abandon the game).

The position of the proponent is much more difficult: he must make assertions (and therefore he can fall in contradiction), and must support them by giving grounds. In a realistic setting the challenge-all trap may be avoided by appealing to shared opinions.

First of all, an opinion may be shared by the parties of the dialogue, that is, the proponent may appeal to ideas that are already adopted by the opponent, who is committed to these ideas either on personal grounds, or because she has publicly endorsed them.

Secondly, the proponent may appeal to opinions that are shared in the social setting where the dialogue takes place. These opinions are usually referred to by using the Aristotelian term *endoxa*, which denotes propositions that are normally accepted in the social context in which the dialogue is embedded. *Endoxa* may indeed be viewed as defeasible presumptions, to be accepted until refuted.[16] The same holds for the so called *rhetorical places* (*topoi*), namely, the theses that can be introduced in any discourse (common places) or in particular disciplines (specific places) being generally accepted and acceptable, though being susceptible of limitations, conflicts and exceptions.

Moreover, as we shall see in the following, when a third party participates in a persuasion dialogue (as a judge or a jury) the decisive step consists in appealing to the opinions of the third party. More generally (consider eg, a political debate) the proponent's position is strengthened when there is an audience, which can sanction the opponent's refusal to concede what is accepted (and appears to require acceptance) by everybody else.

Other Kinds of Dialogue: Information-Seeking, Negotiation and Reconciliation

The pattern of interaction required for the purpose of information-seeking is different from the pattern characterising a persuasion dialogue. In an *information-seeking dialogue*, speech acts are not claims, challenges and concessions, but rather *questions* and *answers*. We may also admit the challenge of a query, which consists in questioning its admissibility or its relevance. As a result of such a challenge, the information-seeking dialogue will embed a persuasion dialogue, where the interviewer tries to persuade the interviewee (or the observers) of the relevance of her question.

In information-seeking dialogues the interviewer plays safe: she does not need to commit to any assertion. On the contrary, the interviewee gets committed to his statements, and incurs the risk of contradicting himself. However, in a co-operative situation, information-seeking dialogues are win-win games: the interviewer succeeds by accessing the information, the

[16] See G Sartor, *Legal Reasoning: A Cognitive Approach to the Law*, vol 5 of *Treatise on Legal Philosophy and General Jurisprudence* (Berlin, Springer, 2005) 78.

interviewee by transmitting it. In contrast, in a non-co-operative situation, when one party is interested in coming to know certain facts, where the other does not want to provide information, the interviewer will win if she extracts the information she wants. In a different sense, the interviewer also wins if the interviewee falls into contradiction, and is consequently discredited. As an example of a (usually) co-operative interview, consider a lawyer examining a witness he has indicated; as an example of a (usually) non-co-operative interview consider a lawyer examining the witnesses indicated by the other party. Similarly, prosecutorial fact-finding tends generally to assume the pattern of an information-seeking dialogue, though there are significant variations in different legal systems.

Still different rules are required for a *negotiation dialogue*. In such dialogues there is a *negotiation space*, namely, a set of negotiated outcomes that both parties prefer to a non-negotiated solution. However, the parties gain differently from different negotiated outcomes. For example, assume that a prosecutor would prefer trial to an agreed penalty lower than five years, and the accused would prefer trial to an agreed penalty higher than 10 years. Within this negotiation space (from five to 10 years) the two parties have to find an agreement. Here the moves are the parties' offers. Each party is committed to his or her offers: if an offer is accepted by the other party, it becomes a binding agreement. Moreover, the subsequent offer of one party must be at least as convenient as the previous offer of that party. The dialogue finishes when an offer is accepted, and thus a deal is made.

In a successful negotiation dialogue both parties win, and the amount of their victory is the difference between the agreed result and the minimum result they were ready to accept (which is determined by the expected value of a non-negotiated solution). In our example, if the agreement is for the accused to plead guilty with a six-year sentence, the prosecutor wins one year (6–5=1) and the accused wins four years (10–6=4). Note that the gains of the two parties may be very different (in a sense, we may also say the party getting the lion's share is the one who really wins). The game also finishes when both parties refuse to make further offers: in this case both parties lose, missing the advantages of co-operation. The loss may even be worse than simple non-co-operation: if in the course of a negotiation threats were issued, now they may need to be implemented, to the detriment of both parties (otherwise the issuer of the threat would lose his or her credibility, and the possibility of using threats in the future).

Still different rules are required for *practical inquiry*, where the parties engage in a common disinterested search for practical knowledge. In these dialogues—a precise account of which has been provided by Alexy's theory of practical reasoning[17]—each one can put forward relevant statements, can defend them through arguments, is obliged to justify his or her statements if required to do so, and can challenge the statements and the arguments of any others. In practical inquiry, defining what counts as winning or losing depends on the purposes of each participant, to wit, on whether they want to achieve an agreement, or rather to increase their individual knowledge or practical wisdom through the interaction with other people, or rather to contribute to the enterprise of increasing collective practical knowledge:

- In the first case, everybody wins if a shared conclusion is achieved, ie, if an argument has been produced which has been capable of surviving all challenges and attacks. Everybody loses if no such argument has been constructed.
- In the second case, one wins if one becomes aware of relevant and insightful arguments supporting or attacking a thesis one is interested in. One loses if no increase in one's individual knowledge and wisdom is obtained through the dialogue.
- In the third case, one wins if one contributes to the development of practical knowledge, viewed as a collective enterprise.

Finally, different rules hold for *reconciliation dialogues*. Here the starting situation is where one party is accused of committing certain offences, the performance of which impairs future co-operation, and which reveal a hostile disposition incompatible with co-operation.

Though very often both parties in a reconciliation dialogue may be in the offender's position one towards the other (as is usually the case after a civil war), it is useful, for analytical purposes, to view reconciliation between reciprocal offenders as consisting in two reconciliation processes going in opposite directions, and thus to keep the idea that reconciliation connects an offender and a victim. The accused party has the possibility either of rejecting the accusation, or instead of admitting his past wrongs while rejecting the disposition that led him to commit such wrongs. The rejection of the accusation would possibly determine a shift into a different type of dialogue, possibly an information-seeking or a persuasion dialogue. The admission would determine a situation where the other party either gives her forgiveness or challenges the change in disposition of the accused. Again this last reply may start a new type of dialogue—possibly an information-seeking or a persuasion dialogue—intended to establish whether such a change has taken place. It is hard to say who wins or loses

[17] See R Alexy, *Theorie der juristischen Argumentation: Die Theorie des rationalen Diskurses als Theorie der juristischen Begründung*, 2nd edn, Frankfurt am Main, Suhrkamp, 1991 (1st edn, 1978) and also the formalisation provided in TF Gordon, *The Pleadings Game: An Artificial Intelligence Model of Procedural Justice* (Dordrecht, Kluwer, 1995).

a reconciliation dialogue, since this largely depends on the psychological attitudes of the parties. We can say that both win if the reconciliation takes place: both parties are now committed to co-operate, and the wrongdoer has changed for good. Both lose if reconciliation fails, which can lead to an escalation of the conflict.

Combination of Dialogues, Dialogue Shifts and Inversion of the Burden of Proof

According to Walton and Krabbe,[18] various other aspects become relevant in describing a dialogue, besides those we considered in the previous sections: the type of conflict (more generally, the type of problem) which has originated the dialogue, the nature of the subject discussed, the degree of rigidity of the dialectical rules, the preciseness of the procedural description of the dialogue, the commixture with other types of dialogues. These aspects too need to be discussed with specific reference to different dialectical systems. For instance, an excessive precision of rules and procedures can play a negative role in a reconciliation dialogue, where excess in formality can prevent people from sincerely expressing their attitudes, while precision can be useful in persuasion dialogues, where it can make interaction quicker and more effective.

The diversity of dialectical systems, and their different ability to cope with different aims and contexts, explains why a *combination of dialogue-types* may be required for handling complex interactions, where more than one purpose is at hand, and parties may take very different attitudes. This is typically the case in legal proceedings.

The basic pattern for reconstructing such proceedings, both in the civil process and in the (accusatorial) criminal process is given by the *persuasion dialogue*. There are indeed many advantages linked to this type of dialogue. It strongly protects the interests of the opponent, and in particular allows him control over his *privacy*, namely, over the decision of what information to disclose at what stage (by conceding the corresponding statement of the proponent). It does not make major psychological demands on the parties: they are fighting one against the other, and there is no need for their having a joint purpose. It may be tightly regulated, since each party reacts to the moves of the other party. Though a persuasion dialogue has these interesting features, it is clear that no legal process could work as pure persuasion.

First, the opponent could always avoid being persuaded (so that he would never lose) simply by challenging every statement of the proponent, even those that are most evident. This can be compensated by introducing

[18] Walton and Krabbe, above n 13.

in the debate an impartial observer, such as a jury (or a judge), with the task of establishing what statements cannot be undermined by a simple challenge, but must be assumed unless proof to the contrary is provided (when *res ipsa loquitur*). The evaluation of the observer may be anticipated by the proponent, who tries to provide reasons that her audience will presumptively accept. The judgement on the presumptive acceptability can also be made directly by the law, by establishing inversions of the burden of proof.

An inversion of the burden of proof, in a persuasion dialogue, starts a new, embedded persuasion dialogue, where the parties switch their roles: in relation to a certain proposition, now the original opponent (the defendant) becomes the proponent while the original proponent (the plaintiff) becomes the opponent. For instance, in the example above once the plaintiff has established that the defendant's cows have caused the damage, the defendant can still avoid liability by showing that the plaintiff's careless behaviour (eg, leaving open the gate to his field) was a decisive precondition for the production of the damage. In regard to this condition, the burden of proof is upon the defendant: she becomes the proponent of this proposition, and she must push the plaintiff to concede it, or provide evidence that convinces the judge. For instance, the defendant can prove that the plaintiff unreasonably forgot to close his gate (knowing that the defendant's cows were grazing in the adjoining field).

Another way to avoid the challenge-all trap consists in embedding inside a persuasion dialogue an information seeking phase, as when a witness is interrogated, an expert provides his opinion, or when one of the parties takes an oath. Again, such a step will (usually) provide an inversion on the burden of proof, which requires the defendant to take the initiative: what results from the embedded dialogue (eg the statements of the witness) will be presumed to be true, unless the defendant persuades the other party (or at least the observers) of the contrary.

Finally, there may be the possibility of embedding negotiation into persuasion, though this would rather consist in moving to a completely different dialogue, as when parties negotiate an agreement to end litigation.

Embedding is an aspect of the more general phenomenon of a *dialogue-shift*, which occurs when a dialogue shades into another dialogue type. This may happen under different circumstances: with the agreement of all participants, according to the intention of only some of them (while others are against the change), or even without the parties being fully aware. For instance, persuasion can become inquiry if the proponent, rather than defending her thesis, confesses her perplexity on the matter, and asks for co-operation in order to solve her predicament. Similarly persuasion can become information-seeking, if the persuader starts questioning her opponent (rather then providing reasons supporting his own statements).

Inquiry can become persuasion when one researcher is so convinced of, or so committed to, her thesis that she just focuses on resisting the challenges against it (rather then impartially considering the merits of the views of others).

In some contexts, such shifts may have a negative impact, since they imply abandonment or distortion of the original purpose of the dialogue. For instance epistemic inquiry (eg, by a committee of experts) can shift to a negotiation when the parties bargain the result of their inquiry (since they can find an outcome whose acceptance would be more convenient to all of them, rather than the acceptance of the conclusion they believe to be true), failing to achieve the epistemic purpose of inquiry (getting to the truth, or at least increasing shared knowledge). Similarly, a persuasion dialogue can degenerate into a quarrel, and so miss the purpose of settling a disagreement. It is even worse when reconciliation dialogue shifts into a quarrel: in this case the parties will attack each other, emphasise their differences, and attribute to each other (and exhibit) features and attitudes that make a future co-operation even more difficult.[19]

DIALOGUES AND PROCEDURES

Dialectical exchanges constitute the essential component of legal procedures. We need, however, to refrain from always imposing a single dialectical model, inspired by an abstract idea of dialectical rationality.

As we shall argue in the next chapter, different procedures serve different aims, in different contexts, and need therefore to be viewed as implementing different types of dialogue.

What Dialogues for What Procedures

Different types of dialogues might contribute to different extents to the different ends which may be pursued through legal processes, as shown in Table 2, which lists the performance of different types of dialogue under different regards.[20]

As appears from Table 12.2, different types of dialogues have different advantages and disadvantages and thus are more or less appropriate for

[19] On the works of the South African Truth and Reconciliation Committee, see among the others EA Christodoulidis, 'Truth and Reconciliation as Risks' (2000) 9 *Social and Legal Studies* 179, who stresses the tension between legal proceedings and reconciliation, and the dangers of a dialogue-shift toward an adversarial paradigm.

[20] The grades indicated just report a very tentative and intuitive personal assessment, which I advance as an example, not being supported by new empirical inquiries nor by the examination of the relevant socio-psychological literature.

	Reach cognition	Avoid mistakes	Promote co-operation	Avoid violent clashes	Promote recognition	Preserve dignity	Promote accommodation	Be self-supporting	Provide efficiency	Psychological ease
Persuasion	L	H	L	H	L	H	L	H	M	H
Negotiation	L	L	H	H	M	M	H	H	H	H
Deliberation	M	M	H	M	M	M	M	M	M	H
Information-seeking	H	L	M	M	L	L	M	L	H	M
Epistemic inquiry	H	H	H	H	M	H	M	H	L	L
Practical inquiry	M	M	H	H	M	H	M	H	L	L
Eristic	L	L	L	M	M	L	L	H	M	H
Reconcilia-tion	M	M	H	H	H	H	M	M	M	L

H=high; M=medium; L=low

different goals: this implies that for achieving the various goals of a legal procedure we will need a combination of dialogues.

For instance, a criminal process inspired only by *persuasion* would correspond to an extreme version of the *accusatorial* system: the accuser is the proponent, the defendant is the opponent, and the jury (or the judge) is an impartial observer. Such a process would have the advantage of maximising the avoidance of wrong convictions, since the burden of proof (of persuasion) would lie on the accuser, but on the other hand it would also minimise the possibility of establishing the liability of the defendant. However, much would depend on what evidentiary strength is required in order that the burden of proof is shifted unto the other party, to wit, on what conditions have to be satisfied for a statement to be considered so evident that it needs to be disproved, rather than proved.

A persuasion-based process would not promote co-operation, since the two parties would have conflicting strategies, but on the other hand it would avoid violent clashes, since whatever one party may say, it will be attributed to the 'logic of the game', rather than to personal attitudes towards the other party (in other words, this would reduce shifts towards quarrel). In fact, the antagonistic position of the parties favours their reciprocal recognition as adversaries in a fair contest. This is different from being partners in a co-operative project, but also from one party having an arbitrary power over the other. A legal interaction modelled according to the persuasion dialogue would tend to be characterised as a win-all or lose-all game. Thus an accommodation that is satisfactory for both parties will not usually be achieved.

The persuasion model is self-sustaining, since it builds upon the interested behaviour of the parties. It is also moderately efficient, and it requires minimal psychological attitudes on the part of the parties: they will likely define their strategies so as to maximise the achievement of their opposite interests, without the need of taking an impartial or co-operative perspective.

Let us now move to a model of the *information-seeking* dialogue. This seems to characterise the model of the *inquisitorial process*. Here the accuser (the judge or prosecutor) is basically an interviewer, who has the task of putting questions to the accused, who plays the role of the interviewee. The accused is thus forced to take a stand, affirming of denying what he is questioned about. In such a dialogue, the dignity and the privacy of the interviewee are at risk, unless appropriate safeguards are taken. There is even the risk that the questions become threats so that the dialogue shifts into mental or bodily abuse, namely, into *torture*.

Also, in an accusatorial process the information-seeking mode is adopted when a person is called to contribute his information (as a witness). The skill of the interviewer consists in facilitating the interviewee in bringing out his entire story, by asking the right questions in the right order. However, if the interviewee is not co-operative, the interviewer may try to force him into contradiction: the interviewee is committed to his answers, in the sense that he is not allowed to provide a contradictory version of the facts. If this happens, the interviewee will have to pay the penalty possibly established for falsehood, and withdraw one of the contradictory statements. Moreover, after detecting a contradiction, the interviewer will probably assume that the interviewee lied in order to protect his interests (or the interests of the party he is trying to support). Thus, the interviewee's falsehood may support the conclusion that the version of the facts that less corresponds to his interests (or to the interests of the party he supports) holds true.

A legal process organised as a pure *negotiation* dialogue would usually take place as an alternative way of resolving a dispute (as when mediation takes place). This also happens in criminal cases when the accused negotiates with the prosecutor the conditions for *pleading guilty*.

There are also some instances of legal proceedings being developed as *reconciliation* dialogues. Here *truth and reconciliation committees* need to be considered, which found one of their highest examples in the South African experience. In such proceedings, the declaration of one's repentance from one's faults and the forgiveness of the other parties are at the foreground. The focus is on psychological attitudes, since the grounds for future co-operation are at issue.

What would make a reconciliation process fall apart is the impression that an exploitative view is taken by the parties to be reconciled, and especially by the wrongdoer: he does not really want to start future co-operation on new bases, detaching himself from his past actions, but simply tries opportunistically to avoid punishment for his wrongful behaviour. Here the 'defendant', when put before his wrongs, should provide evidence of his change of attitude, his rejection of his past, and his commitment for future co-operation, a commitment that should be trusted by the victim, in the first place, and by his other fellows too. The prosecutor (better, the victim) either is satisfied or asks for further admissions and commitments. However, her request should not be viewed as a way of humiliating the wrongdoer (for stigmatising his person, rather than his action), or even of rewarding him for his past wrongs, but rather as a way to ensure that the wrongful damages are restored and to extract evidence that a real change has taken place within the wrongdoer.

Similar kinds of dialectical interactions partially characterise also models of the criminal process inspired by the idea of *restorative justice*.[21]

Legal Dialogues, Cognition and Consent

The above discussion of dialogue types in legal debates is by no means intended to provide an exhaustive survey.[22] However, it should sufficiently justify the thesis that legal reasoning has a collective (interactive) dimension, in regard to which diverse dialectical patterns may be required, according to the goals to be achieved and the context in which they are to be pursued.

The teleological context of such dialogues is quite complex, since on the one hand the goals of the dialectical institution must be distinguished from the goals of the participants, and on the other, the intended goals of a participant (the objectives having a motivational function with regard to the participant's behaviour in the dialogue) must be distinguished from non-intended but possibly accepted (and even positively valued) by-products of participant's action, and from the constraints under which the participant assumes that his or her action is to take place. Moreover, we must distinguish the goals participants endorse individually, from the goals they share collectively, or to which they are collectively committed.

For instance, winning the case is certainly the main goal for a party in a legal case (the goal which mainly motivates her behaviour within the

21 J Braithwaite and P Pettit, *Not Just Deserts: A Republican Theory of Criminal Justice* (Oxford, Oxford University Press, 1990).

22 As another possible kind of dialogue, consider for instance a *brainstorming* or *heuristic* dialogue, namely, a dialogue whose purpose is to generate new interesting ideas, rather then testing their merit. In such a dialogue there is no obligation to provide reasons supporting the theses one states ('I don't know' would be an appropriate answer to a why question), nor to provide the theses one believes to be more justified. There is rather the obligation to provide theses which have not been advanced before, and whose analysis or implementation may lead to interesting developments.

proceedings). However, the party may reasonably assume that by pursuing that goal (given the adversarial framework in which she is acting, and the partiality which such a framework requires in its participants) she contributes to produce a valuable by-product, namely, the correctness of the outcome of the case. And both parties may share the positive appreciation of this by-product and indeed accept certain constraints on their behaviour—such as the prohibition of dishonest behaviour, possibly under the condition that such constraints are shared with the other party—in order to maintain a certain connection between their pursuit of their opposed individual goals (winning the case) and the valuable by-product.

In the following pages I shall consider the connection between the behaviour of the participants in a legal debate and two possible collective goals they may share with other participants in the same debate: (a) contributing to legal knowledge, seen as a common (social) asset, and (b) finding an agreement to a legal outcome.

Some legal dialogues contribute only indirectly to shared legal knowledge, in the sense that providing such a contribution is not the goal which is pursued by the participants, but nevertheless a socially beneficial by-product of their action. For instance, a party in judicial proceedings is usually focused on the goal of winning the case, but his pursuit of this goal may lead him to provide valuable legal information and arguments. These arguments (possibly through their uptake in the judicial opinion), besides contributing to the correctness of the decision of the specific case, may have a further socially advantageous by-product, namely, contributing to the advance of legal knowledge, with regard to how to approach such kind of cases.

By contrast, the goal to contribute to legal knowledge—namely, to increase the information society has at its disposal for approaching legal issues, and to improve the correctness, coherence and usability of such information—should represent the main and overarching goal of legal doctrine. It seems to me that consent, or even reasoned consent, cannot represent such a overarching goal: a researcher should not be worried about the possibility of bringing forward new ideas which may question existing widespread consent, and create new discussions and divisions within legal scholars and practitioners.

We can indeed view legal doctrine as a kind of dialectical *practical inquiry*, namely, as a dialogue whose participants share the purpose of contributing to social cognition concerning a practical issue—the choice of what values, rules, decisions their collectivity should adopt—through sharing their ideas. The reasoners engaged in such an inquiry would publicly express their beliefs on such matters, and also state their critical observations on views by others. Expressed opinions would become part of a common pool of hypotheses to be reasoned about, tested, discussed communally and, consequently, accepted or rejected by each participant independently (no shared decision is required). Here the focus is on collective inquiry, namely, on each one's availability to contribute one's own ideas concerning the best solutions to communal problems, and on each one's availability to take into account impartially the views of others. Practical inquiry is a very appealing kind of interaction with regard to collective choices, which include legal choices: not only does practical inquiry allow for shared advances in practical knowledge, but it also emphasises the participants' active citizenship, their dignity (each being considered as a valid contributor and evaluator of ideas concerning the common good), and their sense of community (each being involved in the collective enterprise of practical cognition).

Some philosophers, and notably Arendt[23] have focused on political action (which is sometimes identified with action *tout court*, in its fullest sense) as the proper domain in which these attractive features can emerge, as opposed to theoretical or technological inquiry. I rather believe that the characterising features of practical inquiry derive from its being a form of collective cognition, an aspect it shares with theoretical science and technological research (eg, in physics or in software engineering), as long as they are developed according to the principles of an open research community. The common purpose of addressing cognitive problems (be they epistemic or practical, scientific or technological, theoretical or applied) and the availability to provide and consider (according to its merit and its relevance) any input which may be significant for this purpose are common to any collective cognitive enterprise, both in the epistemic and in the practical domain.[24]

Dialogues where the fundamental purpose (and collective goal) is increasing common knowledge can be distinguished from dialogues which aim at reaching consent between their participants (given that a shared or collective determination is required). The latter goal may influence indeed the dialectical behaviour of parties involved in deliberation: when the prospect of agreement is near one may reasonably refrain from advancing good arguments (arguments for what one views as the best choice and against choices one views as inferior) if one anticipates that such arguments will be rejected by other participants, and produce new divisions or doubts.

The goal of agreement has a paramount importance when negotiation is at issue. In regard to negotiation, however, we need to distinguish

[23] H Arendt, *The Human Condition* (Chicago, Ill, Univeristy of Chicago Press, 1958).

[24] Consider, eg, the view of science which was advanced by RK Merton, 'The Normative Structure of Science' in NW Storer (ed), *The Sociology of Science* (Chicago, Ill, University of Chicago Press, 1973) 267–78 (1st edn, 1942), for whom communalism (the common ownership of scientific results) and universalism, together with disinterestedness and organised scepticism, are the characterising aspects of scientific research.

negotiation concerning private interest, and negotiation concerning the common good. As an example of the first kind of negotiation, consider bargaining for establishing contractual terms or for settling a private dispute. In this case, as we observed above, each party, within the available negotiation space (possibly under some fairness constraints), tries to maximise the achievement of his or her individual private objectives.

In the second kind of negotiation, by contrast, each participant tries to achieve the agreement that maximises the realisation of his or her view of the common good. Thus, this is the context in which people having different views on what constitutes the common good and on what collective choices most contribute to its realisation, and being aware that such differences are not likely to be eliminated through reasoning and discussion, at least within the available constraints, accept a shared negotiated outcome, though this outcome to each (or to most) of them appears to be inferior to the solution he or she would have preferred.[25] For instance, to find an agreement on a law on reproductive technologies, a bargain may be reached which allows for artificial insemination, but only when the request comes from a stable couple (given that some would ban all forms of artificial insemination and others would always admit it), and which allows for modifying genes, but only to prevent hereditary diseases (when some would reject all intervention on the human genome and others would also admit ameliorative interventions). Similarly, in a decision concerning affirmative action, the agreement may consist in admitting it, but only under restricted conditions (no fixed quotas, no single criteria, and so on).

Negotiation on the common good is different from negotiation on private interests: while in the latter each party aims at maximising his or her gains, in the first each party aims at maximising the implementation of his or her view of the common good, which is different from the view of others. This way of bargaining may take place, for instance, between the political parties forming a coalition government, or between the judges in a panel. An important kind of such negotiation often takes place when a new constitution is adopted. For instance, when the Italian constitution was adopted after the Second World War, different political parties, having very different ideologies (Marxist, Christian-Democrat, Socialist, Liberal-Conservative), converged in a constitutional arrangement representing a compromise between the different values expressed by these ideologies.

[25] The importance of such dialogues is emphasised if we adopt a post-enlightenment view of reason in the practical domain (see GF Gaus, *Contemporary Theories of Liberalism: Public Reasons as a Post-Enlightenment Project* (London, Sage, 2003) ch 1), namely, the view that, though reason can also be applied to practical choices, disagreement on practical matters cannot be reduced to ignorance, mistake or bad faith (on disagreement on legal issues, see J Waldron, *Law and Disagreement* (Oxford, Oxford University Press, 1999).

Each of these parties would have preferred, according to its own ideology (according to its peculiar view of the public good), a different arrangement from the one that was agreed and adopted, but they were able to converge on a satisfactory second best, which was acceptable to all of them. Such compromises often take place at the international level, where Declarations and Treaties on human rights—and first of all the 1948 Universal Declaration of Human Rights—provide the most significant, and most beneficial, example.

Also, negotiation in the common interest presents appealing features: it assumes that participants in the interaction share the purpose of committing themselves to a shared vision of what values to pursue together in what ways, recognise their partners as sincerely expressing their views on the common good, take the views of others seriously, and identify what compromise might be appropriate for convergence.

The separation between the two kinds of negotiation may not always be complete. On the one hand, a party's bargaining for her private interest can be constrained by her view of the common good, there including both her view of what a just or fair division of the benefits of the agreement should be, and her view of how the agreement most advances certain communal values (consider eg, how both commutative consideration concerning contractual justice and further considerations pertaining to social objectives, like increasing productivity or reducing unemployment, may influence negotiations in the labour domain). Moreover, being able to have a vision of the common good (in which her individual interests are impartially balanced with the interests of others), and to sacrifice to such a vision certain individual interests of herself, can be advantageous to the party's individual goals in the long run (in particular, since this will contribute to reaching agreements, having a good reputation, reducing transaction costs, being reciprocated, and so on). On the other hand, the vision of the common good advanced by a party may often be influenced by what private interests of his are going to be advanced by that view. This may be done in bad faith (as when the party, with the hidden purpose of advancing his private interests, argues that something is required for the common good, while he knows that this is not the case), but also in good faith (given our natural tendency to engage in wishful thinking, and to be guided in our inquiries by the need to integrate our views in a coherent whole).

However, it is important to keep these two kinds of negotiation distinct: while negotiation on private interests is in principle inappropriate within political and legal deliberation (unless one presents the satisfaction of one's individual interest as a component of a vision of the common good where everybody's interests are fairly balanced), negotiation on the common good appears to be a very important, and fully legitimate, component of it.

CONCLUSION

A teleological approach to the analysis of legal dialogues leads us to recognise the diversity of the goals which are pursued through dialogues in the legal domain, and thus emphasises the diversity of the dialectical systems which are appropriate to such goals, and the need to combine them, in order to implement legal values in different contexts and with regard to different problems and situations. Recognising the diversity of legal dialogues (and its teleological foundations) is indeed the precondition both for describing dialectical interactions taking place in legal practice, and for improving their performances.

Such diversity, however, does not undermine the importance of a dialectical approach to legal issues, or the significance of dialogues aiming at knowledge and consent, viewed as shared collective goals of the participants in such dialogues. Thus it may possibly complement the analysis of rational legal argumentation produced by Robert Alexy, and even provide a connection to his discussion of the role of values in legal reasoning.

13

The Claim to Correctness and Inferentialism: Alexy's Theory of Practical Reason Reconsidered

GIORGIO BONGIOVANNI, ANTONINO ROTOLO AND CORRADO ROVERSI*

INTRODUCTION

THE CLAIM TO correctness is, needless to say, a key element in Robert Alexy's theory of law. In fact, Alexy uses this claim as one of the argumentative steps on which he bases both the thesis of legal discourse as a 'special case' of practical discourse[1] and the thesis upholding the conceptually necessary connection between law and morality.[2] Even more significantly, the claim to correctness makes up, in practical reasoning, the starting point for some basic rules of rational discourse.[3] Alexy analyses and discusses the claim to correctness in different places, and in each of these the concept acquires a different status. Thus, in his discussion on the outlines of practical reason, Alexy enters into different explanations of the claim to correctness, collectively designed to offer a complex

* An earlier version of this chapter was presented at a Doktorandenkolloquium held at Christian-Albrechts-Universität, Kiel, 11 November 2005. The authors would like to express their gratitude to Robert Alexy for his valuable comments. Special thanks also go to the other participants of the seminar, and, in particular, Carsten Bäcker, Stefano Bertea, Bartosz Brożek and George Pavlakos.

1 R Alexy, *A Theory of Legal Argumentation* (R Adler and N MacCormick (trans), Oxford, Clarendon Press, 1989) 214; R Alexy, 'The Special Case Thesis' (1999) 12 *Ratio Juris* 374 at 375.

2 R Alexy, *The Argument from Injustice: A Reply to Legal Positivism* (S Paulson and B Litschewski Paulson (trans), Oxford, Clarendon Press, 2002).

3 Alexy, *A Theory of Legal Argumentation*, above n 1 at 130. As Alexy puts it, 'the specific rules of discourse which correspond to these claims are those which guarantee the right of all to participate in discourse as well as their freedom and equality in discourse': R Alexy, 'A Discourse-Theoretical Conception of Practical Reason' (1992) 5 *Ratio Juris* 231 at 241.

justification for this claim: the idea behind such a multilayered justification is to avoid the 'weaknesses' involved in basing the claim to correctness on a theoretical foundation. Specifically, Alexy's multilayered approach consists in using arguments based on 'weak' transcendental-pragmatic (or universal-pragmatic) premises that connect with Austin's theory of speech acts and that therefore take into account the presence of performative contradictions.[4] Despite these different levels of analysis, the different arguments can be shown to have problematic points that make it necessary to bring in further theoretical assumptions.

This chapter is aimed at showing that if we are to explain the claim to correctness, it will help to resort to an inferentialist semantics,[5] and in this way we can carry out an analysis of normative and practical discourse that will bring to light the basic features of this discourse and the rational premises connected with it, as well as enabling us to redefine the role of the performative contradiction and highlight the role of normative statements. We will therefore take as our starting point the conviction that 'an inferentialist semantics may be able to shed light on deep connections between *making* a claim and the responsibility to be able to *justify* it'.[6]

The argument that follows is three-fold. First, we intend to show that Alexy's foundation, despite its different levels, draws conclusions that cannot be demonstrated on the sole basis of what are purported to be its own premises. Secondly, we will reconstruct certain contradictions of practical discourse, a reconstruction that will bring to light some possible ways in which the notion of performative contradiction can be interpreted. Thirdly, we will argue that Brandom's inferentialism makes it possible to clarify some open questions regarding the concept of the claim to correctness, the role of the rules of practical discourse, and the grounds of the relation between law and morality.

THE CLAIM TO CORRECTNESS AND THE TRANSCENDENTAL-PRAGMATIC ARGUMENT

(a) In the first stage of his construction, Alexy looks at the role that the claim to correctness plays in practical discourse, and he does so proceeding from Jürgen Habermas' discourse theory.[7] In looking at this theory, Alexy

4 See Alexy, *A Theory of Legal Argumentation*, above n 1; Alexy, 'A Discourse-Theoretical Conception of Practical Reason', above n 3; R Alexy, 'Discourse Theory and Human Rights' (1996) 9 *Ratio Juris* 209.

5 Such as that developed in RB Brandom, *Making It Explicit: Reasoning, Representing, and Discursive Commitment* (Cambridge Mass, Harvard University Press, 1994).

6 RB Brandom, 'Facts, Norms, and Normative Facts: A Reply to Habermas' (2000) 8 *European Journal of Philosophy* 356 at 361.

7 Alexy, *A Theory of Legal Argumentation*, above n 1 at 101.

discusses some 'critical points' but he also points out the arguments that make it possible to have a reconstruction of rational discourse. There are two elements in Alexy's reconstruction that are worthy of note, namely, the critique of Habermas' conception of 'regulative' speech acts, and the view of the 'claims to validity implicated in speech acts' presupposing 'universal-pragmatic' rules. Alexy finds that Habermas, in analysing the claim to correctness, simplifies the structure of 'regulative' speech acts by construing these last as mere 'fulfilments' of norms. This conception overlooks the distinction that 'can and must be made between judging what was done and judging what was said', this because the claim to correctness of regulative speech acts involves not only the performative element but also an evaluation of the locutionary meaning.[8] Alexy thinks it is necessary, therefore, to draw a distinction between different types of speech acts: 'normative' speech acts, properly so called, are those acts that give forth, in their locutionary moment (or utterance), a 'normative statement (a judgement of value or obligation)' the foundation of which needs to be evaluated. This last consideration is important, and yet Alexy does not develop it any further, in that he construes the claim to correctness as dependent on two elements: the locutionary, and hence semantic, moment (and the relevance it carries), on the one hand, and an 'assessment of the facts', on the other. Alexy seems to be saying here that the claim to correctness needs to be evaluated by considering not just the illocutionary but also the locutionary (semantic) element, and that this last element can be evaluated in relation to both an underlying standard and what are assumed to be the facts of the case. The claim to correctness is therefore made to depend on the semantic-locutionary element as well as on the possibility of subjecting this element to verification.

Secondly, Alexy derives from his reading of Habermas a view about the claims that language interaction puts forward as expressions of its transcendental-pragmatic dimension, that is, as conditions 'of the possibility of linguistic communication'. Habermas is primarily concerned with what he calls the basic norms of rational speech, but as Alexy points out, 'they also underlie the claims to validity made in the ordinary transactions of everyday life'. In this sense, we can view as expressions of the transcendental-pragmatic dimension of discourse (in a broad sense of transcendental-pragmatic) not only the claims raised in discourse but also the conditions of its rationality (notwithstanding the fact that these conditions are counter-factual). Alexy regards these conditions differently from Apel, in that he supports Habermas' view whereby this sphere of rationality, too, is a universal-pragmatic sphere: he therefore avoids using

[8] *Ibid* at 110: 'A rule which empowers a non-commissioned officer to issue orders is something different from a rule which lays down what is a good order to issue in a particular situation'.

the term *transcendental*. Alexy finds that if we are to avoid 'misunderstandings', we should rather use the expression *pragmatic-universal*, in that what practical discourse does is not to constitute experience but to produce 'arguments', and he also finds, in parallel, that it proves difficult, in setting out the rules of rational discourse, 'to make a clear distinction between logical and empirical analysis'. These remarks become even more compelling if we take up the weaker form of justification whereby we only commit ourselves to showing that 'the validity of certain rules is constitutive of the possibility of certain speech acts', and that 'we cannot do without these speech acts save by giving up those forms of behaviour which we regard as peculiarly human'. Initially, in *A Theory of Legal Argumentation*, Alexy saw these different forms of justification as raising 'many problems', this by reason of the difficulty involved in establishing, for one thing, what claims and rules should be recognised as 'general and unavoidable presuppositions of possible processes of understanding' and, for another, 'which [rules] are constitutive of which speech acts, and which speech acts are necessary for peculiarly human forms of behaviour'. Alexy seemed little inclined, at this early stage, to go beyond arguing that the claim to correctness is linked to the locutionary meaning of 'normative' acts, and that when it comes to analysing the rules deriving from the claims present in practical discourse, we must leave open the question of these rules' foundation and status (transcendental, constitutive, empirical). A foundation of this sort depends on whether we can show that 'certain rules can be shown to be generally and necessarily presupposed in linguistic communication, or are constitutive of peculiarly human ways of behaviour'.

(b) After *A Theory of Legal Argumentation*, Alexy went back to the transcendental-pragmatic argument and entered further into it by bringing to bear the role of performative contradictions. This makes it more difficult to say how exactly Alexy's thought, and his claim to correctness in particular, relates to the transcendental-pragmatic approach. In fact, Alexy seems to use argumentations of the transcendental-pragmatic kind to support both his claim-to-correctness thesis and his justification of the rules of practical discourse, for in both cases we have an appeal to 'performative contradiction'.[9]

[9] See Alexy, *A Theory of Legal Argumentation*, above n 1 at 215; Alexy, 'A Discourse-Theoretical Conception of Practical Reason', above n 3 at 240 n 23; Alexy, 'Discourse Theory and Human Rights', above n 4 at 214; R Alexy, 'On the Thesis of a Necessary Connection between Law and Morality: Bulygin's Critique' (2000) 13 *Ratio Juris* 138 at 139; Alexy, *The Argument from Injustice*, above n 2 at 37–8. We should note here that Alexy consistently invokes the transcendental-pragmatic justification in connection with discourse theory and the justification of the rules of discourse (cf Alexy, *A Theory of Legal Argumentation*, above n 1 at 185; Alexy, 'A Discourse-Theoretical Conception of Practical Reason', above n 3 at 239; Alexy, 'Discourse Theory and Human Rights', above n 4 at 213, but never in connection

Alexy proceeds directly from the transcendental argument and develops a 'weak' pragmatic version of it. As is known, transcendental arguments consist in the revelation of a necessary presupposition (B) behind a sufficiently self-evident truth (A). This truth is the first premise of the argument; the second premise shows that A has a necessary presupposition B; and the conclusion is the necessity of B.[10] Transcendental-pragmatic arguments have all the features of 'classic' transcendental arguments, plus two other features, namely, (a) they justify a thesis by showing its negation to be absurd (a form of *reductio ad absurdum*), and (b) they need this negation to be concretely uttered in a pragmatic context—in fact the absurdity of the negation is shown by reducing its utterance to a performative contradiction.[11]

In 1992, and in 1996 with specific reference to human rights, Alexy offers a justification of discourse rules on the basis of a 'weakened transcendental-pragmatic argument'.[12] This argument is intended to show that any assertion implies the validity of discourse rules, and particularly of what (in *A Theory of Legal Argumentation*, at 191) he calls 'rationality

with his claim-to-correctness thesis (see Alexy, *A Theory of Legal Argumentation*, above n 1 at 214; Alexy, 'On the Thesis of a Necessary Connection between Law and Morality', above at 139–43; Alexy, *The Argument from Injustice*, above n 2 at 35), where he instead invokes the performative contradiction. The reason may be that, while there cannot be a transcendental-pragmatic justification without appealing to performative contradiction (in fact, the performative contradiction figures centrally in transcendental-pragmatic foundationalism as a primitive concept), the converse case is perfectly possible. On the centrality of the notion of performative contradiction as a primitive concept, see K-O Apel, 'Fallibilismo, teoria della verità come consenso e fondazione ultima' in *Discorso, verità, responsabilità. Le ragioni della fondazione: Con Habermas contro Habermas* (Milan, Guerini, 1997) 143, 150; this work is an Italian translation based on an extended and revised version of K-O Apel, 'Fallibilismus, Konsenstheorie der Warheit und Letztbegründung' in Forum für Philosophie Bad Homburg (ed), *Philosophie und Begründung* (Frankfurt am Main, Suhrkamp, 1987).

[10] On transcendental arguments, see, among many others, B Stroud, 'Transcendental Arguments' (1968) 65 *Journal of Philosophy* 241; B Stroud, 'The Goal of Transcendental Arguments' in R Stern (ed), *Transcendental Arguments: Problems and Prospects* (Oxford, Clarendon Press, 1999); R Stern, *Transcendental Arguments and Skepticism* (Oxford, Clarendon Press, 2000); SL Paulson, 'On the Puzzle Surrounding Hans Kelsen's Basic Norm' (2000) 13 *Ratio Juris* 279; SL Paulson, 'On Transcendental Arguments, their Recasting in Terms of Belief, and the Ensuing Transformation of Kelsen's Pure Theory of Law' (2000) 75 *Notre Dame Law Review* 1775.

[11] The transcendental-pragmatic argument was developed by Apel on the basis of Wittgenstein's language-game argument for the refutation of philosophical scepticism, as presented in the edition of Wittgenstein's *On Certainty* by GEM Anscombe and GH von Wright (eds), (L Wittgenstein) *On Certainty* (D Paul and GEM Anscombe (trans), Oxford, Blackwell, 2004) paras 126, 401, 456, 519. For an overview of Apel's foundationalism in English, see K-O Apel, *Towards a Transformation of Philosophy* (G Adely and D Frisby (trans), London, Routledge, 1980). On the close relationship between Wittgenstein and Apel, see, in particular, K-O Apel, *Towards a Transformation of Philosophy* (Frankfurt am Main, Suhrkamp, 1973) 165, 269; K-O Apel, 'Fallibilismo, teoria della verità come consenso e fondazione ultima', above n 10 at 148–9.

[12] Alexy, 'A Discourse-Theoretical Conception of Practical Reason', above n 3 at 239; Alexy, 'Discourse Theory and Human Rights', above n 4 at 217.

rules', that is, the rules that 'express the universalistic character of the discourse-theoretical conception of practical reason in the cloak of a theory of argumentation'.[13] The reason why Alexy describes this argument as weakened is that its first premise—the universality of the language game of assertion and argumentation—is no longer taken to be necessary, or a priori, but only as empirical (the language game of assertion and argumentation is the 'most general form of life of human beings'[14]), so any conclusion that can be drawn from such an argument will at best be shown to have a high degree of empirical generality.[15] Further, the transcendental basis does not, in this sense, suffice of itself to show that discourse rules are normatively binding, for we also need to this end the purely empirical premise of a 'general human interest in correctness' and an utilitarian argument for the 'maximization of individual utility'.[16]

Contrary to what Alexy says, his argument for the justification of discourse rules is not a transcendental-pragmatic but a 'classic' transcendental argument, and it can be summarised as follows: (1) the language game of assertion and argumentation is the 'most general form of life of human beings'; (2) the speech act of assertion presupposes that the rules of rationality are valid; hence (3), the validity of these rules is 'highly general'. We can see here that even though this argument makes reference to speech acts, it effects no *reductio ad absurdum* of any kind and, further, it does not require any concrete utterance of doubt on the sceptic's part—so we are not looking at a transcendental-pragmatic argument.

Let us see now how Alexy argues thesis (2) above, which is crucial for the success of this 'classic' transcendental argument. Alexy builds a deductive argument as follows:

> [(2.1)] Anyone who asserts something raises a claim to truth or correctness. [(2.2)] The claim to truth and correctness implies a claim to justifiability. [(2.3)] The claim to justifiability implies a prima facie obligation to justify what one has asserted, if asked to do so. [(2.4)] Whoever gives justifying reasons for something raises claims to equality, freedom from force, and universality, at least as far as the justification is concerned.[17]

Alexy presents four sub-theses here, but only in regard to thesis (2.1) does it look as if he is using a genuine transcendental-pragmatic argument. That this is so may not be clear from the article 'A Discourse-Theoretical

[13] Alexy, 'A Discourse-Theoretical Conception of Practical Reason', above n 3 at 236.

[14] See *ibid* at 241; Alexy, 'Discourse Theory and Human Rights', above n 4 at 217.

[15] See Alexy, 'A Discourse-Theoretical Conception of Practical Reason', above n 3 at 239 n 20: 'The whole argument does not lead to an ultimate justification . . .. However it does attempt to expound the view that a universalistic practice admits of a better justification than any other practice.'

[16] *Ibid* at 242; Alexy, 'Discourse Theory and Human Rights', above n 4 at 213.

[17] *Ibid* at 214–16.

Conception of Practical Reason', published in 1992,[18] but it is clearly stated in the subsequent work 'Discourse Theory and Human Rights' of 1996[19]: 'This thesis is supported by the circumstance that *its denial* results in a performative contradiction'. We cannot say the same of thesis (2.2), for here Alexy is asking us to imagine not someone who denies the thesis (saying, 'The claim to truth and correctness does not imply any claim to justifiability'), but someone who does something contrary to what the thesis states, by saying something like, 'I am making such and such an assertion but have no reason to do so'. So this person 'claims that her assertion is true or correct, and at the same time says that there are absolutely no reasons for what she asserts', and maybe this is not even a genuine assertion.[20] Although this argument does differ substantially from a transcendental-pragmatic argument, we can still construe it as such an argument, but only for an incidental reason, namely, that the thesis and the act contrary to what the thesis states are both assertions, which means that the denial of the thesis can be rephrased as an act contrary to the thesis, so that if the act contrary to the thesis leads to a performative contradiction, so does its denial.

This takes us to the argument that Alexy uses to support his claim-to-correctness thesis.[21] This newer argument looks very similar to the one used for thesis (2.2) above but cannot (despite the similarity) be made out to be in any sense a transcendental-pragmatic argument: the thesis is being denied through an *assertion* (someone saying, 'Norms do not imply a claim to correctness'), to be sure, but this denial (because it is an assertion) cannot be understood to be an act contrary to what the thesis states, for the thesis is about norms, and such an act is consequently the *enactment of a norm*, someone saying 'X is a sovereign, federal, and unjust republic'.[22] Hence, in showing that 'a constitutional framer gives rise to a performative contradiction if the content of his act of framing a constitution negates the claim to justice',[23],Alexy does not show that the *denial* of the claim-to-correctness thesis gives rise to a performative contradiction. His argument, then, effects no *reductio ad absurdum*, and so is not a transcendental-pragmatic argument.

What, then, is the status of this argument for the claim-to-correctness thesis? In a sense, by bringing examples of norm enactment that give rise to performative contradictions, Alexy is doing with regard to the act of enacting a norm something very similar to what Wittgenstein does with

[18] Alexy, 'A Discourse-Theoretical Conception of Practical Reason', above n 3 at 240.
[19] Alexy, 'Discourse Theory and Human Rights', above n 4 at 214 (emphasis added).
[20] *Ibid* at 215.
[21] See eg, Alexy, *The Argument from Injustice*, above n 2 at 35.
[22] *Ibid* at 36.
[23] *Ibid* at 37–8.

regard to the act of doubting in *On Certainty*, that is, he is looking to show something about the 'grammar' of norms.[24] In this use, performative contradictions do not serve a foundationalist purpose, as they do in Apel, but rather serve to *show* something about norms and the 'grammar' of the speech act of norm enactment. That this is Alexy's preferred understanding of the performative contradiction seems to come through from the following quotation:

> A performative contradiction does not involve justifying a sentence by means of another independent sentence; for a performative contradiction occurs only in those instances where a rule of discourse is already valid. It is therefore only a matter of a means for *showing* that rules of discourse are valid. It is thus only a question of making explicit something which is assumed to be generally presupposed.[25]

This suggests that we can interpret Alexy's claim-to correctness thesis as a 'grammatical clarification' in a Wittgensteinian sense filtered through Austin's theory of speech acts (and particularly through his use of performative contradictions[26]). In this perspective, the reference to performative contradiction as a means to 'make explicit' the normative claims presupposed by linguistic acts in a pragmatic context leads us to Robert Brandom's inferentialism. Below, we will give an assessment of the performative contradiction in terms of Robert Brandom's semantic inferentialism, and in so doing we will clarify the possible relations between Alexy's claim-to-correctness argument and the status of grammatical clarifications in a rationalistic-pragmatic framework.

(c) What seems to make it necessary to take up a 'weak' transcendental argument is the difficulty involved in defending the assumptions made in Apel's 'strong' argument. This argument assumes that the speech act of assertion is verdictive and commissive, and so sets up an equivalence between assertion and argumentation. This is Apel's starting point, and

[24] See Wittgenstein, above n 11 paras 24, 247–9, 255, 315; also MN Forster, *Wittgenstein on the Arbitrariness of Grammar* (Princeton, Princeton University Press, 2004) 14.

[25] Alexy, 'A Discourse-Theoretical Conception of Practical Reason', above n 3 at 240. The same kind of reasoning is found in Alexy, 'On the Thesis of a Necessary Connection between Law and Morality', above n 9, where Alexy, in making explicit the premises implicit in assertions, is led to construe the performative contradiction as a logical contradiction. In fact, in this paper Alexy takes what, in the original Apelian perspective, could be shown to be necessary through the use of performative contradiction as an heuristic means, and reduces this to a simple clarification of a hidden premise which is logical in nature. It must be noted, however, that this reduction of performative contradiction to logical contradiction is in strong opposition with Apel's view on this matter: In fact, Apel was very well aware of the fact that this kind of reduction cannot but render any argument based on performative contradiction a form of *petitio principii*: see Apel, 'Fallibilismo, teoria della verità come consenso e fondazione ultima', above n 9 at 151.

[26] See JL Austin, 'The Meaning of a Word' in JO Urmson and GJ Warnock (eds), *Philosophical Papers*, 2nd edn (Oxford, Oxford University Press, 1970) 62; JL Austin, *How to Do Things with Words*, 2nd edn (Oxford, Oxford University Press, 1976) 48, 133.

what needs to be demonstrated is its universality, for it is from this universality that Apel transcendentally derives the necessity of discourse rules. The argument by which Apel shows that assertions are verdictive and commissive is based on pure transcendental reflection: this thesis is demonstrated by virtue of its negation, since in denying it we presuppose its truth, and that leads us into a performative contradiction.[27] But this reasoning seems circular, in that the only way we can draw the conclusion is by presupposing what we set out to conclude: here, we must either presuppose that assertions are verdictive and commissive, *or* we must presuppose the immediate evidence of a performative contradiction. Apel seems to opt for the second solution,[28] but this choice introduces in its turn another problem: if we have an evident truth—the falsity of the performative contradiction—how can we justify this evidence and, further, how can we bring it within the framework of a consensual and dialogical theory of truth?[29]

Alexy's solution to this problem is, as we have seen, weaker than Apel's: Alexy confines himself to arguing that the language game of assertion and argumentation is the 'most general form of life of human beings'[30]:

> The thesis about the most general form of life of human beings does not disregard the fact that there are very different concrete forms of life. It says, however, that all human forms of life necessarily include universals of argumentation, which can be expressed by the discourse rules. Those universals may be of ever so little impact in reality due to taboos, tutelage, or terror.[31]

But even with this reduction, we are left with several problems to work out: it seems possible to produce examples of empirical situations in which assertions seem not to have a commissive character (and, in particular, seem not to imply an obligation defined according to the rationality rules of discourse).[32] The problem, then, is, how can we justify the high generality of a language-game in which assertions are in fact commissive and rules of discourse rational?

[27] See Apel, 'Fallibilismo, teoria della verità come consenso e fondazione ultima', above n 9 at 143.

[28] *Ibid* at 141, 147.

[29] It bears pointing out here that Apel offers an answer for this problem, too, by arguing that the evidence of a performative contradiction is 'a priori capable of consensus': Apel, 'Fallibilismo, teoria della verità come consenso e fondazione ultima', above n 9 at 161. But, again, this seems circular, a *petitio principii*.

[30] See Alexy, 'A Discourse-Theoretical Conception of Practical Reason', above n 3 at 241; Alexy, 'Discourse Theory and Human Rights', above n 4 at 217.

[31] Alexy, 'Discourse Theory and Human Rights', above n 4 at 218.

[32] Two simple examples could be a game of soccer, in which a referee can decide without justifying his decisions, and a tribe with reference to the decisions of a shaman. While the latter case can indeed be reduced to a form of taboo, the former cannot: in this case some limitations to rationality rules of practical discourse hold for perfectly rational reasons, ie, they hold in order to guarantee the concrete possibility of the game. Another, and perhaps

It seems that the only way we can answer this question is by taking up a generalised version of Alexy's special case thesis whereby every language-game in which discourse rules are limited *for rational reasons* is a special case of the universal game of assertion and argumentation. This means that in these special case language-games, the rules of assertion and argumentation would hold if that were feasible, but since assertion and argumentation cannot go on without end, and since these particular games require a final result nonetheless, the constraints imposed on the game are necessary and perfectly rational. As is known, Alexy defends this position with regard to the transition from moral rules to legal rules.[33] Now, Alexy's theory of the language-game of assertion and argumentation as the most general form of life of human beings seems to strictly depend on a generalised version of this special case thesis.

This generalised version can be maintained in at least two different ways. The first, very much discussed by discourse theorists, is to account for the *ideal*, *counter-factual* character of the discourse on the basis of the Kantian concept of 'regulative idea'. As Alexy himself notes, the idealised situation in which the discourse rules are effective—that which Apel and Habermas would have called 'ideal speech situation'—is an example of what Kant calls a *regulative* idea, something which cannot exist in the empirical realm, and at which empirical situations should aim.[34] Kant, however, would probably have criticised this transcendental use of a regulative idea.[35] Apel, for his part, says he has drawn this modification of the transcendental perspective from the pragmaticism of CS Peirce.[36] The meaning of this pragmaticist modification of Kant's approach has been explicated by Habermas as follows: 'The rigid "ideal" that was elevated to an otherwordly realm is set aflow in this-wordly operations; it is transposed from a transcendent state into a process of "immanent transcendence"'.[37] It can be said that this appeal to a counter-factual situation and to an 'immanent transcendence' is risky, particularly if we assume it to be the

more interesting, example could be scientific paradigms, as discussed eg in TS Kuhn, *The Structure of Scientific Revolutions* (Chicago, University of Chicago Press, 1962). According to Kuhn, taking for granted some theories and evidence, and temporarily ignoring possible confutations of them, is the condition of possibility of 'normal' scientific discussion.

33 See eg, Alexy, *A Theory of Legal Argumentation*, above n 1 at 207–8; Alexy, 'The Special Case Thesis', above n 1.

34 Alexy, 'Nachwort (1991): Antwort auf einige Kritiker' in *idem*, *Theorie der juristischen Argumentation* (Frankfurt am Main, Suhrkamp, 1991) 414.

35 See I Kant, *Critique of Pure Reason*, in P Guyer and AW Wood (eds), *The Cambridge Edition of the Works of Immanuel Kant* (Cambridge, Cambridge University Press, 2000) B679.

36 Apel, *Towards a Transformation of Philosophy*, above n 11 at 88.

37 J Habermas, 'From Kant's "Ideas" of Pure Reason to the "Idealizing" Presuppositions of Communicative Action: Reflections on the Detranscendentalized "Use of Reason"' in W Rehg and J Bohman (eds), *Pluralism and the Pragmatic Turn: The Transformation of Critical Theory* (Cambridge Mass, MIT Press, 2001) 20.

transcendental basis for the confutation of moral scepticism, and the foundation of moral objectivity. The risk would be that of returning to what the later Wittgenstein called the 'slippery ice where there is no friction', in which 'the conditions are ideal', but on which 'also, just because of that, we are unable to walk'.[38] This is the way Wittgenstein criticised the transcendental use of an idealised image of language he had made in the *Tractatus Logico-Philosophicus* (with particular reference to some of its metaphysical issues[39]). Now, it seems that any attempt to account for the status of the discourse as a regulative idea falls in the same defect of the *Tractatus*, because it rests again, at least in part, on the constitutive function of a counter-factual, idealised situation.

The second way, as we will argue in the following sections, is Robert Brandom's rationalistic pragmatism. Indeed, this approach can be helpful in giving an answer to the problem we have identified, particularly in providing some clarifications on the role of the game of assertion and argumentation (that which Brandom calls 'the game of giving and asking for reasons') with reference to the claim-to-correctness thesis and normativity. In fact, Brandom's expressivism can be interpreted as a form of Wittgensteinian pragmatism that gives a privileged role to the language-game of assertion and argumentation, and, as such, is rationalistic in the same sense as Apel, Habermas and Alexy's discourse theory is:

> Rationalist expressivism understands the explicit . . . in terms of its inferential role. Coupled with a linguistic pragmatism, such a view entails that practices of giving and asking reasons have a privileged, indeed defining, role . . .. Practices that do not involve reasoning are not linguistic or (therefore) discursive practices. . . . By contrast to Wittgenstein, the inferential identification of the conceptual claims that language (discursive practice) has a *center*; it is not a motley.[40]

RECASTING THE CLAIM TO CORRECTNESS

(a) In Alexy's theory of practical discourse, the claim to correctness is necessarily raised by all 'normative' speech acts and this implies that they are open to their justification. If agent Y utters any norm N, Y must be ready to justify N in the context of argumentation. The justification for any 'normative' speech act N has to follow the procedural rules of practical discourse. Rejecting this thesis entails rejecting the very possibility of

[38] L Wittgenstein, *Philosophical Investigations* (GEM Anscombe (trans), Oxford, Blackwell, 1988) para 107.
[39] See eg, L Wittgenstein, *Tractatus Logico-Philosophicus* (DF Pears and BF McGuinness (trans), London, Routledge and Kegan Paul, 1974) paras 2.021–2.1212.
[40] RB Brandom, *Articulating Reasons: An Introduction to Inferentialism* (Cambridge Mass, Harvard University Press, 2000) 14.

argumentation and so of meaningfully asserting N. If so, the pragmatic meaning of N, its normativity, will depend on its susceptibility to be justified within a justification process regulated by the rules of practical argumentation.[41]

The inevitability of the 'claim to correctness' is shown by discussing the idea of performative contradiction. As was mentioned before, this strategy is also adopted by Alexy, who argues that any N raises a claim to correctness because the contrary claim is self-contradictory. Let us return to the following example[42]: suppose a constitutional convention resolves that the following be an article of the constitution:

N_1: x is a sovereign, federal, and unjust republic

Despite the difficulties sketched above, let us admit that N_1, as a norm-enacting performance, corresponds to a special kind of assertion.[43] N_1 is self-contradictory because it states something to be unjust. Justice and practical correctness, according to Alexy, are mutually and strongly linked.[44] So any unjust norm is a fortiori incorrect, leading to the conclusion that N_1 claims to be unjustifiable.[45] But the possibility of asserting a norm depends exactly on the possibility of its being justified.

The peculiarity of performative contradictions is that a certain statement S says the contrary of what is pragmatically presupposed by S itself.

Consider now the following norm:

N_2: All norms ought to be unjust

N_2 likewise determines a performative contradiction because it states that all norms ought to be incorrect. Since all norms, N_2 included, must be

[41] We may say that the rules of discourse state indirectly the pragmatic conditions of the utterance of N as normative, meaning by 'indirectly' that only a second step would show that the notion of correctness is substantiated by referring to the justification process regulated by the rules of discourse. But we may also argue that any process of justification ought to follow the rules of discourse: in Alexy's perspective, we may say that correctness directly presupposes such rules because these last are constitutive of the very possibility of any justification in practical discourse.

[42] Alexy, *The Argument from Injustice*, above n 2 at 36.

[43] As we shall see, this assumption is indeed required by Brandom's theory of linguistic practices.

[44] Alexy, *The Argument from Injustice*, above n 2.

[45] In general, and besides Alexy's own arguments, a claim to correctness does not strictly require a claim to justice. We have three options to link correctness and justice. First, justice implies correctness, but this means that incorrectness implies injustice, not the other way around. Secondly, justice is equivalent to correctness *and* something else. But this implies that injustice can occur even if we have correctness. The third option, that correctness implies justice, cannot be accepted as a starting point. This third option is rather the result of Alexy's argument. The provision N_1 indeed advances a claim to justice. Alexy, in fact, argues that a claim to moral correctness 'can be fulfilled only if the judgment is justifiable on the basis of a correct morality', which directly leads to the concept of justice. As a second step, it is argued that legal correctness necessarily refers to the idea of moral correctness: Alexy, 'On the Thesis of a Necessary Connection between Law and Morality', above n 9 at 144. See Alexy, *The Argument from Injustice*, above n 2 at ch 2.

susceptible of justification, N_2 is self-contradictory. This example indicates that we can identify different degrees of performative contradictoriness. The 'intensity of self-contradictoriness' in N_2 seems to be stronger than in N_1 because N_2 states that *all norms* must be unjustifiable. The occurrence in N_2 of the term 'norm' within the scope of the universal quantifier makes N_2 a sort of 'universal' performative contradiction. Hence, the occurrence of certain terms, and the logical structure of the statement in which they occur, is decisive in assessing the pragmatic self-contradictoriness of this statement. If so, the self-contradictoriness of N_1 and N_2 depends on their 'semantic content', where this last is related to the pragmatic commitment of using certain terms in certain statements and in certain contexts.

Let us consider the following norm:

N_3: All human beings ought to be killed

At first sight, N_3 is not self-contradictory but simply potentially unjust. In other words, we may simply say that N_3 would counter-factually be unacceptable for all potential participants in the argumentation. This point is crucial because it shows the difference between unjust and self-contradictory norms. A norm is unjust if it is not acceptable but is not necessarily unsusceptible of being justified. On the contrary, a norm is pragmatically self-contradictory if it states its unjustifiability.

The impression is that N_3 *directly* violates the Principle of Universalisability (PU) and other rules of the discourse, such as those that forbid that a speaker may be prevented from taking part in a discourse and to introduce and question any assertion whatsoever.[46] In fact, norm N_3 directly expresses that *all* participants in the dialogue should not exist. Thus, this claim constitutes a *conceptual* violation of the idea of reciprocity expressed in PU and of the rules that prescribe that all speakers have the right to enter into the dialogue. N_3 could be pragmatically contradictory, as it is in contrast with the rules that define the conditions of the possibility of justifying any norm. This depends on the fact that the linguistic use of the concept 'human beings' implies that the speaker be committed with the pragmatic requirements connected with the reference to this concept. *Complying with* N_3 determines in theory the impossibility of uttering N_3 consistently. Accordingly, N_3 may appear as a weak form of contradiction, even if it does not properly correspond to a pragmatic contradiction. One may simply find that N_3 does not directly violate the rules of the discourse: N_3 is only potentially unjust.

Hence, the focus on N_3 becomes crucial. If we admit the contradictoriness of N_3, we have two options to account for this conclusion. The first is that of arguing that the content of N_3 is contradictory only if we suppose that practical discourse should be developed along the lines of the Kantian

[46] Alexy, *A Theory of Legal Argumentation*, above n 2.

concept of 'regulative idea', namely, according to the counter-factual character of the *ideal* situation in which the discourse rules are fulfilled. But this solution can be viewed as problematic, since, as was mentioned, we would risk returning to what the later Wittgenstein called the 'slippery ice where there is no friction' (see above). The second option would require showing that N_3 corresponds to a semantic oddity, and, more precisely, that the semantic meaningfulness (or rather meaninglessness) of N_3 is strictly related to the problem of its *actual* justifiability. This second option seems feasible within Brandom's normative pragmatics.

In this perspective, reconsidering the notion of the performative contradictoriness of norms indicates the need to make explicit the interaction between semantic and pragmatic dimensions of norms. This is the suggestion made by Robert Brandom in *Making It Explicit*. Different degrees of performative contradiction suggest that the relation between semantic and pragmatic dimensions of norms may be reconsidered within an inferential semantics. The semantic content of practical assertions depends on the role they play as premises or conclusions in argumentation, and it is shaped with regard to their inferential correctness. Hence, asserting a norm N means committing oneself with respect to N's discursive conditions of appropriateness: 'The practices that confer propositional and other sorts of conceptual content implicitly contain norms concerning how it is correct to use expressions, under what circumstances it is appropriate to perform various speech acts, and what the appropriate consequences of such performances are'. In particular, correctness is based on the pragmatic 'normative positions' of the speakers with regard to any assertional practice. Such deontic statuses basically correspond to commitments (practitioner's obligations to perform) and entitlements (practitioner's permissions to perform). But practitioners may assess each other. This cognitive activity of assessing—acknowledging and attributing deontic statuses—is called scorekeeping and presupposes that speakers, asserting something, have a 'practical mastery' of inferential (material) relations to other assertions (and events).[47]

If normative speech acts 'affect the commitments (and the entitlements to those commitments) acknowledged or otherwise acquired by those whose performances they are', then normative pragmatics is relevant with regard to the construction of the semantic content of norms, since 'propositional contentfulness should be understood in terms of inferential articulation; propositions are what can serve as premises and conclusions of inferences, that is, can serve as and stand in need of reasons'.[48] Thus, the claim to correctness means also a claim to propositional contentfulness and

[47] Brandom, above n 5 at 89.
[48] *Ibid* at xiii–xvii.

the notion of normative self-contradictoriness may be explained, too, in terms of different degrees of semantic meaninglessness.

(b) Usually, we may classify defective speech acts as follows: (1) self-defeating speech acts; (2) inconsistent speech acts; (3) successful but defective speech acts.[49] Self-defeating speech acts cannot achieve their intentions in any context of utterance due to the self-contradictory conditions of success. A paradigmatic example of the first type is 'I promise that I will not keep this promise'. Speech acts of the second type are inconsistent with their contexts of utterance. This is the case when a speaker promises to draw a square with five edges. Speech acts of the third type might achieve their intentions even though some conditions are not obtained. For example, a person can promise to repair her car by some deadline even though she does not believe she can manage to do it. According to what was previously observed, it seems that we have to consider the cases under points (1) and (2). In this perspective, the notion of success (the conditions for any linguistic performance to be meaningful) is the key concept.

Habermas, for example, emphasises the role of communicative action and (rationally grounded) co-operation.[50] The participants are oriented towards mutual agreement and their actions are based on justifying different validity claims raised during communication. Accordingly, the validity claims provide the conditions for commitment. The successfulness of speech acts consists in the speaker's undertaking specific and mutual engagements, while the justification of validity claims corresponds to acting according to the requests because participants believe that these last can be justified.

Brandom is neutral with regard to the necessity of co-operation.[51] He is an Hegelian whose starting point is the late Wittgenstein. In other words, his efforts are oriented to explaining existing practices. And, indeed, there may be moral practices that are pragmatically rational but in which co-operation is not adopted by the participants. We will return to this issue in the next section.

Although Brandom does not extensively discuss the notion of performative contradiction, in his reply to Habermas's review of *Making It Explicit* he says that Apel's notion of pragmatic self-contradiction corresponds to 'undertaking practical commitments materially incompatible with those that are implicit as part of the *form* of those very commitments as

[49] See eg, A Esa and L Kalle, 'Notes on the Success of Speech Acts and Negotiating Commitments' in F Dignum *et al* (eds), *Communication Modeling: The Language/Action Perspective* (Berlin, Springer, 1996).

[50] See J Habermas, *The Theory of Communicative Action*, 2 vols (Boston, Beacon Press, 1984–87).

[51] Brandom, above n 6 at 364.

conceptually articulated'.[52] Two questions must be addressed. First: how can we articulate the above passage in order to provide a definition of performative contradiction? Secondly: according to this definition, are norms N_1, N_2 and N_3 self-contradictory?

It is not hard to answer the first question. As we shall see in the next section, Brandom assumes that any existing practice has some presuppositions, namely some entitlements that are taken for granted the moment one initially takes part in such a practice. Thus, Brandom says that a pragmatic contradiction obtains when a commitment is incompatible with such presuppositions. The notion of incompatibility is defined as follows: two claims B and A are incompatible if and only if commitment to B precludes entitlement to A and vice versa.[53] This means that the material articulations of B and A lead to, or presuppose, incompatible patterns of inferences. The asserter Y, who commits a performative contradiction B, does undertake the commitment to B but also vindicates (as a scorekeeper) the entitlement to A, which is supposed to be a reason for B. But this is not enough. Brandom in effect says that the incompatibility regards the form of commitments. Hence, what must be added is that Y's commitment to B precludes her entitlement to any claim A that is supposed to justify B. In other words, commitment to B precludes entitlement to any other claim that Y is disposed to advance to justify B. If A is among such presuppositions, and so is implicitly undertaken by Y, then we have a pragmatic contradiction.

Let us look at this idea from a different perspective. Consider a generic practical argument by which Y justifies the claim B on the basis of A:[54]

$$\frac{A}{B} \Rightarrow N \tag{1}$$

N is the norm that, assuming a sufficient linguistic competence of Y, makes explicit the normative sense of the link between premise and conclusion. However, (1) is *materially* correct independently of N. If claiming B is self-contradictory, this means that no A can support B, and so that no appropriate circumstance can occur where B is meaningful. Therefore, there is no normative assertion N that can make explicit the practical link between B and any A. Notice, in addition, that (1) should

[52] *Ibid* at 374 n 12. See J Habermas, 'From Kant to Hegel: On Robert Brandom's Pragmatic Philosophy of Language' (2000) 8 *European Journal of Philosophy* 322.

[53] Brandom, above n 5 at 160, 196; see Brandom, *Articulating Reasons*, above n 40 at ch 6. A radical critique of the consequences of Brandom's notion of incompatibility is developed in S Rosenkranz, 'Farewell to Objectivity: A Critique of Brandom' (2001) 51 *Philosophical Quarterly* 232. Rosenkranz's arguments sound indeed convincing, even though they are based on a particular interpretation of Brandom's analysis. However, we will not consider here these difficulties.

[54] See Brandom, above n 5 at ch 4; Brandom, above n 40 at ch 2.

produce reasons for action. This implies that its result, from the assertional perspective, is that of having a practical commitment, namely, the linguistic counterpart of intentions. Meaningless practical conclusions (intentional commitments) are such that no action is meaningful in the sense of fulfilling the corresponding commitments. Thus, the claim B does not correspond to a normative reason for any action. Of course, we can assume that A is among the default entitlements of the practice. This fact makes sense, in terms of pragmatic contradiction, if it is considered from different viewpoints, namely, if it is placed within the interpersonal social practice of giving and asking for reasons. Indeed, an interlocutor X may ask of Y reasons for B—this cannot be excluded—and so X, as a scorekeeper, will endorse the deontic attitude of not attributing to Y any entitlement to any A. This analysis thus makes it necessary to understand the role of disagreements in Brandom's theory, an issue that will be considered in the next section.

The second question is whether N_1, N_2 and N_3 are pragmatic contradictions. N_2 clearly is so: indeed, it is the most general kind of practical performative contradiction. According to the above analysis, if taken to be justified (if all speakers undertake and attribute it to others), the content of N_2 says that no practical inference is meaningful in any context of the practice, that practical reason, independently of any material articulation, cannot provide any intelligible and significant reasons for action. What about N_1 and N_3? N_1 excludes in itself that its content can be materially articulated, unless we are disposed to produce materially incompatible claims. But, if taken to be justified, this does not exclude the very possibility of asserting other norms with different contents, namely the very possibility of practical reason in actual practices. As we noted, the problems reside in N_3. In this case, its potential contradictoriness corresponds exactly to the fact that others are not disposed to undertake it. Again, this makes it necessary to focus closely on the problem of interpersonal disagreements.[55]

[55] Notice that the problem of degrees of contradictoriness can be framed also using the same argument developed in M Klatt, 'Semantic Normativity and the Objectivity of Legal Argumentation' (2004) 90 *Archiv für Rechts- und Sozialphilosophie* 51 at 58. Given Y's claim B, Klatt focuses on degrees of semantic clarity of such an assertion. The assessment depends on the ability to answer the following four questions: (1) To what circumstances is Y committed by B? (2) Based on what circumstances is Y entitled to B? (3) To what consequences is Y committed by B? (4) To what consequences is Y entitled by B? This analysis can be extended to cover pragmatic contradictoriness, because Brandom's idea of semantic significance depends on his normative pragmatics.

INFERENTIALISM, THE CLAIM TO CORRECTNESS AND PRACTICAL DISAGREEMENTS

Brandom's theory of practical reason is a specification of his very general view about assertional practices. Given some assertional circumstances, where these are inferentially articulated, some consequences will thereby follow. In the case of practical reason, in particular, linguistic consequences have, as discursive exit transitions, intentional attitudes and actions. This mechanism is based on an inferential semantics according to which inferences are materially correct independently of their logical form and of any additional (normative) premises, which at most can only *make explicit* the link between premises and conclusions. The normative vocabulary (the different meanings of 'ought'), in this sense, plays the same role in practical reason as the logical vocabulary does in theoretical reason.[56]

An aspect worthy of note is that Brandom specifies, in addition to assertions (claims), some auxiliary speech acts that are needed to account for the social model of assertion (and so of practical reason) defined by the function of scorekeeping.[57] First, we may consider deferrals, namely, the possibility of referring to the authority of others, thus making possible the inheritance of entitlements. In addition to that, we may have disavowals, queries and challenges. These aspects connect with an important issue underlined by Brandom's theory: the *problem of disagreement* in assertional practices. Indeed, the fact that an interlocutor may, eg, challenge assertions made by others (in the light of her own scorekeeping attitude) means that material articulations are far from being predetermined in the practice. Disagreements are thus an essential component, essential at least depending on whether an explanatory attitude is adopted towards real-world practices. In addition, they are essential in light of the very sense of scorekeeping, which presupposes a normative pragmatics and revolves around the social nature of asserting. This leads directly to another crucial problem, which is one of the basic starting points of Alexy's theory of practical reason and of discourse ethics: how to deal with explicit justificatory processes and how to avoid *the regress of rules* in such processes. To be clear, the search for practical agreements requires providing, if requested, justifications for practical assertions. The justification process, however, if it is not grounded in some way, is apt to open an infinite regress of reasons.[58]

[56] See Brandom, above n 40 at ch 2.

[57] Brandom, above n 5 at 191.

[58] Hence, the transcendental-pragmatic account of practical reason and of the status of discourse rules, as we have previously commented, is a possible solution to the problem of regress.

Brandom is not a foundationalist. As for the later Wittgenstein, for him actual practices come first, and only within these practices does normativity emerge.[59] In this sense, the potential regress of justificatory processes can be avoided in the perspective of any person who successfully takes part in actual and concrete practices. This is the reason why Brandom maintains that material inferences are in a way correct in themselves without relying on any form of foundationalism: this is so precisely because the actual inferential know-how (knowing how to draw inferential relations between premises and conclusions) comes first, whereas the know-that (the ability to make explicit the link between such premises and conclusions) eventually follows. Indeed, what is made explicit is not required in general to provide grounds for inferential articulations of practical assertions. As the logical vocabulary, normative vocabulary has as well an *expressive* role. In this perspective, the search for the universal normative presuppositions of practical reason, in whatever sense we view them, seems not to belong to Brandom's project.[60]

However, this does not mean that Brandom lacks sensitivity to the problem of regress of warrants. It is rather, more simply, that in his view the functioning of each assertional practice requires only *formally*, and is based on, any *actual* set of default entitlements that permit the practice to exist and work. Brandom calls this fact the 'default and challenge structure of entitlement': on this basis, the asserters 'are innocent until proven guilty'.[61] This implies that the material articulation of assertions is linked to normative (social) pragmatics, but this does not lead one to assume any universal material presuppositions. In fact, for any actual practice, what is needed is simply any package at all of background commitments and entitlements mutually attributed among interlocutors, and which, holding prima facie, make it possible to carry on the same practice.

If that is so, are we sure that the foundationalist challenge is really rebuffed? Normative pragmatics is such that the problem of regress of warrants is the other side of the coin of disagreements. Let us consider again schema (1). Suppose first that the asserter Y advances claim B. Suppose an interlocutor X challenges this claim. Indeed, (1) provides Y with a justification in reply to such a challenge. Then, X may attack B trying to defeat this material inference. X has different but related strategies to do this.[62] Let us see roughly how the attack may be developed. X can rebut the inference by publicly undertaking a commitment to A but alleging that an incompatible claim is the direct conclusion of A. Secondly, X can discard the inference by attacking A, as by publicly not attributing

59 Brandom, above n 5 at chs 1 and 2.
60 See Brandom, above n 6.
61 Brandom, above n 5 at 206.
62 See J Pollock, *Cognitive Carpentry* (Cambridge Mass, MIT Press, 1995).

to Y an entitlement to A. This can be done for reasons that are independent of B, or because the commitment to B itself is, directly or indirectly, incompatible with A. The third option is properly to undercut the inferential link of (1). In this sense, X may try to undermine the link between A and B by asserting that the commitment and entitlement to A do not materially imply anything that pragmatically licenses the claim B. In this case, X and Y do not agree on the normative (material) articulation that leads to B from A. Notice that X cannot in practice exclude that there can be potential reasons that follow from A and so also license the claim B. But as far as X knows, this is not the case. Therefore, X may conclude prima facie that, indirectly, the undertaking of the commitment to A is incompatible with B. Assume now that Y is sufficiently competent to publicly make N explicit in conversation and that she does so. N is in its turn an assertion, and so the arguments above can be reiterated. Attacking N seems again a kind of undercutting. Even if Brandom's pragmatist approach to inferentialism denies that (1) conceptually requires N to be correct—the intelligibility of N rather depends on (1)—this does not exclude the reverse argumentative direction, namely, that rejecting N does undermine (1). If that were not so, what else is the role of N? Indeed, the expressive role of N, and its being attacked, may mean defeating (1) and this remark is not problematic: even incorrect arguments can, prima facie, make other assertions intelligible.

This analysis seems to reintroduce a weak form of regress. In particular, an inferential regress of commitments can also embed an indefinite nesting of deontic statuses, because each scorekeeper is always allowed to make public and second-level assertions about the different deontic statuses vindicated by other asserters and scorekeepers. Brandom maintains that default entitlements 'can be brought into question later', but 'one initially is entitled to whatever one is in practice taken as entitled to; *deontic statuses* must be understood in terms of practical *deontic attitudes*'.[63] This sounds good in so far as the practice actually works and exists, but if the 'primitive' claims are later challenged, what are the consequences of this? Brandom's point is that:

> The very notion of one propositional content being an inferential consequence of another essentially involves a crucial relativity to social perspective: Are the auxiliary hypotheses (the premises to be conjoined with the claim in question in assessing its consequences) to be those the scorekeeper assessing the propriety of the inference undertakes commitment to, or those the scorekeeper attributes to the one whose statuses are being assessed? Neither answer is correct. The fact

[63] Brandom, above n 5 at 206 (emphasis added).

> that proprieties of inference a claim is involved in can be assessed from either of the two social perspectives ... is fundamental to the very notion of a propriety of inference.[64]

For any propositional content, the fact of having different social perspectives is then 'an essential part of its being the content it is'.[65] This is the reason why Brandom argues that, in real practices, deontic statuses enter into scorekeeping specification as the object of deontic attitudes. On the other hand, the interplay between different perspectives obtains in terms of the joint attributing of commitments/entitlements to others and the undertaking of them.[66]

We have here two problems. First, in the context of practical reason, we have to deal with reasons for action, and actions may affect interests and values endorsed by other interlocutors. Hence, in the perspective of justification, Brandom's answer is not sufficient: Competing speakers should at least attempt to achieve some agreement. Secondly, as noted by Ronald Loeffler, given an authoritative background of commitments, 'is this background authoritative for the scorekeeper in the given context, because every participant in fact acknowledges it (in that context)? Or does everyone acknowledge it because, for them, it is authoritative?'. According to Loeffler, the second option is the right one: Participants 'acknowledge it in this context because they (assume to) know how to display, *across different contexts*, the portions of this background as tailored to each other and to experience in a smooth and enlightening way'.[67] If that were not so, the background would not be objectively binding, and the true normative dimension of pragmatics would therefore be lost.

Again, suppose that Y asserts B. X may query or challenge this claim. Then Y replies advancing claim A. Does this response alter X's score? X keeps track of the deontic score on the basis of the commitment- and entitlement-preserving inferences and incompatibilities she takes as good. Now suppose that X does not consider A as a reason for B, because, say, A is incompatible with B. X says this openly, but Y is not willing to disavow either B or A. So, according to X, claim B may retract Y's entitlement to A. What, then? Does the deontic score of X have to be based on her own good inferences, or should she also take Y's inference into some consideration? In the first case, X will be continuing to assess Y's claims, being aware that Y was meaning something different. But in this case, we will have a dialogue in which one of the interlocutors is in effect 'deaf', at least if X is not willing to settle the disagreement. Without this willingness, the

[64] *Ibid* at 197.
[65] *Ibid* at 197.
[66] Brandom, above n 5 at ch 8; Brandom, above 40 at ch 5.
[67] R Loeffler, 'Normative Phenomenalism: On Robert Brandom's Practice-Based Explanation of Meaning' (2005) 13 *European Journal of Philosophy* 32 at 50.

social and actual dimension of normativity could be lost. In fact, if practical problems are at stake, and these affect both X and Y, then X may be interested in settling the disagreement. This same argument can be reversed and applied to Y, who is a deontic scorekeeper towards X. If Y behaves like X, then we will have a dialogue between two 'deaf people'. This is probably the sense of Habermas' criticism of Brandom.[68] Brandom rejects this criticism.[69] In fact, the absence of willingness to settle disagreements *does not deny the possibility (significance) of the practice*—the dialogue between X and Y will work in some way—nor does it undermine the *possibility of practical reason*. What Brandom's rational pragmatism requires is just that the speakers be sensible to the normativity of the practice.[70]

On the other hand, normatively, such an absence should be socially admitted only when X and Y are playing the role of a third party, not that of being each other's direct interlocutors. Competing scorekeepers may co-exist, but this, if applied extensively for all participants in the practice, would lead to non-social social practices in which, eg, deferrals do not make sense. The crucial aspect of Brandom's theory is that each scorekeeper is also an interlocutor to other scorekeepers, who in turn are also interlocutors. This makes interesting the social construction of the web of pragmatic dependencies between the participants. The third-party perspective refers to the single deontic attitudes of each subject towards the others, but it is not enough; for otherwise, the social nature of practical reason would vanish into a sort of solipsism.

This conclusion is linked to the problem of the existence of semantic norms that bind the material inferences of the speakers. According to Brandom, scorekeepers treat linguistic performances as governed by objective semantic norms. But, as we noted in commenting on Loeffler, such treatments cannot 'explain the obtainment of objective semantic norms'.[71] Loeffler argues that the only way to explain the objectivity of semantic *norms* regulating material inferences is to eliminate them: this makes room only for semantic *normative attitudes*. But this is not enough, as we said. According to Loeffler, Brandom himself suggests how to bypass the problem:

> Each perspective is at most locally privileged in that it incorporates a *structural* distinction between objectively correct applications of concepts and applications that are merely subjectively taken to be correct. But none of these perspectives is privileged in advance over any other. At first glance this egalitarian attitude may seem just to put off the question of what is really correct. ... The alternative is to

[68] Habermas, above n 52 at 342.
[69] Brandom, above n 6.
[70] Brandom, above n 5 at chs 8 and 9; Brandom, above n 40 at chs 5 and 6.
[71] Loeffler, above n 67 at 57.

> reconstruct objectivity as consisting in a kind of perspectival form, rather than in a nonperspectival or cross-perspectival content. What is shared by all discursive perspectives is that there is a difference between what is objectively correct in the way of concept application and what is merely taken to be so, not what it is—the structure, not the content.[72]

This means that, in the end, there are no predetermined objective contents, since 'there is no bird's-eye view above the fray of competing claims from which those that deserve to prevail can be identified'.[73] But the nature of practices does not necessarily entail a linguistic non-objectivism. Indeed, Loeffler's thesis is that some form of objectivism is guaranteed if the structural distinction between 'being objectively correct' and 'being merely taken so' is actually endorsed by all scorekeepers. This means that normativity is shaped by the *actual* developing of the practice of giving and asking for reasons. This practice, we argued, should have some constraints, at least in order to avoid the strange consequences of what we called non-social social practices. But these constraints should properly be interpreted as the *grammatical structure of normative assertions*, and not within a weak transcendental perspective. The way in which we can articulate the *grammar of the structural objectivity* of practical reason is not clearly addressed by Brandom. However, in this new perspective, it seems to us that Alexy's approach can be helpful here. In particular, we have at our disposal a systematic view with which to account for the normative structure of the practice of giving and asking for reasons (for action). In this sense, something very close to Alexy's rules can be viewed as the constitutive rules defining the grammar of practical justification.[74]

FINAL REMARKS

Let us provide some brief conclusions. In this chapter, we have discussed three related issues:

(a) first, we tried to highlight some problematic aspects of the notion of the claim to correctness in so far as this is considered within a transcendental perspective;
(b) secondly, we suggested that it would be more appropriate to interpret this notion in terms of a 'grammatical clarification' of the nature of norm enactment and, in general, of normative assertions;
(c) thirdly, we tried to show how Brandom's rationalistic pragmatism may

[72] Brandom, above n 5 at 600; see Brandom, above n 40 at 196–204.
[73] Brandom, above n 5 at 601.
[74] *Idem* at ch 9.

prove useful in the effort to outline a picture of what this grammatical clarification should look like, and what the role of discourse rules in it should be.

If what is stated in the foregoing turned out to be plausible, then the claim-to-correctness thesis could be reframed as follows.

The notion of claim to correctness (and the claim to justice with which, according to Alexy, the claim to correctness is linked) can be articulated as corresponding to the concept of constitutive rule defining normative speech acts (and, for this reason, defining norm enactment). In this perspective, the fact that 'the claim to correctness in the case of a resolution passed as a constitutional provision is essentially a claim to justice'[75] should be conceived of as based on a constitutive rule akin to that according to which making a promise means undertaking an obligation. This would allow for an interpretation of the claim to correctness—and of the *Verbindungsthese*—as a descriptive (theoretical), rather than a normative, thesis, even if the normative consequences could be drawn from it in a way similar to what John Searle attempts in 'How to Derive "Ought" from "Is"'.[76] The final result would be that of providing an explanatory view of the claim to correctness in terms of a grammatical clarification of existing and actual practices of practical assertion. However, this solution is challenging because it seems to shift the burden of proof upon an exhaustive analysis of normative assertions (and in particular, of norm enactments) in the framework of speech acts theory, an analysis that does not necessarily turn out to be in support of the claim-to-correctness thesis, and which, in addition, has not been attempted so far.

It must be emphasised, however, that there are at least two further interpretations according to which the claim to correctness seems still viable (though, as we have seen, potentially problematic).

According to a first view, the claim to correctness is something revealed by the self-evidence of performative contradiction. In this sense, this is a solution which could be accepted by Apel. But, clearly, this solution requires the performative contradiction to be a primitive concept, and does not admit any logical reduction of it, as the reduction proposed by Alexy, for example, in the article 'On the Thesis of a Necessary Connection between Law and Morality: Bulygin's Critique'.[77] In fact, as Apel himself notes with regard to the transcendental-pragmatic approach, any logical reduction of the performative contradiction, and then any attempt to cast the claim-to-correctness argument in a deductive form, would end in a

[75] Alexy, 'On the Thesis of a Necessary Connection between Law and Morality', above n 9 at 140.

[76] J Searle, 'How to Derive Ought from Is' (1964) 73 *Philosophical Review* 43 at 55.

[77] Alexy, 'On the Thesis of a Necessary Connection between Law and Morality', above n 9 at 139–40.

petitio principii.[78] But it must be conceded that the reliance on the simple, immediate and direct evidence of performative contradiction seems rather problematic, particularly in the frame of a consensus theory of truth.

In a second perspective, the claim-to-correctness thesis could be conceived of as a substantive (metaphysical) normative statement. In this way, Alexy's view would imply committing ourselves to a quasi-realistic stance towards meta-ethics.[79] Hence, we would be able to recover from the radical eliminativism of semantic norms implicit in Brandom's model of practical reason, thus enabling us to acknowledge some substantive boundaries for the propositional contentfulness of practical claims (such as the boundaries set by the system of human rights). But this substantive and realistic approach would probably be rejected by Alexy.

[78] See Apel, 'Fallibilismo, teoria della verità come consenso e fondazione ultima', above n 9 at 151.

[79] See G Pavlakos, 'On the Necessity of the Interconnection between Law and Morality' (2005) 18 *Ratio Juris* 64.

14

The Concept of Validity in a Theory of Social Action

CARSTEN HEIDEMANN

INTRODUCTION

THIS CHAPTER WILL centre on the thesis that the discourse theory, as developed by Jürgen Habermas and Robert Alexy, exhibits two different characters which are not easily re-conciled with each other. On the one hand, it is a multifacetted theory of social action, reconstructing critically the perspective of a participant. On the other, it is a theory of cognitive validity. This double-aspect is not peculiar to discourse theory, but characteristic of quite a lot of (other) pragmatist theories, as well.

At first glance, this blend of conceptions seems to offer an ideal way of founding objective validity, and especially normative validity, neither in an outer world-in-itself nor in some mysterious faculty of reason, but simply in social practices. But a closer scrutiny reveals that it is flawed.

One preliminary remark concerning the notion of a 'theory of validity' or *Geltungstheorie*: a theory of validity in the sense meant here is a theory about the universal conditions which must be fulfilled for any judgement to be objectively valid, ie for the corresponding sentence to be true. Especially for neo-Kantians, this kind of theory is of fundamental importance, because it takes the place of ontology. Accordingly, the concept of validity is one of the most basic concepts in the writings of neo-Kantian authors. Heinrich Rickert, to name one prominent example from the Baden School, contrasts it with the concept of existence, taking validity to be even more basic.[1]

And, in the present context, Rickert's theory is important in another respect, as well: his philosophy of value and culture deeply influenced Max

[1] Cf H Rickert, *Der Gegenstand der Erkenntnis*, 4th/5th edn (Tübingen, Mohr, 1921) 229.

Weber, whose work in turn left a distinct mark on the theory of Habermas. In fact, Rickert's theory possibly laid the foundation-stone for the tension, found in Habermas' theory, between the results of a reconstruction of social practices from an internal perspective and the demands which any theory of objective validity must satisfy. I will return to this point at the end of this chapter.

THE DOUBLE ASPECT OF DISCOURSE THEORY, AS DEVELOPED BY HABERMAS

Discourse theory, as developed by Habermas, may be assigned to two different theoretical mainstreams: (1) to those varieties of linguistic philosophy which claim to be legitimate successors of traditional metaphysics; (2) to those parts of hermeneutic sociology which are concerned with the nature of social—and particularly communicative—action.

(1) According to Habermas, the historical development of metaphysics or 'First Philosophy' is characterised by two changes of paradigm[2]: originally, metaphysics was ontological in nature and dealt with the essence of being or existence. In the wake of the 'Cartesian revolution', it was superseded by philosophy of consciousness and cognition which focused on the necessary conditions of recognising something as being or existing. Philosophy of consciousness in turn was transformed in the course of the Fregean-Wittgensteinian revolution by incorporating a 'transcendentally moulded conception of language', according to which the constitution of facts by cognition necessarily takes language as its medium. In the beginning, this 'linguistic turn' resulted in semanticism, ie it was confined to language as an abstract body of rules. A further development was achieved by the insight of discourse theory, the most mature form of *prima philosophia* , according to which the 'transcendental capacities' cannot be ascribed to the grammatical systems of linguistic rules as such, rather, the linguistic synthesis is the result of successful acts of communication.[3] Therefore, its starting point is linguistic pragmatics, and, by its conception of communicative acts, it takes into account the priority of practice over theory in founding objective validity.

(2) But at the core, Habermas' theory is sociological in character. His original aim is to establish a critical theory of society. Part of this theory of society is his conception of 'universal pragmatics', which goes hand in hand with discourse theory. It is the task of universal pragmatics to 'identify and reconstruct the universal conditions of the possibility of

[2] Cf J Habermas, *Nachmetaphysisches Denken* (Frankfurt am Main, Suhrkamp, 1988) 20–1.

[3] *Ibid* at 56.

communication [*Verständigung*]'.[4] As action aiming at communication is, for Habermas, the basic type of social action, universal pragmatics may be taken to be reconstructing the necessary presuppositions of social action from the perspective of a participant. Explicit speech acts are, for universal pragmatics, just one form, though the most important one, of communicative acts.

On first glance, these two explanations of the status of Habermas' theory do not seem to differ in a serious way; in fact, they seem to complement each other. No matter which theoretical framework we prefer, the theory aims at elaborating the universal presuppositions of communicative or speech acts. But the perspective is different. If discourse theory is taken to be the legitimate successor of ontology-superseded-by-epistemology, it is fundamentally a theory of objective validity, and as such it is primarily concerned with the pragmatic conditions of the possibility of objectivity. In so far as it deals with the conditions of the validity of assertive sentences, it may be understood as a theory of truth. In contrast, universal pragmatics as a theory of social action is not fundamentally a theory of validity; rather, it focuses on the conditions of an 'agreement' between social actors—'agreement' in the meaning of a 'successful communication'.

This can be shown by reconstructing Habermas' argument.

Elements of the Speech Act

The typical method of communication is, according to Habermas, communicating by speech acts. There are three different modes of communication and three co-ordinated types of speech act which are characterised by their respective 'thematic content': the cognitive mode of communication is coupled with assertive speech acts stating a fact ('That's marmalade in that bowl over there'), the expressive mode of communication is coupled with representative speech acts pointing to the speaker's inner-world ('I hate marmalade'), and the interactive mode of communication is coupled with regulative speech acts ('Take that marmalade away!').[5]

Each of these three types of speech act has in turn three differently weighted functions: to represent something, to express the speaker's intention and to establish an interpersonal connection between the speaker and the listener. In order for a speech act to be successful, the speaker has to guarantee all three functions: as for the cognitive function of representing, he has to raise a claim to truth and, if necessary, justify it by giving

[4] J Habermas, 'Was heißt Universalpragmatik?' in K-O Apel (ed), *Sprachpragmatik und Philosophie* (Frankfurt am Main, Suhrkamp, 1976) 174.
[5] *Ibid* at 246.

reasons; as for the expressive component, he has to raise a claim to sincerity and, if necessary, justify it by acting consequently; as for the interactive function, he has to raise the claim to normative correctness and, if necessary, redeem it by justifying it. In all these cases, 'redeeming' the claim means that the validity of that which is claimed is established.[6]

Necessity of Discourse from the Perspective of a Participant

Though the claim to sincerity which is raised by a speech act cannot be redeemed by performing a discourse, the claims to truth and normative correctness can and must, according to Habermas, be redeemed on demand in a real discourse.[7]

Why this should be necessary, remains somewhat in the dark. As far as Habermas' theory is taken to be a sociological theory of communication, he may point to the fact that any agreement fails if a claim raised by a speaker is doubted and nevertheless is not further reasoned for by the speaker—he is violating some regulative rules governing the speech act of asserting something. But as far as his theory is taken to be a theory of validity, Habermas' argument remains vague. Starting the argument with the speech act of asserting seems to lead into a dead end when investigating the necessary conditions of objective validity.

On the one hand, Habermas in his earlier writings appeals to the thesis that any correspondence theory of truth is untenable: a fact is only the apparent objective correlate of an assertion, and the correspondence theory of truth attempts in vain to escape from the realm of language. For facts as such appear as objects only internal to the communicative enterprise of discourse, and only as long as the cognitive claim raised with an assertion is made the subject of discussion.[8] So the meaning of 'fact' cannot be explained without pointing to discourses in which suspended claims raised by assertions are checked.[9]

On the other hand, Habermas appeals to Wittgenstein's 'private language-argument'. There is, he maintains, a close connection between validity and linguistic meaning, and meaning is something which necessarily implies intersubjectivity: 'You cannot follow a rule *privatim,* and you

[6] *Ibid.*

[7] Cf J Habermas, 'Diskursethik – Notizen zu einem Begründungsprogramm' in J Habermas, *Moralbewußtsein und kommunikatives Handeln*, 5th edn (Frankfurt am Main, Suhrkamp, 1992) 69.

[8] J Habermas, 'Wahrheitstheorien' in J Habermas, *Vorstudien und Ergänzungen zur Theorie des kommunikativen Handelns*, 3rd edn (Frankfurt am Main, Suhrkamp, 1989) 134.

[9] *Ibid* at 135.

cannot continuously use an expression with an identical meaning as an isolated subject';[10] accordingly, validity presupposes intersubjectivity, as well.

A more detailed argument can only be found for the case that claims to *normative* validity must be redeemed by discourse: in everyday communicative practices, these claims play an important role in co-ordinating actions. Co-ordination of actions presupposes a real consensus. If normative validity claims are contested, they can only be redeemed by intersubjective recognition. This demands a real discourse, where everybody may utter her own undistorted interests and has to expose them to the critique of others.[11]

Necessary Presuppositions of Discourse

If redeeming validity claims demands the performance of a real discourse, then, Habermas maintains, acting according to the rules which, as necessary presuppositions of any argumentation, condition the possibility of a real discourse, is at the same time a necessary condition of validity at large. These rules can be made out by the fact that their negation in a discourse results in a performatory contradiction.[12] There are three different kinds of argumentative presuppositions: 'logical presuppositions from the level of products, dialectic presuppositions from the level of procedures, and rhetoric presuppositions from the level of processes'.[13] From the bulk of them, an argumentative rule for practical discourse may be derived, namely, the principle of universalisation (U). According to this principle, a contested norm may only be consented by the participants in a practical discourse,

> if the consequences and side-effects for the satisfaction of the interests of each individual which may be expected to follow from the general realisation of the norm can freely be accepted by everybody.[14]

Taking this as a basis, discourse ethics may be reduced to the 'economical' principle (D), that only those norms may claim validity which meet the consent of all persons affected (or which might meet their consent) when taking part in a practical discourse.[15]

[10] Habermas, above n 2 at 118.
[11] Habermas, above n 7 at 77–8.
[12] Cf *ibid* at 93.
[13] *Ibid* at 97.
[14] Cf *ibid* at 103.
[15] *Ibid*.

Plausibility of Habermas' Argument

What kind of argument is this, and how can the validity of normative or assertive sentences be established by it?

Unlike Apel in his theory of 'transcendental pragmatics', Habermas denies that the argument leading to the principles of U and D can be called a 'transcendental argument'. Instead, he takes the necessary rules of discourse simply to be derived from a reconstruction of social practice which in itself is not necessary. This is an important point. For as long as discourse theory is taken to be a *prima philosophia*, it makes no sense to say that it is just an analysis of the presuppositions of a social practice. It must be the pragmatic equivalent of either ontology or the conditions of any cognition of objects.

To be sure, Habermas comes close to offering such an equivalent by forwarding a consensus theory of truth and pointing to the private-language argument. But, although Habermas' argument against the correspondence theory of truth is convincing, the consensus theory of truth is by no means the only alternative, and, as a comprehensive theory of truth, it is deficient, too. This, however, need not be elaborated here, for there was a major change in Habermas' theory recently: influenced by philosophers Cristina Lafont, Albrecht Wellmer and Lutz Wingert, he gave up the idea that there is any constitutive relation between truth and consensus. I will return to this point later.

Habermas' pointing to Wittgenstein's private-language argument in order to explain the necessary relation between truth and performing a discourse is not helpful either, because he does not give a thorough analysis of the argument. Not even the exact meaning of the private-language argument, let alone its validity, is established, so that Habermas' reference to Wittgenstein is far too vague to be convincing. He formulates the conclusion of the private-language argument as follows:

> Nobody can follow a rule just for himself, in a solipsist way; for to be able to handle a rule competently presupposes a capacity to take part in an established *social* practice which, for any subject, is 'given', as soon as he reflectively realises his intuitive knowledge in order to justify himself vis-à-vis other subjects.[16]

But this falls short of the aim of showing that there is an internal connection between discourse and truth. In fact, there is a strong suspicion that the argument is even counter-productive to Habermas' enterprise. For Wittgenstein's conception of 'rule-following', which is fundamental to his

[16] J Habermas, *Kommunikatives Handeln und detranszendentalisierte Vernunft* (Stuttgart, Reclam, 2001) 72.

private-language argument, focuses on the idea that learning and maintaining the competence of following rules is a matter of 'training' (*Abrichten*)[17]—which is exactly what taking part in a discourse, as a reflective activity, is not.

Although Habermas' argument for the necessity of a real discourse to establish the validity of *normative* sentences is more plausible, it destroys the parallel between the (primary) claims to truth and to normative correctness raised by assertive and regulative speech acts, respectively. Besides, it is based on the concept of a common 'interest', which is rather ambiguous but at first glance more a matter of sociology or a theory of democracy than of a theory of objective validity, unless one postulates an ethical 'meta-principle' running somewhat like 'exactly those norms are objectively valid which correspond to the common interest'. But postulating such a principle would destroy the fundamental character of discourse theory and reduce the discourse to an heuristic device.

Anyway, according to Habermas, performing a real discourse is necessary so that anyone who is possibly affected by the prospective measure may utter his own undistorted interests and expose them to the critique of other participants in the discourse. But it is difficult to see why the rules of a discourse concerning the validity of normative sentences should imply that any participant in the discourse should get the opportunity to present his private undistorted interests; one would rather have expected that the participants get a chance to present the rules of actions which they privately hold to be valid, and to give arguments in their favour.

On first glance, it might seem as if this problem of 'ascending' from particular interests, introduced into the discourse by its participants, to an objectively valid norm as the result of the discourse could be solved by applying the principle of universalisation introduced above: according to Habermas, this principle is a 'bridging principle' comparable to the principle of induction in the natural sciences; by virtue of the aspect of impartiality contained in it, it makes possible the transition from the particular interests to an objectively valid 'common interest' that is embodied in exactly those norms which could be recognised by any participant in a real discourse in which all rules constituting the ideal speech situation have been observed.[18]

But there are problems. On the one hand, it is doubtful whether the principle of universalisation immediately follows from the presuppositions of any discourse, as Habermas would have it when introducing this principle. It is more likely that it just explicates the basic intuition of some

[17] Cf L Wittgenstein, 'Philosophische Untersuchengen' in *Werkausgabe* vol 1, 5th edn (Frankfurt am Main, Suhrkamp, 1989) , para 206 [page 346].

[18] Habermas, above n 7 at 73–5.

cognitivist ethics: Habermas himself concedes this point in passing.[19] On the other hand, it is doubtful whether the principle really necessitates performing a discourse—the way in which Habermas formulates it does not make this conclusion compelling. More important, though the principle may permit the transition from particular interests to an objectively valid common interest, it cannot, free of circularity, found the necessity of a real discourse, because it is valid itself only if a real discourse is necessary to constitute objectively valid norms. For, according to Habermas, the principle follows from those rules of discourse which belong to the rhetorical presuppositions of any argumentation and which, therefore, are valid only relative to a non-monological discourse.[20]

Habermas' contention that a real discourse is necessary so that the particular interests of those affected by a future regulation may be articulated by themselves without any distortion might be explained by conceiving of discourse theory as a theory of solving social conflicts. If practical discourse is just a means of solving current social conflicts, then it seems to be necessary indeed that those possibly affected by the outcome of the conflict should get a chance of articulating their particular interests and to expose them to the critique of others so that a solution might be achieved which is acceptable for everybody. Such a procedure would, if successful, result in a 'compromise'; the discourse would consist in speech acts of negotiating, and it would not in the least be a pragmatic equivalent of a cognitive procedure leading to objectively valid norms.

Accordingly, Habermas explicitly turns down such an interpretation of the practical discourse. He does not want to do without the ambitious role of discourse theory as a *prima philosophia*, as a theory of objective cognitive validity: even if the discourse is taken to be essentially a strategy to solve conflicts, he argues, the conditions of arriving at a rational agreement by discourse must not be confused with the conditions of negotiating to reach a fair compromise:

> In the first case we assume that the participants recognise what their common interest consists in; in the second case we assume that there is no interest at stake which is universalisable at all. The participants in a practical discourse try to get clear in their minds about a common interest; whereas, when negotiating about a compromise, they try to reconcile conflicting particular interests.[21]

But as soon as a theory of solving social conflicts is enriched in this way by adding elements of a theory of objective validity,[22] it becomes doubtful

[19] *Ibid* at 73.
[20] Cf *ibid* at 103.
[21] *Ibid* at 83–4.
[22] The conception is 'enriched', because it assumes that a discourse which aims at solving social conflicts is concerned with finding out a common interest, understood as an objective normative entity.

why there should be more than a heuristic need to give those persons possibly affected by a regulation the chance to utter their particular interests in a real discourse.

It is difficult to see how Habermas might avoid the following dilemma: if the practical discourse is a cognitive procedure aiming at objectively valid norms, it can scarcely be made plausible why those possibly affected by the norm should *necessarily* have the opportunity to utter their particular interests. If, conversely, the practical discourse is a matter of negotiating with the aim of reconciling conflicting interests, it cannot be demonstrated why the outcome should be a universally valid norm.

In any case, if the practical discourse is concerned with establishing objective normative sentences, then the utterance of a particular interest should not be regarded as a genuine contribution to the discourse. Rather, a genuine contribution concerns the question as to what might be regarded as the 'common interest'; and the utterances of particular interests would merely provide the material for an application of the principle of universalisation. So there are, in fact, two different kinds of discourse: in the first discourse, all those persons who are possibly affected by a prospective regulation would utter their particular interests and expose them, to allow for a correction of their self-interpretation, to the critique of others.[23] This kind of discourse does not aim at co-ordination, but at compiling and possibly purifying the particular interests of the participants. In a second discourse, which is the genuine practical discourse, the results of the first discourse serve as material for determining which interest might be regarded as the 'common' interest.

But this duplication of discourses would give rise to new problems. If the necessity of having a real non-monological discourse stems from the fact that only a person affected by the result of the discourse herself can utter her particular interest in an undistorted way, then performing the discourse is necessary merely on the level of the 'discourse of interests' which precedes the genuine practical 'discourse of validity'. The discourse of validity, which concerns the establishment of the common interest, might as well be a monological affair. What is more, the 'discourse of interests' would not even be a genuine discourse, because it serves just to provide data—and the process of obtaining information is exactly what Habermas wants to exclude from a genuine discourse.[24]

[23] Habermas, above n 7 at 77–8.
[24] J Habermas, *Erkenntnis und Interesse* (Frankfurt am Main, Suhrkamp, 1973) 386.

Habermas' New Conception

Some years ago, Habermas modified his theory in several crucial respects. This is not the place to give a detailed discussion of his complex and problematic conception of a rational discourse and its role concerning the truth or correctness of its results. In this context, I can only offer a short sketch of some of the most important changes.

It seems that Habermas now distinguishes between two different concepts of truth, namely, the realist and non-epistemic life-world concept of truth, and the discourse-theoretical concept of truth. Truth in the realist sense is independent of justification, discourse-theoretical truth is more or less identical with justification under ideal conditions. But Habermas cannot sufficiently explain how these concepts hang together. This is shown examplarily by the paradoxical last sentence of the following passage:

> The non-epistemic concept of truth which is operative in practice, without being made subject of discussion, invests the claims to truth which are made subject in discourse with a point of reference which is inde-pendent of any justification. *It is the aim of all justification to discover a truth which is independent of any justification.*[25]

Besides being hard to digest, this conception further endangers the status of discourse theory as a theory of validity, at least for non-normative sentences. Moreover, Habermas now favours a conception which he calls 'weak naturalism'; it is based on the thesis that there is a continuum between nature and culture.[26] This is highly problematic, for it is scarcely compatible with the dualism between the hermeneutic approach adopted when reconstructing the perspective of a participant of the life-world, and the objectivist approach which is characteristic of natural sciences. And there is another problem with naturalism. Although Habermas still sticks to his original conception of normative truth/cor-rect-ness as being dependent on a rational discourse, thus destroying the parallel between truth and correctness , it is scarcely conceivable how a weak naturalism can allow for an autonomous sphere of normativity. To be sure, Habermas maintains that there is a 'meta-theoretical' level which not only allows for the statement that there is a continuum between natural sciences and hermeneutics, but which also assigns a certain amount of autonomy to both perspectives.[27] But he fails to explain how this joining of perspectives might work, and what kind of perspective it is which is employed on the

[25] J Habermas, *Wahrheit und Rechtfertigung* (Frankfurt am Main, Suhrkamp, 1999) 53 (emphasis added).

[26] Cf *ibid* at 37–40.

[27] *Ibid* at 38–9.

meta-level. For the time being (further developments are to be expected), Habermas' new conception offers no real change for the better.

THE DOUBLE ASPECT OF DISCOURSE THEORY, AS DEVELOPED BY ALEXY

Practical Discourse

Alexy's discourse-theoretical conception of normative cognition is based on that of Habermas, but it is more obviously designed to be a theory of validity, lacking the sociological roots of Habermas' conception. Alexy appropriates the discourse theory in the course of designing a theory of legal argumentation; he takes discourse theory simply to be a procedural theory of practical correctness according to which a norm is correct or valid if it might be the result of a rational practical discourse.[28] But there are also strong elements of a theory of social action throughout Alexy's writings.

Basically, Alexy's argument resembles Habermas': establishing a norm as valid requires performing a real discourse that lives up to the rules which are constitutive for an ideal speech situation. The most important rules of discourse are the rhetorical ones; they are non-monological in character and resemble the right of speech and opinion. These rules would, on the level of argumentation, embody the liberal ideas of universality and autonomy; they are, according to Alexy, necessary conditions of any rational practical reasoning. They entail the principle of universalisation, which is worded by Alexy in a way similar to that of Habermas:

> In any discourse, a norm may be consented to by all those affected by it only if they can accept the consequences of a general compliance with this norm for the satisfaction of the interests of any individual.[29]

Seen in the light of the central tenet of discourse theory, that, first, consenting in a discourse depends on arguments, and that, secondly, there is a necessary relation between a universal consent under ideal conditions and the concepts of correctness and moral validity, the basic principle of discourse ethics may thus be formulated as follows:

[28] Cf R Alexy, 'Grundgesetz und Diskurstheorie' in W Brugger, *Legitimation des Grundgesetzes aus Sicht von Rechtsphilosophie und Gesellschaftstheorie* (Baden-Baden, Nomos, 1996) 343–60, 343. Actually, things are a lot more complicated: Alexy distinguishes between an ideal and a real discourse, relative and absolute correctness; he concedes the possibility of a monological discourse, and at the same time he presupposes that any participant in the discourse has the 'power of judgement'. But, in the present context, these refinements may be neglected.

[29] Cf *ibid* at 345.

Exactly those norms are correct, in an ideal sense, and thus valid in this sense, which would be judged as correct by any participant in an ideal discourse.[30]

Necessity of Performing a Real Discourse

Whether Alexy succeeds in founding universally valid dialectic or rhetoric rules which constitute the ideal speech situation and are, thus, necessary conditions of any objective knowledge depends on whether he successfully demonstrates that there must be a discourse before any norm of morality might be called correct or valid.

Alexy mentions essentially two different reasons why forming practical judgements—judgements about moral norms—should necessarily depend on performing a discourse:

(1) Contrary to Habermas, forming practical judgements does not just aim at ascertaining a *common* interest, but at a just balancing of *particular* interests. This balancing is possible only by weighting the particular interests, which affords an argumentation. There is a normative reason why such an argumentation should include those affected by the regulation, namely, the 'principle of autonomy': whosoever denies that the interpretation and weighting of some individual's interests is, in the end, this individual's own affair, does not respect her autonomy; he does not take her seriously as an individual.[31]

(2) In addition, there is an 'external' reason for the necessity of a non-monological discourse: someone who is not omniscient, but is interested in truth or correctness, will value the discourse as a source of arguments.[32]

The second argument need not be examined further in this context, because it may at best establish a heuristic, but not a constitutive relation between the performance of a real discourse and the objective validity of its result, so that it does not live up to discourse theory's claim of being a theory of validity.

It is, however, not so easy to assess the first argument. Though Alexy avoids the problematic thesis that the practical discourse is concerned with establishing a common interest, he nevertheless concentrates on the concept of an 'interest', and the procedure of balancing interests remains vague. He explains it as follows:

> [To solve a conflict of interests in a normatively correct discursive way,] the differing factual opinions of the participants concerning the just settlement of the

[30] *Ibid.*
[31] Cf Alexy, above n 28 at 346–7.
[32] *Ibid* at 347.

> conflict of interests are subjected to a rational processing. In this processing, the interpretation of one's own interests and those of the other participants and the modification of these interpretations on the strength of arguments play an important role.[33]

This conception must meet with doubts, because, similarly to Habermas' conception, it mixes the process of gaining information with the process of constituting valid normative judgements: the interpretation of one's own interests which might be influenced by arguments is just a matter of acquiring data for the genuine practical discourse; for applying the principle of discourse demands that one should be acquainted with the particular interests.

Moreover, appealing to the principle of autonomy is problematic. This principle is not implied in the rules of discourse; it is, for discourse theory, an external element which is in the end based upon a certain conception of personality. Though it is legitimate to introduce it into discourse theory, it gives rise to the question whether this does not shift the burden of proof from discourse theory to quite a different philosophical tradition.

To be sure, Alexy tackles this problem by trying to demonstrate that the principle of autonomy is a presupposition of any rational practical discourse, after all. He does so by expounding the notion of a 'genuine participation' in discourse:

> To get at the principle of autonomy, the notion of genuine participation in a discourse has to be given another, stronger interpretation. According to this interpretation, a genuine participation in a discourse presupposes that the participant really wants to solve social conflicts by an agreement which was achieved and controlled by discourse. . . . Whosoever wants to solve social conflicts by an agreement which was achieved and controlled by discourse, accepts the right of his interlocutors to orientate their behaviour by standards which, after sufficient consideration, they judge to be correct and, therefore, valid.[34]

This argument, however, is doubtful: on the one hand, it might serve to found the thesis that we should grant other persons the right to orientate their behaviour by standards they judge to be correct; but it does not follow that we should grant them the right to give expression to their particular interests, as well. On the other hand, and more importantly, the argument tends towards an interpretation of the practical discourse as (simply) aiming at the solution of social conflicts. This objection is anticipated by Alexy; he makes the following rejoinder:

[33] R Alexy, 'Antwort auf einige Kritiker' in R Alexy, *Theorie der juristischen Argumentation*, 2nd edn (Frankfurt am Main, Suhrkamp, 1991) 408.

[34] R Alexy, 'Diskurstheorie und Menschenrechte' in R Alexy, *Recht, Vernunft, Diskurs* (Frankfurt am Main, Suhrkamp, 1995) 149–50.

> It might seem as if this interpretation of a genuine participation replaces the concepts of truth and correctness by the concepts of consensus and autonomy. But this would be wrong. Even for somebody who is interested only or chiefly in moral truth or correctness, this interpretation is preferable. Only a permanent review of all action norms on the basis of autonomy can prevent lasting moral mistakes.[35]

But this argument seems to be qualified merely in order to raise the practical discourse to the level of a heuristic requirement. Again, it does not do justice to discourse theory's claim that there is a *constitutive* relation between the agreement achieved in a rational practical discourse and the validity of the normative content which the participants agreed upon.

This aside, the following objection against justifying the necessity of a real discourse by the principle of autonomy which in turn is based on the concept of a genuine participation in discourse seems to be decisive: there is a *petitio principii* where the principle of autonomy is employed to justify the necessity of a discourse for establishing objectively valid norms, as long as this principle itself is valid only in relation to a real discourse. But this is the case, because the conception of a genuine participation in discourse presupposes that a discourse is *really* performed—and not just in monologue, ie, in the mind of a solitary thinker.

SPEECH ACT THEORY AND VALIDITY

Comparable to Habermas' analysis of the claims raised by speech acts, Alexy gives another discourse-theoretical justification of the presuppositions of objective validity, starting at the speech act of assertion and analysing its normative implications. It is no pure discourse-theoretical justification, because it contains several arguments alien to discourse theory: there is a tran-scendental-pragmatic argument relying on the normative implications of the claim to correctness raised along with any speech act of asserting something, a utilitarian argument, according to which it is helpful at least to pretend to keep to the rules implied by asserting something, and even an anthropological argument, according to which human beings are interested in correctness and, furthermore, it would mean not taking part in the most fundamental of all human life-forms never to utter an assertion.[36]

On the one hand, the argument avoids the problem of justifying the necessity of a real discourse for reaching at universally valid norms, for its starting-point *is* an element of or a trigger for a real discourse: the speech

[35] *Ibid* at 150.
[36] *Ibid* at 132–3.

act of asserting something. On the other hand, the necessity of backing the transcendental-pragmatic argument with further, rather heterogeneous arguments indicates that it is well nigh impossible to leap from a speaker's faithfully observing all rules which are connected with the speech act of asserting something to the truth or correctness of the content of his speech act.

It is interesting enough that Alexy does not even seem to attempt to accomplish this feat; his main concern is the proof that the rules necessarily connected with the speech act of asserting oblige the speaker to treat her interlocutors in a certain way, that these rules are universally valid, and that they have some impact as rules of action outside the discourse, as well. He dubs this procedure a 'direct' justification of norms by discourse theory, in contrast to an 'indirect' justification which is delivered if certain norms are shown to be the outcome of a correct discourse-theoretical procedure.[37]

This is no longer a theory of validity in the classical sense, and the conception is not in a genuine discourse-theoretical vein either. Furthermore, it is highly doubtful whether the rules of a special language-game may be said to be 'universally' valid and to have an impact on general norms of action. For, on the one hand, the argument is purely hypothetical: we are obliged to keep to the rules of asserting if, and only if, we perform this speech act; but we are not obliged to assert something. If we react to an argument by beating the speaker, he cannot coherently reproach us for having violated the rules of asserting, for it was not our intention to assert anything. On the other hand, if it were true that in a successful act of asserting we necessarily presuppose that we and our interlocutors have, principally, equal rights, this does not oblige us to treat them as equals outside the narrow context of our transient participation in a language-game. As far as Alexy gives further strategic reasons for keeping to these rules, this can, of course, not justify their objective validity but only support the case that one should pretend that they are objectively valid.

SUMMARY AND CONCLUSION

To summarise very briefly: there is a strong internal tension to be found in the discourse theories of Habermas and Alexy, for they couple elements of a classical theory of validity with elements of a theory of social action. In the course of this enterprise, the differences among the following questions are blurred:

[37] *Ibid* at 146.

(1) What are the necessary (and/or sufficient) conditions of objective (normative) knowledge?
(2) What are the necessary (and/or sufficient) conditions of an agreement or consensus amongst participants in a certain practice?
(3) What are the necessary (and/or sufficient) conditions of successfully performing a certain speech act, especially the speech act of asserting something?

It is obvious that there must be (or at least can be) very different answers to these questions. Only the first question is a genuine concern of a theory of validity; to answer the second and third questions is the task of a theory of social action. Accordingly, neither a theory of the presuppositions of communication nor a theory of the presuppositions of certain speech acts is, without 'bridging' or 'overarching' theories, able to yield universal conditions of objective validity. Exploring, vice versa, the necessary conditions of objectively valid assertive or normative judgements does not yield the necessity of a real discourse—at least, this has not been argued for convincingly by Habermas and Alexy. And to detect universally valid moral norms in the results gained by answering the second and third questions is not only contrary to the spirit of discourse theory, it is highly doubtful as well, for the results would necessarily be merely hypothetical: only if (and only as long as) we take part in a certain practice, or aim at a genuine agreement, or assert something, would we be bound to observe these rules.

There are several possible ways to relieve this tension. One solution is to divest the notions of 'truth' and 'correctness' or 'validity' of their absolute nature so that the discourse just aims at 'truth relative to a certain community at a certain time': both Habermas' and Alexy's theories sometimes point in this direction. Another solution would be to drop the claim that the discourse theory offers an ana-lysis of the universal conditions of objective validity. It would then still retain its worth as a reconstruction of the necessary conditions of solving social conflicts by achieving a rational agreement or of taking part in certain social practices; and, of course, its worth as a heuristic theory. A third, more ambitious solution would be to bridge the gap between sociology and theory of validity by adducing a sound argument to the effect that objectivity presupposes intersubjectivity, or—and this seems to be more promising—that subjectivity, intersubjectivity and objectivity are 'equiprimordial'. This solution, however, would ask for a metaphysics more basic than discourse theory which, so far, cannot be found in the writings of either Habermas or Alexy.

One final remark on the relation between Habermas' and Rickert's theories which was mentioned in the beginning: in his epistemology, Rickert distinguishes a 'subjective' or immanent way of transcendental philosophy from an 'objective' or transcendent way. The subjective way starts with the factual act of judgement and explores its presuppositions. One result is that in any act of judgement, an 'ought' is recognised, ie, a norm which is directed at the cognitive subject and demands that she should judge in a certain way. But recognising this ought alone is not enough to lend objective validity to the meaning-content of the act of judging. For in starting the investigation by examining the factual process of judging:

> we remain stuck to the psychological process. The object, the theoretical value is not set free. It appears in the form of a norm directed at a human being, and everything appears in an anthropomorphic colour. We have to realise that the value in its validity soars high above everything human, and thus above any acts of judgement or recognition.[38]

Therefore, there must be an objective way of investigation, as well, starting not with any process of judging, but directly with the objectively valid theoretical value. As may be imagined, one of the main problems of Rickert's epistemology is that he cannot give a convincing answer to the question of how to determine the relation between the 'immanent ought' and the 'transcendent value' (and how to get at the transcendent value).

This dualism between 'immanence' and 'transcendence' reappears in Rickert's theory of cultural sciences which was very influential, having an impact especially on Max Weber's sociology.

It is difficult to say whether there are any germs of Rickert's philosophy buried deep down in Habermas' theory, having been passed on by Weber, but the fact that his theory is troubled by a similar problem is obvious: the relation between 'immanence' (reconstruction of social practices from the perspective of a participant) and 'transcendence' (determining the presuppositions of the objective validity of certain meaning-contents) is not determined in a satisfactory way.

[38] Rickert, above n 1 at 243.

15

The Weight Formula and Argumentation

BARTOSZ BROŻEK*

INTRODUCTION

IN THIS CHAPTER I would like to consider the role of Robert Alexy's 'weight formula' (WF) within the framework of his theory of legal argumentation. I will start with a brief overview of the latter, highlighting those aspects thereof which are crucial given the chapter's aims. Next, the WF will be presented and analysed against the background of another mode of legal reasoning advocated by Alexy, ie the 'subsumption scheme' (SS). Finally, I will argue for the necessity of replacing classical logic with so-called defeasible logic as 'the correct' form for modelling legal argumentation.

ALEXY'S ARGUMENTATION THEORY

Alexy maintains that legal discourse is a special case of general practical discourse (the so-called 'special case thesis'). Therefore, in order to understand what (rational) legal discourse consists in one has to have a grasp of what general practical discourse amounts to. I shall not go into the details of Alexy's conception.[1] Instead, I will try to sketch the general idea behind it. Painting with a broad brush one can say that any such discourse consists in putting forward arguments backing certain theses and deciding which of the arguments prevails. Therefore, one can distinguish

* Chair of Theory and Philosophy of Law, Jagiellonian University, Kraków. This chapter was written during my stay at the University of Kiel as Alexander von Humboldt fellow. I wish to express my gratitude to Robert Alexy and George Pavlakos for discussing early drafts of the chapter.

[1] See R Alexy, *A Theory of Legal Argumentation* (Oxford, Clarendon Press, 1989).

(although only conceptually) two 'stages' or 'levels' of argumentation. The first of them boils down to constructing particular arguments. The second consists in comparing arguments.

To the two enumerated stages of argumentation there correspond two sets of rules. As Alexy puts it himself:

> [the rules of the first group] are also applicable in the context of monologues, and it can be assumed that no theory of rational practical argumentation or justification can dispense with them. This makes it clear that discourse theory in no way replaces justification by merely producing consensus. It fully embraces those rules of rational argumentation, which are applicable to arguments. Its distinctive feature lies exclusively in the fact that it adds a second level to this one, namely that of rules referring to the procedure of discourse.[2]

Therefore, a complete theory of general practical discourse must include two sets of rules, namely rules for constructing arguments and rules 'referring to the procedure of discourse', ie rules which govern the comparison of arguments. These are precisely those two sets of rules that encapsulate the rationality of discourse. Any discourse that is carried out according to the rules may be deemed rational, and only such a discourse. What follows, an outcome of a discourse that observes all the rules, can also be called rational or justified.

It is convenient to quote here some of the rules of general practical discourse, especially those which will be important for the discussion below (I use Alexy's own numbering from *A Theory of Legal Argumentation*).[3]

Of the rules which regulate the construction of arguments one can mention the following:

(1.1) No speaker may contradict him or herself.

(1.3) Every speaker who applies a predicate F to an object a must be prepared to apply F to every other object which is like a in all relevant respects.

Rule (1.1) is of special interest as it constitutes the requirement that all the arguments should be constructed according to the rules of logic.[4]

Among the rules of general practical discourse of the 'second stage' of argumentation the following can be mentioned:

(1.4) Different speakers may not use the same expression with different meanings.

(2.1) Everyone who can speak may take part in discourse.

[2] R Alexy, 'A Discourse-Theoretical Conception of Practical Reason' (1992) 5 *Ratio Juris* 232.

[3] All the quoted rules may be found in Alexy, *A Theory of Legal Argumentation*, above n 1 at parts B and C.

[4] See *ibid* at 188–9.

(2.2) (a) Everyone may problematise any assertion; (b) Everyone may introduce any assertion into the discourse; (c) Everyone may express his or her attitudes, wishes and needs.

(2.3) No speaker may be prevented from exercising the rights laid down in (2.1) and (2.2) by any kind of coercion internal or external to the discourse.

In addition, Alexy identifies several rules concerning the allocation of the burden of proof, the so-called justification rules and transition rules (the latter concern transitions from practical discourse to theoretical, linguistic-analytical and discourse-theoretical discourses).

Alexy maintains, further, that legal discourse is a special case of general practical discourse. The special case thesis is:

> supported on the ground that: (1) legal discussions are concerned with practical questions—that is, what should or may be done or not done; and (2) these questions are discussed under the claim to correctness; ... [and] (3) legal discussions do take place under constraints [imposed by the valid law].[5]

It is the third thesis that distinguishes law from other normative discourses. Therefore, among the 'special' legal rules of argumentation there are rules of valid law. Among them one can, as in the case of general practical discourse, distinguish between rules concerning the process of constructing arguments and rules concerning the 'comparison' of arguments. The former are, especially, the rules of the so-called internal justification. The simplest form of internal justification has the structure of the SS:

(J.1.1)

(1) $\forall x\ (Ax \rightarrow Bx)$

(2) Ao

---

(3) Bo

where (1) is a general legal norm, with A being the conditions of the rule's application and B the rule's conclusion. (2), in turn, is a description of the case, ie a statement of facts. Finally, (3) is the legal judgment expressing the solution to the case at hand.

Other requirements for constructing arguments include:

(J.2.1) At least one universal norm must be adduced in the justification of a legal judgment.

(J.2.2) A legal judgment must follow logically from at least one universal norm together with further statements.

On the other hand, among the rules of the 'second stage' of argumentation the following can be mentioned:

(J.8) Determinations of the relative weights of arguments different in form must conform to weighting rules.

[5] *Ibid* at 212–13.

(J.9) Every possibly proposable argument of such a form that it can be counted as one of the canons of interpretation must be given due consideration.

The picture sketched above looks, roughly, like this. Legal discourse consists in putting forward arguments backing certain theses (legal decisions). The arguments must be built according to the first level rules; those rules include, among others, also the logical requirements. In other words, legal arguments must be constructed in compliance with the rules of logic. Then, the arguments which back contradictory (or otherwise incompatible) theses must be compared in order to reach the decision which of the (competing) arguments prevails. This process has to comply with the rules of the second level.

A peculiar feature of Alexy's conception has to be noted here. The rules of the second level are too general to yield a unique decision in every conceivable case. As Alexy puts it himself:

> observance of the stated rules and utilization of the described forms of argument do indeed increase the probability of reaching agreement on practical issues, but they do not guarantee that agreement can be reached on every subject nor that any agreement obtained will be final and irreversible.[6]

Therefore, the rules decide only which theses (legal decisions) are discursively rational. It is not unusual, therefore, for there being a case in which both of the two incompatible outcomes are equally justifiable with regard to the rules of the second level.

> In those instances in which two incompatible normative statements or rules can be justified without violating any of the rules of discourse, one can speak of '*discursive* possibility'.[7]

In other words, the rules of discourse demarcate only what is discursively justifiable (possible) from what is discursively untenable (impossible).

ROLE OF THE WEIGHT FORMULA

Let us now consider the following question: what is the role of the WF within the framework of Alexy's argumentation theory? We have to begin with a formulation of the WF. Alexy maintains[8] that whenever there is a conflict between two legal principles, it should be decided by the following formula:

$$W_{i,j} = \frac{I_i \cdot W_i \cdot R_i}{I_j \cdot W_j \cdot R_j}$$

[6] *Ibid* at 206.
[7] *Ibid* at 207.
[8] See R Alexy, 'On Balancing and Subsumption: A Structural Comparison' (2003) 16 *Ratio Juris* 433.

where $W_{i,j}$ stands for the concrete weight of the principle P_i relative to the principle P_j, ie relative to the case at hand; I_i stands for the intensity of interference of P_j with P_i; W_i stands for the abstract weight of the principle P_i, ie irrespective of any circumstances. Finally, R_i stands for 'the reliability of the empirical assumptions concerning what the measure in question means for the non-realization of P_i and the realization of P_j under the circumstances of the concrete case'.[9] The principle that has a greater weight prevails in the concrete case over the other principle. The final legal decision is then taken according to what Alexy deems the 'law of conflicting principles' (LCP): the circumstances under which one principle takes precedence over another constitute the conditions of a rule which has the same legal consequences as the principle taking precedence.[10]

In order to illustrate how the WF works let us use a modified version of HLA Hart's notorious 'vehicle in the park' example. The example reads as follows:

An ambulance carrying a seriously injured person has to go to a hospital. The shortest way to the hospital is through the park. However, if the ambulance was allowed into the park it would cause serious pollution. The question arises whether the ambulance can enter the park.

Be the case as naïve as it may, it constitutes a nice illustration of a conflict between two principles. The principles are:

(P1) Human life and health should be protected by the law.

(P2) The environment should be protected by the law.

The application of (P1) results in allowing the ambulance to enter the park and the application of (P2) bans the entrance. Therefore, the principle (P1) reshaped to fit the example can be formulated as follows:[11]

(1) $\forall x\ (AHIx \rightarrow EPx)$

where AHI stands for 'is an ambulance carrying a seriously injured person' and EP for 'may enter the park'. (P2), in turn, becomes:

(2) $\forall x\ (Vx \rightarrow \neg EPx)$

where V stands for 'is a vehicle'. The set of the case's facts C includes:

(3) AHIa

(4) Va

where a is a name of a specific ambulance.

Let us assume, further, that the application of the WF yields the following result: in the described case it is the principle (P1) that takes precedence over (P2). Therefore, according to the LCP the following legal rule should be applied in the case:

[9] *Ibid* at 446.

[10] R Alexy, *A Theory of Constitutional Rights* (Oxford, Oxford University Press, 2002), 54.

[11] This transformation is problematic. For a discussion see B Brożek, 'The Logic of Rules and Principles' (2005), unpublished manuscript.

(5) (AHIa ∧ Va) → EP*a*

I would like to argue that, within the above sketched framework of Alexy's argumentation theory, this reconstruction of a conflict between two legal principles is mistaken.

We should start with clarifying the role the WF plays within argumentation. There are two interpretations possible. According to the first, the WF serves for 'producing' an argument. Therefore it is a device to be used on the first level of argumentation. There is one reason backing this claim. It has to do with the LCP, which states that: the circumstances under which one principle takes precedence over another constitute the conditions of a rule which has the same legal consequences as the principle taking precedence.

The LCP together with the WF serve to produce a case-relative legal rule, like:

(5) (AHIa ∧ Va) → EPa

This rule, in turn, is used to construct an argument which decides the case.

I believe, however, that this interpretation is mistaken. It follows from it that the WF is used *before* the process of argumentation even starts, what is highly controversial. We are misled here, so I argue, by the wording of the WF and the LCP. Instead of speaking of resolving conflicts between principles, it would be much more convenient to say that the WF decides conflicts between two arguments based on legal principles. This mode of speaking supports the second interpretation, according to which the WF plays its role on the 'second level' of argumentation, the one that serves to compare arguments. It is further backed by the fact that both principles which are in conflict when the WF is applied are *valid* legal norms, so a decision which of two valid norms to apply has to be a result of an argumentation process.

The WF, therefore, is not a scheme of constructing arguments. It is a device that serves comparing different, competing arguments. It belongs to the second level of argumentation. Let us recall our example. We have two principles, (P1) and (P2). They have to be compared with the use of the WF for the simple reason that they make it possible to construct two competing arguments, one based on (P1) and the other on (P2). Schematically, we can present it as follows:

(ARG1)
(1) ∀x (AHIx → EPx)
(3) AHIa

---

(6) EPa

(ARG2)
(2) ∀x (Vx → ¬EPx)
(4) Va

---

(7) $\neg EPa$

It has to be stressed that both (ARG1) and (ARG2) have to be constructed according to the rules of logic (rule (1.1)), and they are. Now, the role of the WF is to decide which of the two arguments, (ARG1) or (ARG2), prevails. The WF does it by balancing both principles involved in the formulation of (ARG1) and (AG2) relative to the case at hand.

An important problem concerning the role of the WF within legal argumentation is its relation to the rules of discourse. As we said, the WF serves to resolve conflicts between arguments based on principles. Therefore, the urgent question is, whether the outcomes of applying the WF lie within what is characterised by the rules of the second level as discursively possible. If this is the case, then those outcomes (decisions) can count as rational or justified. If not, the WF is useless from the point of view of the theory of legal argumentation.

I would like to propose the following solution to this problem. When a conflict of two arguments based on principles occurs, there are two possibilities. It may be the case that one of the arguments is discursively impossible. If so, then there is no need to apply the WF, as the outcome is obvious: it is the discursively rational argument that prevails. Otherwise both arguments are discursively possible and that is when the WF has to be applied.

The role of the WF within argumentation should be contrasted with the role of the SS. The SS is a valid form of argument:

(SS)

(1) $\forall x\ (Ax \rightarrow Bx)$

(2) Ao

---

(3) Bo

where (1) is a general legal norm, with A being the conditions of the rule's application and B the rule's conclusion. In turn, (2) is a description of the case, ie a statement of facts. Finally, (3) is the legal judgment expressing the solution to the case at hand.

It is obvious that the SS serves for constructing arguments. Alexy says so literally, formulating the rule of discourse (J.1.1).[12] Another point is that, as the WF decides conflicts between two arguments, legal principles (and conflicts between them) cannot be handled with the WF alone: the arguments based on principles must be constructed as deductive arguments in compliance with rule (1.1). It contradicts what, taken literally, Alexy says. He maintains that legal rules are handled with the SS, while legal principles, with the WF. He goes on to say that:

[12] *Ibid.*

> in both cases a set of premises can be identified from which the result can be inferred. ... The relation between those premises and the result is, however, different. The Subsumption Formula represents a scheme which works according to the rules of logic; the Weight Formula represents a scheme which works according to the rules of arithmetic.[13]

It is clear that the difference between legal rules and principles does not boil down to the fact that rules are handled with the SS scheme and principles with the WF. On the first level of discourse, both arguments based on rules and arguments based on principles must have the form of deductive schemes. The difference lies somewhere else, namely on the second level of argumentation. Conflicts between principles (or, more precisely, of arguments based on principles) and conflicts between a rule and a principle (an argument based on a rule and an argument based on a principle) are decided by the WF. As regards the conflicts of rules, the story is completely different. Precisely speaking, if the validity of a legal rule is established, there can be no argument based on another legal rule incompatible with the argument based on the rule at hand. This is in compliance with what Alexy says:

> conflicts of rules are played out at the level of validity; since only valid principles can compete, competitions between principles are played out in the dimension of weight instead.[14]

LOGIC

In such a setting there immediately occurs a logical problem. If we accept the thesis that the WF decides conflicts between two arguments based on principles, arguments that are both deductively valid, we cannot use the classical logic to deal with the problem. The issue may be illustrated with our earlier example. Recall that on the basis of (P1) and (P2) we constructed the following two arguments:

(ARG1)
(1) $\forall x\,(AHIx \rightarrow EPx)$
(3) AHIa

---

(6) EPa
(ARG2)
(2) $\forall x\,(Vx \rightarrow \neg EPx)$
(4) Va

---

(7) $\neg$EPa

[13] Alexy, above n 8 at 448.
[14] Alexy, above n 10 at 50.

Having those two arguments we move on to the second 'level' of argumentation applying the WF to decide the conflict (and there, naturally, is a conflict, as the conclusion of (ARG1) is contradictory to the conclusion of (ARG2)). The application of the WF leads us to preferring (ARG1) over (ARG2), ie to rejecting the conclusion of (ARG2), ¬EPa. This is, however, highly problematic. If we accept that (ARG2) is a deductive argument which is based on true (or valid) premises, then it is impossible for the conclusion of the argument to be rejected under any circumstances. It is simply the way classical logic works.

In order to avoid this problem, a shift to another formalism is needed. The so-called defeasible logics can serve our aims well. Let me present, therefore, a sketch of a simple defeasible formal system. Let us start with a definition of defeasibility:[15] a rule of the form $A \supset B$ is defeasible if and only if there are situations in which A is fulfilled but B does not follow.

It is easily observable that $\supset$ cannot be read as the material implication $\rightarrow$, for in such case it is impossible that $A \rightarrow B$ and A are true and B is not.

Let us now describe the formal system.[16] Our defeasible logic (DL) operates on two levels. On the first level from a given set of premises arguments are built; on the second level the arguments are compared in order to decide which of them prevails. The conclusion of the 'best' argument becomes the conclusion of the given set of premises.

The language of DL is the language of the first order predicate logic extended by addition of a new sentential connective, the so-called defeasible implication, for which we will use the symbol $\Rightarrow$. For defeasible implication there exists the defeasible *modus ponens*, analogical to that of the material implication:

$A \rightarrow B$

A

―――

B

The difference between material and defeasible implications is visible only on the second level of DL.

The language of DL serves for building arguments. Let us recall our example:

[15] The notion of 'defeasibility' was introduced into legal philosophy by HLA Hart in 'The Ascription of Responsibility and Rights' in A Flew (ed), *Logic and Language* (Oxford, Blackwell, 1951). Hart speaks there of defeasibility of legal concepts. Here, a widely accepted rephrasing of Hart's idea is used: defeasibility is predicated of rules. For more details, see B Brożek, *Defeasibility of Legal Reasoning* (Kraków, Zakamycze, 2004).

[16] The fundamental ideas of the simple system I present here are those of Prakken's logic; see H Prakken, *Logical Tools for Modelling Legal Argument: Study of Defeasible Reasoning in Law* (Dordecht, Kluwer Academic Publishers, 1997). See also J Hage, *Reasoning with Rules: An Essay on Legal Reasoning and its Underlying Logic* (Dordecht, Kluwer Academic Publishers, 1997) and Brożek, above n 15.

(1) AHIx ⇒ EPx
(2) Vx ⇒ ¬EPx[17]
(3) AHIa
(4) Va

This set of premises enables us to construct two arguments, applying defeasible *modus ponens*:

(ARG1)
(1) AHIx ⇒ EPx
(3) AHIa

---

(6) EPa
(ARG2)
(2) Vx ⇒ ¬EPx
(4) Va

---

(7) ¬EPa

The arguments lead to contradictory conclusions. In such a case we have to move to the second level of DL, on which the arguments are compared in order to decide which is 'better' and, in consequence, which of the sentences, EPa or ¬EPa, shall be regarded as the conclusion of our set of four premises.

On the second level of DL two concepts play a crucial role: *attack* and *defeat*. We shall say that an argument A attacks an argument B if the conclusions of both arguments are logically inconsistent.[18] In our example it is the case since EPa and ¬EPa are contradictory: consequently, (ARG1) attacks (ARG2). If two arguments attack one another, one has to know how to decide which of the arguments prevails, ie which *defeats* the other. Various ways of comparing attacking arguments have been developed. The easiest and most flexible is the following. One checks what the defeasible implications that served to build the attacking arguments are. It is assumed that those implications are ordered. In a comparison an argument wins which is built with the use of a defeasible implication that is higher in the ordering. Let us assume that in our example it is the defeasible implication (1) that is higher in the ordering than (2).

The conclusion of the argument that prevails in comparison of all attacking arguments built from the given set of premises is the logical conclusion of this set. Therefore, it is EPa that is the logical conclusion of our set of premises (1) to (4).

The logical system sketched above can easily be applied to conflicts between legal norms and it is the ordering of defeasible implications that

[17] Note that material implications have been replaced by defeasible implications.
[18] As our presentation is elementary, we apply here a simplified definition of attack. Cf Prakken, above n 16.

ultimately decides the outcome. In case of a conflict between two rules the ordering can be established *in abstracto*, ie irrespective of the given legal case. This captures the idea that 'conflicts of rules are played out at the level of validity'. Conflicts of legal principles or of a principle and a rule are decided relative to the given case. Within the framework of DL, it is the WF that decides the ordering of defeasible implications representing principles. For instance, in the case of our example, where the principle (P1) outweighs the principle (P2), the WF decides the ordering such that (P1)>(P2) (or in other words, (1)>(2)) and, consequently, it is the argument based on (P1) that prevails over the argument based on (P2). In this way the logical mechanism of applying legal rules is the same as in the case of principles, but the difference between the two kinds of legal norms is captured in the way the ordering of defeasible implications is decided.

Thus we get exactly what is needed. The arguments based on principles are deductively valid. It is true that the validity in question is a local one, ie the arguments have valid forms and proceed from true premises, but their conclusions do not necessarily belong to the set of the consequences of the given set of premises. The set is decided, ultimately, by comparison of conflicting arguments. In this way the conclusion of (ARG2), ¬EP*a*, follows deductively from the premises (2) and (4), but nevertheless it is not included in the set of the logical consequences of the set of premises {(1), (2), (3), (4)}. However, unlike in the case of classical logic, DL provides us with a formal mechanism which makes such a situation possible. Moreover, the proposed solution enables us to get rid of the LCP, which was the main source of confusion as to the role the WF plays in argumentation. It is evident from what we said, that the LCP was needed because of the underlying assumption that it is the classical logic that has to be used to formally model legal reasoning.

I would like to say, also, that there are some additional reasons justifying the abandoning of the classical logic in favour of DL. One of them concerns the formal mechanisms governing resolution of the conflicts between two legal rules, two principles or a rule and a principle. The use of classical logic in this context requires taking advantage of the notion of revisability, which is acceptable in the case of a conflict between two legal rules but is troublesome in the remaining two cases. However, as this problem exceeds the scope of this chapter, I will not pursue it here.[19]

[19] It is addressed in detail in Brożek, above n 11. See also B Brożek, 'Revisability vs. Defeasibility' (2005), unpublished manuscript, for the distinction between revisability and defeasibility and Brożek, above n 15 for other reasons for preferring defeasible logic over the classical.

CONCLUSIONS

The findings of the present chapter may be summarised as follows. The first thesis I defended may be put forward in the following way:

(T1) The weight formula plays its role at the second level of argumentation, ie at the level at which arguments are compared.

The thesis is backed both by the distinction between two levels of argumentation and by the fact that the very idea of the WF is to settle a controversy, ie the WF cannot be thought of as a device applicable for constructing arguments, or, so to speak, before the argumentation starts. There are several corollaries[20] that follow from this:

(C1) What the WF ultimately compares are not two principles but two arguments based on principles.

(C2) The WF plays an essentially different role within argumentation than the SS; the former is applied on the second level of argumentation, the latter on the first.

(C3) The difference between legal rules and principles does not boil down to the fact that rules are 'handled with' the SS and principles with the WF. Both rules and principles are used to construct deductively valid arguments. The difference between them lies in the question whether, and in what circumstances, they can face opposing arguments and how such conflicts are decided.

(C4) The LCP is misleading. It suggests that the WF plays its role on the first level of argumentation. Therefore, it should be abandoned.

The second thesis I advocated reads:

(T2) Legal discourse should be modelled with the use of defeasible logic rather than classical logic.

This claim is based on the fact that it is impossible to reconcile (T1) and (C1) to (C4) with the classical logic approach. A corollary from (T2) is the following:

(C5) A shift from the classical logic to the defeasible logic enables one to abandon the LCP.

[20] I allow myself the use of the notion 'corollary' somewhat loosely.

Part V

Comments and Responses

16

Thirteen Replies

ROBERT ALEXY*

AN AUTHOR'S DELIGHT in finding readers is enhanced many times over when a reader engages the author, asking questions, offering criticism and another viewpoint. Lack of clarity, even error, may lie comfortably unnoticed in long-held, cherished notions, only to be discovered in the bright light of criticism. New terrain must be explored. New ideas emerge from the give and take. It is in the spirit of this vital exchange, then, that my replies to my critics are accompanied by an expression of my gratitude to all of them. I should add that my replies are not, of course, comprehensive, and for that I ask the reader's indulgence.

REPLY 1 TO NEIL MACCORMICK

On a superficial reading Neil MacCormick's thesis that 'law claims nothing' (at 59)[1] might give rise to the impression that any claim whatever ought to be kept completely away from the law. Nothing, however, would be more mistaken than this. MacCormick emphasises that legislation involves not only the claim that one have the authority to legislate as conferred by the constitution (at 64), but also the claim to serve 'justice and the common good' (at 66). The claim to justice is said to be a claim that is always raised by legislation: 'In legislative politics, there is always some underlying claim about just demands and the demands of justice' (at 66). An act of legislation that has a title like 'Unjust Poll-Tax Act 1987' would be 'politically self-defeating' and 'politically absurd' (at 66). Openly to 'proclaim the maintaining or the maximising of injustice as the point of law is to maintain what is not seriously sustainable' (at 66). The latter

* I should like to thank Stanley L Paulson and Bonnie Litschewski Paulson for suggestions and advice on matters of English style.

1 The articles are cited in the text with page numbers between parentheses.

comes at least close to the performative contradiction.[2] All of this simply goes to show that the main tenets of the claim thesis are shared by Neil MacCormick. His thesis that 'law claims nothing' is not directed against the claim to correctness in law at all. It merely amounts to the argument that it is not 'law itself' (at 67) that is raising the claim, but those who make, apply or execute the law: 'This "claim to correctness", if such it be, is that of the law-maker, not that of the "law"' (at 67). The reason for this is, first, that law is a 'normative order' (at 60), secondly, that '[t]he existence of a normative order is … a state of affairs' (at 60), and, thirdly, that states of affairs are 'incapable' of having intentions, performing speech acts and making claims (at 60). Therefore, '[t]o say law claims anything, meaning this literally, is a category mistake' (at 59). To mean it, however, not literally, would be 'an unhelpfully metaphorical way of expressing what can be stated more clearly' (at 67).

Neil MacCormick is, without any doubt, right in maintaining that the law as such is incapable of raising, in a literal sense, any claim, and he rightly quotes a remark of mine in which I expressly concede this point by saying that '[i]n a strict sense, claims can only be raised by subjects having the capacity to speak and to act'[3] (at 59 n 3). But does the fact that claims can be raised in a fully qualified or strict sense only by subjects having the capacity to speak and act really mean that talk about law's claim to correctness is 'unhelpful' (at 59, 67) or misleading? It is not clear to me that this is the case. The reason why talk about law's claim to correctness seems to be sensible stems from the idea of what might be termed an objective raising of this claim. Raising a claim objectively has as its counterpart raising the claim subjectively. A subject that makes, applies, executes or interprets law raises a claim subjectively, if the subject wants or decides to raise it. In this respect, the claim can also be termed 'personal'. In contrast to this, a claim is raised objectively if everyone who performs an act-in-law or submits a legal argument necessarily has to raise the claim, whether he wants to do so or not. The objective claim is not a private matter; rather, it is necessarily connected to the role of a participant in the legal system. It could also be designated as 'official', using the term in a broad sense.[4] The objective or official character becomes most evident in the case of a judge who raises the claim to correctness qua representative of the legal system, but it is present even in the case of a citizen who addresses

[2] R Alexy, *The Argument from Injustice: A Reply to Legal Positivism* (B Litschewski Paulson and SL Paulson (trans), Oxford, Clarendon Press, 2002) 35–9.

[3] R Alexy, 'My Philosophy of Law: The Institutionalisation of Reason' in LJ Wintgens (ed), *The Law in Philosophical Perspectives* (Dordrecht, Kluwer, 1999) 23–45 at 24.

[4] See R Alexy, 'Law and Correctness' in MDA Freeman (ed), *Legal Theory at the End of the Millennium* (Oxford, Oxford University Press, 1998) 205–21 at 206.

publicly the issue of what the law demands. It is this role of a representative of the legal system that is necessarily held by those who are empowered to perform acts-in-law and necessarily occupied by those who merely argue what the law of the land is, which is what makes talk about law's claim to correctness sensible. The representatives of the law do not act or argue for some other subject, nor for nothing. Rather, they act and argue on behalf of a common institutionalised enterprise and an idea.

REPLY 2 TO STEFANO BERTEA

An objection often raised against the non-positivist concept of law is that non-positivism jeopardises legal certainty, one of the main purposes or values of law. If it should prove to be true that legal non-positivism cannot do justice to legal certainty, then non-positivism would, indeed, be rendered untenable. The main point of Stefano Bertea's chapter is that an adequate non-positivistic concept of law 'can suitably accommodate certainty' (at 71). I think he is right. The question is how non-positivism ought to be conceived such that legal certainty can play the role it ought to play.

All non-positivist theories of law defend the connection thesis, which says that there is a necessary connection between *legal* validity or *legal* correctness on the one hand, and *moral* merits and demerits or *moral* correctness and incorrectness on the other. This thesis, however, lends itself to very different interpretations, which lead to very different versions of non-positivism. The most radical version says that each and any moral defect yields legal invalidity. An example is the position defended by Deryck Beyleveld and Roger Brownsword, according to which 'immoral rules are not legally valid'.[5] To be sure, Beyleveld and Brownsword are well aware of the problems for legal certainty posed by this formula, and they attempt to delimit the unlimited effects of their formula, but this matter will not be considered here.[6] Only one point is of interest here. A version of non-positivism that precluded the legal validity of authoritatively issued and socially efficacious norms in all cases of conflict between law and morality would not be acceptable. One might term this version of non-positivism 'exclusive non-positivism'.[7] Owing to the inherently controversial nature of moral issues, exclusive non-positivism would be tantamount to anarchism.

[5] D Beyleveld and R Brownsword, *Human Dignity in Bioethics and Biolaw* (Oxford, Oxford University Press, 2001) 76.

[6] See R Alexy, 'Effects of Defects—Action or Argument? Thoughts about Deryck Beyleveld and Roger Brownsword's *Law as a Moral Judgment*' (2006) 19 *Ratio Juris* 169 at 170–1.

[7] *Ibid* at 173.

Bertea designates the connection thesis that underlies exclusive non-positivism as 'unqualified' (at 78). Its counterpart is a 'qualified' (at 79) connection thesis, one that is based on the distinction between a qualifying and a classifying connection between law and morality.[8] The qualification of this version of non-positivism consists, so to speak, in taking account not only of classifying connections between law and morality, but also of qualifying connections. Bertea is right in saying that the distinction between a classifying and a qualifying connection can 'be interpreted as designed to retain the connection thesis without thereby having to let go of legal certainty' (at 79). It is, indeed, a main purpose of this distinction to achieve an 'incorporation of morality into law' that 'does not involve sacrificing certainty beyond what is reasonable' (at 79). Perhaps it should be added that there exists a second main purpose in defence of this distinction, namely, in not sacrificing justice beyond what is reasonable. An unreasonable sacrifice of justice would occur if appropriately issued and socially effective norms retained their legal validity even though the threshold of extreme injustice has been crossed (classifying connection), or if appropriately issued and socially efficacious norms remained legally perfect norms even though they suffered from moral defects or demerits (qualifying connection). The ground for these two directions of the distinction between a classifying and a qualifying connection is the dual nature of law. The claim of law to correctness refers both to law's factual or authoritative dimension and to law's ideal or critical dimension, and demands, in comprising the real as well as the ideal side, for an optimal coupling of legal certainty and justice. In this sense, the concept of correctness is the most fundamental or, as it were, the all overarching concept.

REPLY 3 TO GEORGE PAVLAKOS

The concept of objectivity presupposes the distinction between what we say or believe and what is actually the case. If this difference really exists, and if there exist ways to connect the one with the other, then objectivity is possible.

In order to solve the problem of objectivity in law, George Pavlakos begins with a dilemma. Its horns are conventionalism on the one hand, and essentialism on the other. Pavlakos sees conventionalism not only in Hart's theory but also in Dworkin's earlier writings, and he sees elements of essentialism in Dworkin's more recent work.

According to conventionalism, the criteria of the correctness of a legal proposition are internal to the practice of a legal community, whereas they

[8] Alexy, above n 2 at 26.

exist independently of it according to essentialism (at 90). The dilemma is said to stem, on the one hand, from the fact that a community can go wrong, which leads, in the end, 'to a total loss of objectivity' (at 90), and on the other, from the fact that essentialism presupposes 'some (mysterious) legal essences in the environment', which counts as such a strong condition of objectivity that 'it makes objectivity unattainable' (at 90). The dilemma, however, is said to be 'far from compulsory' (at 90).

The decisive point in Pavlakos' argument is that 'both horns of the dilemma can be traced back to the same notion of criteria' (at 97) for the objectivity or correctness of 'normative propositions' (at 100). Conventionalism as well as essentialism are said to rest on a 'static' conception of criteria (at 97). Criteria are 'static' if they are 'ultra-determinants' (at 99). Ultra-determinants are criteria that 'invest single facts with absolute power of determination (be they facts about the semantic behaviour of the participants of the practice or about law's "real" essence)' (at 99). They determine the result monotonically. Owing to their respective static or monotonic conceptions of criteria, Pavlakos characterises conventionalism as well as essentialism as 'shallow' (at 97, 99).

Taking the concept of shallowness together with its counterpart, the concept of depth, as a fork in the road provides a way out of the dilemma posed by conventionalism and essentialism. The path of shallowness leads to the dilemma; the path of depth offers a solution. Now one might well expect that conventionalism as well as essentialism will reappear on the path of depth. Pavlakos, however, seems to consider only a 'deep conception of practice' (at 99), that is, a deep conception of conventionalism, as workable. This, however, will be noted here only in passing. The relationship between a 'deep' conception of practice and a 'deep' conception of essence is a topic that goes beyond the scope of these remarks.

Pavlakos claims that discourse theory can help to provide for a deep conception of practice. One might come to think that deep theories must be strong theories. The opposite, however, is the case. Pavlakos is right in pointing out that a deep theory of objectivity has to be a 'modest' (at 84) theory of objectivity, whereas only a shallow theory of objectivity can pretend to be a strong theory of objectivity (at 84).

The pivotal question, therefore, is whether discourse theory can explain how objectivity qua weak objectivity is possible. This issue has many aspects. In George Pavlakos' chapter they appear under the heading of 'two conditions of depth' (at 99): first, the 'dynamic character' (at 99) of the criteria for correctness and, secondly, a structure that Pavlakos describes by means of the concept of 'multi-levelled discursive grammar' (at 100).

Discourse is a procedure that is characterised by openness. Anyone may take part in discourse, anyone may render problematic any assertion, anyone may introduce any assertion whatever into the discourse, and anyone may express his or her attitudes, wishes and needs.[9] Thus, nothing whatever is placed beyond scrutiny, while everything is considered a possible source of argument. Discourse, therefore, is an essentially non-monotonic and holistic enterprise. For this reason, a legal or moral system based on discourse has to be a flexible system. It cannot be static. It has a dynamic character in the sense of this concept understood by Pavlakos.

Flexibility as such, however, does not suffice for generating objectivity. One can be wrong in a highly flexible way. At this point, Pavlakos brings in the concept of grammar. A grammar is a system of rules and forms. A discursive grammar must comprise rules and forms that provide not only for flexibility but also for rationality. Such a system might well be termed a 'code of practical reason'.[10] Rationality is not possible without reflexivity. Discourse is reflective not only with respect to its objects, that is, in our case, with respect to law and morals, it is also self-reflective. Its form of self-reflexion is discourse-theoretic discourse.[11] In this respect the discursive grammar is indeed, as George Pavlakos terms it, 'multi-levelled' (at 100). Objectivity seems to be intrinsically connected with a reflective activity that is governed by rules and inspired by spontaneity.

REPLY 4 TO PHILIPPOS VASSILOYANNIS

Philippos Vassiloyannis' central issue is the place occupied by discourse in the relation between law and morality. According to Vassiloyannis, there exists the possibility that discursive proceduralism qua formalism might well boil down to a rather crude version of positivism: 'a merely procedural claim to correctness, a formalistic legal discourse ..., [that] leads to a belated revival of *Begriffsjurisprudenz* (the distinctive type of German legal positivism of the nineteenth century) and to the so-called *juristische Methode*' (at 111). The question is raised whether a discourse theory of law as I conceive it is '[l]acking a moral bridge that would take us from moral to legal argumentation (in other words, without a moral justification of the form of law), the discursive conception of legal argumentation cannot but reproduce the positivistic distinction between law and morality, and ends up a mere apology for legal discourse' (at 109). According to Vassiloyannis, discourse ethics can stay clear of the danger of formalism and positivism only 'by virtue of purely moral reasons: in short, from a moral justification of the form of law' (at 110).

[9] See R Alexy, *A Theory of Legal Argumentation* (R Adler and N MacCormick (trans), Oxford, Clarendon Press, 1989) 193.

[10] *Ibid* at 188.

[11] *Ibid* at 187, 206.

This sounds as if two versions of discourse ethics were possible: a formalistic one that lacks any reference to substantive morality and a non-formalistic one that includes moral reasons. My reply is that discourse, by its nature, is always intrinsically connected with morality. A purely formal conception of discourse ethics is, therefore, impossible.

To be sure, one can find in Habermas' writings the thesis that his universalisation principle[12] 'does not prejudge substantive regulations, as it is a rule of argumentation only',[13] and Vassiloyannis is right to point out that Habermas himself stresses the 'formal'[14] character of his universalisation principle. At the same time, however, Habermas maintains that his rule of argumentation 'is not compatible with all substantive legal and moral principles'.[15] This implies that Habermas' universalisation principle, notwithstanding its character as a rule of argumentation, is related to moral content. Habermas has, indeed, a strong tendency to delegate the selection of moral and legal content to real discourses. Even in his case, however, 'formal' or 'procedural' does not mean 'compatible with any content'.

In my work I have attempted to establish a considerably stronger relation between discourse rules on the one hand, and moral and legal rules on the other, than that set out by Habermas. The linchpin of this connection is the thesis that human rights can be based on the presuppositions of discourse. Vassiloyannis seems to agree with the result but not with the way it is achieved. According to my view, a main problem consists in the transition from discourse rules as rules of speech to human rights as rules of conduct.[16] Rules of speech such as 'Everyone may problematise any assertion', 'Everyone may introduce any assertion into the discourse', and 'Everyone may express his or her attitudes, wishes, and needs'[17] give expression to the idea of autonomy in discourse. As such, they do not imply a right to autonomy that concerns not only speech but also action, which right might be formulated as follows: 'Everyone has the right to judge for himself what is right and good, and to act accordingly'.[18] In order to arrive at this right—which might well be considered the Archimedean point of a substantial moral and legal system—one needs additional

[12] Habermas' universalisation principle demands that 'all affected can *freely* accept the consequences and the side effects that the *general* observance of a controversial norm can be expected to have for the satisfaction of the interests of *each individual*'. See J Habermas, 'Discourse Ethics: Notes on a Program of Philosophical Justification' in *idem*, *Moral Consciousness and Communicative Action* (C Lenhardt and S Weber Nicholsen (trans), Cambridge, Polity Press, 1992) 43–115 at 93 (emphasis in original).

[13] *Ibid* at 94.

[14] *Ibid*.

[15] *Ibid*.

[16] R Alexy, 'Discourse Theory and Human Rights' (1996) 9 *Ratio Juris* 209 at 222.

[17] Alexy, above n 9 at 193.

[18] See Alexy, above n 16 at 226.

premises. These additional premises can be characterised by means of the concept of serious or genuine participation in discourse.[19] The underlying idea is that whoever takes discourses seriously also takes seriously autonomy in social life. Discourses that are taken seriously by their participants are discourses in a fully-fledged sense. To be sure, discourses in a fully-fledged sense are by no means ideal discourses, but they are real discourses that seriously strive to be as ideal as possible in all aspects. The decisive point is that a right to autonomy that is not implied by any discourse rule qua rule of speech is indeed implied by the concept of fully-fledged discourse. This shows that seriousness is the missing premise or link. Now, to be serious or not is a—perhaps the—paradigmatic existential decision.[20] The thesis that rules of action cannot be derived from rules merely expressing presuppositions of speech aims at elucidating this existential moment in the concept of discourse.

REPLY 5 TO MATTIAS KUMM

The question of whether proportionality analysis adequately describes the structure of constitutional and human rights is highly contested. Mattias Kumm's answer is neither a simple 'yes' nor a simple 'no'. He claims that the 'proportionality structure is rightly a central feature of rights reasoning, but it is merely one of three distinct structural elements central to reasoning about rights as a matter of political morality. Other structural features of rights discourse include the idea of excluded reasons and the prohibition of certain means-ends relationships' (at 132–3). These structural features are to be complemented by 'institutional considerations that sometimes justify imposing additional requirements on the justification for an infringement of a right, requiring reasons of special strength' (at 133). These additional elements are said to be corollaries of three basic ideas of political liberalism which Kumm refers to as antiperfectionism, anticollectivism and anticonsequentialism.

Antiperfectionalism insists that 'reasons relating to the realisation of demanding perfectionist ideals of any kind, may not be used to justify infringements of individual liberty' (at 143). In this sense, they are excluded reasons. Excluded reasons are reasons that are ruled out where any participation in balancing is concerned. This implies that they can never serve to justify a limitation of rights. With respect to those reasons, rights are trumps in the full sense of the word. One of Kumm's examples of an excluded reason is promoting 'a Christian way of life' (at 143).

[19] *Ibid* at 223–4.

[20] See R Alexy, 'Menschenrechte ohne Metaphysik?' (2004) 52 *Deutsche Zeitschrift für Philosophie* 15 at 21.

The phenomenon of excluded reasons is not foreign to proportionality analysis. Kumm correctly describes the proportionality test as having 'four prongs': suitability, necessity, legitimate ends and balancing (at 137). The third prong on this list, legitimate ends, is identical with the idea of excluded reasons. Promoting a Christian way of life is an excluded reason on the ground that it 'would not count as a legitimate government purpose' (at 144). Illegitimate ends, like invalid principles,[21] can never justify any limitation of any right. It therefore makes no sense to employ them in the balancing procedure. If they were employed, it would be with the value of zero. This would deprive them of the capacity to outweigh anything else. As possessing the value of zero, they would be excluded, moreover, from representing a divisor in the weight formula. Participating in balancing without any weight is, however, not really to participate in balancing.

Therefore, proportionality analysis has no difficulty in describing the formal structure of excluded reasons. It is, however, not in a position to justify which reasons are to be excluded. This is a question of substantive moral and political theory. For this reason, Kumm rightly claims that the 'idea of excluded reasons complements' (at 148) proportionality. Participation in the proportionality test turns on a presupposition, and this presupposition is not to be excluded—a presupposition, again, that cannot be justified by a proportionality test. Perhaps one might distinguish here between unlimited and limited balancing. Unlimited balancing encompasses all principles, values or aims to participate in balancing with a value higher than zero. Limitations on balancing begin at the point at which at least one principle, value or aim is graduated as zero—is, namely, excluded.

The second basic idea of political liberalism is anticollectivism. The central tenet of anticollectivism is that rights 'enjoy priority over the "general interest" or the "collective good" in some way' (at 142). This corresponds to the idea of 'rights as shields' which 'points to a structure of rights reasoning—the requirements of reasons of a special strength' (at 152). Kumm is right to emphasise that 'proportionality analysis can easily incorporate' this understanding of the priority of rights (at 148). The test of proportionality in the narrow sense, ie, the first law of balancing (Kumm characterises it as the 'last prong of the proportionality test' (at 149)) 'provides a space for the reasoned incorporation of an understanding of liberties that expresses whatever priority over collective goods is substantively justified' (at 149). That conception of rights as shields that aims at the protection of rights 'beyond what proportionality requires',

[21] R Alexy, *A Theory of Constitutional Rights* (J Rivers (trans), Oxford, Oxford University Press, 2002) 61–2.

would 'overprotect certain interests' (at 151). Kumm correctly points out that there can be no justification for such a conception of rights at the level of substantive reasons (at 151).

Kumm terms a conception of rights exclusively based on reasons of political morality a 'first-order account' (at 151). Its counterpart, a second-order account, is a conception of rights that reflects not only considerations of political morality but also institutional requirements. An example of the latter are the 'biases of courts and other institutions' (at 152) with respect to negative secondary effects that are said to stem from granting homosexuals the right to serve in the armed forces. In such cases the empirical claims lending support to the thesis that the fighting power and operational effectiveness of the army would be endangered if homosexuals were not excluded from it must be of special strength in order to 'counteract the epistemic biases in favour of finding such effects with regard to suspect activities of unpopular groups' (at 152).

Now, the problem of the reliability of empirical premises underlying the justification of a limitation of rights is not unknown to proportionality analysis. Proportionality analysis seeks to resolve the problem by means of a second law of balancing, which runs as follows: 'The more heavily an interference in a constitutional right weighs, the greater must be the certainty of its underlying premises'.[22] Both laws of balancing give expression to the idea that the capacity of rights to withstand interference increases the more intensive the interference becomes.[23] This shows that the conception of rights as principles by no means stands in opposition to the idea of rights as shields. It attempts to give that idea as rational an expression as possible. Proportionality analysis is, therefore, compatible with anticollectivism.

Anticonsequentialism is the third basic idea of political liberalism. This idea is not so easily reconciled with proportionality analysis. Kumm maintains that 'the proportionality structure is inadequate' on the ground that 'it imposes a structure on rights reasoning that is consequentialist. As a consequentialist structure, it is unable to reflect the deontological nature of at least some rights' (at 153). He illustrates this point by means of the well-known trolley problem. The trolley problem addresses the question of whether it is allowable to kill a smaller number of persons (here one) in order to save a greater number (here five). The decision of the German Federal Constitutional Court of 15th February 2006[24] on the Air Security Act, enacted in the wake of September 11th and allowing that a passenger plane be shot down by the German Airforce if this is deemed to be the only way to avert a clear and present danger to human life, shows that this

[22] *Ibid* at 418.
[23] *Ibid* at 103.
[24] Decisions of the German Federal Constitutional Court, vol 115, 118.

problem has by no means merely theoretical significance. Kumm's point is that the answers to these questions depend on 'the structure of the means-ends relationship', which, he contends, cannot 'be appropriately captured within the proportionality structure' (at 162–3). In the trolley case, two constellations are to be considered. In the first constellation, five people can be saved if a bystander diverts a runaway trolley onto another track where the trolley will kill only one person. In the second constellation, the runaway trolley will kill five people if the bystander does not push the 'fat man' (at 153) onto the track in order to stop the trolley. The fat man will die in the process.

Kumm maintains that the two situations exhibit an essential difference. The fat man is being used as a means to bring about the end of saving the five. He is an *enabler*. By contrast, the one person killed in the first situation is merely a *disabler*. It would be permissible to divert the trolley if he did not exist, and the question is whether his standing on the track disables the bystander from saving the five. The claims of the disabler are assumed to be 'susceptible to proportionality analysis' (at 154), whereas the claims of the enabler are said to impose strict deontological constraints that cannot be outweighed. Proportionality analysis qua consequentialist reasoning is, however, unable to grasp this difference.

In order to reply to this reproach to proportionality analysis vis-à-vis consequentialism one has to know what is meant by the concept of consequentialism. The notion of consequentialism is often associated with utilitarianism, namely, as referring to the greatest utility of the greatest number. Proportionality analysis is, however, clearly to be distinguished from utilitarian considerations. An important class of cases to be resolved by proportionality analysis are cases of a collision between two rights. In such cases, the question is whether the intensity of infringement in the one right outweighs the infringement in the other right that would be brought about by omitting the infringement in the first right. In many cases this is a question concerning the relationship between the rights of simply two persons. The number of persons does not, then, play any role. If one wants to term this structure—a clear example of a proportionality structure—'consequentialist', the notion of consequentialism is reduced to a single feature, namely, that the resolution of the collision problem is made dependent on the intensity of the interferences. A consequentialist approach is, then, simply an approach that allows for or demands balancing, ie, a non-categorical approach.

This brief look at the concept of consequentialism as used by Kumm shows that the central issue of anticonsequentialism is not the number of persons involved but the categorical or absolute nature of the constraints. It is not possible to discuss here the question of whether and for what reasons there exist absolute or categorical rights. Our question is simply this: what would it mean for proportionality analysis if there existed absolute rights based on means-ends considerations that, as such, could not be grasped by proportionality? The implications would be two in number. The first is that there would exist a domain from which balancing is excluded. In antiperfectionism some reasons are excluded in all cases from taking part in a balancing procedure; anticonsequentialism excludes balancing as such in some cases and, in this way, excludes all reasons, in some cases, from taking part in a balancing procedure. This, too, can however be grasped by means of the weight formula. As already mentioned, in case of excluded reasons this can be done by attributing to them the value of zero. In case of categorical constraints this can be achieved by giving them an infinite value. Participating in balancing with an infinite value is, just like participating with the value of zero, not really participating in balancing at all. In this sense, the two extreme values give expression to the notion that the limits of balancing have been reached. The fact that balancing has limits of this kind is not to say, however, that proportionality does not remain at the centre of rights analysis.

The second implication would be, namely, that there exist rights based on a structure of argument that, as such, cannot be captured by proportionality analysis. Kant's thesis that man as '*an end in itself*' has an 'absolute value'[25] is an example. But this, too, is not to say that proportionality analysis does not find itself at the core of reasoning about rights. Proportionality analysis is, as the weight formula shows, a formal structure that essentially depends on premises provided from outside.[26] Kant's end-in-itself thesis can be conceived as an argument justifying the attribution of an infinite value to a certain right. In this way, the means-ends consideration acquires the status of an argument justifying the substitution of a value for one of the variables of the weight formula. To be sure, this would count as an extreme case of substitution. Normal cases concern judgements about the intensity of an infringement in a principle or the degree of its abstract weight as measured by such factors as light, medium or serious. The normal cases, however, share with extreme cases the need for justification of these judgements by means of arguments that, again, cannot be submitted to proportionality analysis. Proportionality without those arguments would be arbitrary and mechanical. Rights analysis must come to terms with this. Kumm's scrutiny into excluded reasons and deontological constraints represents a genuine contribution here.

[25] I Kant, *The Moral Law: Kant's Groundwork of the Metaphysic of Morals* (HJ Paton (trans), London, Hutchinson, 1948) 95 (emphasis in original).

[26] See R Alexy, 'On Balancing and Subsumption: A Structural Comparison' (2003) 16 *Ratio Juris* 433 at 448.

REPLY 6 TO JULIAN RIVERS

Constitutional rights have two dimensions. One is substantive or material; the other is formal or procedural. The substantive dimension of a constitutional right concerns the questions of what the right demands and the question of the conditions under which the right can be limited in favour of other constitutional rights or public interests. The formal dimension of constitutional rights concerns the institutional problems of constitutional review. Here, formal principles such as the principle of the democratically legitimised decision-taking competence of the legislature come into play. I have attempted to adjust the relationship between substantive and formal principles in a theory of discretion in which two 'laws of balancing' play a pivotal role. The first law of balancing concerns the relationship between the intensity of an interference in a constitutional right and the substantial weight of the reasons justifying the interference. This law lends itself to different formulations.[27] A version with maximal structural congruence to the formulation of the second law in the Postscript runs as follows:

> The more intensive an interference in a constitutional right is, the greater must be the weight of the competing principles.

By contrast, the second law of balancing refers not to the substantive importance of the reasons justifying an interference but to their epistemic quality. It runs as follows:

> The more intensive an interference in a constitutional right is, the greater must be the certainty of its underlying premises.[28]

Julian Rivers argues 'that this formulation of the second law of balancing is incomplete' (at 170). '[I]t betrays a tendency to downplay the significance of formal principles', for it fails 'to take full account of these principles' (at 170). Thus, it 'requires reformulation' (at 170).

Rivers presents a most impressive list of problems that have to be resolved in order to achieve a 'full account' of the role played by formal principles in a theory of legislative discretion. It is impossible to consider all of them here. I will confine myself to some comments on the interpretation of the second law of balancing, as introduced in the Postscript, and on Rivers' proposal for reformulating it.

My first point concerns the understanding of the concept of certainty as used in the second law of balancing. This concept lends itself to two different interpretations. It can be understood either as probability or as reliability. Rivers argues that only the second interpretation is correct, and I fully agree with him on this point. Rivers, however, maintains that I have

[27] See Alexy, above n 21 at 102, 418–19.
[28] *Ibid* at 419.

a 'preference for the probability formulation' (at 183). Perhaps I have not expressed myself clearly enough. Be that as it may, when I introduced reliability (R) as the third variable on both sides of the weight formula, I did so by way of an explanation of reliability as a gradual epistemic property that can be expressed by epistemic grades such as: certain or reliable (r), maintainable or plausible (p), and not evidently false (e).[29]

All this serves to show that the second law of balancing in the formulation quoted above has the character of an epistemic rule referring to the certainty of empirical premises. Now, Rivers' main point is that the second law of balancing should be conceived not merely as an epistemic rule referring to the certainty of empirical premises but, what is far more, as a general rule 'determining the intensity of review, wherever the court has the power to review more or less intensively' (at 187). Rivers expresses this general rule as follows:

> the more serious a limitation of rights is, the more intense should be the review engaged in by the court (at 187).

This generalisation of the second law of balancing qua epistemic rule extends its scope of application considerably. The generalised second law of balancing refers to all possible sources of legislative discretion. From this point of view the reproach of incompleteness (at 170), as addressed to the epistemic version, explains itself. It is a reproach of lacking generality.

Rendering our thoughts more general is a bit like a regulative idea of research. For that reason, Rivers' proposal of a generalisation of the second law of balancing is an inspired idea, one that contributes a great deal to the theory of balancing in constitutional law. It should, however, be noted that the extension of its scope of application alters the status of the second law of balancing. The second law qua epistemic rule is part of the weight formula, a part that is represented by 'RP_iC' and 'RP_jC'[30] in a first and by 'R_i' and 'R_j'[31] in the more recent simplified version of the formula. By contrast, the general notion of intensity of review relates to a number of features that are not expressed by any of the variables of the weight formula. This, however, does not mean that these features bear no relation to the weight formula.

Scalar discretion is an example. Rivers aptly points out that increasing the fineness of a scale implies a decrease in the discretion of the legislature (at 184). The rule that the more serious the limitation of a right is, the greater the fineness of the scale of evaluation should be, seems to be well founded. This rule is a corollary of the general idea that the capacity of a right to withstand interference increases in proportion to the intensity of

[29] *Ibid* at 419 n 97.
[30] *Ibid* at 419.
[31] Alexy, above n 26 at 446.

interference, and it corresponds to the observation that our ability to distinguish degrees of interference increases with the extremity of the interference.

At the same time, however, it is obvious that a scalar rule cannot define a new variable of the weight formula. Scalar rules are by definition confined to the determination of the scales by which the factor represented by the variables is to be classified. They do not say what has to be classified. Still, as determining how to classify they are an indispensable element of the theory of balancing. Without scales, balancing would not be possible.

REPLY 7 TO JAN SIECKMANN

Discourse theory is grounded on the assumption that assertions are the basic elements of argumentation. Assertions are necessarily connected with a claim to correctness. This implies that discourse theory is necessarily connected with a claim to correctness. Jan Sieckmann raises six objections against this conception of practical discourse and its implications.

According to his first objection, it is inadequate to consider assertions as basic elements of argumentation. Assertions claim to be true and purport to state facts. This, according to Sieckmann, gives rise to a problem for discourse theory as a procedural theory of justification: 'the problem of how a statement of a normative fact, which might be the result of discourse, can be made at the beginning of a justificatory procedure' (at 195). Does this not 'render a procedural justification redundant'? (at 195). My reply is that assertions qua speech acts merely claim or purport to express a true proposition or to state a fact. The mere fact that someone asserts something does not imply that what is asserted is true. It is possible to assert something that is false. It is not possible, however, to assert something without claiming that it is true. Claims, for their part, can either be fulfilled or not fulfilled. Discourse is a procedure that aims to establish that what is claimed to be true is really true. In order to do so, an assertion must be both the starting point of discourse and also its result.

Sieckmann's second objection concerns the classical problem of the relationship between correctness or truth on the one hand, and justifiability or warranted assertability on the other. This is not only a central theme for discourse theory, but, indeed, a perennial issue in philosophy generally. Steering discourse theory through this battlefield, my main instrument is the distinction between a relative procedural concept of correctness and an absolute non-procedural concept of correctness. The results of real or actual discourses are always relative to the participants, the time and the degree of fulfilment of the discourse rules and principles.[32] For that reason, even a well-reasoned consensus can never be more than an expression of relative procedural correctness. This relativity is most obvious in the case of merely discursively possible results.[33] In contrast to this, the absolute non-procedural concept of correctness says that a normative proposition 'p' or [p][34] is true, if and only if p. According to Sieckmann (at 197), the:

> distinction between a relative procedural concept of correctness and an absolute non-procedural concept of correctness ... leads to the conclusion that an individual cannot use in his reasoning a procedural conception of justification and therefore cannot base his normative justifications on discourse theory.

This, however, has to be contested, and for two reasons. The first is that the procedural concept of justification presupposes the absolute non-procedural concept of correctness as a regulative idea. Otherwise, the participants of discourse would miss a common direction and a permanent aim. The second reason runs not from justification to correctness (or truth), but from correctness (or truth) to justification. There may be some justification-transcendent truths such as 'There is intelligent extra-terrestrial life', but even in this case truth and justifiability remain interdependent. If we had no grasp at all of what made the proposition about extra-terrestrials warrantedly assertible, we would have no grasp of the truth of this proposition. The impossibility of grasping its truth would somehow be similar to the impossibility of grasping the truth of 'There is a violent eternal comma'. For this reason, as Künne puts it, 'having at least an implicit conception of justification is a necessary condition for having the concept of truth'.[35] Given this background, a procedural conception of justification is altogether compatible with the idea of absolute correctness.

Sieckmann's third objection concerns the thesis that a claim to correctness comprises not merely an *assertion* of correctness but also a *guarantee* of justifiability and an *expectation* of acceptance. Sieckmann maintains that this is too strong. A guarantee of justifiability implies not just that 'reasons are given but that these reasons are sound' (at 198). With that, the guarantee of justifiability refers to the result of the discourse. If it were possible to guarantee, at the outset, the results of discourses, discourses would be redundant. Now, the expression 'guarantee' might indeed be infelicitous, for it has the connotation of infallibility. It belongs to the nature of claims that they can fail. On the other hand, the claim to correctness not only includes the notion that there are some reasons, whether they be sound or not. It comprises, too, the claim that these

[32] R Alexy, 'Problems of Discourse Theory' (1988) 20 *crítica* 43 at 61–3.

[33] On the concept of discursive possibility see Alexy, above n 9 at 207.

[34] '[p]' shall form a singular term which designates a particular proposition. See on this W Künne, *Conceptions of Truth* (Oxford, Clarendon Press, 2003) 337.

[35] *Ibid* at 450.

reasons are sound. The claim to have sound reasons lies between the claim simply to have some reasons, whether sound or not, and the guarantee of soundness. For this reason, for the expression '*guarantee* of justifiability'[36] one should perhaps substitute something like '*affirmation* of justifiability'. Indeed, such an affirmation of justifiability anticipates the result of the discourse. But this must be so. Discourses are enterprises in which claims to correctness and soundness are examined. Not all claims succeed. If, however, a claim succeeds, the initial affirmation is confirmed. Something similar applies to the expectation of acceptance. For discourse theory 'concedes that reasonable disagreement is possible' (at 199). But this does not mean that the participants of discourse cannot begin with the claim that their solution is the right one. They must do so if discourse is to be carried out as a serious enterprise and not simply as an intellectual game.

Sieckmann's fourth objection concerns the necessity of the claim to correctness. It is indeed true that the claim to correctness evaporates once one begins 'to avoid making assertions' (at 199), or something approximating them. This applies to assertions in general as well as to normative assertions. Sieckmann considers, with reference to Mackie's 'error theory',[37] the possibility of changing the practice of normative discourse by making normative statements without an 'assertoric claim of the correctness of normative statements' (at 200). The reply to this is that discourse theory is able to show that rational practical argument is possible, and with an eye to this possibility, it would be far more peculiar to give up the claim to correctness residing in our normative practice than to take it seriously.

Sieckmann's fifth point concerns the implications of the claim to correctness. Sieckmann maintains that this claim, if understood as a claim to truth, 'does not suffice for any normative conclusions' (at 200). The ideas of ideal discourse or rational acceptability may have normative implications, but truth as such has no implications of this kind. Sieckmann is, indeed, correct in stating that 'truth is different from' (at 201) rational acceptability or justifiability. But his argument presupposes more. It presupposes that truth and justification are completely independent from each other. In my reply to Sieckmann's second objection, I argued that the distinguishability of truth and justifiability does not exclude the notion that truth is internally related to justification. If such an internal relation exists, the claim to truth, via the claim to justification, can have normative implications.

Sieckmann's sixth point concerns the justification of human rights. Sieckmann argues that human rights qua moral rights can only be justified

[36] See Alexy, above n 4 at 208.
[37] J Mackie, *Ethics: Inventing Right and Wrong* (London, Pelican, 1977) 35.

by way of moral reasons, not by way of reasons referring to rational self-interest. For this reason he deems it 'unsatisfactory' that my argument 'begins as a transcendental argument and ends up referring to the long-term interests of dictators' (at 201). To be sure, Sieckmann is well aware that recourse to the maximisation of individual utility is only an extension of 'the core argument' (at 202). But, he argues, such an extension is not sound, for moral justification has to be distinguished and separated from rational justification in terms of self-interest. Now there is little doubt that both have to be distinguished. But what has to be distinguished need not be separated once and for all. The transcendental argument attempts to establish what is universally and categorically correct. The maximisation of utility is added in order to take account of those persons who take no interest in moral correctness. It concerns not the level of moral judgement but the level of motivation. At the level of motivation the maximisation of utility is introduced as a non-moral reason for morally correct action.[38] Now I think that a comprehensive theory of the justification of human rights might well include questions of motivation in a quite comprehensive way, provided that the distinction between moral judgement and the motivation to act accordingly, for whatever reasons, is not blurred.

REPLY 8 TO JONATHAN GORMAN

Jonathan Gorman's main point is that the principles of rational discourse cannot be applied directly to legal decision processes. The rules and forms of discourse are said to be 'two-person principles' (at 219). As such, they apply to debates between two persons as well as to those among more than two persons. The latter is the case, for the two-person structure is preserved when more than two persons participate in a dispute, provided that all participants have the same rights or competences. Participants in discourse have the same rights or competences if none of them has the authority to decide, alone or together with others, who is right in cases of a disagreement that cannot be resolved by means of argument. Given this condition, which may be termed the condition of equality, if more than two persons engage in a process of reasoning, the relation of each participant to every other participant is a two-person relation. Once the concept of a two-person dispute is coined in this way, one may indeed say that a 'multi-person procedure' (at 218) performed under the condition of equality has a two-person structure.

If disagreement cannot be eliminated by means of argument, that is, by means of a two-person justification, then resorting to other devices for conflict resolution will be necessary if the conflict must be settled. In law,

[38] See Alexy, above n 16 at 219–20.

this other means is a judge or court. According to Gorman, the structure of justification essentially changes by means of this transformation of the two-person situation into a '*three*-person situatio[n]: two parties and a judge' (at 219).

Gorman's description of the transition from a two-person procedure to a three-person procedure corresponds in certain fundamental aspects to the conception of institutionalisation proposed by discourse theory. The basis of this conception is a four-stage model.[39] General practical or, broadly speaking, moral discourse comprises the first stage. The rules of general practical discourse by no means lead in every case to exactly one answer. But the resolution of social conflict demands just one answer. This makes an institutionalised procedure of law-making necessary at the second stage, in which arguments are made and, in addition, decisions are taken. A paradigmatic example of such a procedure is the legislative procedure of a democratic state. Even a law-making procedure, however, is not capable of establishing in advance a single solution to every case. This gives rise to the necessity of a third procedure, that of legal discourse. Just like the first procedure, legal discourse qua argumentation procedure is not institutionalised, but unlike the first procedure it has an obligation to respect statute, precedent and legal doctrine. In this way, uncertainty of outcome is reduced to a significant extent. The abundance of legal disputes shows, however, that uncertainty is by no means totally eliminated. This seems to be the point of Gorman's legal disagreement in the two-person situation. Disagreement in legal discourse leads to the necessity of a fourth procedure, once again a strictly institutionalised procedure, namely that of a judicial process in which, as in the legislative process, there is not only argument or justification but also decision. This stage corresponds exactly to Gorman's 'three-person justification situation' (at 221).

Up to this point agreement prevails. Doubts, however, arise once Gorman's concept of a three-person justification is considered. According to Gorman, it is essential for a three-person justification (ie, for the justification of a judge) that it 'is different from the justifications offered by either of the parties to the dispute' (at 217). Gorman explains this essential difference, as he sees it, as follows: 'For the judge's decision, we seek a reasoned justification which has an internal justificatory quality which does not import bias or beg the question by being identical with the justifications used by either of the parties' (at 218). The question is whether it is really true that the justification of the judge must always be different from that of both parties. What is the case when the judge, after careful consideration, arrives at the conviction that the justification of the one party is correct in all aspects as well as complete in the sense that no

[39] Alexy, above n 21 at 370.

further reasons are available, whereas the justification of the other party is wrong? It is the task of the judge to hand down a correct decision, backed up by a correct justification. For this reason, he has in the case described here no possibility other than to give a justification that is identical to the correct justification of the one party. Naturally, in most cases the justifications of the parties are neither correct in all aspects nor complete. But here, too, the judge may adopt good reasons presented by the parties in so far as they are correct. Should he avoid them simply because they have been put forward by a party, and take recourse, then, solely to reasons newly concocted by himself or taken from sources outside the process? If so, the arguments of the parties as articulated in the courtroom would have the function of excluding just these arguments from the justification of the court. Putting forward an argument would mean destroying it. This, however, would be incompatible with the claim to correctness that is necessarily raised by both parties in arguing before the court.[40]

There is a further reason why a court is never prevented from using good reasons independently of whether they have previously been presented by a party. The arguments of a court are addressed not only to the parties but also to other courts, the legal profession, and to the general public. Given these relations, the justification offered by the court is an argument in a general legal discourse. This might well be described by means of Gorman's distinction between two-person justification and three-person justification. The authoritative three-person justification that has been given to the parties turns into a non-authoritative two-person justification that has to withstand critical examination in a general legal discourse. The reasoning of the court can pass the test, withstand this scrutiny, only if the court is able to use each and every argument in its justification that counts as a good argument in legal discourse.

REPLY 9 TO MAEVE COOKE

The starting point of Maeve Cooke's chapter, 'Law's Claim to Correctness' is the most fundamental difference between the positivist's and the non-positivist's interpretation of law's claim to correctness. For the positivists, if they connect law with such a claim at all, the claim to legal correctness refers only to standards already established in the prevailing legal system. Non-positivists need not deny that the claim of law to correctness has this factual or real dimension, and normally they in fact do not deny this.

[40] Alexy, above n 9 at 218–19.

Rather, they insist that this dimension of the claim to legal[41] correctness has to be complemented by an ideal or critical dimension. This means that law's claim to correctness transcends the established law. Cooke gives expression to the point as follows: 'non-positivists attribute a *context-transcending* component to the claim to correctness raised for legal norms and decisions' (at 226).

Maeve Cooke's main concern is captured by the question: how is one to understand the context-transcending component of law's claim to correctness? According to Cooke, neither Habermas' nor my account of the context-transcending component is convincing. Habermas' interpretation is said to be 'overly contextualist', for, so Cooke argues, 'he curtails the context-transcending power of law's claim to correctness by restricting its validity to the inhabitants of a particular democratic order' (at 227). Notwithstanding a 'deep ambivalence' (at 238) in his theory, Habermas is said to fall short of a 'genuinely context-transcending conception of validity' (at 239), for 'he seems to posit the community of citizens in a particular democratic order as the ultimate reference point for the validity of democratic decisions' (at 234).

The problem that runs parallel to being overly contextualist is being 'overly universalist', and Cooke directs precisely this charge to my attempts to understand the claim of law to correctness (at 227). In what follows I will confine myself to this line of criticism.

Legal argumentation always takes place within the institutional framework of a legal system. Sometimes the decision is more or less determined by authoritatively issued legal rules; sometimes, owing to the often described open texture of law, this is not the case. The question is what law's claim to correctness demands in such 'hard cases'. My position, according to Cooke, is that the reasons on which legal decisions have to be grounded in hard cases must 'be construed as moral reasons' (at 228). In this way, the reproach of being overly universalistic boils down to the charge of having reduced legal reasoning in the open sphere of positive law to moral reasoning. The alternative to this, Cooke contends, is a construction that conceives the non-institutional reasons admissible in hard cases 'as a bundle of moral, ethical and pragmatic reasons' (at 228). This position is attributed to Habermas.

Still, Maeve Cooke quite clearly recognises that according to my view legal discourse is a special case not of moral but of general practical discourse and that in a general practical discourse 'moral reasons (eg, reasons appealing to human rights), ethical reasons (eg, reasons appealing

[41] For non-positivism it is crucial that it is legal correctness that comprises an ideal dimension. Otherwise this dimension could not be considered as necessarily incorporated into the law. Criticism based on this dimension would then be criticism from outside the legal system, not from within.

to collective self-understandings) and pragmatic reasons (eg, reasons appealing to the resources available in the given circumstances or in the foreseeable future)' (at 230) are not only connected in one way or other but, moreover, 'are joined in a complex interrelationship that, in concrete cases of practical judgement makes it impossible to disentangle one from the other' (at 229). For this reason, I think, Maeve Cooke and I agree on the point that 'general practical discourse is not a simple combination of moral, ethical and pragmatic reasons but "a systematically necessary connection expressing the substantial unity of practical reason"'[42] (at 230). It is exactly at this point that I am said to have set off in the wrong direction (at 231–2):

> At this point, however, Alexy makes a surprising move. In light of his acknowledgement that deliberation on questions of justice involves moral, ethical and pragmatic reasons, one would expect him to locate the context-transcending aspect of the claim to correctness in the *substantial unity* of practical reason. Instead, surprisingly, he locates it in the *moral* component of practical reason: in its reference to what is just and reasonable from the point of view of what is equally in everyone's interests. His jump from the argument that legal discourse is a special case of general practical discourse to the argument that there is a necessary connection between law and a universalistic morality is not just surprising; it is also ill-advised.

Maeve Cooke is, indeed, right in pointing out that there are formulations of mine that can be interpreted as saying that the non-institutional dimension of the claim of law to correctness refers solely to morality understood as universalistic morality. The clause 'just and reasonable',[43] for instance, might be interpreted in this way. Such an interpretation, however, would not be compatible with one of the most fundamental assumptions of my theory of legal argumentation, the special case thesis. The special case thesis says that legal discourse is a special case not of moral discourse but of general practical discourse, which comprises a moral as well as an ethical and a pragmatic dimension.[44] This implies that the claim to correctness refers to moral correctness as well as to ethical and pragmatic correctness. The moral dimension of the claim of law to correctness does indeed establish a necessary connection between 'law and a universalistic morality',[45] and in this respect the claim surely has a

[42] The quotation within the quotation is from R Alexy, 'The Special Case Thesis' (1999) 12 *Ratio Juris* 374 at 379.

[43] *Ibid* at 382.

[44] *Ibid* at 378.

[45] R Alexy, 'On Necessary Relations between Law and Morality' (1989) 2 *Ratio Juris* 167 at 180.

context-transcending character. But this implies in no way whatever that the ethical and the pragmatic dimension are lacking in context-transcendence.

The decisive question, therefore, is whether correctness is connected with context-transcendence only in case of moral correctness or also in case of ethical and pragmatic correctness. If one understands pragmatic correctness as correctness with respect to the factual possibilities of action, then context-transcendence does not create any problems. Mistaken assumptions about the suitability of a means to an end ought to be revised even if these assumptions are deeply entrenched in a cultural context. This is a minimal requirement of practical rationality expressed by rules and forms of argument that refer to consequences,[46] connect practical with empirical discourse[47] and require that the actually given limits of realisability be taken into account.[48] Things are not so easy in cases of ethical correctness. The ethical dimension refers to what is good according to our individual and collective self-understanding, and, in this sense, according to individual and collective values. Now, self-understanding seems to be a paradigm case of particularity. If any claim may be connected with it, then only a claim to authenticity,[49] not a claim to correctness. A closer look, however, shows that here, too, a context-transcending dimension exists. This context-transcending dimension stems from two sources: first, from the dependence of questions of justice on questions of self-understanding or value, and, secondly, from the discursivity of self-understanding. That there exists a permeation of the just by our self-understanding can be recognised, eg, by the fact that the choice between a liberal or a libertarian conception of justice depends essentially on how one conceives oneself and the community in which one lives. This does not rule out the possibility that the adherents of each of these conceptions of justice might well raise a claim to correctness as against everyone. In this way, the ethical component has context-transcending character as an element of the 'substantial unity of practical reason'.[50]

Maeve Cooke talks about a 'balance' that is to be achieved 'between the requirements of universalisability, particularity and expediency' (at 233). There are, surely, aspects of balancing or weighing in the construction of a complex unity of these three elements, but there are also other unifying operations as, eg, the transition from the concept of justice to a conception of justice with the help of values that express a self-understanding, which, as such, raises a claim to correctness. The last point leads to the second

46 Alexy, above n 9 at 198–9: (4.2) and (4.3).
47 *Ibid* at 206: (6.1).
48 *Ibid* at 205: (5.3).
49 See J Habermas, *Zwischen Naturalismus und Religion* (Frankfurt, Suhrkamp, 2005) 93.
50 Alexy, above n 42 at 379.

source of the context-transcending character of the ethical dimension of general practical discourse. It is the discursivity of self-understanding as such, and not only as related to justice. It is possible to exchange arguments about questions of individual and collective self-understanding. Arguments, which submit ethical convictions to a critical testing in terms of their genesis, are but one example.[51] The discursivity of self-understanding does not mean, however, that the moral and the ethical dimension can play the same role in public deliberation. This is excluded by the limits set to the democratic process by constitutional rights. Democracy allows, on the one hand, ethical considerations to have influence on the decisions of the majority. On the other hand, however, constitutional rights protect the ethical convictions of minorities. Constitutional rights obtain their power by constitutional review, which, again, has a discursive nature. In this way, discourse theory leads to a complex system, which might be designated 'discursive constitutionalism'.[52]

Discursive constitutionalism is an attempt to reconcile the factual or real and the ideal or critical dimension of law. Maeve Cooke's thesis that 'there is an ineliminable gap between correctness and all actual articulations of it' (at 243) points to an important aspect of this dialectic between the ideal and the real. Her connection of the concept of correctness with the concept of a 'transcendent object' (at 244), gives rise, however, to the question of whether correctness as a transcendent object must not make demands on rational discourse that it cannot possibly meet. Maeve Cooke proposes interpreting 'discursively reached consensus' as a regulative idea that is, qua idea 'a representation of correctness as opposed to correctness itself' (at 244). But here, too, the status of the concept of correctness remains indeterminate. Perhaps it would be preferable to understand not the concept of a discursively reached consensus but the concept of correctness itself as a regulative idea, which is, as such, related to discursive justification.[53] This might well explain how practical correctness can be, at the same time, discourse-transcendent and discourse-immanent. It always transcends the actual results of discourses, but in transcending them it does not refer to something that can be established outside of discourse. In this sense, practical correctness has a discourse-immanent (or justification-immanent) discourse-transcendent (or justification-transcendent) nature.

[51] Alexy, above n 9 at 204–5: (5.2.1) and (5.2.2).

[52] R Alexy, 'Balancing, Constitutional Review, and Representation' (2005) 3 *International Journal of Constitutional Law* 572.

[53] See Alexy, above n 32 at 58–9.

REPLY 10 TO GIOVANNI SARTOR

Giovanni Sartor's main point is that goal-oriented or teleological considerations play a pivotal role in the analysis and evaluation of dialogues. The concept of dialogue is used by Sartor in a rather broad sense, namely, as pertaining to 'linguistic exchanges between two or more people' (at 249 n 1) that are organised as a 'dialectical system' (at 252) in one way or other. The highly diverse phenomena comprised by this wide concept of dialogue can be classified in quite different ways. Sartor distinguishes 'eight kinds of dialogue: persuasion, negotiation, deliberation, information-seeking, epistemic inquiry, practical inquiry, eristic, reconciliation' (at 256). Discourse theory can, indeed, profit a great deal from Sartor's 'teleological approach' (at 274), which relates a diversity of goals or values to a diversity of dialogues not only for purposes of description and analysis but also for purposes of evaluation and improvement. There remains, however, a difference. In Sartor's teleological approach, the different kinds of dialogue seem to have, at least in principle, the same standing. Which one is preferred or recommended depends on the situation and the values or purposes that one wants to realise. No form of dialogue has, then, a fundamental status. One might term such a view 'phenomenological'.

In opposition to this, discourse theory proceeds systematically. Discourse as such is the Archimedean point to which all dialogical phenomena are related. This by no means implies that all forms of social interaction performed by speech acts are to be interpreted simply as discourses, or, if such an interpretation is not possible, are to be transformed into discourses defined by freedom, equality and absence of coercion. Discourse theory comprises an ideal as well as a real dimension. The main issue of the real dimension is the introduction of law and legal institutions.[54] The decisive point is that the ideal dimension remains vivid in this process of institutionalisation. Discourse theory requires a design of legislation that comes as close as possible to the idea of deliberative democracy, and it demands an organisation and a practice of adjudication that make it possible to realise discursive rationality to as high a degree as possible.

According to Sartor (at 266):

> [d]ialectical exchanges constitute the essential component of legal procedures. We need, however, to refrain from always imposing a single dialectical model, inspired by an abstract idea of dialectical rationality.

Sartor is, indeed, right in emphasising that we cannot identify legal procedures such as parliamentary legislation or judicial proceedings with discourse in the sense of non-coercive unfettered communication. But he is mistaken if he wants to reject the inspiration they draw from the general

[54] Alexy, above n 3 at 32–41.

idea of discursive rationality. The rules of legal procedures must be justifiable in general practical discourses, and the arguments put forward in, eg, judicial proceedings raise a claim to correctness that is internally connected to general practical correctness.[55] The details are complex, and Giovanni Sartor aptly points out that there are many combinations and shifts (at 264–6). He is also right in maintaining that a diversity of goals apart from correctness have to be considered, eg, legal certainty, efficiency and autonomy. But the idea of correctness retains a certain role with respect to these additional values. The degree of their realisation as well as the balance between and among them, including the value of correctness, must be correct. In this way, the idea of correctness turns out to be an overarching idea. The idea of correctness, however, is intrinsically related to the concept of discourse. This, in turn, brings about a necessary relation between, on the one hand, all kinds of legal procedures, however small their discursive dimension may appear on first glance, and, on the other, the idea of discourse.

REPLY 11 TO GIORGIO BONGIOVANNI, ANTONIO ROTOLO AND CORRADO ROVERSI

Discourse theory is an essentially universalistic theory. It claims, first, that all human beings participate (apart from unusual circumstances) in the practice of asking, asserting and arguing; secondly, that this practice necessarily presupposes universals of reasoning that can be expressed by rules of discourse; and, thirdly, that the practice of discourse is oriented towards truth or correctness as regulative ideas.

Giorgio Bongiovanni, Antonio Rotolo and Corrado Roversi confront this universalistic enterprise with the question: 'how can we justify the high generality of a language-game in which assertions are in fact commissive and rules of discourse rational?' (at 283) and they propose a highly interesting answer: 'It seems that the only way we can answer this question is by taking up a generalised version of Alexy's special case thesis whereby every language-game in which discourse rules are limited *for rational reasons* is a special case of the universal game of assertion and argumentation' (at 284). It is here that the problem arises. The generalised version of the special case thesis, according to our three authors, is open to two different readings. The first interpretation underlines the *ideal* dimension of discourse in that the concept of correctness is understood as a regulative idea. This is the view of classical discourse theory. The second interpretation stresses the pragmatic and *real* character of discourse. A main representative of this approach is Robert Brandom. Bongiovanni, Rotolo

[55] Alexy, above n 4 at 214–21.

and Roversi emphasise the 'actual and concrete' (at 293) character of Brandom's 'social practices of giving and asking for reasons',[56] and they claim that this pragmatic approach is preferable on the ground that it is able to avoid a risk inevitably connected, according to the three authors, with ideals: 'The risk would be that of returning to what the later Wittgenstein called the "slippery ice where there is no friction", in which "the conditions are ideal", but on which "also, just because of that, we are unable to walk"'[57] (at 285).

Does discourse theory really compel us to walk on slippery ice? This would be the case if the fact that discourse theory includes an ideal dimension implied that it does not rest on the 'rough ground'[58] of reality. Discourse theory, however, claims that precisely the opposite is the case. It is one of discourse theory's main tenets that the ideal dwells in the real. Real discourses always strive to be as ideal as possible, but in doing so they remain real discourses. Wittgenstein's critique of the ideal to which Bongiovanni, Rotolo and Roversi refer concerns the 'crystalline purity of logic'[59] which was the ideal of his *Tractatus logico-philosophicus* of 1921. Discourse theory's dialectic between the real and the ideal has little to do with this ideal of the early Wittgenstein.

Something different would be true only if regulative ideas demanded of us that we forsake the realm of reality and pass into an ideal world. This, however, is not the case. The concept of a regulative idea, as it is used here, stems from Kant. Kant stresses the point that regulative ideas can never constitute an object. They 'cannot tell us *what the object is*, but only *how the empirical regressus is to be performed* in order for us to arrive at the complete concept of the object'.[60] This applies not only to empirical knowledge but equally to practical knowledge. Regulative ideas do not express what is 'given'; rather, they tell us what is 'set as a task'.[61] In doing so, they refer not to any 'object that supposedly corresponds' to the idea, but 'to the understanding's use as such'.[62] In this way 'transcendental ideas have a superb and indispensably necessary *regulative* use: viz., to direct the understanding to a certain goal'.[63] To be sure, this goal 'lies entirely outside the bounds of possible experience',[64] but everything that is set in

[56] RB Brandom, *Articulating Reasons* (Cambridge, Mass., Harvard University Press, 2000) 35.

[57] The quotations in the quotation are from L Wittgenstein, *Philosophical Investigations* (GEM Anscombe (trans), Oxford, Blackwell, 1963) para 107.

[58] *Ibid.*

[59] *Ibid.*

[60] I Kant, *Critique of Pure Reason* (WS Pluhar (trans), Indianapolis, Hackett, 1996) B 538 (emphasis in original—trans altered).

[61] *Ibid* at B 536 (trans altered).

[62] *Ibid* at B 671.

[63] *Ibid* at B 672 (emphasis in original).

[64] *Ibid.*

relation to it must remain inside the bounds of experience. In this sense, the use of regulative ideas must always remain 'immanent'.[65]

If the concept of correctness is related to real discourses in this way, the risk of 'slippery ice' seems to vanish. This, however, is only the one side of the matter. The other side is the fact that Bongiovanni, Rotolo and Roversi's emphasis on discourse as actual and concrete social practice cannot completely dispense with the employment of concepts that have at least in some aspects the character of regulative ideas. The three authors refer to Brandom's distinction 'between objectively correct applications of concepts and applications that are merely subjectively taken to be correct'[66] (at 296) The mere possession of the distinction between being correct and being merely taken to be correct seems to imply a commitment to correctness qua regulative idea.

REPLY 12 TO CARSTEN HEIDEMANN

Discourse theory is a procedural theory of practical correctness or truth. The basic tenet of all procedural theories of correctness is that the correctness of a normative proposition depends upon whether or not the proposition is or can be the result of a certain procedure. It is an essential feature of discourse theory that this procedure not be a bargaining or decision procedure but rather an argumentation procedure. Discourses are argumentation procedures that are defined by a system of discourse rules that demand, eg, non-contradiction, clearness of language, empirical truth, consideration of consequences, weighing of reasons, the analysis of the genesis of normative convictions, everyone's right to participate and freedom and equality in discourse.[67]

In one of the main objections brought against discourse theory, the claim is raised that there exists no necessary relations between discourse, on the one hand, and correctness, truth or objective validity, on the other. One always has to reckon with the possibility that a normative judgement is the result of a discourse but is not correct, or that it is correct but is not the result of a discourse.

The relation between correctness and discourse is, indeed, one of the most serious problems of discourse theory. Carsten Heidemann's critique concerns some important aspects of this issue. His main point is that discourse theory must fail on the ground it cannot establish 'a constitutive relation between the performance of a *real* discourse and the objective

65 *Ibid* at B 671.

66 RB Brandom, *Making It Explicit* (Cambridge, Mass, Harvard University Press, 1994) 600.

67 See Alexy, above n 9 at 188–206.

validity of its result' (at 312, emphasis added). This, however, cannot undermine discourse theory in the form in which I would like to defend it. It is a central point of discourse theory that it is always possible that there exists a divergence between what is correct or objectively valid and what is achieved as a result of a real discourse.[68] The reason for this is the context-transcending character of the claim of correctness, which is an expression of the dialectic between the ideal and the real that is essential for discourse theory. The participants of discourses are real persons in concrete historical situations who attempt to achieve correct moral judgements with respect to ideal rules of argumentation that never can be completely fulfilled. Under these conditions only an approximation to correctness is possible. For that reason, a consensus achieved in a *real* discourse cannot, indeed, be constitutive of correctness or objective validity. Such a consensus can never be more than an attempt to provide an answer to a practical question that meets correctness qua regulative idea to the extent possible.

A consensus achieved in a real discourse could only count as a definitive criterion of correctness if discourse were conceived of as a kind of bargaining or decision procedure. This, however, would completely miss the point of discourse. For discourses are just the opposite of bargaining or decision procedures. They are argumentation procedures. This, however, leads to another objection against discourse theory as a theory of practical correctness. If the notion of argument is the crucial concept, then the question may arise as to why correctness might not be connected directly with argument or justification. Things would then become far more simple. Discourses presuppose a non-monological or communicative structure. In contrast to this, arguments can be produced and assessed by a single person, ie, they are, at least in principle, compatible with a monological structure. One might term this objection the objection of the possibility and sufficiency of monologue, in short, the monologue objection.

Heidemann raises the monologue objection in asking why practical argumentation 'should include those affected by the regulation' (at 312). A reply to this objection has to show why practical justification has to have a communicative or non-monological character. I have argued that the autonomy of those affected is the reason for the necessarily communicative character of practical justification.[69] Heidemann objects that the principle of autonomy 'is not implied in the rules of discourse' (at 313). This, however, is only half true. One of the basic distinctions of discourse theory is the distinction between rules of discourse as rules merely relating to speech as such, and rules relating to social action, including, for instance,

[68] Alexy, above n 32 at 61–4.

[69] R Alexy, 'Nachwort (1991): Antwort auf einige Kritiker' in *idem*, *Theorie der juristischen Argumentation*, 2nd edn (Frankfurt, Suhrkamp, 1991) 407–10.

the human right to freedom of speech as a social rule. The rules of discourse express the idea of autonomy of judgement; the human right to autonomy guarantees the possibility of acting in accordance with one's autonomous judgement. Now, the autonomy of judgement and argument is implicit in the discourse rules. It is, apart from universality, their main point.[70] To this extent, Heidemann is mistaken. On the other hand, the principle of autonomy in discourse does not imply, as such, the principle of autonomy in social life. For this, additional premises are necessary. Here Heidemann is right. This, however, shows that his reproach of a *petitio principii* (at 314) is wrong. The step from one proposition to another proposition with the help of further propositions is not a *petitio principii*, even if the first proposition carries a name that is similar to that of the second one.

Far more interesting than this is the question of whether autonomy in discourse really implies a communicative structure of practical justification and judgement. The answer to this question depends on what the subject of moral questions is. Moral questions may concern either the relation between different persons or the relation of a single person to himself. Here, only the first relation will be taken up. Moral questions concerning the relation between different persons are essentially questions about what is a correct or just solution of a conflict of interests. A correct solution of a conflict of interests can only be achieved by considering the relative weights of the conflicting interests. There exists, however, no absolute—and in this sense, objective—scale that makes it possible to measure and compare the conflicting interests. For this reason, it is indispensable that one refer to the interpretation of interests made by those who have them. On first glance, this seems to boil down to complete subjectivism. But interpretation oriented towards correctness is argumentation. This implies that the assumptions about the importance of one's interests have to be transformed into arguments that relate to the arguments raised by those who have competing interests. In this way, interests and arguments are connected in discourse. This connection is necessary if a balance of interests is to be achieved, a balance backed by arguments that meet the claim to correctness as far as possible. In this way, a communicative structure, ie, discourse is required by correctness.

REPLY 13 TO BARTOSZ BROŻEK

The basis of Bartosz Brożek's analysis of the role of the weight formula in legal reasoning is a distinction between 'two "stages" or "levels" of argumentation' (at 320). The first of these is a matter of constructing

[70] Alexy, above n 16 at 216.

particular arguments, while the second consists in comparing arguments. Brożek's central point is that the 'subsumption formula'[71] belongs to the first level, whereas the weight formula has its place at the second level where conflicts of arguments are to be resolved.

This assignment to different levels is said to have significant consequences. Brożek seeks to illustrate them by means of a modified version of HLA Hart's[72] well-known example of the vehicle in the park: 'An ambulance carrying a seriously injured person has to go to a hospital. The shortest way to the hospital is through the park. However, if the ambulance were allowed into the park it would cause serious pollution. The question arises whether the ambulance can enter the park' (at 323). It is, indeed, not difficult to recognise that this case is a case of a collision between two principles. Brożek aptly identifies them as follows (at 323):

'(P1) Human life and health should be protected by the law.
(P2) The environment should be protected by the law.'

Brożek is also correct in maintaining that the 'application of (P1) results in allowing the ambulance to enter the park and the application of (P2) bans the entrance' (at 323). The problems begin, however, when Brożek argues that the principle (P1) 'reshaped to fit the example can be formulated as follows' (at 323):

(1) $\forall x\ (AHIx \rightarrow EPx)$

where 'AHI' represents 'is an ambulance carrying a seriously injured person' and EP 'may enter the park'. Brożek himself remarks in a footnote that '[t]his transformation is problematic' (at 323 n 11). It is indeed. (1) is not (P1) in some other shape or form but is something completely different. (1) is a concrete, case-relative rule that is, according to the 'law of competing principles',[73] implied if principle (P1) takes precedence over principle (P2) in circumstances AHI (C). The same applies, in turn, to the 'transformation' of (P2) into:

(2) $\forall x\ (Vx \rightarrow \neg EPx)$

where 'V' stands for 'is a vehicle' (at 323). If one adds

(3) AHIa

to (1) and

[71] Alexy, above n 26 at 433–4.
[72] HLA Hart, *The Concept of Law*, 2nd edn (Oxford, Clarendon Press, 1994) 128–9.
[73] The law of competing principles runs as follows: 'If principle P_1 takes precedence over principle P_2 in circumstances C: $(P_1PP_2)C$, and if P_1 gives rise to legal consequences Q in circumstances C, then a valid rule applies which has C as its protasis and Q as its apodosis: $C \rightarrow Q$'. Alexy, above n 21 at 54.

to (2), then one can generate two subsumptions with contradictory conclusions:

(ARG1)
(1) $\forall x\ (AHIx \rightarrow EPx)$
(3) AHIa
(5) EPa

(ARG2)
(2) $\forall x\ (Vx \rightarrow \neg EPx)$
(4) Va
(6) $\neg$EPa

Brożek argues that this reconstruction shows that the theory of principles is mistaken at several points. I will consider three.[74] The first concerns the thesis that subsumption is the form of the application of rules, whereas balancing is the form of the application of principles. Brożek objects: 'On the first level of discourse, both arguments based on rules and arguments based on principles must have the form of deductive schemes' (at 326). This objection will clearly prevail if one identifies the premises (1) and (2) in (ARG1) and (ARG2) with (P1) and (P2), respectively, in a 'reshaped' (at 323) form—if, that is to say, one identifies (1) and (2) as principles. Precisely this, however, would be mistaken. For (1) and (2) are, as already noted, concrete, case-relative rules, ie, the very opposite of principles.

There is, however, an aspect of Brożek's argument that is correct. Principles, like norms in general, cannot refer to cases without being applied to them. If it were not an ambulance but rather 'a toy motor-car electrically propelled'[75] that is of concern, an application of (P1) would not result in our allowing the toy motor-car in the park. Now, principles qua optimisation requirements are applicable only if the rights or goals protected by them are, in some way or other, either promoted or impaired by some feature of the case. One might classify this as a subsumption under an optimisation requirement—a decisive point. In this sense, any application of a principle begins, then, with a subsumption. With an eye to the fact that the law of competing principles requires a subsumption at the end of the balancing procedure, one might therefore say that subsumption stands at the beginning as well as at the end of balancing.

Brożek's second point is that the weight formula 'plays an essentially different role within argumentation' than that played by the subsumption

[74] Brożek connects his considerations about the role of the weight formula with the proposal to substitute classical logic by defeasible logic, and he refers in this context to Prakken (at 327). See on this R Alexy, 'Review: Henry Prakken (1997), *Logical Tools for Modelling Legal Argument. A Study of Defeasible Reasoning in Law*' (2000) 14 *Argumentation* 66.

[75] Hart, above n 72 at 129.

formula (at 330). The weight formula is said to be unable to 'produce' (at 324) or construct (at 330) any argument. As belonging to the second stage it is to be confined to the 'comparison of arguments' (at 320). This might, perhaps, be true if the realm of argument were confined to a level where arguments of a simple form such as (ARG1) and (ARG2) are produced. This, however, would be to underrate the scope and the power of argument. Arguments appear at all levels of reasoning, and, what is more, arguments at different levels are capable of being connected to complex argument structures.[76]

In order to grasp the complex structure of balancing, the weight formula must be distinguished clearly from preferential statements of the form:

(7) $(P_i P P_j)\ C$

$(P_i P P_j)\ C$ is a preferential rule[77] which says that the principle P_i takes precedence over principle P_j in circumstances C. The weight formula, ie:[78]

$$(8)\ W_{i,\,j} = \frac{I_i \cdot W_i \cdot R_i}{I_j \cdot W_j \cdot R_j}$$

tells us how $(P_i P P_j)\ C$ is to be justified. It does so in attributing to $W_{i,\,j}$, ie, to the concrete weight of P_i relative to P_j, a value that is connected in the following way to $(P_i P P_j)\ C$:[79]

(9) $W_{i,\,j} > 1 \rightarrow P_i P P_j$
(10) $W_{i,\,j} < 1 \rightarrow P_j P P_i$
(11) $W_{i,\,j} = 1 \rightarrow$ stalemate

In this way, a complete chain of reasoning is established, a chain that connects the weight formula via a concrete preferential rule or statement with the law of competing principles, which, again, implies the concrete, case-relative rule within which the final subsumption takes place. This chain comprises, indeed, different levels, but this does not mean that at the level above subsumption, as Brożek seems to be assuming, no arguments are 'produce[d]' (at 324). The opposite is true. In cases of balancing the decisive arguments find their place at the higher level. To be sure, as second-order arguments they presuppose the existence of first-order arguments. Presupposing the existence of other arguments does not, however, preclude the structure in question from being an argument.

The analysis of balancing as a part of a complex argument structure shows that the law of competing principles plays a pivotal role in this structure. Brożek's third point is that precisely this law is 'misleading' because it 'suggests' that the weight formula 'plays its role on the first level

[76] Alexy, above n 9 at 92–3.
[77] *Ibid* at 201.
[78] Alexy, above n 26 at 443–6.
[79] *Ibid* at 444–5.

of argumentation. Therefore, it should be abandoned' (at 330). I think that just the opposite is the case. The law of competing principles is not only an indispensable bridge between balancing and the final decision, it also fulfils this function without 'suggest[ing]' (at 330) that the weight formula plays its role on the first level. It has already been remarked that the concept of a first level as used by Brożek suffers from a certain equivocity. If it refers to the subsumption under concrete, case-relative rules, the weight formula definitively does not play its role on the first level. If it refers to the application of principles as the first step of any engagement in balancing, this, too, does not confer any role upon the weight formula on the first level. The weight formula comes into play only if a first application of principles has led to a collision. A, so to speak, mingling of levels is excluded in both interpretations.

Index

Lightning Source UK Ltd.
Milton Keynes UK
UKOW07n1918110115

244191UK00011B/70/P

9 781841 136769